MW00826486

Center for Basque Studies
Occasional Papers Series, No. 14

CAMERON J. WATSON

Basque Nationalism and Political Violence: The Ideological and Intellectual Origins of ETA

Center for Basque Studies
University of Nevada, Reno
Reno, Nevada

The Center for Basque Studies wishes to gratefully acknowledge the generous financial support of the Bizkaiko Foru Aldundia / Provincial Government of Bizkaia for the publication of this book.

Bizkaiko Foru Aldundia
Kultura Saila

Diputación Foral de Bizkaia
Departamento de Cultura

CAMERON J. WATSON

Basque Nationalism and Political Violence: The Ideological and Intellectual Origins of ETA

This book was published with generous financial support from the Basque Government.

Center for Basque Studies
Occasional Papers Series, No. 14
Center for Basque Studies
University of Nevada, Reno
Reno, Nevada 89557
http://basque.unr.edu

Library of Congress Cataloging-in-Publication Data

Watson, Cameron, 1967-
Basque nationalism and political violence : the ideological and intellectual origins of ETA / by Cameron J. Watson.
p. cm. -- (Occasional papers series ; no. 14)
Includes bibliographical references and index.
ISBN 978-1-877802-75-1 (hardcover) -- ISBN 978-1-877802-76-8 (pbk.)
1. Political violence--Spain--Pais Vasco--History. 2. Nationalism--Spain--Pais Vasco--History. 3. País Vasco (Spain)--History--Autonomy and independence movements. 4. ETA (Organization)--History. I. Title. II. Series.

HN590.P275W37 2007
303.60946'609045--dc22

2007032010

TABLE OF CONTENTS

Acknowledgments

This work is based on my Ph.D. dissertation, submitted in December 1996, at the University of Nevada, Reno. I would like to thank my original dissertation coadvisors, Martha L. Hildreth and William A. Douglass, for the encouragement they afforded me to keep going (and going), as well as the extraordinary attention to detail they gave the original text. I would also like to acknowledge grants from the (then) Basque Studies Program at the University of Nevada, Reno, that afforded me to undertake research in both Europe and the United States. While in the Basque Country to undertake research for the dissertation, Javier Corcuera and José Luis de la Granja were especially generous in giving up their time and discussing with me the emergence and development of Basque nationalism.

Special gratitude is due Joseba Zulaika for his continuing inspiration and friendship through the years. Thanks, also, to Dennis Dworkin, Hugh Shapiro, Imanol Galfarsoro, Pauliina Raento, Maggie Bullen, Iban Ayesta, Iñaki Barcena and Alfonso Pérez-Agote for many stimulating discussions on both Basque and other issues that broadened my intellectual horizons, and to Richard English and Pedro Ibarra for their thoughts on the book manuscript. Credit is, moreover, due to all my students in Reno, Donostia and Eskoriatza for many wonderful and thought-provoking discussions. Any errors in the text are, of course, my own.

Two colleagues also deserve particular mention, not least because they have taught me just how much other people, not just the authors themselves but editors, copy editors, translators, book designers, indexers and proof readers, are involved in creating a finished book: Bud Bynack's contribution was invaluable in ironing out the syntactic wrinkles of the book manuscript, challenging me to focus my ideas and sharpen my vocabulary. And Jose Luis Agote transformed the finished manuscript into book form with his usual composure and professionalism.

Finally, I would like to thank all those who provided moral (and often material) support, as well as many treasured memories during the time I spent putting this work together: Jerry Ansell, Jose Javier Aretxabaleta, Iñaki Azkarraga, Jill Berner, Kate Camino, the Carlson family, Will Diaz, Pedro Feijóo, Dan Golding, Mike Lequericabeascoa, Ted McCarthy, Dave Smith, Tim Walker, Ivor Westmore, Linda White and Joanna Ziclinska. Finally, very special thanks to Edurne Erkizia, the Erkizia Jauregi fami ly, and my own family. *Mila esker denei.*

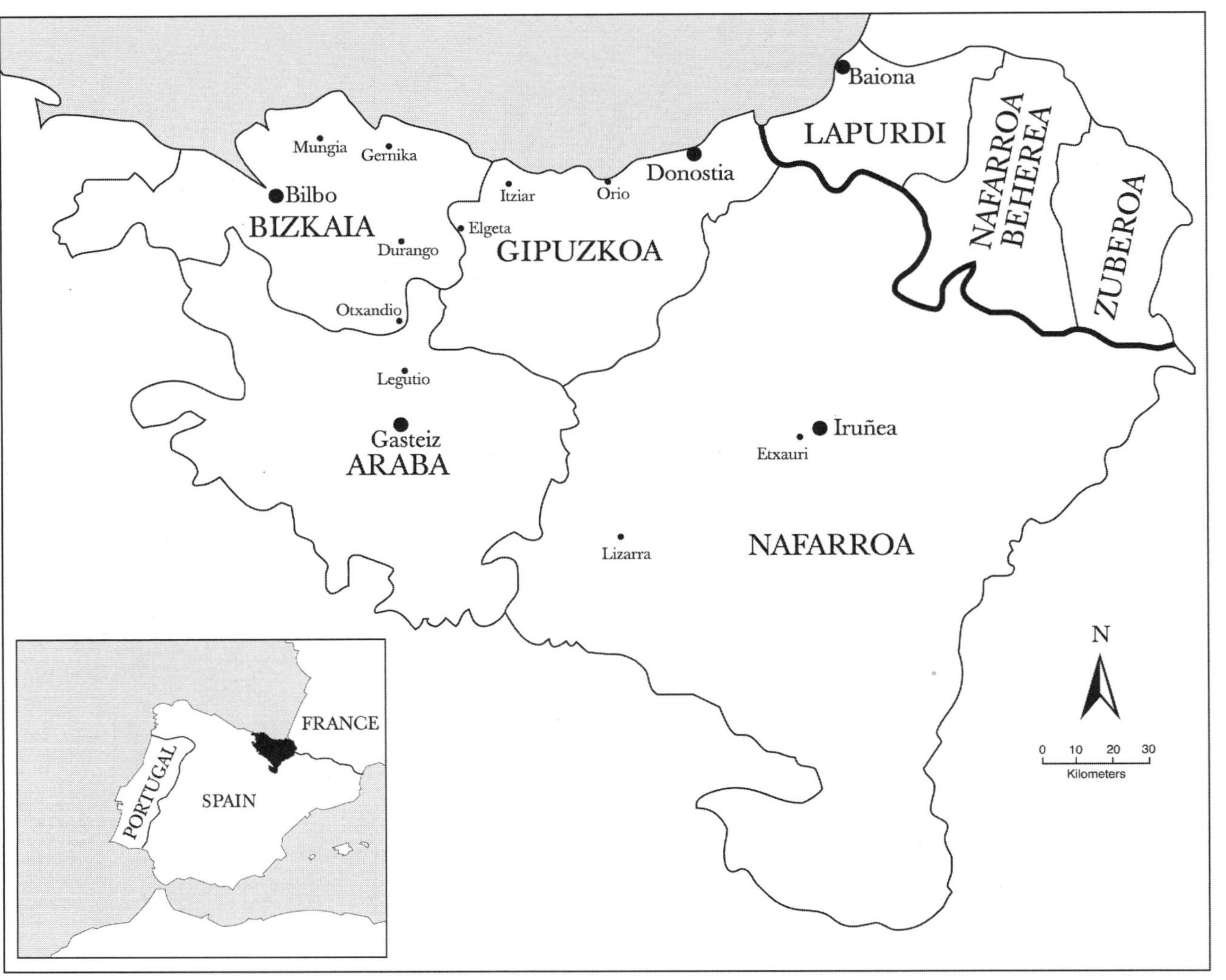

The Basque Country: Principal Cities and Towns Mentioned in the Book.

INTRODUCTION

Culture, History, and Identity

Anyone with an interest in Basque culture or history cannot escape the issue of political violence. Routinely, it is the first question to arise in a conversation with someone who has no special connection to or interest in the Basque Country. Indeed, I was drawn to studying political violence through an interest in Basque culture, rather than the other way around. What follows, then, is the result of an original wish to explore modern Basque culture, a decision that led me into considering the broader connections between nationalism and political violence, the relationship between nation and state, and the construction and maintenance of identities, ideologies, and ideas. This accounts for the focus of the present work and explains why I seek to understand through predominantly cultural means what is typically posed as a political problem. At root, however, I believe my aim is quite simple: I want to understand how and why some Basque nationalists decided to incorporate the potential use of political violence into their struggle with Spain at the close of the 1950s.

This work seeks to interrogate the relationship between ideas and action through a historical account of how images of violence and warfare pervaded the discourse of Basque nationalism through the twentieth century. I will examine the historical context of such images within the culture of Basque nationalism and argue that there was a culture of political violence within the historical discourse of this same nationalist movement. This genealogy incorporated symbolic as well as strategic representations. That is to say, historically, violence was used both as a symbolic construct and a potential strategy of the Basque nationalist movement. After identifying the founding myths of Basque nationalism in which this culture emerged, I will trace their evolution as core symbols in the development of nationalist discourse. ETA (Euzkadi [later, Euskadi] ta Askatasuna–Basque Country and Freedom), an organization employing armed struggle in the name of Basque nationalism, is generally viewed as separate from the moderate conservative nationalism of the Partido Nacionalista Vasco (PNV), or Basque Nationalist Party. While there are obvious ideological and tactical differences between the two, they share a common heritage. Indeed, as I will demonstrate, a culture of political violence emerged within the structure of the PNV prior to the formation of ETA in 1959.

Basques have been historically categorized as a mystery people with an archaic language and simple cultural traditions, devoid, for example, of any great literary tradition and prone to hostility and racism toward non-Basques. Basque nationalism is commonly seen as reactionary, and the violence of ETA is perceived to be part of the conspiracy of international terrorism. I argue here that Basque culture is neither archaic nor simple. Nor is it somehow unique or special. Rather, I consider Basque culture much as one would any other. To borrow a phrase from Raymond Williams, Basque culture is ordinary.[1] As such, it can be defensive (and hostile) to other cultures, just like any other culture. I will suggest here, for example, that Spanish culture can claim no moral high ground with regard to this question. There is, however, an important link between some elements of Basque culture and the political violence that has afflicted the Basque Country for almost forty years, a link that can be traced back to the inception of the Basque nationalist movement during the last century.

The connection between the ordinary nature of Basque culture and the extraordinary nature of political violence implies a mirror for our own experience, for I believe it is too easy to pose the dangerous terrorist as exoticized Other. This distance masks the potential of any culture (our own included) to engage in terror and/or political violence. Removing the mask of terrorism, so to speak–that is, attempting to understand it on its own terms–is to some extent my goal here. In this task I follow the pioneering research of Richard English, who, in his work on political violence in Northern Ireland, observes that "contrary to popular opinion, the IRA is in fact utterly comprehensible: their actions can be systematically explained, and their arguments clearly set out and analysed."[2]

In embarking on this investigation, I also acknowledge the words of Joseba Zulaika, commenting on the connected nature of cultures (in this respect, those of the Basque Country, Spain, and the Americas):

> Addressing the uses of history in the context of Basque Studies forces us to question the epistemic value of traditional disciplines such as anthropology, art, or literary criticism, as well as the more recent theoretical formations aligned around Cultural Studies or Subaltern Studies. It leads us to issues of disciplinary practices, discursive hegemonies, and various forms of institutionalization of knowledge. Debates concerning deconstruction, essentialism, strategic essentialism or hybridity come immediately to the fore.... [Thus] an inaugural issue is how to create a space for thinking these interrelationships beyond a field of merely reactive positions. Is there an emergent field of critical reason that will transform the very dynamics in which these adaptive and contrastive interdependencies can be dealt with? As an example, can the transnational framing transform the terms of debate beyond the imperatives of either the nation-state or the natural community?[3]

Indeed, one of the major historiographical additions to the academic treatment of Basque nationalism that I have benefited from in recent years has been the emergence of a series of diaspora theories and studies. This has revolutionized thinking about varieties of Basqueness, away from closed conceptions of being Basque within Spain (always problematic given the cross-border nature of the Basque Country) to a more open, flexible interpretation or awareness of Basqueness as transgressing state borders.

In fact, tracing the cultural origins of ETA led me to contemplate the history of not just the Basque Country and Spain (the two most obvious starting points for this particular investigation), but also significant events in (among other places) Cuba, Ireland, and Morocco. It also led me to consider the principal philosophical trends of modern Europe: the rise of modernity itself, its links to the growth of the modern nation-state,[4] and its twentieth-century challenges, from postcolonialism to existentialism and postmodernism. This book addresses culture and its influence on politics; social and economic transformation, including migration and industrialization, and their influence on culture; nationalism,[5] both of substate and statist varieties, and nation-state formation; political violence, in theory and practice; ideologies and ideas and their articulation; and the multiple and complex way in which identity is defined, articulated, and transformed. Although focusing on the Basque Country in Spain, the work also explores (I hope) what it means to be European and the interplay between European and other forms of identity (North and South American and African, for example).

Cultural Representations

So that we might first understand how Basque culture is viewed from the outside, I have selected two authors. These authors, both acknowledged authorities in their own right, typify for me the closed approach or fixed meanings mentioned above. They are by no means the only authors to follow this line of analysis regarding Basques. Nor, probably, are they the most extreme in their respective approaches.

Louis L. Snyder, a respected authority on global nationalist movements, claims that "hot-headed Basque extremists ... turn to bullets, bombs, and grenades," preferring "the way of the Irish Republican Army; the Palestine Liberation Organization; the Baader-Meinhof gang, or Red Army faction, in West Germany; and the Red Brigades in Italy."[6] Furthermore, Euskara the Basque language, is viewed as "one of the most complex of all tongues" and a "guttural" language, with Basque nationalism in general dismissed as "a proud, highly sensitive" movement.[7]

In the first example, an unscholarly reference to "hot-headed extremists" serves only to reify its subject as deviant from the still-undefined, yet ever-present, norm. I would contend, for example, that it would be more accurate to assume that a successfully functioning direct-action or terrorist group would more likely be cool-headed. How, otherwise, could ETA operate successfully (understood on its own terms) during these past forty years? In the conclusion to his history of the IRA, for example, English contends that "it seems important for the historical record to recognize that the Provisionals [the IRA] were as rational as any other political player tends to be" and that "the IRA act with just that mixture of the rational and the visceral that one commonly finds throughout human history, and with a combination of interwoven motives such as one would find in other political organizations."[8]

"They" are further isolated or distanced from "us" (normal, responsible, level-headed people) by their association with a cadre of international terrorist groups. In establishing a connection to the threatening category of international terrorism, Snyder reinforces their otherworldliness or outsider status. This not only removes ETA rhetorically from the culture out of which it emerged (and that continues to sustain it), but offers a neat conclusion to the thorny problem of terrorism.

Snyder's argument rests on an assumption that terrorism can be easily and simply identified as an international conspiracy with its own self-sustaining dynamic. The specificity of cultural or historical precedent can, in this way, be disregarded in favor of a global or universal and ahistorical interpretation of political violence. Consequently, the interpretation assumes a vague and ill-defined allegiance to "freedom" and "democracy" as positive and morally sound, juxtaposed with terrorism (by way of an opposing or other status) as negative and evil.

Moreover, Snyder describes the Basque language as a "complex" tongue, although in relation to what remains unclear.[9] Chinese script, for example, possesses some fifty thousand characters and two ways (through both an alphabet and a pictographic-ideographic system) of rendering speech into writing.[10] It is questionable, however, if this fact would be regarded as a salient point in discussing the sociopolitical realities of modern China. Similarly, it seems to me unclear why Basque being a "guttural" language should detract from the power of a nationalist movement. Perhaps the "highly sensitive" nature of Basque nationalism may have something to do with it.

Not only does such discourse reify Basque culture in general, it veers drastically away from most of the standard and accepted norms of academic behavior. Why, for example, in a work of political science, does Snyder introduce emotional references? I suspect that the answer to this lies in the emotional nature of political violence itself. Terrorism does indeed charge our emotions, but should we allow this to blind us to critical and objective understanding? Should we allow terrorism–as something so terrible to our contemporary senses–to stand outside the force of history? I believe not.

If such image production were solely confined to the academic world, then perhaps we might still be able to explore the topic of Basque political violence critically. Unfortunately, this seems not to be the case. In 1992, on the dual occasion of the World Exposition in Seville and the Barcelona Olympic Games, the British Broadcasting Corporation commissioned a television series to survey contemporary Spain for English-language viewers around the world. A book based on the television series was subsequently published. Titled *Fire in the Blood: The New Spain*, it was intended not for the specialist, but for those who may have felt an "incipient interest in modern Spain and might be considering a visit."[11]

Ian Gibson, the presenter of the series and the author of the book, is a widely known commentator on Spanish affairs, yet his views on Basque culture and the contemporary political situation recall another age. Basques in general are considered "a mystery race and their language an enigma,"[12] while the description of Basque women almost defies belief:

> the [Basque] women have a characteristically "Red Indian" look, with a pointed nose (which tends to get hooked in old age), square shoulders and small buttocks and breasts. When a Basque woman wears her hair plaited and dons moccasin sandals she looks as if she has come straight off the set of a Western. Sometimes, through the industrial pall of a winter evening in Bilbao, you can see, standing at a bus-stop or crossing a street, a breath-taking female apparition from *Hiawatha*.[13]

Furthermore, Basques are viewed as "sexually more timid than other Spaniards," their language (based on a random writing sample) "is heavily dependent on Spanish for its terminology," and sympathizers of ETA are "a wild, irrational bunch."[14]

Quite apart from the offensive stereotypes offered by the book, we might critically pose a number of questions. For example, in the randomly chosen language passage, great play is made of the fact that Basque has borrowed words from Spanish. This is unquestionably true. The words *negoziazio* (negotiation), *diskurtso* (speech), *politikoaren* ([pertaining to] politics), and *erreferentzia* (referendum) are indeed borrowings from Spanish, just as an English speaker might also recognize them as original adaptations of both Greek and Latin.[15] Would this point, I wonder, be made about a piece of text in Spanish?

The history of language is a history of borrowing and adaptation, and it would be rare for even the most wild and irrational extremist to deny the influence of Spanish on Basque. For over two thousand years, the Basque language has, indeed, borrowed from Celtic, Latin and Romance, Arabic, and most recently, English. Consider, for example, the following sentence in Basque: "*Bere hobbiak jogging-a, futbola, rock bideoak ikustea, eta whisky edatea dira*"–"His hobbies are jogging, soccer, watching rock videos, and drinking whisky." In Spanish, the same sentence would be, "*Sus hobbies son footing, fútbol, ver videos de rock, y beber whisky*." Might we therefore conclude in, say, a general introduction to the language and culture of Spain, that Spanish is reasonably dependent on English for its terminology?

The core of the Basque vocabulary–including numerals below one thousand, pronouns and grammatical words, kinship terms, geographical features, natural phenomena, indigenous animals and plants, plus most common adjectives and verbs–is indigenous.[16] And Gibson's argument, like his evaluation of Basque women, is outdated and insulting. Furthermore, I would assume, from the evidence of the book's treatment of Basque culture, that it seems unlikely that anyone considering a visit to Spain would bother traveling to the region.

Of the many photographs that complement *Fire in the Blood*, two refer specifically to the Basque Country. One shows a city scene of Bilbao (also spelled Bilbo), replete with morning smog and an accompanying phrase alluding to the environmental problems caused by heavy industry. The other shows the burned-out shell of a car targeted by ETA. There are no images of the natural environment of the Basque Country, comprising as it does a complex variety of ecological zones within a relatively small area, or of the picturesque towns and villages of both the coastal and interior mountain regions, which have attracted generations of visitors.[17] Conversely, Andalusia, in the south of Spain (author Ian Gibson's specialty region), is portrayed in three images as the region of the Alhambra (a Moorish palace noted for its architectural beauty), quaint folk festivals, and the visually stunning Doñana National Park. This when Gibson could have included photographs of the industrial port city of Málaga, with its symbols of urban decay as striking as those of Bilbao, or visual references to Andalusia's social problems–for example, high unemployment, widespread poverty, drug addiction, and so on.

Even Catalonia, also known for its nationalist aspirations, is pictured as a combination of artistic innovation (a statue of a dragon by Gaudí in Barcelona's Güell Park), technological progress (Barcelona's Spanish Industrial Park), and world cultural venue (Barcelona's Saint Jordi Olympic Sports Hall). This despite the fact that Catalonia, and in particular its capital, Barcelona, is home to one of Spain's most virulent racist movements.[18] And any celebration of Barcelona's Olympic success in 1992 should be tempered by the fact that the city seemingly had no problems in removing certain socially undesirable elements from its streets in anticipation of foreign visitors.[19]

Any reader opening the pages of this book, reading the text, and looking at the photographs would tend to conceive of the different regions in specific ways. We might say that Andalusia appears dramatic and wild, the repository of a bygone age, of the stereotypically passionate Spain; Catalonia seems dynamic and progressive, with Barcelona exuding the confidence of a vibrant international city; by contrast, the Basque Country appears sad, beset by industrial pollution, and rife with terrorism.

However, by way of a critical intellectual exercise aimed at highlighting the power of representation and imaging, let me propose an alternative vision of the three regions at the time Gibson wrote. Andalusia might accurately be portrayed as rife with decay, unemployment, and crime. Perhaps we would add an old photograph of unemployed heroin addicts roaming the streets of La Linea, the (at the time) economically depressed frontier town opposite Gibraltar, to emphasize the sense of despair. We might view Barcelona as one of Europe's premier racist cities. Why not include an image of the many skinheads who terrorize immigrant neighborhoods in the Catalan capital?

By contrast let me propose a different perspective of the Basque Country: The view is that of a region where crime levels are lower than in other areas of Spain, where the racism that plagues Madrid and Barcelona surfaces much less in Bilbao, and where traditional culture is still strong in picturesque rural areas. We might choose photographs of the technological park in Zamudio sponsored by the Basque government or the new metro and Guggenheim Museum in Bilbao, arguing that they represent a real commitment to move the Basque Country into the twenty-first century through concerted efforts at urban regeneration. Or we might show pictures of the mountains, forests, rivers, and lakes that form the surprisingly complex natural environment. Such a view would, likewise, be highly subjective and lack a perspective of the gritty realities of day-to-day life in the Basque Country, but that is the point: Limiting such views to one perspective or another, we inevitably distort the wider picture.

The point of examining the works of Snyder and Gibson is to introduce the reader to the images popularly associated with the Basque Country and how they feed into both academic and political discourse. I view such conclusions as reflective of a trend more usually associated with those who participate in the creation and consolidation of cultural authority on the part of one group over that of another.[20] It is this approach to the analysis of Basque political violence that I wish to question and displace. The task of cultural analysis is not to reproduce the ways in which cultural hegemony is produced and perpetuated, but to understand it in specific situations.

Aims of the Work

If they are understood simply as merely reacting to the assertion of cultural hegemony by Spanish society, those Basque nationalists advocating an armed struggle in favor of their cause are immediately represented as alienated, as something other than the norm. Their gestures, in the form of extreme acts of violence, then are seen as constituting acts of defiance, contempt, and refusal to conform to the prescribed methods of political behavior. "Today Basque culture must be above all a counter-culture," argued Jean-Paul Sartre in 1971: "the praxis which arises from man's oppression by man in the Basque country."[21] Sartre's observation sums up the twin themes of dominant culture and oppression and of the subsequent victimization experienced by a subculture. Seen in this way, the gestures of armed resistance by some Basque nationalists, as the case with most subcultures, appear both impotent and powerful: As an expression of minority sentiment, they are unlikely to effect the change they desire. At the same time, their symbolic power is unquestionable.[22]

However, by reducing the contemporary evaluation of Basque political violence to a subcultural context, there is a concomitant tendency to condense the phenomenon to the status of a rational equation, a problem to be solved. This disregards both the historical and cultural role that political violence (in the form of ideological representations of struggle and warfare) has played in the development of Basque nationalism. It is my hope that a greater appreciation of this dual role will actually alleviate the burden of seeking such solutions. Instead, investigation would more reasonably profit from an understanding of the cultural motivations and historical legacy that Basque political violence possesses.

My aim, then, is to examine the themes of myth, war, heroism, and tragedy in the historical trajectory of Basque nationalism in an attempt to explain the cultural legacy that bequeathed Basque nationalists a strategy of political violence.[23] I should clarify a key point about myth and symbolism, words the reader will encounter frequently in the following pages. In the introduction to Luke Gibbons's exploration of contemporary Ireland, *Transformations in Irish Culture* (1996), the author contends that "understanding a community or a culture does not consist solely in establishing 'neutral' facts and 'objective' details: it means taking seriously *their* ways of structuring experience, their popular narratives, the distinctive manner in which they frame the social and political realities which affect their lives." Indeed, continues Gibbons, "the very existence of a *symbolic* dimension in human action requires a historical method that goes beyond literalist assumption, and scientific norms of causality and certainty."[24]

Specifically, I will explore two ideas: that the contemporary history of the Basque Country has been marked by an intensity of warfare and violent social upheaval and that as a consequence, war and violence have been historically a strong factor in Basque ideological constructions. Thereafter I will extend these considerations to the particular trajectory of Basque nationalism and examine how much these original ideas or mythical creations have changed over time.[25]

Culture is involved in history to the same extent that history is involved in culture. For example, a Basque oral tradition fed into an emergent written ideology, and vice versa. Understanding that this has been a historically flexible and fluid process is one of the key themes of this investigation. There is also another motive propelling the present study: I want to argue for the validity of taking the Basque experience with nationalism and political violence as an example of more universal concerns–the struggle for cultural authority, the construction of identity, cultural representation, and the contest between different discourses, definitions, and meanings.

Given the timeframe that the work occupies–a period between the last decade of the nineteenth and middle of the twentieth centuries–it also deals with broader questions of modernity, crisis, and change. A theme of the work is, therefore, the importance of what Bertrand Russell terms "instances" of universals (the historical representation of Basque political violence for example), rather than the universals (the study of terrorism) themselves.[26] Understood this way, an examination of Basque political violence, and in particular its development from symbolic rhetoric to actual participation, can be taken as a metaphor of the wider changes affecting Basque, Spanish, and European society through the first half of the twentieth century.

If modernity can be historically regarded as a universal trend toward the triumph of reason, as represented by the primacy of scientific and technological rationality as and manifested most evidently in advanced capitalist rationalization, then the emergence of Basque nationalism in part reflected a challenge to this globalizing tendency based on the premise of multiple local struggles.[27] Furthermore, there is a tendency to limit theoretical explanations of Basque nationalism to either a purely Spanish, or at best, European context, but here I would also like to emphasize both the connections (and discontinuities) between Basque nationalism (historically constructed) and other movements (nationalist/national liberation/anticolonial, and so on) in Cuba, Morocco, Ireland and, of course, Catalonia, without forgetting its principal historical adversary, Spanish nationalism.

The Catalan case is worth noting at the outset, for academic treatment of Basque nationalism seems invariably drawn to comparison with Catalonia. While there are obvious connections between the two movements, I do no limit my examination to analyzing Basque nationalism within a purely Spanish or even Hispanic context. To illustrate this, I have borrowed much from the parallel historical and cultural experiences outside the strictly Spanish context: Cuba and Ireland, for example, formed and form crucial reference points for comprehending the historical evolution of Basque nationalism and have been overlooked in much of its historiography.

In its initial phase, Basque nationalism might accurately be described as the rearguard action of a Romanticist imagination. Yet as the century progressed, the Basque nationalist movement, particularly the strand most responsive to more extreme ideas, began to adopt another challenge to modernity–an approach encompassing many of the qualities associated with its Romantic forebears, yet somehow different.[28] If indeed "modernity does not represent the end of history," then we have not "yet seen any conclusion of the transactions between modernity and all the cultural experiences of the past."[29]

Basque political violence is the contemporary manifestation of a past cultural experience: the original conceptualization of Basque nationalism by its founder, Sabino de Arana y Goiri (hereafter referred to as Sabino Arana). Any talk of "resolution," of such political violence as a problem, then, must take account of the challenge of direct action–or political violence or terrorism–to the modernizing project itself.[30] As I will suggest, Arana bequeathed Basque nationalism a suspicion of modernity that required a rearguard action. Thus, the emergence of ETA can be viewed as symbolic of a wider issue, that of the relationship between nationalism, political violence, and cultural change.

My aim, then, is to examine the process by which a cadre of Basque nationalist images emerged in the nineteenth century and developed through the following six decades until, during the 1950s, a small group of young men came to articulate a specific ideology that theoretically involved armed insurrection against the Spanish state in favor of Basque nationalism. This is not intended to be a study of ETA per se, but rather of the historical context that allowed for ETA's articulation as something more than a mere idea. It will, therefore, be an examination based on historical and cultural constructions and the meaning of these constructions, or an account of the conditions that gave rise to the creation of ETA. This account will focus more on the historical representation of Basque nationalism than on the specific motivations of the founders of ETA.[31]

The general thesis that political violence is part of a larger story of nationalist development involves three themes relating to the emergence of ETA in 1959. The work begins with a theoretical consideration of the importance of culture as a site of political contest. Second, it contends that both Spanish and Basque nationalism vied with one another to control this site–not in a simple process of cultural hegemony imposed on and creating a subculture, but in a dialectical relationship. Finally, it argues that within the history of Basque nationalism itself, and partly as a reaction against the Spanish state-building project (or Spanish nationalism, to be discussed later), there has been a conception of struggle and warfare as twin themes in a constant potential strategy to be employed. However, I maintain that the idea of what actually constituted the potential tactic changed in response to both the evolution of Basque and Spanish society and developments outside the Spanish state.

Culture: Some Theoretical Considerations

I take culture to be a battleground on which political struggles are fought. Cultural representation and appropriation accordingly form the central focus of this study. In terms of cultural authority, this becomes a question of relevance not only to the Basque case, but to the whole issue of center-periphery relations in Europe and beyond.

I propose here an analysis of the relationship between Basque nationalism and political violence through and examination of cultural history. But what of the word "culture" itself? As Williams notes, any form of cultural analysis must, inevitably, define the concept of culture, and this consciousness must at the outset be seen as historical.[32] I do not, however, view culture as historical simply in terms of the past as social cause or aesthetic precedent. Rather, culture is process–process as the renewal and refiguration, contestation and articulation of our daily lives, where the "'past-present' becomes part of necessity, not the nostaligia, of living."[33] When the meaning of this articulation is lost, and cultural authority is ambivalent or unconvincing, we have the raw material of cultural analysis, the critical moment or contested refiguration of the past.

Let us first consider the European context of this cultural analysis, for after all, it is my intention to portray this story as an integral chapter of European history. I agree with Jan Nederveen Pieterse that there is a multicultural reality to the Europe that has been ignored by the generalizing tendency of historical scholarship.[34] However Nederveen Pieterse is himself guilty of broad generalization regarding what he considers "Europe" to mean. European appropriation and cultural authority in fact reflects only a specific part of the continent as a whole: what may be termed the Western, metropolitan, literary, scientific, and rational culture of Europe. And some Europeans, those Europeans falling outside the above categories, have also been reduced to the status of the exotic. This is an especially salient point when considering the contemporary Basque experience.

Certainly Snyder's evaluation of the complex and guttural nature of the Basque language, and hot-headed Basque extremists implies an otherworldliness in opposition to a normal world based on rational understandable languages and political behavior. This is also the case with Ian Gibson's trivialization of Basque culture based on gender and racial stereotypes. This reduction of Basque culture (and its consequent political manifestations) to the status of abnormal or exotic is important in regard to the central argument here: When a political struggle is refracted through cultural concerns, it subsumes categories–the manners and customs by which people live their everyday lives–and as such assumes ontological proportions. At this point, the struggle has entered cultural territory.

In order to make sense of such cultural preoccupations, I will attempt to think them out in a Gramscian way. Antonio Gramsci configured his own political crisis by realizing that historical, political, and cultural change is best conceived as process, rather than event. Consequently, the "moment," a notion for Gramsci that is not just temporal but also implies specificity (a distinct feature or aspect) and is the result of some kind of historical motive force, becomes crucial in a process where difference and specificity matter. According to Gramsci, hegemony (the ideological control exercised by a dominant social group) is a fluid concept involving constantly evolving, moment-to-moment relations between different groups that share a degree of consensus.[35] It is thus a combination of cultural, political, and economic dimensions.[36] Following Gramsci, I take cultural hegemony to be the outcome of a constant and ever-changing struggle between competing groups, resulting in the creation and consolidation of cultural authority on the part of one group over another or several others. I hope, moreover, to expand the general rubric of this process–politics and economics–to include (among others) sexual, moral, intellectual and psychological considerations.[37] These considerations will underpin the cultural focus of the work.

The work is, then, an examination of modernity itself, of the triumph and crisis involved in the process of transformation within the modern European experience. Again thinking in a Gramscian way, I conceptualize this as a struggle to create a singular modern identity. This struggle has historically been between the state (with its political and administrative structures) and civil society (nonpolitical organizations, religious and other beliefs, customs, or a way of life). Indeed modern identity depends on the relationship between these two forces.[38] I therefore consider it important to include an examination of the ideological struggle between the state and civil society. For the purposes of my argument, this is best explored in addressing the relationship between Spanish and Basque nationalism.

Spanish and Basque Nationalism

As I will demonstrate, the struggle between Spanish and Basque nationalism is an excellent example of Gramsci's concept of the shifting processes by which cultural hegemony is produced, maintained, contested, and subverted. However, this focus was not part of my original intention. Indeed, at the outset of my investigation, I had no idea that Spanish nationalism even existed. General works on Spain tended to confuse Spanish nationalism with what is commonly referred to as the more neutral concept of a state-building project. Such notions have ignored the fact that nationalism, as Craig Calhoun clearly points out, "can be employed equally in the service of unification or secession." Thus, he continues, "the scope of the national unit is not determined by the *form* of the nationalist discourse. It is a content given, in large part, by the relationship of national integration, cultural tradition and contraposition to other states within the world system."[39] While the question of regional[40] identity and nationalism within Spain is well covered in the relevant historiography, for many years Spanish nationalism itself remained fairly untouched by scholarly inquiry, save for the period of Franco.[41] One influential study of nationalism in both the Basque Country and Catalonia, for example, makes no reference whatsoever to their Spanish counterpart.[42] However, I would echo the comments of Josep M. Fradera:

> the intellectual goal in writing about Spanish and other nationalisms should be a complex integration that includes . . . diverse political and ideological developments. Nationalisms need to be integrated into shared spaces in the colonial and metropolitan world, while the importance of the different sorts of "imagined communities" . . . in the historical process must be acknowledged. We need to focus not only on specific variants, but also on their multiple interconnections.[43]

"Normally," Stanley G. Payne argues, both "in general and comparative studies [of nationalism], the Spanish example shines by its absence."[44] Often, examples of Spanish nationalism have been overlooked within the liberal or modernizing tendency of the Spanish intellectual tradition or artistic forms.[45] However, there have been some notable historiographical developments from the mid-1990s onward.[46] Via several concrete examples, I will argue that a dialectic emerged between Spanish and Basque nationalism and that the emergence of Basque nationalism was due, at least in part, to the state-building project of the Spanish Restoration system (1876–1923). Although it would be too simplistic to view Basque nationalism as merely a response to the emergence of modern Spain, one cannot deny that the liberal state played a critical role in shaping the Basque nationalist movement.

A final point I would like to underscore here at the outset is that Spanish history is not just a peninsular narrative, but also one that stretches across Europe and traverses the Atlantic. Thus, historiographical notions that fix Spain within the supposedly neat borders where it finds itself today demonstrate (an admittedly skillful) ability to forget what *was* "Spain"–the Netherlands, Portugal, Latin America–in favor of retroactively projecting the modern state onto a historical canvass.

An Ideology of Struggle and Warfare in Basque Nationalism

Like "culture," the word "ideology" has been discussed at length without satisfactory common consent as to its real meaning or importance. I confirm Terry Eagleton's conclusion that ideology is a matter of "discourse," rather than of "language"–of certain concrete discursive effects, rather than of any signification as such. It represents the points where power impacts upon certain utterances and inscribes itself tacitly within them.[47] When we think about ideology, we are thinking about discourse and power. This in part explains the formal aspect of ideology and its close connection to, for example, political philosophy.

Regarding the theme of the present study, George Rudé seems a particularly relevant theoretician, given his work in relation to popular protest. According to Rudé, there are two elements involved in "popular" ideology:

> The first is the "inherent," traditional element–a sort of "mother's milk" ideology, based on direct experience, oral tradition or folk-memory and not learned by listening to sermons or reading books. In this fusion the second element is the set of ideas and beliefs that are "derived" or borrowed from others, often taking the form of a more structured system of ideas, such as the Rights of Man, popular sovereignty, nationalism, socialism, or Marxist-Leninism.[48]

In effect, the two elements constitute "inherent" and derived ideas. The problem with this dichotomy is that everything, in a sense, is constructed or derived. And yet Rudé has captured something: two elements, potentially, of the same derived consciousness. These two elements overlapped in Basque nationalist discourse to consolidate an ideology of protest that involved symbolic images of struggle and warfare.

Furthermore, as Rudé rightly cautions, the original message that is communicated does not always survive intact.[49] This is a critical point to consider, for, in our rational worldview, we tend to imagine a certain coherence in ideology that does not really exist. Ideology is and indeed always must be a more fluid or flexible configuration of different subjects, identities, projects, and aspirations. This *is* the strength of ideology, the point of what Gramsci conceived as organic ideology–a coherence or unity that emerges out of difference.[50]

In the Basque case, a nationalist ideology emerged that made liberal use of symbolic and metaphorical references to struggle and warfare. Part of this ideology involved the cultural appropriation of Rudé's "mother's milk" ideology, such as tales of the nineteenth-century Carlist Wars.[51] Thereafter, through the twentieth century, this original symbolism (redolent of folkloric ideology) gradually assumed a greater reality in the sense of actual physical confrontation. Initially, this took place in street skirmishes with other political factions (most notably with the similarly expanding socialists) and culminated in the supreme reality, war: the Spanish Civil War of 1936–39. A basis, then, had been laid for what Charles Townshend identifies as "an almost mystical belief in the transformative potential of violence" as a means of exposing "the deeper reality of collective allegiance."[52]

This work seeks to trace the evolution of an original discourse based on symbolic representations of blood to the reality of spilling that blood on a large and ultimately disastrous scale. It is an evolution that subsumes and discards different subjects, identities, and aspirations. It is this very fluidity that, indeed, provides the discourse with the essential unity of organic ideology.

This kind of interpretation involves a degree of subjectivity. As with most political movements, after the initial founding of the Basque Nationalist Party, it became increasingly difficult to speak in terms of one single nationalism. The Basque example is as noteworthy for its plurality as any other, and there is certainly a case for arguing that a large group within the Basque nationalist movement (the majority, even) has consistently eschewed violence as a means of achieving its objectives. Yet within the contemporary historical context, and ever since the assassination of Archduke Franz Ferdinand by a Serbian nationalist, Gavrilo Princip, in 1914, multiple examples have demonstrated that nationalism has been a potent factor in generating the use of political violence.[53] Since its inception, Basque nationalism has in part been imbued with at least a mythical recourse to violence. If nothing else, this may explain the Basque Nationalist Party's successful mobilization of its members and sympathizers into well-organized and disciplined fighting units during the Spanish Civil War.

The work therefore seeks to identify the original symbols of struggle and warfare as they emerged within the Basque nationalist discourse and to follow their development through to the Civil War. Particular attention will be paid to how the symbols themselves changed over time, that is to say, how they were articulated and perceived according to circumstance. And I will argue that throughout the course of Basque nationalism, there has been an identifiable (although flexible and constantly changing) ideology or even culture of political violence. This may go some way to explaining the context in which ETA emerged in the 1950s.

The Scope of the Work

After a general historical introduction the work is, in effect, divided into four sections. The first of these will examine the creation of Basque nationalism in the 1890s and the symbolic rhetoric with which it established its ideology. In the second section, the effect of social tensions in the early twentieth century (particularly the period from 1917 to 1923) on the course of Basque nationalism will be examined. Then a discussion of Basque nationalism in the 1930s (with special emphasis on the Civil War) will assert that an ideology of political violence had become an integral part of nationalist discourse by the conclusion of the conflict. Finally, there will be a discussion of the influence that this ideological development may have had on the context in which ETA was founded in 1959.

Unless otherwise noted, translations supplied in the text of Spanish, Basque and French sources cited here are my own. For the most part, the Basque orthography of place names will be used in the present work, with parenthetical references to their Spanish (or French) equivalents. Elsewhere, both the Basque and Spanish versions are used.

CHAPTER ONE

Overlapping Identities in Spain and the Basque Country

In the late nineteenth century, Europe was experiencing a widespread change in the structure of both its society and its economy–modernization via industrialization. Most Europeans were increasingly aware of this change, however small or insignificant its particular effects may have seemed at any given time. In some places, the transformation was gradual; in others, it was relentlessly swift. Spain as a whole did not really begin to feel the full weight of modernization until after the turn of the century. Yet in the Basque province of Bizkaia (Vizcaya), one single generation witnessed an upheaval that irrevocably altered a long-established social pattern. The industrial revolution in Bizkaia, in the opinion of one observer, brought with it real structural violence–in other words, an enforced change in the way people led their lives and viewed the world–of a type that would subsequently have a major influence on the region's politics.[1]

Faced with a change of such basic human proportions and building on the foundations of Enlightenment rationalism, late nineteenth-century European thinkers increasingly sought to explain scientifically both their own origins and the contemporary society around them. And central to their explanations were the themes of struggle and conflict. In Darwin's theory of evolution, the critical variable–natural selection–in a world of flux and change depends on just such a struggle; Marx revolutionized philosophical explanations of humanity with his insistence on the primary importance of material reality, emphasizing the struggle of classes in the dialectic of history; and Freud, in his quest to unearth human personality development through psychoanalysis, argued that the human mind is a field of struggle and conflict between unconscious instincts and desires and cultural or societal constraints.[2] Such intellectual restlessness would also underpin the critical reframing of both Spanish and Basque culture in the nineteenth century, leading to a conflict of identity that increasingly assumed such ontological proportions, conceived as it was in an either/or dichotomy germane to the very basis of modernity itself, that its legacy would reverberate for a century afterward and ultimately result in an all too real violent struggle.

Although nineteenth-century Spain frequently has been seen as isolated and exempt from these sweeping conceptual developments within the general narrative of modern European history, it was not so different as some would contend. The myth of an unchanging, rural Spain owed (and owes) much to both the so-called black legend–anti-Spanish historiography promoted by predominantly Protestant, northern-European historians–and nineteenth-century Romantics who traveled to the country in search of a preindustrial paradise.[3] It is, however, rooted in a degree of reality. Modernization and the liberal revolution came late to the country, although this should not obscure the fact that Spain went through the normal historical processes of the nineteenth century: economic modernization, albeit in uneven fashion.[4]

This was the background against which Basque nationalism emerged in the province of Bizkaia, a fact that immediately refutes the myth of Spanish economic backwardness. In the late nineteenth century, indeed, within the space of a generation, Bizkaia became one of the world's most important industrial centers. And with this industrial change came a profound social transformation, revealing much about the aforementioned philosophical and scientific inquiries into the nature of human society and its patterns of change. In the Basque Country, for example, where previously one had taken a basic identity from family, farmhouse, village, and church, there were new challengers to the position of guarding individual consciousness, among which the state and class were the most prominent. Together, these patterns of identity only confirmed the historical process of building Spain, a process marked by both conflict and accommodation between its constituent regions.

Spain and the Basque Country: From the Late Fifteenth to the Early Nineteenth Centuries

The initial unification of what would eventually become Spain began with the alliance of the crowns of Castile-León and Aragón-Catalonia in 1479 and ended with the annexation of Navarre in 1512. This took place within the context of two crucial processes for the later articulation of Spanish identity that both, ironically, date from 1492: the culmination of a series of wars on the Iberian Peninsula between Muslims and Christians (specifically, the four medieval kingdoms of the Iberian Peninsula, Aragón-Catalonia, Navarre, Castile, and Portugal),[5] lasting several centuries, with a victory for the latter that imprinted a religious; and, later (during the sixteenth-century Counter-Reformation), a specifically Catholic dimension to this identity[6] and the beginnings of an overseas imperial expansion that would reward the new country with a wealth of riches and resources at its very birth.

The Habsburg monarchs who subsequently ruled the country in the sixteenth and seventeenth centuries presided over a vast and varied number of lands, stretching from the Iberian Peninsula through territories in western Europe into the Americas. However, this auspicious and omnipotent starting point for the Spanish Empire was, almost at its inception, challenged by its different subjects. Specifically, in the sixteenth and seventeenth centuries, there were several major separatist revolts. Two were successful (in Portugal and the Netherlands), and three were not (in Castile itself, Aragón, and Catalonia). These revolts highlighted the uneven and fragmented nature of the Spanish Empire.[7] José Álvarez Junco stresses the decidedly nonnationalist nature of these revolts: "in the early modern period, those struggles were the result of competition among elites for *privileges*, with little resemblance to a clash over *sovereignty* in terms of cultural collective personalities." However, he does see, in the "extraordinary political success" of the Catholic kings and the Habsburg monarchs, the beginnings of "some kind of collective identity in 'Spanish' terms," although this identity was neither national nor state based.[8]

The emergence of a unified polity, then, was delayed beyond the initial point of unification in 1512, and this process began to take place only between the early eighteenth and early nineteenth centuries, a timeframe marked by the initial unifying measures of the new Bourbon dynasty in the eighteenth century and the proclamation of the 1812 Cádiz Constitution. Spain, therefore, emerged in a gradual and distinctly diverse way. Indeed,

> the [Spanish] state was born of different entities (feudal states, principalities, kingdoms) amassed by the dynasties of the old regime through successive wars, marriage alliances and accidents of fate. The concept of power was regarded as the patrimony of a few interchangeable people, inheritable or conquering depending on their strengths and ambitions. This power had been geographically attributed as Spanish or Hispanic but had never had any national significance. It was in the year 1812 . . . that Spain was defined for the first time as a sociopolitical concept, as identifying a community called "the Spanish nation."[9]

It is difficult, then, to speak of a single Spanish identity before the early nineteenth century,[10] in that "from the fifteenth to the nineteenth centuries, both particularist and national-state identities–never clearly differentiated–made use of a repertoire of aggressive images derived from external, expansionist imperial or missionary experience, alongside a sort of shared resistance to outside influences whose emotional core was expressed through the idealization of the local."[11] Indeed, it is probably fair to say that such an idealization of the local, provincial, or regional formed the historical foundation on which Spain was constructed.

Since the Middle Ages, the Basque provinces of Gipuzkoa (Guipúzcoa), Araba (Álava) (both 1200), and Bizkaia (1379) had been part of the kingdom of Castile, albeit with distinct institutional systems. The peasant agricultural organization of the Basque provinces provided for a stable and relatively egalitarian social organization based on three separate groups: self-sufficient and independent small farmers living in isolated and introverted rural communities; similar, dispersed fishing communities sheltered by a number of natural harbors dotting the Basque coastline; and a small, but emergent merchant class whose fortunes were linked to maritime trade patterns developed after the expansion of the Spanish Empire to the New World.[12] Indeed, following Paul Gilroy's groundbreaking examination of the reflexive nature of culture and identity as it traversed back and forth across the Atlantic,[13] one should perhaps see these developments as part of a wider process of multiplying Basque consciousness.

Traditional Basque social organization also had parallels in civic life. Although officially a part of the kingdom of Castile since medieval times (Araba, Bizkaia and Gipuzkoa) and, during the early modern period (with the incorporation of the kingdom of Navarre in 1512) subjects of the unified Spanish crown, the four Basque provinces enjoyed their own financial, legal, and administrative structures.[14] These structures were codified under the *fueros*, a set of charters conceding special privileges and local rights. Although these laws existed throughout the kingdom, they were especially important in the Basque provinces, ceding an autonomous system stronger than existed in any other region.[15] Indeed, if one interprets the *fueros* as the legal foundation of the historical relationship between the Basque provinces and Spain, it is worth bearing in mind that Araba, Bizkaia, and Gipuzkoa, at least, accepted the king of Castile as their sovereign as the result of an agreement codified in these charters, rather than as the result of direct military conquest, as was the case with Navarre.[16]

The degree of local organization was such that each Basque province retained its separate identity, based on a coherent system of councils (at both the municipal and provincial level) that were sovereign within their province. For example, each province retained the power to tax property and to mobilize soldiers, not being automatically subject to the authority of the royal army. There was also a provision to review and possibly to veto any laws introduced by the king. Finally, as a symbol of royal allegiance, any ascending Spanish monarch had to travel to the Basque provinces in order to swear an oath of loyalty to their *fueros*. In the case of Bizkaia, this act took place under the oak Tree of Gernika (Guernica), traditionally the meeting place of the Bizkaian representatives. From the early sixteenth to the late eighteenth centuries, then, Basque society maintained a large degree of social and economic autonomy within the emergent Spanish state.

There was, furthermore, a distinctive cultural identity within the Basque provinces. In a predominantly rural society the Basque language, Euskara (also spelled Euskera), was the primary language of communication.[17] At the forefront of its use were some Basque village priests, reflecting the increasingly important role of the church at the local level from the Counter-Reformation onward. Their role was both spiritual and community-oriented, and their interests, linked to those of the communities that they served, aimed at preserving the existing stable framework of their society.

Yet this stability was also challenged by several important changes within the same period, most notably the emergence of a vibrant commercial class. The expansion of the Spain's European trade opened a commercial route between landlocked Castile, through Araba, to the coastal provinces of Bizkaia and Gipuzkoa. Further, by the eighteenth century, mineral excavations were under way in Bizkaia, with a concomitant growth in tentative manufacturing industries. Within this transformation, the merchant class associated with these developments increasingly eschewed Euskara in favor of Castellano, that is, Spanish, the language of trade, empire, and profit. At the same time, this class began to support the ideas of Enlightenment liberalism, with its emphasis on progress through education, technology, urbanization, and economic growth.

In Spain, too, there were important changes. After the ascendancy of the Bourbon dynasty in 1701, attempts were made to centralize the Spanish state in accordance with coherent policies of economic expansion. An administrative system modeled on that of absolutist France was introduced, stressing the importance to efficiency of one state language. The other languages of the country were therefore relegated to a lower status–the domain of the peasantry and their local clergy.[18] This inevitably led to tension, especially with the Basque provinces that, up until that time, had enjoyed the advantages of regional privileges while at the same time making use of their commercial connections with Madrid.[19] There was also a rising tension within the Basque provinces as an increasingly bipolarized society positioned the majority traditionalist peasantry against a minority, though ascendant liberal merchant class.

The division of Basque society took shape around a variety of forms: Although the foral system, the system of the *fueros*, provided for a theoretical legal equality of citizens, there was increasing political inequality, framed around the peasant-merchant dichotomy. Linked to this division was the increasing use of Spanish within the Basque provinces as the language of politics, trade, and commerce. Euskara was consequently relegated to the illiterate masses.[20]

By the turn of the eighteenth century, a political dichotomy between liberals and traditionalists had emerged within Basque society. Liberals defined themselves according to their belief in an emerging market economy and envisioned a society open to change in both political and economic terms. Traditionalists viewed change with suspicion and sought the maintenance of a society based on faith and (a perceived) stability. This division, representative of an underlying challenge to ancien régime Spain, would provide the dominant sociopolitical theme for the next century and beyond. And the emerging struggle would be played out predominantly on the battlefield, with the Basque provinces taking a leading role.

One catalyst of the challenge to ancien régime Spain was provided by revolutionary France. In 1793–95, France invaded Spain, annexing Gipuzkoa, with some degree of help from enlightened liberal leaders in Donostia–San Sebastián. The war against Napoleon's forces did much to unleash a Romantic or cultural form of Spanish nationalism whereby the nation was seen as an innate reality, beyond the will of the individuals who constituted it.[21] At the same time, the French occupation had three important consequences for the future emergence of Basque nationalism. It highlighted the strength of centrifugal tendencies within the Basque provinces, allowed for the reinforcement of Basque myths of original independence, and provided a context in which the concept of war as a viable means of solving problems attained its own dynamic.[22] Furthermore, between 1808 and 1814, the country was subject to a large-scale invasion and occupation. The ensuing War of Independence saw a majority of Basques fight *against* the French invaders, in defense of traditional, foral Spain.

Although the effect of foreign occupation is credited, by one observer, with forging for the first time a sense of communal Spanish nationhood,[23] it should be added that this view anachronistically employs the modern conception of nationalism, an ideological creation aimed at cementing state unity. Indeed, as Joseba Gabilondo (following Álvarez Junco) points out, the term "War of Independence" was invented after the event (in the 1830s and 1840s), most likely inspired by the Latin American wars of independence against the Spanish Empire itself between 1810 and 1825. As a result, Gabilondo contends, "the Spanish nationalist model now derives from Latin American nationalism and thus ultimately responds to a (post)colonial imagination and logic: the (post)colony imagines the (post)empire, not the other way around."[24]

Away from the coast, deep in the heart of the rural Basque society, the invading French found few allies. The occupation subsequently came to incorporate the expropriation of property, deportation, and incarceration in French jails. The response of the Basque peasantry was to form small insurgent units, establishing an effective network of groups among the sympathetic rural population. The tactic of guerrilla warfare, first employed in Navarre at the outbreak of hostilities, thus came to be closely associated with the Basque peasantry. The concept of the guerrilla, however, implies more than a mere military tactic. The guerrilla came to symbolize a heroic figure, the humble peasant engaged in a noble struggle against the greater forces of an organized army. Basque guerrillas enjoyed the unconditional support of the rural populace from which they emerged, and they pursued a precisely defined ideology: the defense of rural Basque interests. There was also a sense of tragedy associated with the guerrillas in that they could triumph only in their native surroundings, and these triumphs would always be of a localized nature. They could win battles, but without a regular army, they would never win a war.[25]

During the French occupation, the Spanish king, Fernando VII, was forced into exile. This left a power vacuum in the country and allowed an ascendant Spanish liberal class to create a centralized and more representative regime. In 1812, the Cortes of Cádiz proclaimed a liberal constitution that effectively abolished the *fueros*, providing for a uniform system of government, administration, and law,[26] although these provisions also allowed for clear local and regional decision-making powers through *ayuntamientos* (city halls) and *diputaciones* (provincial councils).[27] In general terms, the Cádiz Constitution established three clear and connected elements that thereafter would be central to Spanish history: revolution (to abolish *ancient régime* feudal society), nation (to open up a new space of power), and Spain (as the single political reality with which citizens should identify).[28] Further, the Cádiz Constitution also integrated two important declarations as regards the future construction of Spanish nationalism: the identification of the Spanish nation with Catholicism and a postfeudal place for the hereditary monarchy.[29]

Interestingly, the constitution also spoke of a "coming together of all Spaniards from both hemispheres," a clear attempt to create a transatlantic community or nation–this, precisely at a time when several Latin American colonies had began to revolt against the Spanish Empire. However, this concept was withdrawn from subsequent legal definitions of the nation as Spain gradually lost its colonies through the nineteenth century. From the 1830s onward, then, "the nation's sovereignty belonged exclusively to the Peninsula. Moreover, in the name of these national, peninsular interests, equal conditions were denied to the [remaining overseas] territories... which remained part of the Spanish state," and therefore "Spain as a nation was established, not only on the basis of ideas, but, above all, on the basis of governing interests that nationalized church and common property, abolished customs duties and protected markets.[30]

Between 1814 and his death in 1833, Fernando VII ruled Spain in absolutist fashion, although with a curious secularizing tendency, the likely consequence of a certain institutionalization of liberal values in 1812. That said, liberal sympathizers revolted in 1820, returning to power briefly before a conservative counterrevolution in 1823. On his death in 1833, Fernando named his infant daughter, Princess Isabel, as his successor (Queen Isabel II) in opposition to his younger brother, Don Carlos María Isidro, and a dynastic struggle thus ensued, crystallizing many of the rising tensions in a Spain stumbling in its evolution from a traditional to a modern society. Indeed, there would be no swift change, because the forces of ancien régime Spain prepared to defend their society against the oncoming liberal transformation.

The Nineteenth-Century Carlist Challenge

The resultant crisis led to the First Carlist War. Although initially motivated by the claims of Fernando's younger brother, Don Carlos, there were several other factors leading to the outbreak of hostilities: for example, the general debate over the position of the church in Spain, how the country should plan its economic future, and of course, the question of foral privileges.[31]

It was at this time that Carlism emerged as a political ideology, and a majority of Basques rallied to this cause. Carlism was a rural, religious, and traditional sociopolitical outlook, reflecting the fears of a society under threat from the escalating importance of secular capitalism. In the Basque Country, it assumed a specifically defensive tone, linked to the central question of the *fueros*. This defense was in turn connected to the protection of what was perceived as an authentic Basque culture, with a certain idealization of concrete liberties and social harmony as guaranteed by the foral regime. These ideas were seen as representing the true Basque way of life, as opposed to the "godless" forces of liberalism.[32] The Carlist cause thus went beyond a simple defense of monarchical privilege, because it encapsulated the defense of Basque culture itself. Indeed, regional liberties were central to the ideological formation of Carlism.[33]

The First Carlist War, which broke out in 1833, was a brutal civil war of attrition. Lasting seven years, it was marked by a number of atrocities among both the liberal and Carlist ranks. The conflict began, ended, and was largely conducted as a guerrilla war in which Basques, well schooled in this type of warfare, played a prominent role.[34] It was also a response to the brutalities of martial law, which included arbitrary arrest, confiscations, and the execution of prisoners: "This policy, adopted by government commanders from the middle of 1834 on, gave the war a viciously sanguinary policy, with no quarter offered on either side."[35]

The strength of Carlism lay in the rural Basque peasantry, and it was from this peasantry that the Basque culture of guerrilla warfare emerged. In 1838, the English traveler George Borrow visited the Basque provinces, recording the following observations:

> Whilst listening to ... [Basque songs] it is easy to suppose oneself in the close vicinity of some desperate encounter. We seem to hear the charge of the cavalry on the sounding plain, the clash of swords, and the rushing of men down the gorges of hills. In person the Basques are of middle size, and are active and athletic.... Their bravery is unquestionable, and they are considered as the best soldiery belonging to the Spanish crown.[36]

One does wonder, however, to what extent Borrow was guilty of a desire to represent Basques as noble and quaint–as a nineteenth-century noble savage or something *other* than the metropolitan Europe from which he hailed.[37]

During the hostilities, government forces found the Basque countryside completely inhospitable to regular troops carrying arms and equipment.[38] Yet Carlism's strength, its rural character, would also be its downfall, for the Carlists could not win the war outside their native mountains.[39] This bequeathed Carlism a fatalism that would resonate in later struggles. Furthermore, as Martin Blinkhorn remarks, "already by 1840 violence had assumed for the Carlists a mythical role which had little or nothing to do with rational assessment of the chances of victory."[40] Nevertheless it is difficult to accept that the war represented a struggle between the Basque provinces and Spain. It was not a war of national liberation, but rather a conflict between two ideas, two different visions of what actually constituted Spain: the aforementioned liberal and traditionalist visions. It was, furthermore, a struggle in which different sections of Basque society allied with one or other of the competing forces.[41]

The First Carlist War lasted from 1833 until 1839, yet it became increasingly clear that, through a combination of indecisive leadership, internal divisions, and the grueling nature of combat, the Carlists would not triumph. The Compromise of Bergara (Vergara) in August 1839, signaling the end of the war, referred the foral question to Madrid, and in October of that year, a law was passed that, although actually confirming the Basque *fueros*, also stipulated that they should not infringe the constitutional unity of Spain. In effect, the seeds had been sown for the erosion of the foral system.

In 1844, for example, the Basque veto on royal decrees (the *pase foral*) in the Basque provinces was abolished, and the customs border was once and for all transferred from the Ebro River to the coast and the French border.[42] That same year, the Spanish government created the Guardia Civil (Civil Guard) as a theoretical civilian counterbalance to the army in questions of public order. It subsequently became *the* representative of state authority in Spain, particularly at village level.[43] Successive liberal governments from 1835 onward also oversaw a process by which the state gradually took control of the educational system, creating new schools throughout all municipalities, a state-run system of secondary schools and teacher-training institutions,[44] with the key change taking place in an 1857 law on national education.[45] This attempted, among other things, to centralize public education so that, for example, in the Basque Country, non-Basque-speaking teachers could now instruct primarily Basque-speaking children. As a consequence, "Euskera was stigmatized as the language of the stables, the language of unsophisticated rustics in contrast to Spanish, the language of refinement, culture, education and urban success."[46] From the end of the First Carlist War onward, Basque politics gradually came to be dominated by a growing upper-middle-class liberal elite taking full advantage of the erosion of the foral system.

Spain was again beset by a political crisis, however, in 1868, when a military coup by the more radical Progressive Liberals in Madrid forced Queen Isabel II to abdicate. A democratic monarchist system was subsequently installed, with Amadeo of Savoy taking the throne in 1870,[47] ushering in a wave of anticlericalism that in turn produced a revival of Carlism, and once again, the Carlists found solid support among the peasant masses of the Basque Country. Then, when the democratic monarchy itself fell in 1873, a second war ensued.[48]

The immediate cause of the Second Carlist War was the proclamation of the first Spanish Republic, a radical, anticlerical regime that for the first time distanced itself from any constitutional arrangements with potential monarchs. Yet the war, which lasted until 1876, did not assume the mantle of the previous struggle. The Carlist pretender to the throne, Carlos "VII," was more overtly political, in a modern sense, and is described by one observer as "one of the first modern Spanish nationalists."[49] He did not enjoy widespread support within Spain, and the Basque Carlists were gradually worn down by the more powerful government forces.

In 1874, a new pretender to the throne emerged: Alfonso, the son of Isabel II. With the war reaching its climax, he was proclaimed King Alfonso XII in an alliance with moderate and conservative liberals. At the close of hostilities, a new constitution was proclaimed heralding the beginning of the Restoration Monarchy, a regime that would last until 1923. With respect to the Basque provinces, the 1876 Constitution marked the end of the foral system, a triumph for Spanish liberalism and the final defeat of Carlism as an important political force.

The Restoration Monarchy: Political Modernization and Industrial Takeoff

The constitutional monarchy of Alfonso XII sought something of a middle ground between the progressive positions of the Republicans and the traditionalism of the Carlists. Through the influence of the most important politician of the era, Antonio Cánovas del Castillo, a two-party political system was created consisting of the Conservative Liberals (popularly known as the Conservatives, and led by Cánovas himself) and the Constitutional Liberals (or the Liberals, led by Práxedes Sagasta). At the same time, the Republicans and Carlists remained politically isolated due to internal divisions after their recent defeats. Composed of notable members of Madrid's political society, both major parties reflected a common ideology: the defense of oligarchical interests in the centralizing state. These interests were linked to the agrarian upper middle classes and to the emergent industrial bourgeoisie of Spain,[50] with power emanating from the central alliance between the king and his ministers.[51]

To say that the state was a working democratic monarchy, however, would be misleading. Cánovas was deeply affected by what he saw as the decadence of the "Spanish race"[52] and was a great admirer of the British political system, with its "natural" ebb and flow between the two major political parties. Consequently, he sought to impose this system on Spain, although there was no democratic tradition to allow for its natural emergence. Free elections would have revealed this, for while Republican and Carlist power had been curtailed, it had not been completely subdued.

Thus, in the absence of such a natural ebb and flow, Cánovas invented his own democratic tradition: Elections were fixed to allow for the efficient transfer of power between the Conservative and Liberal parties, the two political groups dedicated to the success of Restoration Spain. This election rigging involved the complicity of the civil governors (the state's representatives in each of its constituent provinces) in tandem with the Home Office in Madrid. The civil governor would "prepare" the provinces by selecting the right men for the job to be placed in the municipal authorities. They would be both Conservative and Liberal, even a moderate Republican here and there, so as to allow for the efficient creation of a workable political system. The municipalities would then draw up the lists of eligible voters to elect from a choice of officially sanctioned candidates. In the more compact, populous towns, the civil governors could keep a careful eye on the development of the system.[53] In smaller, more dispersed towns and rural areas, this control was left to local luminaries known as *caciques*.[54] Stability was thus the overriding theme of Restoration Spain, because Madrid sought to provide a solid basis for its economic policies. According to Jaime Vicens Vives, "The Restoration was, essentially, an act of faith in Hispanic coexistence.... Cánovas wanted to establish a legal state, not an arbitrary one, but one that would be backed by the vital forces of the nation–agricultural landowners, industrialists, and bourgeoisie–and by an army with no capricious desires for a pronunciamiento," a military coup.[55] The political modernization of the state entailed a greater degree of centralization than ever before. In the Basque case, this meant a radically changed relationship with Madrid.[56]

In an 1873 text, Cánovas himself had quite clearly stated that Basque "particularity" had no place in his vision of a modern Spain:

> I believe a day will come when those honorable [Basque] provinces acknowledge that in their current relations with the other provinces of Spain they are unintentionally violating the clearest juridical principles. Forming a gradual and successive alliance over time for the providential purpose of constituting state and nation, this does not imply an obligation on the non-Basque regions of Spain to remunerate with the profits of their own labor the general services which their privileged and exempt brothers need and require neither more nor less than they do. And it is even less appropriate that other Spaniards should be considered to be under a perpetual obligation to risk their lives in defense of the moral and material inter-

> ests, which the Basques enjoy equally through the state or common nation, unless this is a mutual relationship with equal obligations for all.[57]

For Cánovas, it was not a question of abolishing the *fueros*, but rather of extending their provisions throughout Spain: "The local freedoms of the Basques, like all those engendered and created by history, benefit those who enjoy them, and do not harm anyone, unless it is regarded as harmful because of the righteous envy it arouses in others."[58] However, he did not envisage a federal Spain. Rather, he sought to implement a solidly unitary state.

As a consequence, and building on previous nineteenth-century initiatives, an even more centralized educational system was introduced that actively promoted Spanish as the official language of the state while at the same time discriminating against the other languages of Spain, Basque included.[59] One contemporary observer recorded the increasing influence of the Spanish state in Basque regional affairs, noting that the central government sought the eradication of Euskara. For example, it was now compulsory to learn the catechism in Spanish. In a deeply religious society such as that of the Basque provinces, this represented a profound challenge for Basque culture.[60] Indeed, for Cánovas, Euskara was antithetical to modernity itself:

> The Basque (or Bizkaian, or whatever you want to call him) being enclosed in his solitary language, which is totally unknown in other nations, and being even more isolated in his impassable mountains, has until now defied the impetuous current of new ideas, not allowing them to infiltrate except slowly and gradually into his mind, and only then after having carefully digested and assimilated them. The same can be said for his language.[61]

The only remedy, then, was for Basque to disappear to allow for the necessary modernization of Spain. "Centralization," remarks Adrian Shubert, "was one watchword of Spanish liberals. The other was homogeneity."[62]

Yet there remained a degree of fiscal autonomy within the Basque provinces, for Madrid could not afford to alienate the increasingly powerful (and liberal) Basque business class. Through a *concierto económico*, or fiscal pact, the economic privileges enjoyed by the Basque Country under the foral system continued in modified form. According to the first of these pacts, promulgated in 1878 and renewable thereafter, the treasury in Madrid assessed a total tax contribution for the Basque provinces. Thereafter, the collection of these taxes was left to the discretion of the provincial governments. This compromise between administrative centralization and economic autonomy stabilized the new regime and provided a basis for a spectacular industrial takeoff in the Basque provinces.

Already during the 1850s and 1860s, there had appeared in Bizkaia the first stirrings of a boom that may have been unequalled anywhere else in Europe.[63] The invention of the Bessemer process in 1856 allowed for the relatively cheap, efficient processing of steel using high-grade nonphosphoric ore.[64] As a consequence, the low-phosphorous red ore of Bizkaia began to attract industrial concerns in France and Germany and particularly in Britain. After the 1876 settlement, a wave of foreign capital flooded the provinces of Bizkaia

The Ripa Wharf, Bilbao, late nineteenth century. The River Nervión, dissecting Greater Bilbao, allowed ships access right into the city center. Here, vestiges of a preindustrial age–the use of animals–blend with machine power to capture a moment of economic and social transformation. By permission of Editorial Iparaguirre Editorial, S.A. archives.

and Gipuzkoa. By the turn of the century, 21.5 percent of the world's iron ore was produced in Spain, predominantly in Bizkaia.[65] Furthermore, this mining boom and the iron ore exports it produced stimulated home-based industries in Bizkaia and led to the creation of metallurgical, shipping, paper, chemical, banking, and hydroelectric companies. By century's end, the bulk of heavy industry, the largest merchant fleet, and the most powerful financial institutions in Spain were concentrated in Greater Bilbao.[66] This industrial growth, in turn, produced a social diversification previously unknown in the Basque provinces as immigration from non-Basque regions of Spain swelled their populations. In the period from 1877 to 1910, the Bizkaian population rose from around 190,000 to just under 350,000, and that of Gipuzkoa increased from approximately 167,000 to nearly 227,000.[67]

The dual process of industrial growth and social modernization would have one important result: the emergence of a Basque nationalist movement. The appearance of Basque nationalism came as a direct response to the changes occurring within Basque society. Similarly, in the industrial towns of Bizkaia and Gipuzkoa and the working-class areas of Bilbao, an emergent proletariat began to embrace socialism,[68] while at the same time, the new Basque urban middle class adopted the ways of nineteenth-century European liberalism.[69]

Spain and the Crisis of the 1890s

In 1885, King Alfonso XII died of consumption. This prompted the incumbent Conservative prime minister, Cánovas, who was fearful of Carlist and Republican rebellions, to usher in a Liberal ministry, because he believed that such outbursts could be best controlled by the opposing party. The Liberals duly took office under the regency of María Cristina, the wife of Alfonso. While political stability ensued, Restoration Spain had taken its first step toward its own demise.

Liberal governments in the period between 1885 and 1890 introduced a set of sweeping reforms, including a law of association, trial by jury, and universal male suffrage. To a great extent, this helped to assimilate a number of Republicans into the political system, thereby extinguishing the fire of their cause. Yet it also allowed for the institutional emergence of *caciquismo*, government by local politico-economic elites, a product of the wish to preserve traditional conservative interests. In a predominantly peasant society, there was little widespread interest in politics. This left the system, bolstered by the suffrage legislation, open to abuse by the *caciques*. The universal vote was thus transformed into a means of preserving vested, property-tied interests. After 1890, the institutionalization of *caciquismo* gradually eroded the balance of Restoration Spain, a stability further affected by social and economic pressures both from within and outside the country.

The economic takeoff enjoyed during the early years of the new regime endured until the late 1880s, when, in common with predominantly agricultural societies elsewhere, the country suffered an agricultural crisis. Spain's two staple products, wine and wheat, both suffered a dramatic fall in price, and there were renewed calls for protectionism. As the state responded with a growing wall of tariffs, the intervention of Madrid in local economic affairs became readily more apparent. This was especially the case in the more dynamic economic areas of Catalonia and the Basque provinces, compounding their own social and regional tensions.

Madrid intervened in the provinces in other ways, as well–ways that led to increased violence. Prior to 1890, anarchism had been almost entirely associated, in Spain, with the large estates of Andalusia in the south. However, with the growth of the Catalan economy, Barcelona became the focus for a widespread migration of impoverished southern Spanish immigrants. Some brought anarchist ideology with them, and it flourished in Barcelona of the 1890s. Indeed, the image of Barcelona during the decade became one of enduring social violence, reflecting the increasingly violent nature of Spanish society as a whole.[70] The reaction of the Spanish state was swift and uncompromising: Two antiterrorist laws were passed, in 1894 and 1896, respectively, that placed the death penalty on any act carried out with explosives.[71] They also licensed a repressive police response that included the harassment and torture of suspects. This, in turn, engendered yet more anarchist violence.[72]

Catalonia, with its commercial hub in Barcelona, had emerged in the 1840s as the principal industrial center of Spain. At the same time, and as in the Basque case later on, a cultural renaissance occurred in tandem with the increasing modernization of the region. A regionalist spirit gradually emerged, principally literary in outlook and based on the Catalan language.[73] There were, moreover, also important economic motives driving a burgeoning Catalan regionalism: Industrial gains had to be protected, and with this in mind, economic protection was the order of the day in the period from 1840 to 1868.[74]

During the 1880s, literary and economic regionalism gave way to an increasing emphasis on political rights. In 1887, the Lliga de Catalunya (Catalan League) was formed to safeguard Catalan interests.[75] It would subsequently form the principal force for Catalan nationalism, a phrase that was first used in the 1890s. Furthermore, in 1891, the newly created Unió Catalanista (Catalan Union) argued for a form of autonomy within the Spanish state.[76]

With economic discontent dividing Spanish society along both class and regional lines, toward the coming of the 1890s, it seemed as if the triumph of liberal Spain was to be short lived. This was not only the case within the peninsula, for the mood of separatist nationalism had spread to the last remnants of the Spanish Empire, and it was from there that the threat to an eternal, indivisible Spain appeared even greater. Abroad, Cuba remained the principal point of friction. In an intense period between 1810 and 1825, Spain lost all its colonial possessions in Latin America except Cuba and Puerto Rico, leaving these (together with the Philippines) the only remnants of its once mighty empire. Like the eighteenth-century rebellion of the North American colonists against Britain, these revolutions were the result of a changed economic relationship between the imperial center and its transatlantic peripheries, resulting in the creation of Argentina (1816), Chile (1818), Colombia (1819), Venezuela (1821), Mexico (1822), Peru (1824), and Bolivia

(1825). These losses contributed in no small part to a developing crisis. At the end of the century, Cuba became for Spain what Ireland was to Britain: a problematic contemporary reminder of a glorious imperial past.

Although the Cuban insurrection mirrored the political conflict between Britain and Ireland, there were also significant differences. Nineteenth-century British policy in Ireland encouraged general economic (and specifically industrial) development in a reduced area–in and around Belfast in the northern province of Ulster–at the expense of the rest of the island and especially of its traditional economic center, Dublin. One of the most infamous episodes related to this lack of development was, of course, the aftermath of the Irish potato famine, with an inadequate British government response to the disaster and the death and migration of millions of people. However, the situation in Cuba was different. Through the course of the nineteenth century, the island actually acquired greater economic value for Spain, becoming the largest slave society in Latin American history and also central to Spanish capitalist development.[77] Indeed, in 1882, for example, of the 40,721 people who migrated to the Americas from Spain that year, 30,730 went to Cuba.[78] However, a corrupt colonial system left power and profit in the hands of Spanish officialdom while denying the island a policy of free trade and its inhabitants basic political rights.[79] Cuba rose in rebellion during the years from 1868 to 1878, yet peace was not truly assured. One contemporary observer remarked that "for sixteen years–that is, from 1879–1895–Cuba was not precisely in a state of insurrection, but it was never quiet."[80] After the "Long War" of 1868–78, the Cuban Autonomist Party emerged on the island, principally to safeguard the interests of the Creole elite. A home-rule movement was thus born, but the tension remained between this elite and the Spanish colonial community. With the approach of the 1890s, this tension increased to the point of further insurrection.

Cuban nationalism found its most eloquent exponent in José Martí, whose call for Cubans to look within their own culture, rejecting that of Spain, would have echoes in the peninsula itself during the 1890s: "The government must be born of the country. The spirit of the government must be that of the country. The form of the government must adjust to the inherent structure of the country. Government is nothing more than the balance of the natural elements of the country."[81] According to Martí's argument, Cuba's ills stemmed from the application of Spanish culture in a non-Spanish context. Further, resistance to this idea could be based only on Cubans' looking within their own cultural traditions.

In the Philippines, a similar system of Spanish control was in effect, with the same results. In 1887, José Rizal's novel *Noli me tangere* (literally, from Latin, Touch me not) articulated native resentment, placing Filipinos at the center of their own narrative to "imagine" a community for future Philippine nationalists.[82] In 1892, Rizal formed the Liga Filipina (Philippine League), which found a clandestine counterpart in the Katipunán, an organization dedicated to direct confrontation with the Spanish authorities.[83]

Spanish Nationalism: The Cultural Politics of State and Nation

The threat of regional discontent at home and colonial unrest was nothing new in the history of Spain. Neither were several of the Spanish responses that sought to reaffirm the territorial unity and integrity of Spain. This could well be termed "Spanish nationalism"–a relatively new subject in the academic treatment Spanish history, but one I believe to be crucial for understanding the complex unfolding of national tensions in nineteenth-century Spain. And as a focus of intellectual inquiry, understanding Spanish nationalism helps us unravel the intricate connections between center, periphery, and empire that constitute this history. To quote Juan Sisinio Pérez Garzón,

> if we really want to overcome the misunderstandings and tensions that have characterized relations between the different national cultures within the Spanish state, then we must deconstruct the myths that have emerged over the last two centuries as part and parcel of the building of what we know today as *Spain*. And some of the most pernicious myths are those produced by Spanish/centralist nationalism, which has the curious ability to present itself as if it were something more than a species of nationalism, as if its aims were immanent, natural, and therefore, beyond question or analysis.[84]

Joseba Gabilondo, echoing this view, accuses the influential thinker, Jon Juaristi, of perpetuating just such a myth: "Juaristi actively legitimizes Spanish nationalism by denying its nationalist nature, thus emphasizing its democratic, rational, modern, and transparent character, a transparency that is always a sign of hegemony, as when race, gender, class, or ethnicity are not 'our' problem but a 'minority problem,' 'their problem.' Nationalism is not a Spanish problem; 'it's theirs, the Basques.'"[85]

Spanish nationalism, of course, had emerged prior to the Restoration. Article 2 of the 1812 Cádiz Constitution declared "Love of the Fatherland" a fundamental obligation of all Spanish citizens, and from then on, there were constant appeals to the fatherland as a means of justifying official state policies.[86] One of the best examples of nationalist fever gripping the country (and with a clearly demarcated Other) occurred in the war of 1859–60 in North Africa.[87] Actually, the offensive was no more than a policing action, designed to protect the Spanish garrison towns of Ceuta and Melilla from attack. Although a subservient sultan ruled the country, he could not control the people of the Rif mountains, the Berber clans whose sporadic offensives against the Spanish enclaves incensed public opinion in the peninsula.[88]

The subsequent offensive took on the highly charged atmosphere of a crusade, incorporating the vague idea of an African mission with the image of battle against the modern-day Moors.[89] Victory in the campaign, including the capture of Tetuan in 1860, ensured widespread enthusiasm for "national feeling" throughout the country, not least of which occurred in Catalonia.[90] "With the 1859–1860 war Spanish nationalism became a respectable enterprise for Catholic conservative forces," Álvarez Junco points out: "Patriotism was finally embraced by the clergy and absolutist elites who thus far had relied on religion and tradition as their only legitimizing discourse."[91] Another legacy of the "crusade," however, would be the continued insurrection of the Rif clans, for complete military conquest of the area was virtually impossible, given the difficult geographical conditions.[92]

It was, then, "unquestionably in the middle decades of the nineteenth century that *Spanishness* was configured as something supposedly immutable, that had descended across the centuries, as the definition of an eternal political nation, and a unique cultural essence."[93] And Restoration Spain principally promoted this immutable quality of Spanishness through the centralizing tendencies of its educational policies.[94] Indeed, some observers contend that "the greatest impact of the state's formulation of a nationalist ideology was in education," with the new educational system transforming "the former subjects of a dynasty into citizens of one nation and patriots with the same interests" so that "all the resources of the new liberal society were deployed in order to preach the civic religion of a whole nation whose image was superimposed upon its constituent parts and its social conditions."[95]

The importance of education and its relation to an emergent idea of Spanish nationalism were also evident in the private sector. In 1876, the Institución Libre de Enseñanza (Free Institute of Education) was founded by Francisco Giner de los Ríos. Although originally intended to be a free and independent university, it actually became an experimental primary and secondary school, private and secular, whose roots lay in the ideas of the 1868 revolution and the general philosophy of the German thinker Christian Krause. This philosophy stressed individual civic responsibility and the importance of culture in the process of modernization. Perhaps more than any other institution, it represented the zeal of modernization in Spain. And in many ways, it was an attempt on the part of a liberal intelligentsia to drag the country into modern Europe. Ultimately, it was successful in its immediate goal of creating a new cultural and political elite to lead modern Spain, yet this elite had no access to a general public capable of responding to its ideas.[96] Its overall influence was also limited by the control exercised by the state in educational matters, but, like its public counterpart, it did promote an idea of Spain intimately associated (indeed confused) with Castile. In fact, it was an institution completely dedicated to Spanish nationalism.[97]

In addition, there was a concerted effort in the nineteenth century to shape a specific collective memory through the invention of a Spanish national heritage by placing statues in public squares and gardens, establishing national museums, and commissioning grand monumental paintings depicting a shared and glorious past based on heroic figures such as Columbus and the Catholic kings: Thus, for example, *The Surrender of Granada* by Francisco Padilla and *Roger de Flor's Assault on Constantinople* by Moreno Carbonero decorated the Senate Conference Hall.[98]

Similarly, an ideology devoted to promoting the concept of a unitary Spain was more than evident in the principal historical works of the time. For example, Manuel Merry y Colón's historical interpretations were standard textbooks for both seminary and university students. Both his *Compendio de historia de España* (1889) and *Elementos de historia crítica de España* (1892) stressed the essential unity of Spain through its Catholic faith[99] while at the same time emphasizing the "mission" of Spain and the greatness of the Spanish race and its heroes such as the Cid, also condemning Jews and *conversos* (Jewish converts to Christianity after 1492) "with remarkable ferocity for their heresy, antipatriotism, and greed."[100] Similarly, the widely read Modesto Lafuente offered a more liberal (yet still nationalist) vision of Spanish history–for example, in his thirty-volume *Historia de España* (originally published between 1850 and 1867 and reissued in 1889).[101] One might even contend that the middle decades of the nineteenth century marked the beginning of the political use of history through the prism of education, a debate that continues to this day[102] and one that reveals the crucial role of history in political transitions.[103]

Music, too, was at the vanguard of an expanding Spanish nationalism. In his 1891 nationalist manifesto *Por nuestra música* (For a music of our own), Felip Pedrell called for a national opera to integrate Spanish musical traditions with those of Europe. The influence of Pedrell and his manifesto bequeathed Spain its first truly internationally recognized composers of the twentieth century: the former Pedrell pupils and pan-Hispanic nationalists Isaac Albéniz and Enrique Granados.[104]

Finally, in keeping with nationalist mythology across Europe, the public celebration of national anniversaries was also promoted, perhaps most famously on the four hundredth anniversary of the discovery of the Americas in 1892, an occasion in which the royal family and government took part in promoting public parades, and the Spanish press celebrated the unique quality of the nation in its overseas conquest: "According to *La Época*, the faith and monarchist patriotism of this achievement expressed the destiny of a 'chosen people,' while for *El Liberal* it signified the superiority of a nation that had brought progress to the Americas. They all agreed that it was the most significant contribution of a united Spain, strengthened by the Catholic Kings."[105]

To coincide with this auspicious occasion, the Royal Spanish Academy of the Language commissioned a text by the philologist, historian, and literary critic Marcelino Menéndez y Pelayo to articulate the literary connections between Spain and the Americas. As might be expected "from one of the main contributors to the construction of Spanish national identity based on the Catholic faith," his *Antología de poetas hispano-americanos* (Anthology of Spanish-American poets, 4 vols., 1893–1895) celebrated Spain's "civilizing mission" in the Americas precisely on the eve of its final downfall.[106] In the introduction to the work, Menéndez y Pelayo unapologetically spoke of this mission as rooted in one of the two great languages of the civilized world, Spanish (the other being German, with its Protestant individualism), which represented Catholic Latin Europe, and as incorporating a significant racialist dimension that dismissed most foreign and indigenous cultures.[107]

When all these elements are taken together, one cannot but stress the importance of an ideology of Spanish nationalism in the era of the Restoration. Building on initial attempts to promote a single Spanish national identity in the late eighteenth and early nineteenth centuries, this ideology became especially important in late nineteenth-century liberal Spain. Indeed, the Restoration "allowed [Conservatives and Liberals] to use Spanish nationalism as an ideological alibi when confronted with any competing ideology (like federalism or internationalism) that might undermine their own economic and social hegemony."[108] Such nationalism was also reflective of more general European trends of that time, when the emergence of modern states marked an increased awareness on the part of state builders of the need to augment their work by promoting a right-wing statist nationalism that served as a bulwark against potential threats from more democratic, leftist, or even substate nationalist movements. Indeed, despite charges that Spain was a weak nation, it has been claimed that, "the [Spanish] nation-state established during the nineteenth century had sufficient strength to support cultural nationalism."[109]

According to Jon Juaristi, the liberal Spanish state achieved the apogee of its construction in 1889 when, with the promulgation of the Civil Code, Spain finally became a modern country.[110] This seems a somewhat precipitous conclusion, however, given the events of the twentieth century, when Spain imploded into the bloodiest civil war in a recent history marked by numerous civil conflicts. Furthermore, it is questionable whether many states could claim to be fully constructed in the 1880s,[111] and Spain was, in this case, certainly no exception. Indeed, events in Spain through the nineteenth century demonstrate the same pattern that is found in many other nation-states in Europe: an attempt to shape a national identity through the invention of a collective memory, aimed fundamentally at creating a uniform middle class capable of leading the country through a capitalist transformation.[112]

At the heart of nineteenth-century Spanish nationalism there remained two fundamental weaknesses: the failure to liberate the Spanish national myth from the Catholic faith, thereby associating any attack on the church as an attack on Spain itself and thus delaying a potential liberal social (as opposed to economic) transformation, and the equation of Castile with Spain, which, although originally serving an important purpose in explaining the mythical core of the Spanish nation-state and empire, now prevented inclusion of the most dynamic economic regions of the country, Catalonia and the Basque Country, and indeed led to the emergence of nationalist movements there. "Thus," it has been contended, "both the arguments of the regional nationalists . . . and the reactions of the defenders of a single, centralist state provoked the cultural fracture of Spain as a nation."[113]

Furthermore, while the nation-state envisaged by the 1812 Cádiz Constitution established a concept of national sovereignty as a means of controlling and developing modern, liberal notions of property, production, and political activity and in the process creating a Spanish middle class, subsequently (as in other countries) this same social sector came to dominate and to control the very state that had given rise to it in the first place. This, in turn, meant that the nineteenth-century Spanish nation-state did not have, in the words of Eduardo Manzano Moreno and Pérez Garzón, "the exclusive cultural control that could have created a single historical memory, a single cultural, linguistic and artistic tradition and a single patriotism for all the people of the country." To be sure, there were attempts to impose a "centralist and Castilian-centered paradigm," and the general population, thanks to improved communications, military conscription, education, and so on, was less heterogeneous than in previous centuries. "However," they conclude,

> In nineteenth-century Spain, unlike in other European countries, these processes, initiated by the state, were accompanied by tendencies toward cultural pluralism and political federalism. The liberal state established itself in Spain on the legacy of peoples whose rulers promoted a different cultural memory and who were strong enough to demand their own share of power. Consequently, since the nineteenth century various historical memories have been constructed in Spain, one fostered by the state, focused on Castile and claiming hegemony, and others that foster alternative, popular national identities.[114]

Or as another observer more bluntly concludes: "In the 1890s in Spain there were still too many local or religious *fiestas*, too many guild traditions and regional identities; there was no need and no room for the nation."[115]

In sum, between the promulgation of the 1812 Cádiz Constitution[116] and the cultural initiatives of the mid-nineteenth century promoting a Castilian-based sense of Spanishness (educational reform, military conscription, and so on), statist Spanish nationalism emerged. This government-inspired and elite-inspired ideology, however, was far from embracing a truly civic form of nationalism. Instead, it alienated its two most dynamic regions, making a sense of feeling Catalan or Basque culturally difficult or incompatible with that of feeling Spanish. It is therefore plausible enough to contend that nineteenth-century Spanish nationalism encouraged the emergence of its Catalan and Basque counterparts.

Restoration Spain of the early 1890s was not a confident country. Violence was increasingly endemic within a society having great difficulty adjusting to the pressures of modernization. Inequality, so often the theme of class relations, was, in Spain, given a regional edge that only compounded the already existent social divisions. The unity of Spain was further threatened from abroad by a growing series of anticolonial nationalist movements. Increasingly, they moved toward outright insurrection in the face of Spanish duplicity about effecting colonial reform. It was against this background that a young Bizkaian, Sabino de Arana y Goiri, rallied to the defense of what he perceived to be traditional Basque society. Arana was to articulate the first political statements of Basque nationalism in his book *Bizkaya por su independencia* and in the speech with which he inaugurated his program: the Larrazábal Address. And in so doing, he bequeathed to Basque nationalism a legacy of a symbolic recourse to violence that pervaded the movement into the next century. To an analysis of the legacy we now will turn.

CHAPTER TWO

Sabino de Arana y Goiri and the Emergence of Basque Nationalism

Sabino Policarpo de Arana y Goiri (hereafter Sabino Arana), the founder of Basque nationalism, was born on January 26, 1865 in Abando (Bizkaia). Although a separate town at the time, Abando was subsequently incorporated as a neighborhood of the expanding metropolis of Bilbao. He came from an economically comfortable family, yet unlike the new and growing middle classes in and around Bilbao, they were not liberals. Their money had been made in the "preindustrial" and traditional Basque industries of shipbuilding and arms manufacturing. Santiago, his father, was a Carlist who, together with the family, had been forced into exile (in the northern or French Basque Country) for three years during the Second Carlist War.[1] Arana consequently received a strict Catholic and traditionalist upbringing, even contemplating becoming a Jesuit priest.[2]

The young Arana experienced an adolescence of profound seriousness in a family atmosphere that increasingly rejected both a rapidly changing society and the political system that sustained it. There was also a sense of hopelessness linked to this rejection, because the changes seemed progressively more irreversible. After 1876, the traditionalist class in the Basque Country was in crisis.[3] The foundations of its power and influence had been the *fueros*, religion, and traditional industrial concerns, yet these were the very values that were now most threatened by a centralizing liberal state promoting modern industrial capitalism. The Arana family, for example, lost a lot of money through both its financial support for the Carlist cause and the restructuring of Basque shipbuilding from the traditional wooden to the modern iron-clad hulls.[4] An older Arana is reputed to have commented that he "was born in order to arrive for the death of the fatherland."[5]

Politically, Arana considered himself a Carlist like his father until a conversation with his brother Luis in 1882. During that conversation, Luis convinced Sabino that the Basque people are distinct from the Spanish through their blood, race, and traditions and that those distinctive qualities had been endangered by the liberal victories of 1839 and 1876.[6] From that moment on, the younger and devoutly religious Arana began to develop a personal moral code that drew inspiration from an idealization of traditional Basque society. It was, he argued, a society with both physical and moral rights, and its only salvation could be achieved through liberation.[7]

The values Arana associated with traditional Basque society included an increasing conception of Basqueness as a separate identity from the Spanishness promoted by the new Spanish state.[8] Carlism stressed only the regional nature of the Basque provinces within this state, and he sought a more precise and separate definition of what it meant to be Basque. Although Arana's family was ethnically Basque, they did not speak Euskara. The family had earned its wealth and social status, in part, at least, by adopting Spanish as the language of trade and commerce. Thus, from an early age, he suffered a dual isolation: Socially and culturally, he remained distant from his own idealized Basqueness, and politically, although from a middle-class background, he could not adapt to the modern and more secular emergent liberal state in Spain.

Between 1883 and 1888, Arana studied law in Barcelona, although he never finished his studies, preferring instead to learn Euskara. His time in Catalonia coincided with the rise of bourgeois Catalan nationalism. "It is difficult to assess the importance of this," William A. Douglass observes. His stint there coincided with the publication of Francisco Pi i Maragall's *The Nationalities* (1877), a work calling for a federal Spain, and the presence of a young Philippine student, José Rizal, the future father of Philippine nationalism. "Clearly," Douglass concludes, "Arana was at least indirectly affected by Catalanism, and particularly the reverence accorded the language."[9] It was during these years that Arana began to conceive of a new ideology encompassing the foralism, traditional values, and moral vision of his upbringing and a regionalism that rejected the modern Spanish state: Bizkaian (rather than Basque) nationalism. This ideological conversion was prompted by both the specific nature of his upbringing and the changing society around him. It was in many ways an ideology rooted in rejection, alienation, and isolation. In 1888, Arana published the first results of his philological research in *Gramática elemental de Euskera bizkaíno* (An elementary grammar of Bizkaian Basque). That same year he also returned to Bilbao with the intention of developing his philosophy regarding the essential differences separating Bizkaia and the other Basque provinces from the rest of Spain.

Greater Bilbao in the late 1880s was a rapidly changing city. Its population in 1857 was just over 40,000, yet by 1900 it had risen to nearly 168,000.[10] Fin-de-siècle Bilbao was also a liberal stronghold. The Liberals (whether of the conservative or moderate variety, and sometimes in alliance with Republicans) represented the city in the Spanish Parliament without serious challenge between 1876 and 1895. Bilbao liberalism was monarchist, modernizing, and supportive of the post-1876 Spanish state. It envisaged a unitary Spain, in contrast to the regionalism of the traditionalist Carlists. In common with the rest of Spain, however, Bilbao was increasingly prone to *caciquismo*, centered on the important industrial families of the time.[11] Though *caciquismo* was not as rampant in the Basque provinces as elsewhere during the early years of the Restoration, at least, that handful of influential families, principally those who had gained from the industrial changes of the mid and late nineteenth century, viewed their own success and power as dependent on that

Plaza del Mercado, Bilbao, late nineteenth century. The central marketplace in Bilbao was located between the city's old quarter and the principal immigrant neighborhood just across the river, and was a place of daily interaction between Basques and non-Basques. By permission of Editorial Iparaguirre Editorial, S.A. archives.

of the Spanish state.[12] And Restoration Spain saw its economic future intrinsically linked to the productivity of trade and industry in Bizkaia. Most of those families, therefore, were supportive of the constitutional monarchy, although there were a variety of political allegiances, ranging from traditionalism and independent Catholicism to republicanism.[13]

The twenty-four-year-old Arana was shocked by what he saw. His Bizkaia was changing at an alarming rate, with rural Basques migrating to the Americas and non-Basque immigrants swelling its towns and cities. Indeed, migration was a dominant social theme of the time, with a significant population shift both from Spain to the Americas and within the country itself.[14] Transatlantic migration was, of course, a key feature of nineteenth-century Europe. Between 1870 and 1914, Spain contributed the third-highest number of transatlantic migrants, many of whom were Basque.[15] In the southern or Spanish Basque Country, this was especially felt in Arana's natal province, Bizkaia, where chain migration from several smaller towns led to the establishment of a Bizkaian social, cultural, and economic network of transatlantic relations.

Gloria P. Totoricagüena isolates four salient factors in nineteenth-century emigration from the Spanish Basque provinces: the social and economic effects of the two Carlist Wars (including general economic hardship as the result of so many years of warfare and a new demand of the emerging modern Spanish state: military conscription), the liberalization of emigration laws by the Spanish government after 1853, the Basque primogeniture inheritance system, and overpopulated rural areas.[16] Although the number is difficult to calculate with total certainty, William A. Douglass and Jon Bilbao estimate that perhaps as many as two hundred thousand Basques migrated to the New World from both Spain and France over the course of the nineteenth century.[17] This is a remarkably high figure in light of the fact that the total Basque population, throughout the seven provinces at the end of the nineteenth century was something in the region of eight hundred thousand.

At the same time that Basques emigrated to establish new transatlantic networks of cooperation and, indeed, new configurations of Basque identity,[18] there was a concomitant migration into the Basque Country that would also have important ramifications for the shaping of Basque identity. Attracted by the new opportunities offered by industrialization in and around Bilbao, massive waves of poor, predominantly rural people migrated to Bizkaia and later to Gipuzkoa from surrounding regions of northern Spain: Castile, León, Cantabria, Asturias, Aragón, and Galicia. These were the people who effectively populated and built Greater Bilbao, settling in the towns along the left bank of the River Nervión, where most of the industry was based.[19] However, living and working conditions were harsh, and the new immigrant population quickly came to constitute a classic, nineteenth-century proletariat. In the space of a generation, Basque society had been transformed economically, socially, and demographically.

Arana sought refuge from the physically changing urban landscape around him in hunting. This was both literally and figuratively an escape from the shock of the new, enabling him to experience rural Bizkaia physically. One might even speculate that hunting served as a kind of rite of passage for the young Bizkaian.[20] It was during his time spent hunting that Arana began to contemplate an ideology based on a rural mysticism in which the true repository of Bizkaian (and Basque) values was to be found in peasant culture.[21] Accordingly, he defined traditional Basque rural society within the framework of complex relationships between the agrarian family and its household, Roman Catholicism, and rural mythology.[22] The *baserri*, or traditional farmstead, for example, enjoys a central position within rural Basque society as a primary focus of identity, blending social, economic, and cultural factors in its character as a "total institution" or unit of production. It is the symbol of traditional Basque culture par excellence, the fundamental delimitation of social organization in rural Basque society.[23] It is no wonder, then, that Arana sought to include the *baserri* within the symbolic constructs of his ideology.

These values subsequently formed the cornerstone of Arana's reactionary, essentialist, and dualist nationalism[24] or moral ideology, which conceived of life on Earth as the product of the Creation, with a precise "end" (the Final Judgment) and specific temporal and spatial divisions between these two events.[25] Indeed, religion bequeathed Arana's program a series of ideas, from moral lessons to political realities, that underscored Basque difference and the need to free the Basque Country from the (morally and politically) corrupt Spanish state.[26] "For him," Daniele Conversi observes,

> political centralisation... meant a conspiracy to deprive the Church of its hold over society and dilute Catholic values of piety and justice in the name of materialism and avarice. Hence, Spain was dominated by sinister anti-clerical forces epitomised by the Liberals and their corrupt electoral system. His own was a crusade against the irreligion and 'immorality' of Spanish reformers who were leading devout souls astray. Indeed, his whole campaign was to provide a new morality and set of values for the emerging Basque society at the very moment when they were lacking and very much needed.[27]

Indeed, Arana's whole program rested on one basic premise: "a struggle for the religious salvation of the Basque race," and that "salvation was to be won through complete isolation from other peoples, especially Spaniards."[28]

As Arana searched for an ideal society amid the violent upheaval of modernization affecting Bizkaia, he recalled the mythological foundations of the rural society he so idealized. He concluded, in broad terms, that redemption was the key, redemption carried out through the heroic effort of struggle. This was a lesson learned from the rural mythology he so desperately wished to imitate.[29] In this endeavor, Arana differed little from other nationalist leaders in seeking a way to confront the challenge of social transformation.[30] "*To redeem those who lived in the past* and to turn every 'it was' into a 'thus I willed it,'" wrote Nietzsche in 1888, "that alone should I call redemption."[31] Arana, striving for a way to will the destiny of his nation, was in many ways a typical product of the age in which he lived. He pursued his Holy Grail, the spiritual redemption of the Bizkaian nation, by seeking to create an ideology that, for him, would awaken the people from the slumber of Spanish occupation.[32] The fashioning and dissemination of this ideology would involve a number of devices designed to effect such a redemptive awakening, devices that might be described as a combination of arts, artifacts, and artifices.[33]

What is particularly important in analyzing the creation of Basque nationalist ideology is the manner in which Arana configured Bizkaian (and later Basque) identity as a nationalist identity. For William A. Douglass, this was the "visionary" dimension to Arana's thought, for "in articulating his radical Basque nationalism (i.e., independentism), he underscored the Basques' shameful dilemma in being colonized by Spain, and thereby anticipated the subsequent internal colonialism arguments of Lenin, Gramsci, Preobrazhensky, Bukharin, and Hechter."[34]

As an "imaginative construction"[35] and part of a wider cultural production, the process by which Arana arrived at the linkage of identity with struggle and conflict is best viewed through the texts he produced to illustrate and define Bizkaia and the Basque nation and, in them, the symbols he appropriated to articulate Basque identity. In one way or another, all involved regeneration through violence, a symbolic recourse to violence in a conflictual world, a topos that was intimately rooted in nineteenth-century European culture.

Bizkaya por su independencia

Whereas Arana's discursive propaganda of the 1880s had been essentially philological and cultural in tone, from the 1890s onward, he framed his political discourse in historical terms that he hoped would awaken Bizkaians to their historic destiny and at the same time deliver them from the Spanish yoke to achieve the redemption he believed was coming for the Basque nation.

Between December 1889 and March 1890, he published four articles in the short-lived monthly review *La Abeja*. Collectively referred to as the "Four Glorious *Patrias*," they were reissued as a book in November 1892, under the title *Bizkaya por su independencia* (Bizkaia throughout its independence), which went on sale to the general public in May 1893 with an initial print run of two thousand copies.[36] As the first explicitly political public statement by Arana,[37] there is good reason to date the specific origins of Basque nationalism with the publication of this work.[38]

Taken at face value, the book would scarcely merit such attention. The main argument, adapted from the earlier articles, presented a Romantic view of four Bizkaian battlefield victories over Castile or León at Arrigorriaga in 888, Gordexola (Gordejuela) and Otxandio (Ochandio) in 1355, and Mungia (Munguía) in 1470. Throughout the text, an explicit dichotomy is drawn between the Basques (as represented by Bizkaia) and the Spanish (Castile/León), the resultant message being that throughout their history, Basques had been ready to fight and die in order to preserve their independence. Furthermore, these texts claim, that original independence had continued to exist, in modified form, until 1876.

Although Arana claimed it was a historical study, the work itself contains little of historiographical merit.[39] Its prose style relies heavily on Romanticism, and its focus is essentially its contemporary political message. It was, to all intents and purposes, history as artifice.[40] This was made clear in the foreword, which served as a criticism of the social and political changes affecting his birthplace:

> If we open our doors to the Spanish invasion in such a way . . . the greater part of the senior officials and provincial employees and the municipal authority of Bilbao is in the hands of foreigners. . . . Why should that bother us?! But . . . if the Philippine *indios* try to break the chains with which the Spanish oppress them . . . if the Yankee makes love to Cuba. . . . Oh! Then the patriotic spirit flares up, the blood is inflamed and pen tears paper to shreds with indignation on seeing the integrity of the *patria* in danger or national dignity offended!!![41]

This is the kind of rhetoric that has moved many observers of Basque nationalism to concentrate on its xenophobic aspects. Without doubt, the kind of selective categorization emphasized by Arana bequeathed his cause an exclusivist (and racialist) legacy.[42] Yet it is equally important to understand the communicative power of the underlying symbols stressed in *Bizkaya por su independencia*, a power understood by Arana as he switched early on from contemporary political comment to allegorical account. That is why, here, I rely more on metaphorical interpretation than on literal evaluation.[43] As Walker Connor rightly maintains, "it is not chronological or factual history that is the key to the nation, but sentient or felt history,"[44] and myth and symbol would provide Arana with the power to transmit a sentient history.

The most immediately striking image of the book was the title, which incorporated the words "Bizkaia" and "independence." This reflected both the art and the artifice in Arana's coding of history: an imaginative and striking heading implying an independent Bizkaia that never really existed. This marked a significant change, highlighting the development of his thought from literary or philosophical protest to concrete political proposals. Thus, independence emerged as a preexisting state to be recovered, the remedy or precise "end" to the ills of Bizkaia.[45] This, as William A. Douglass points out, was "the truly 'revolutionary' part of his political agenda" and was explicitly stated in Arana's very first political treatise.[46]

It would be misleading, however, to judge the work simply on its political merits (or lack thereof).[47] In the realm of symbolic representation, a rich source of ideology came together in Aranist ideology. Indeed, in articulating the Basque nationalist program through a historico-cultural discourse, Arana not only echoed Matthew Arnold's use of culture as a response to the rational, secularizing effects of industrial capitalism, but was also shrewd enough to appreciate the power of culture as what Terry Eagleton terms "a second-rate surrogate" for religion: "if religion offers cult, sensuous symbolism, social unity, collective identity, a combination of practical morality and spiritual idealism, and a link between intellectuals and the populace, so does culture."[48]

Although he spoke of lost political and judicial *rights*, Arana's vision was much wider: "It is not a legal pact that was violated and broken, but a religious alliance, a metaphysical bond with Mother Earth; the solution cannot be politico-judicial alone, [but] a *total regeneration, from the root* [up] is essential, and the root is that betrayed Land itself."[49] The primordial images used to convey this sense how regeneration was to be achieved are important: Land, blood, and the hunt were the central images of Basque nationalist ideology at its beginning.

One observer sees "Land" as the central character in the work, because it is precisely what encourages the heroic exploits of its inhabitants.[50] In this way, Arana's ideology evoked three critical sentiments of nationalist ideology: territory, history, and community,[51] and indeed, the words Arana employed to configure Basque identity were clearly shaped by geographical and social space and specifically defined by natural images. Edward Said speaks of such images as constituting a "cultural topography" where "structures of location and geographical reference appear in the cultural languages of literature, history, or ethnography, sometimes allusively and sometimes carefully plotted."[52] Through both artifact and artifice, Arana managed to construct what Zulaika refers to as a "primordial cognitive map"[53] or a cultural map of the imagination. Identities and memories are thought *with* rather than *about*.[54] Even the use of artifice, if successful, will enter the imagination, perhaps even forming an integral part of an individual or group identity. This imagining of the Basque community subsequently came to pervade nationalism with the above images,[55] proving the timeless persistence of nature myths in the context of modern society.[56]

Arana represented the mountain, for example, as more than a mere physical presence. For him, it symbolized the true essence of the Basque community: a pure, peaceful place where freedom could be enjoyed.[57] He projected an image of topographical scale as a guardian of the *euskaldun*, or Basque speaker.[58] This is a category that goes beyond a simple linguistic categorization, because the *euskaldun* is also a symbolic figure: one of the principal repositories of rural Basques' cultural values.[59] It was, then, according to Arana, in "all those mountain villages that, between the plains of Araba and the sea, they [the Basques] lived free from Saracen [Muslim] domination and ... spoke a certain crude and barbarous language."[60] This mountainous terrain was a safeguard, a symbol of freedom for the Basques and their language, and a location of undisturbed stability when, "in those essentially warlike times that followed the Saracen invasion of the eighth century ... the Bizkaian people generally lived peacefully in their mountainous territory, without ... change."[61] Here the idea of change was clearly associated with a threat to traditional Basque values, most emphatically emphasized by the profound social and economic upheavals affecting Bizkaia.

Eric Hobsbawm attacks the idea of a residual sentimental attachment to land in the late nineteenth century: "Nationalism and the state took over the associations of kin, neighbours and home ground," he contends, "for territories and populations of a size and scale which turned them into metaphors."[62] However, this argument, while accurate as regards the statist nationalism of nation-states, must be qualified in regard to Arana's program. Clifford Geertz, for example, views culture as composed of an ordered system of meanings and symbols through whose context social action takes place and a social system as the pattern of that same interaction.[63] Hobsbawm is guilty of confusing the two. People in the late nineteenth century, perhaps more than ever before, needed such metaphors, and topography still commanded the individual imagination, even within expanding state systems.[64] This is more than evident in the work of Arana, which reflected not only an attempt to capture the minds of potential followers, but the inner turmoil of individuals confronted by aggressive social and cultural change. Indeed, it is to the latter that we should perhaps look in assessing the communicative power of *Bizkaya por su independencia*, for in articulating a Bizkaian (and later Basque) nationalist discourse, Arana projected his own individual sense of conflict and strife onto those collective aspects of a personal identity that would produce a sense of identification with others.[65]

The central metaphor for that strife was bloodshed. Throughout history, Arana argued, Basques had been prepared to spill their own blood and the blood of others to defend their peaceful, pure, and independent existence in their own land. Through this argument, he artfully combined the artifice of the myth of independence with the symbolism of the Basque Country's actual landscape to provide an emphatic image for the Basque imagination, an image that, in Arana's opinion, had definite political ramifications in the late nineteenth century: "Blinded and stubborn, only the terrible blow of their fall into the dark abyss of slavery (the nineteenth century) can wake up and show [the Basques that] their only way to purification [is] to save themselves and be reborn as their dignity demands and which the blood that has bathed their mountains demands."[66]

This emphasis on the shedding of blood was a principal element in his call for ritual purification[67] and implied the precise "end" to the myth: liberation through struggle. As René Girard maintains concerning such purifications, "the community must effectively be emptied of its poisons. It must feel liberated and reconciled within itself. This is implied in the conclusion of most myths."[68] And it is in this context that we can read Michel Foucault's association of sanguinary images with systems of power: blood "owed its high value ... to its instrumental role (the ability to shed blood), to the way it functioned in the order of signs (to have a certain blood, to be of the same blood, to be prepared to risk one's blood), and also to its precariousness (easily spilled, subject to drying up, too readily mixed, capable of being quickly corrupted)."[69]

That power does indeed speak *through* blood became one of Arana's central metaphors. The nation was represented not merely as a political or judicial aggregate, but as a living organism, connected through blood and intimately associated with the land that sustained it.[70] According to Arana, the freedom of Bizkaia was "well worth the blood of its sons," for its very independence was "as old as its blood and its language." He later made a specific connection between images by stressing, in a reference to the oak tree of Gernika under which Bizkaian foral representatives traditionally met, that "the Tree of Liberty has no greater sap than the blood of its sons."[71]

Arana implied that glory awaited those who were prepared to sacrifice themselves for the land of the Basques. Indeed, if any evidence is needed of the symbolically sacramental quality of nationalism, it is to be found here.[72] He sought to awaken the Basque national spirit by challenging his compatriots to a number of tests–almost initiation rituals–in an attempt to prove their Basqueness. Indeed, that "boys become men by passing exacting tests of performance in war, economic pursuits, and procreativity"[73] is one of the principal messages of *Bizkaya por su independencia.*

Hunting is likewise both a test of masculinity and a rite of passage to adulthood, and in it one can also observe human attitudes toward the struggle between life and death, peace and war. "In all the rich catalogue of human hypocrisy," Robert Ardrey argues, "it is difficult to find anything to compare to that dainty of dainties, that sugared delicacy, the belief that people do not like war."[74] War is a specifically human product that reproduces the hunter's urge to kill. There is no moral repugnance at killing one's prey, for that represents the ritual purification of what is perceived as one's own territory. Arana adapted this notion to his emerging conception of nationalism in its will to have what it did not possess–in hunting terms, the prey, and in a political sense, liberation.[75] Hunting allowed Arana to appeal to primordial instincts prior to the complications of modern industrial civilization.[76] "At the sensorial level, in hunting a regression to smell and touch takes place . . . In a hunting morality there is no repugnance at killing . . . From the hunter's compulsion to kill we may gain significant insights into the military compulsion to destroy the enemy target."[77] The hunt would thus provide him with a metaphoric example for Basques to follow.

Hunting is also an activity that is intimately associated with territory. Hunters respect the terrain on which they hunt, and the progressive acquisition of hunting skills has been important to the human experience of territorial domination.[78] Indeed, hunters establish their own human social space in the wild terrain on which they hunt–a cultural separation and strategic division that marks the context of their hunt.[79]

The hunter, of course, also can be the hunted, and nature, in the late nineteenth century, was definitely seen as a scene of Darwinian strife, red in tooth and claw. At the battle of Arrigorriaga, for example, Arana wrote, the Bizkaians were threatened by the "armed foreigner . . . like an eagle to its prey" and reacted by "thrust[ing] forward against the invader with the fierceness of a lion against an antelope." By the time of the battle of Gordexola, the Bizkaians had become "the wolves that beat the Spanish lion." And at the conclusion to the battle of Otxandio, Arana maintained, there was the following rallying cry: "Little Basque wolves against the Spanish lion? *Veni, vidi, vici!*"[80]

Animal imagery forms an integral part in the human endeavor of establishing categories,[81] and Arana thus envisaged a clear image to represent Bizkaia: the wolf. This was a clever choice. As both hunter and killer,[82] the wolf was free from any ontological ambiguity. Further, lupine adjectives normally involve aspects of cunning or guile, vital traits when your enemy is physically stronger. In traditional Basque culture, moreover, the saying "*otsoak ez du bere haragirik jaten*" (literally, "the wolf does not eat its own meat") would translate into English as "blood is thicker than water," an essential expression of family and group identity.[83]

The act of hunting is also a basic cultural performance. As Zulaika observes, "when periods of critical transformation force upon a society new acts of creation and violence, the return to the original roots gets partly expressed in tacitly assuming modes of performance long sanctioned by cultural tradition."[84] With the publication of *Bizkaya por su independencia* in 1893, Arana initiated the beginning of a just such a performance: the Basque nationalist program.[85] This was, of course, political rhetoric, designed to awaken nineteenth-century Basques to their historical destiny. But it should also be read as a skillful presentation of ideas through an articulation of core images that might readily appeal to a collective Basque consciousness.

The regeneration of the Basque Country via the purification of the land by blood placed struggle at the center of the founding myth of Basque nationalism.[86] And martyrdom in the name of the cause is also crucial to nationalist ideologies. Although Arana did not make an outright call for armed resistance, on two occasions in *Bizkaya por su independencia* he observed that it is better to die free than live enslaved.[87] The battles to which Arana referred, moreover, he characterized as "wars of independence" against "Spain."[88] This, again, is historical artifice, for it is difficult to justify Bizkaian independence in the modern sense, and, as we have noted, it is problematic to discuss Spain historically in anything other than geographical terms, given the continuous struggle over what actually constituted Spanish identity.[89]

The message for contemporary Basques, however, was clear. The Basques' independence, "as old as their blood and their language,"[90] had to be preserved:

> TODAY–Bizkaia is a province of Spain
> TOMORROW– . . .?
> Nineteenth-Century Bizkaians can respond . . . the future is dependent upon their behavior.[91]

If one phrase gave birth to Basque nationalism, it was this, and with these words–and the invitation to fill in the spaces of the ellipses–came an imagery of struggle, most definitely symbolic, but resonating with importance for the subsequent development of the nationalist movement. Art, artifact, and artifice had combined to create Basque nationalism.

The Breakthrough of 1893: The Larrazábal Address and the Summer of Discontent

Bizkaya por su independencia went on sale in May 1893, a tumultuous year in Spain, when the growing social and economic crises of the late 1880s and early 1890s finally began to spill over into the political arena. The period thereafter was characterized by an escalation of social and political violence, marking the challenge to liberal Spain of both organized labor and nationalism.[92] It was in this context that, having established a selection of core images with which to articulate the ideology of Basque nationalism, the next logical step for Arana was to try to disseminate these ideas to a wider public. As is history's wont, the chance fell to Arana at a moment when at least some of his fellow citizens would be receptive to these new ideas.

Although the triumph of human action is often emphasized in the litany of nationalist historiography, the most important feature of the "breakthrough" year of 1893 was the social unrest enveloping the Basque provinces. In 1893, there were widespread protests in the Basque provinces against a proposed tax increase that particularly singled out Navarre. In addition, it comes as no surprise to find that Spanish society in 1893, rather like other European societies, was preoccupied with imperial matters, and unlike in previous assertions of European expansionist might, a new critical attitude toward political references such as "imperialism," "colonialism,"[93] and "race" had begun to filter into the European imagination. Spain faced growing colonial problems in both Cuba and Morocco. These problems were exacerbated by the complicated nature of the Spanish state-building project, and this same project encouraged, to some degree at least, the birth of Basque nationalism. Both of these developments would provide opportunities for the dissemination of Arana's nationalist ideas.

The reforming zeal that had marked Spain's Liberal ministry of 1885–90 came to an abrupt end when the prime minister, Práxedes Sagasta, was implicated in a corruption scandal. Yet two years of Conservative rule did little to resolve these social and economic problems. Indeed, if anything, the general mood of the country actually worsened. Sagasta returned to power in December 1892 with hopes of reestablishing the spirit of change associated with his earlier period in control, but Spanish society in 1893 was different from what it had been in 1885. In the March general elections, *The Times* of London felt the need to emphasize that events had taken place "with complete order in the capital," although "at some few places . . . there was some fighting at the polls."[94] Sagasta was immediately confronted with two issues that would define the course of Spanish politics throughout the coming year and that would influence the shape of Arana's vision of Bizkaian nationalism, as well: Cuba and the colonial problem in general and a reform of Spain's financial system that also implied a review of the regional question.

Cuba remained the thorniest of Spain's remaining colonial problems. Sporadic rebellions continued to break out, demonstrating to Madrid the need to resolve a rapidly escalating problem. Already in the spring of 1893, Cuba's governor general had called for troop reinforcements to bolster the island's defense system.[95] Sagasta, in turn, recognized the need for a quick resolution of the issue, given its potential influence on domestic regionalist movements. To this end, he sought a minister of colonies who was capable of instituting reform in regard to Cuba while at the same time placating traditional Spanish interests on the island. One man stood out: Antonio Maura.

Maura's mere presence could silence a room full of people. He was conservative, autocratic, and clerical. By nature, he was opposed to compromise. Even by Spanish standards, he was a reactionary. Yet he was also a man of integrity and natural humanity who believed that government could exist only with the consent of the governed.[96] Born in Majorca (the Balearic Islands), he retained a sense of distance, a separation from the *madrileño* society of court and government. Paradoxically, he was a comfortable member of that society, reveling in the traditions of Castilian centralized power. It was precisely this ease that bequeathed him a sense of both assured self-confidence and overpowering egotism. Although a Carlist by nature, he accepted the Restoration monarchy and the liberal political system. However, as a former Carlist, he remained sympathetic to the demands of regionalism in Spain.[97]

The appointment of Maura as minister of colonies was an astute choice. He was a member of the new generation of Restoration politicians who were convinced by the ideal of making society more just and yet were still comfortable members of the social and political elite, well to the right of the Liberal Party and devoted to the stability of a regime that had come under increasing pressure since the turn of the decade.[98] Maura's remedy for everything, based on his experience as a lawyer in civil and constitutional matters, was reform–not the short-term reform of self-interested politicians, but real reform dedicated to programs of change. He believed any problem could be solved by passing the right law, for this would encourage people to better society.[99]

With regard to Cuba, Maura was converted to the idea of home rule because the island did not function under the official colonial system. Too much power was concentrated in the hands of the Spanish elite, an axis of economic, political, and military luminaries composed of Cuba's large landowners, administrators, and soldiers. The system left no room for a potentially vibrant Creole class desperate for recognition. In 1893, Maura came up with a program of home rule for Cuba. It was specifically designed not for any political gain (as with the liberal reform of the 1880s), but instead to effect long-lasting change, or rather, to make Cuba a peaceful and stable part of Spain's dwindling empire. The plan included a complete financial reorganization of the island to clamp down on the concentration of wealth by purely Spanish interests, the adaptation of Spain's military presence to purely strategic and technical needs, and the extension to Cuba of the social and political reforms that had been introduced in the peninsula in the 1880s.[100] The colony would thus be granted a single assembly to oversee domestic matters, and it would then consult with both the captain general and Cuba's 'live forces' (the economic and political elite) in governing the colony. It was a bold and idealistic plan. Although seemingly conciliatory to Spanish interests, it would still have weakened the electoral power of the peninsula's political parties.

Maura presented the proposed reform, "which practically amounted to autonomy,"[101] on June 3, 1893. As was later recalled,

> This Bill was violently opposed in the Chambers by the representatives of the [Cuban] Unionist party of all denominations, and the Conservatives, Republicans and Carlists alike, as well as many of the Government supporters, stigmatized Señor Maura's project as an attempt to foist Home Rule on the country under the guise of reform. The result of this organized opposition was to compel Señor Sagasta to dissolve the Cabinet, and Señor Maura retired from the Ministry and the project was shelved.[102]

The bill might have been passed if Sagasta had been willing to risk losing some political ground at home, but he was not. For the sake of party unity, he thus distanced himself from the minister of colonies, and Cuba's first home-rule bill failed. By the time a second bill was proposed, the reform, as in Ireland, came as too little and too late,[103] and once more, in 1895, the island erupted in rebellion.

On the domestic front, the new administration sought a review of the 1876 settlement whereby the Basque provinces enjoyed a level of financial autonomy through fiscal pacts known as the *conciertos económicos*. This was an issue that challenged people to question once more the nature of Spain, for it raised the issue of the unity of the state. In fact, according to one observer, it was precisely the financial issue that defined the struggle between center and periphery in Restoration Spain.[104]

The man charged with carrying out this economic reform was Germán Gamazo, a serious-minded lawyer with *cacique* ties to the wheat-growing interests of Valladolid. As Sagasta's minister of finance, he introduced a plan to revise the *conciertos económicos* in 1893, a revision that would significantly alter the beneficial financial status of the four provinces by increasing regional payments to Madrid. While Araba, Bizkaia, and Gipuzkoa managed to halt the plan as unconstitutional, Navarre remained vulnerable to Gamazo's proposed reform. The result was a popular protest in all four provinces that recalled the spirit of the Carlist Wars and that coincided with the emergent political program of Arana. An organization known as Laurak Bat (the four in one, in Basque) emerged to defend Navarrese foral privileges and it served as a sharp reminder that popular unity within the four provinces had not gone away with defeat in the Second Carlist War. Naturally, it attracted Arana, and from the spring of 1893 on, he took part in a series of demonstrations in favor of Navarre and against the central government in Madrid.

That May, when *Bizkaya por su independencia* went on sale to the general public in Bizkaia at the price of one peseta in an atmosphere of escalating regional protest against Madrid's policies, it succeeded in attracting the attention of a group of Bilbao liberals with foral sympathies. The group, known as the Sociedad Euskalerria (Basque Country Society), favored a secular liberal program of modernization, yet was also suspicious of centralizing political authority. It was sympathetic to the historical rights of the Basque provinces, and for this reason, several of its members were determined to find out more about Arana's proposals.

They organized a dinner, ostensibly to inaugurate the book, but also as a way to hear Arana explain his program in more detail. The leader of the Euskalerriacos (as its members were known), Ramón de la Sota y Llano, had originally met Arana through the activities of Laurak Bat. Yet this alone did not guarantee that Arana's more obviously political agenda would appeal to the group.[105] The dinner took place at the Larrazábal restaurant on June 3, 1893, the same day that Maura had unsuccessfully presented his home-rule proposals for Cuba. Arana opened the proceedings by explaining the doctrine behind the publication of *Bizkaya por su independencia*, this being the principal reason for the occasion.[106] The Larrazábal Address (as it was subsequently known) expanded on the ideas already presented in the book and emphasized an emergent doctrine that used the fierce symbolism of historical struggle to get its point across.

Throughout its history, Bizkaia, in Arana's view, had preserved its "independence through the blood of its sons, conquering in a thousand battles the Muslim, the Spaniard [*hispano*], the Gaul, and the Saxon."[107] As in his published work, Arana's ideological construction was prepolitical in that it relied less upon ideological explanation and more upon the primordial attachment to sanguinary images. This subsequently became a dominant feature of Basque nationalism and can be dated back to its earliest appearance.[108] Arana described Bizkaia as "fearless at sea [and] strong on land," appealing to the geographical division that defines the Basque Country,[109] and called for a spirit of redemption to unite all Bizkaians "in the mountain and in the street,"[110] that is, in the countryside and in the cities. Again, his use of natural images was striking and reflected the respect felt by Basques for their noble fisherman and peasants. "The life of the man of the ocean," wrote Carmelo de Echegaray in 1893, "is a life of denial, sacrifice, and heroism."[111] Such a description might easily have been used by Arana himself in articulating his cause.

Occupational settings are clearly seminal in the construction of any identity. In Basque society (as in all others) this was particularly the case, with a basic division between the rural peasantry and the town dwellers. Indeed, this division has been described in terms of the social space between that of the *kale* (street) and the *baserri* (farmstead). Each may be said to define the other, principally in terms of "not being like the other."[112] In calling for these opposites to come together, Arana was symbolically calling for all sections of Bizkaian society to unite. Indeed, this might have been a carefully constructed piece of wording. After all, the Euskalerriacos were members of urban Basque society, as indeed was Arana. This may be evidence that at an early date, Arana was capable of contemplating the integration of nationalism into modern society, a policy favored officially only much later on.[113]

Arana continued his speech by referring to Bizkaia being plagued by a Spanish "virus" and "torn apart by foreign violence."[114] In a clear projection of pariah status on Spanish historical influence in Bizkaia, Arana appealed to the mythological construct of the diseased outsider.[115] Furthermore, he accused the Spanish of bringing violence to Bizkaia and, by implication, alluded to the just cause of repelling the "invader."[116] Arana explained that his discovery of nationalism came as a result of constantly encountering instances of the "Spanish invasion that was cutting down our mountains" and causing the death of his homeland.[117] The struggle was a difficult one, and he himself had often considered giving up the cause, but at such times of crisis, he would repeat the following words: "You have not beaten me. I will fight you alone and will only cede ground when ... I see you overpowered; if you should ever see me defeated on this Earth, I will abandon my *Patria*."[118] Defeat, in his worldview, would spell death for his nation. He was unwilling, therefore, to cede ground (either metaphorically or in reality) until he had gained the upper hand. It was a mindset framed in terms of right and wrong whose central belief relied on the strength of negation: the power to overcome difficulty by rejecting the outsider's ability to win.[119]

"Right this very minute," he concluded, "and not [only] once but a hundred times, I would sacrifice my throat to the knife, without even expecting memory to recall my name, if I knew that with my death I had revived my *Patria*."[120] Here, in the closing sentences of the speech, Arana once again called upon the most sacramental image he could offer–that of martyrdom. It was an appropriate conclusion, for in the speech, Arana combined several ideas that go some way to establishing the nature of his "imagined" ideology. The sacrament of Basque nationalism was thus formed from three sources: the sanctity of accepting evil as an opponent in the form of Spain, the chivalrous vengeance to be inflicted on that opponent for a perceived wrong, and the bearing of witness to one's faith through martyrdom.[121]

Arana's willingness to offer his own life for the cause, albeit rhetorically, also calls attention to the mythical role that sacrifice plays in the construction of political ideologies. Sacrifice is a sacred act, traditionally a means of binding social cohesion through an act of purification. This act of purification binds both the community and the victim, for the latter is sacrificed for reflecting ills that affect that community.[122] By consistently emphasizing the need to rid Bizkaia of Spanish influence, Arana again was most probably projecting onto his program some of his most personal feelings. He was, after all, the product of a class and society that was intimately connected to Spain's historical reality within the Basque Country. This accounts for the partly agonized quality of this nascent Basque nationalism, its sense of tragedy, loss, and sacrifice, a feature stemming from Arana's combination of idealism and catastrophe in his vision of Basque historical destiny.[123]

In the context of the speech, his words were inflammatory. Not only had he gone beyond the expectations of the gathering, but he had actually extended the argument of *Bizkaya por su independencia* from accounts of Bizkaia's independence in the past to a call–through his willingness to die in return for a "revival" of the *patria*–for outright independence from Spain in the future. In the course of the speech, he also managed to criticize the very group that had come to listen to him by attacking their anti-Bizkaian activities. Although the criticism was actually aimed at all the political parties in Bizkaia, this naturally implicated the Euskalerriacos, as well.[124]

The immediate reaction was a stunned silence; the Euskalerriacos were particularly shocked by Arana's violent tone.[125] Although asked to do so, Arana refused to answer questions about the speech. He was there, as he later explained, only to explain his ideas, and not to discuss them.[126] Sota's group, according to Arana, were liberal and *españolista* (centralist, or pro-Spanish), and it was this accusation that inflamed the proceedings. "An Euskalerriaco, the drunken one, began to insult us," recalled Arana, "and Koldobika [his brother, Luis] and I almost came to blows with everyone."[127]

Although the meeting was a failure, Arana took a curious strength from the proceedings. It was neither the first nor last time that he felt invigorated by confrontation, especially when opposed by apparently overwhelming odds. Throughout the early months of 1893, a decision had been looming for Arana as regards the future of Bizkaian nationalism. The answer was now clear. Five days after the meeting, he printed the first copy of a journal, in reality no more than a leaflet, entitled *Bizkaitarra* (The Bizkaian). This first edition followed the line established by Arana in *Bizkaya por su independencia* and the Larrazábal debacle. It contained just one article, which was devoted to a historical discussion of the insurrectionary attitude demonstrated by sixteenth-century Bizkaians toward King Felipe III, forcing him to retire a tax he had introduced contrary to the spirit of the *fueros*. And this article, written during the escalating tension of Gamazo's proposals for Navarre, had important contemporary ramifications.[128]

Once again, the theme of sacrifice was prominent as Arana alluded to a supposed letter written to the king by a Bizkaian representative: "We remain obliged to defend our dearly beloved and loved *Patria*, to the extent of seeing this [territory] burned and destroyed and the deaths of women... children and famil[ies]." He concluded that a search was necessary for Bizkaians "worthy of this name" who had not succumbed to the creeping attentions of the Spanish plague.[129] The effects of this propaganda are difficult to gauge, although the future nationalist leader, Engracio de Aranzadi ("Kizkitza"), remembered that on reading *Bizkaitarra* several months later, "from the first moment, on becoming aware of the significance of *sabiniano* thought, I accepted it as true and perfect, without contest, without worry, as if I had never felt *españolismo*, writing to Sabino to tell him that he had me by his side."[130] Arana could not have hoped for a more devoted response.[131]

Meanwhile, the social tensions in the Basque Country at this time were mirrored elsewhere on the peninsula. In Madrid, an anarchist bomb exploded prematurely outside the house of Cánovas, the leader of the opposition Conservatives, killing one of its carriers.[132] In the Andalusian capital, Seville, the discovery of yet another bomb several days later forced the city into a state of emergency, leading *The Times* of London to report that "armed guards are kept stationed outside many houses with orders to fire upon any one approaching during the night."[133] In July, Gamazo actually agreed to forego the proposed tax increase for Navarre if the opposition could find an equal source of revenue to finance his proposed budget,[134] but they could not. Maura's failed home-rule policy in Cuba, furthermore, had incited tension on the island, where between "the native element" and the "Spanish Europeans" there was "no mutual understanding," with events "growing worse, while dissatisfaction [was] extending."[135]

By August, the traditional vacation month in Spain, there had been no improvement the situation in Spain, which instead was worsening. Within the Basque provinces, the protest at Gamazo's reforms for Navarre continued to capture the attention of the general public. As a result, the foral protest group Laurak Bat, realizing the value of using a month when people generally had the time to participate in such events, advocated a series of demonstrations. Specifically, and with the intention of honoring a visit to Bilbao by the Choral Society of Pamplona (Iruñea), the Navarrese capital, Laurak Bat organized a series of commemorative acts to take place in Gernika to coincide with the celebrations taking place on August 16, the town's patron saint's day. Both Arana and Sota (the leader of the Euskalerriacos) had been involved in planning these acts and attended the event in person, as did Carlists and foral sympathizers of all persuasions, including large numbers of people from Navarre itself and some members of the Catalan protonationalist group Unió Catalanista.

That day, the small town was swelled by the arrival of thousands of people of different political persuasions. Many of the town's balconies, for example, were draped with Spanish flags, demonstrating that not all Bizkaians were hostile to Madrid. After a lunch organized by Laurak Bat to honor the Pamplona Choral Society, however, someone from the Carlist ranks shouted "Death to Castile!" This was followed by the shout of "Death to Spain!" to unanimous applause. Events escalated in the afternoon as the gathered assembly of foral protesters went into the streets of Gernika. On coming across the site of the Sociedad Guerniquesa (the Gernikan Society), with the Spanish flag aloft on its balcony, they attacked the emblem with the intention of burning it. The flag was pulled down, and a street battle ensued between several of the protesters and two Civil Guards, aided by four locals. After a scuffle, the protesters withdrew, shouting "Long live the Basque Country [Euskeria]!" and "Death to Spain!" The group returned to Bilbao, where they held a demonstration into the night.[136]

Three days later, Arana published the second edition of his newsletter, in which he related the recent events. The cries of "Death to Spain!" did not, in his opinion, imply any wish to destroy Spain. Rather, he advocated that Spain should abandon "our territory" and go back to its own land. Bizkaians, he continued, had the right to govern themselves and be left in peace and freedom: "If justice is done . . . we will not veer from Spanish legal ways to achieve independence . . . if justice is not done, but disregarded, then . . . right is on our side, and we will wait [until] we are strong [enough]."[137]

With a momentum of popular protest building, events then switched to Gipuzkoa. With the Spanish Parliament in its summer recess, Prime Minister Sagasta left Madrid on August 24 to visit the queen regent at her summer residence in Donostia–San Sebastián. He wanted to secure royal support for a proposed reform of the Departments of Justice, although he also needed to gain the confidence of the crown for the continued rule of his administration. "It is feared in some circles that the party now in power will be unable to cope with the increasingly complicated situation," judged *The Times* of London; "those who entertain this view loudly declare that a strong military Government is required in order to save the existing constitutional *régime*."[138] With the Spanish premier in the town, the Basque foral protesters could not overlook the opportunity to follow up their actions in Bizkaia with further demonstrations in the neighboring province. It was a traditionally liberal town, though, and toward the end of August full of visitors on vacation. A demonstration was planned for August 27, to coincide with the customary bull fight, but it did not take place.[139]

That same Sunday, however, after an evening concert by the town's municipal band, several members of the audience requested a version of the Basque Carlist anthem, "Gernikako Arbola" (The Tree of Gernika). The band refused, and this led to cries of "Long live the *fueros*!" and "Death to Sagasta!" as a group of people began to march toward the hotel where the Liberal leader was staying, resisting all efforts by the police to stop them. "They stoned the hotel and also the police who tried to disperse them," observed *The Times*; "the Civil Guards and the troops were then called out, but they, too, were stoned, and the troops therefore opened fire... order was then restored."[140] As a result, three people were killed and many others wounded.[141] According to Engracio de Aranzadi, the Civil Guard opened fire without warning. He viewed it as the "villainous murder of a defenseless people," carried out because of the queen regent's presence in Donostia–San Sebastián: "For this reason, without doubt, the military elements attacked without mercy."[142]

The violence of the event certainly brought public attention not only to the level of social protest within the Basque provinces, but also to the actions of the Civil Guard, an organization associated with the institutionalization of the liberal state in Spain.[143] Indeed, it was the raison d'être of the organization to serve the Spanish government, whatever its political complexion, against any opposition.[144] The incident also reflected that although a liberal state had been institutionalized, traditional recourse to force, a staple tactic of Spanish government throughout the century, had not been relinquished.[145] The evidence suggests, then, that the liberal state in Spain was not as tolerant as may have been perceived.[146] That same day, a strong military presence had been posted to Bilbao in order to offset republican demonstrations in the city.[147] It was clear from the level of social protest of varying political persuasions that Spain was suffering a grave domestic crisis. However, what was perhaps most significant about the Donostia–San Sebastián disturbance was the scene of these events itself, a place of liberal tradition and the summer residence of the monarchy.[148]

News of the killings spread quickly throughout the Basque Country, and a wave of protest against Sagasta's administration swept both Gipuzkoa and Bizkaia. Trouble in the Gipuzkoan capital continued throughout the next few days, causing three thousand visitors to leave the town.[149] Aranzadi later recalled the atmosphere as marking the first stirrings of popular Basque nationalist sentiment,[150] although the indignation was probably more reflective of a widespread dissatisfaction with the liberal state throughout Spain, encompassing many political views. In September, for instance, there were a number of peasant riots directed against tax gatherers in the provinces of Tarragona, Córdoba, Oviedo, and, of course, Navarre.[151] Such riots were intrinsic forms of protest in rural Spain, an enduring remnant of preindustrial society that entailed short-lived, spontaneous, and violent outbursts without any coherent organization.[152] In the Basque Country, too, a tradition of rural protest survived, such as the broad-based riot known as the Zamacolada against the imposition of greater tax levies in Bizkaia during the first decade of the nineteenth century.[153] Furthermore, the comparatively new phenomenon of anarchist violence was beginning to infiltrate Bilbao, where "precautionary measures" were reported to be in place.[154]

This was the immediate context in which Arana began to conceive of a political expression of Bizkaian difference from Spain: a summer of violent protest that witnessed a greater popular unity of Basque interests than at any time since defeat in the Carlist Wars. This protest did not, however, involve the majority of Basques. As was evident from events in Gernika, there was a sufficient degree of Spanish feeling within the region to defend against the symbolic attack on the national flag. Similarly, the increment of urban protest had more in common with class interests than with any awareness of a separate Bizkaian identity. Between 1890 and 1911, there were five general strikes and 169 minor protests in Bizkaia. These socialist-organized strikes were noteworthy for their violence–used as an instrument of negotiation in the absence of any formal arbitration process between workers and owners.[155] It is therefore also worth noting the increasing importance of class as regards the complex nature of Basque society.[156]

However, by the end of the summer of 1893, a number of foral protesters, principally (although not exclusively) from Carlist backgrounds, had become aware of Arana's ideas, and he could take inspiration from the active, participatory turn that the protest had taken. Indeed, he actually demonstrated a somewhat subtle political acumen in realizing that there was an opportunity to capitalize on such sentiment, especially given the declining state of its former political expressions, foralism and Carlism, which were, respectively, in the words of two observers, "a political corpse" and "chronically sick" at that time.[157]

Meanwhile, the issue of Cuba had split both country and government, and as the year drew to a close, attention switched to Morocco. With Spain already gripped by fear concerning its domestic political situation,[158] Madrid could not afford to let matters get out of hand abroad. After several more outbreaks of the sporadic unrest against Spanish interests in Morocco, the mood in Spain turned to thoughts of a war. And this, in turn, led to a renewed wave of Spanish nationalism like that associated with the conflict of 1859–60. According to *The Times* of London: "If one were to judge from reading the newspapers and listening to the rumours here of public subscriptions, of reserves being called out, of ladies' committees and of Red Cross societies one would imagine that Spain was on the eve of a war with one of the great powers at the very least."[159]

In the Spanish garrison town of Melilla, the subject of several attacks by Rif tribesmen, the waiting troops were increasingly restless with the government's indecision regarding a possible offensive.[160] Following a well-established pattern, they ultimately had to make do with a minor offensive that did more harm than good. Arana responded with his most damning condemnation of Spain to date, framed once more in the symbolic use of animal imagery. In an article titled "The Spanish Lion," he came out in open support of the Rif clans, the "ferocious black lion of the Atlas," against Spain as the "timid white lamb of Burgos." Moreover, Spanish troops, according to Arana, were afraid to enter battle, doing so only under the threat of death by their own commanders. At the sound of retreat, he concluded, they scattered like sheep.[161]

The anticolonial aspect of Arana's discourse has been overlooked,[162] while most observers focus on the repeatedly proffered xenophobic symbols for the Spanish in his articulation of Bizkaian identity. (In)famously, he coined derogatory terms for the Spanish immigrants fueling the industrialization of Bizkaia and swelling Bilbao's population, contrasting inferior racial stock of the *Maketos* (a pejorative term for non-Basques) to that of the pure Basques. His vision of Basque purity meant that even foreigners willing to learn Euskara, for example, would still not be acceptable. In his own words, "many who are Basques do not know Basque. This is bad. There are several *Maketos* who know it. This is worse."[163] Moreover, just as Bizkaia, like Morocco, was occupied by the Spanish, it, too, had to be "deoccupied."[164] In order to cultivate this idea, he used a number of symbols to confer an outsider status on all things Spanish and to distinguish between good Basques as patriots who preserved their heritage and bad Basques as collaborators who were no better than the occupiers who polluted it.

According to Conversi, "it is not certain how justly Arana can be accused of being a racist" because "at the root of his isolationist posture lay a pervasive insecurity and pessimism over the possibility of assimilating foreigners."[165] For Juan Díez Medrano, however, Arana was a racist, espousing a "discourse... motivated... by culturally and class-determined ethnic competition between immigrants, who supported a more secular lifestyle and represented a challenge to property relations, and the Basque petty bourgeoisie, who resisted secularization and staunchly supported private property."[166]

The racial dimension of Arana's thought did not, of course, come out of nowhere. Zulaika situates Arana's discourse within a European context in which new academic disciplines such as archaeology, anthropology, ethnology, and folklore sought race theories to explain human difference. Enthusiastic European anthropologists, for example, were obsessed with the Basque "race." "The Basque[s] were the subject of a fetishistic interest," contends Zulaika; "they were at once a rarity and an object of desire." In turn, "such scientific exercises in orientalising the Basque[s] significantly shaped their own perceptions of themselves."[167] Indeed, such "racial essences were discovered and turned into scientific objects by European anthropology before Sabino Arana... was even born."[168] While it seems highly unlikely that Arana was familiar with this European academic discourse, it is still not unreasonable to assume that it may have contributed to cementing a certain fixed notion of Basque identity, employing the rhetorical devices of defining Basques a mysterious, noble, and pure race. Therefore, "in situating Arana within fin-de-siècle Europe," contends Douglass, "the issue was not who was a racist, the rarity was the non-racialist."[169] The more obvious intellectual origins of Arana's thought are to be found in what José Luis de la Granja Sainz defines as the "remote precursors" of Basque nationalism: Basque writers, beginning in the fifteenth century, who articulated myths of Basque origins in order to defend foral privileges.[170] However, these writers did not employ the concept of race to the extent that Arana would.[171]

There was little historical merit to Arana's vision of Bizkaia as an occupied nation and Bizkaians as a colonized people. However, certain sectors of Basque society (such as the Basque speakers mythicized by Arana) were excluded from the Spanish national and statist program. That is to say, the emergence of the liberal state in Spain made no attempt to include among its founding identity myths large aspects of Basque culture, as well as other sectors of Spanish society. This was one of the reasons for the emergence of a weak liberal state in Spain. Indeed, the limitations of the Restoration system would be felt into the next century as Spain continued to suffer from both tensions between liberal and traditionalist sectors and the failure to integrate its population fully. Juan Aranzadi seems to suggest that the rural Basque world had disappeared during the latter stages of the nineteenth century,[172] thereby absolving liberal Spain of its failure to develop the civic nationalism so favored in many current intellectual circles. Yet at least one contemporaneous account rejects this idea,[173] and according to Eduardo Jorge Glas, by 1900, the primary (rural) sector still accounted for one third of Bizkaia's active population.[174]

The previously discussed educational policy of Restoration Spain is just one example of how Spanish nationalism was progressively institutionalized in monocultural form from the mid-nineteenth century onward at the expense of the plural and diverse nature of the country itself. As José Mª Basarrialde commented in 1893, "we see today that [even] in the most humble village peasants learn to spell in Castellano, [a] language they learn by force, *force*! [and] if not by the school book, by military decree."[175] Interestingly, an Andalusian cultural form, *flamenco*, was embraced and encouraged within the Spanish national consciousness of the twentieth century.[176] In contrast, native Basque traditions such as *bertsolaritza*, the Basque troubadorial tradition of extemporaneous versifying, remained outside this same consciousness.[177] Indeed, a salient trait of contemporary historiography on Basque culture seems to adopt the same (Spanish nationalist) position, as shown by Shlomo Ben-Ami's observation that "Basque literature remained the archaic, 'savage' and primitive concern of dedicated, narrow parochial minds."[178] However, Ben-Ami's demeaning characterization of Basque literature overlooks the myriad qualities of cultural expression–disregarding, for example, *bertsolaritza*, which, although an expression of oral culture, was indeed also literature.

Undoubtedly, in late nineteenth-century Europe, where wealth and success potentially awaited all those who wholeheartedly embraced modernity (and its official language of state), many sectors of Basque society rejected their traditional culture.[179] Indeed, such sectors had long demonstrated a desire to integrate into the high culture of metropolitan Europe. Culture, to borrow a definition from Edward W. Said, is an "overlapping experience," and to ignore "the interdependence of cultural terrains in which colonizer and colonized coexisted and battled each other through projections as well as rival geographies, narratives, and histories, is to miss what is essential about the world in the past century."[180] I do not want to suggest that the political relationship between Spain and Bizkaia was one of colonizer and colonized, as Arana did. However, there is an element of truth in Said's definition regarding the cultural effects of imposing Spanish nationalism on the Basque Country in the nineteenth century. "Cultures are involved in one another," continues Said; "none is single and pure, all are hybrid, heterogeneous, extraordinarily differentiated, and unmonolithic."[181] It is customary for this idea, with reason, to serve as the principal criticism of the kind of exclusivist nationalism favored by Arana. It should, however, be extended to incorporate the emergence of many liberal nation-states and their concomitant statist nationalism. The nascent nineteenth-century Spanish liberal state did not recognize its own overlapping cultures and diverse nature–a charge so often made against stateless nationalist movements. And this failure was in turn a principal motivator behind the ascendancy of Basque particularism.[182]

For Jon Juaristi, the anti-Basque sentiment of Spanish national feeling reflects a weak and secular version of anti-Judaism: it is an inclusive nationalism that requires a Basque presence to justify its own existence. Whereas for him, the reverse, anti-Spanish feeling in Basque nationalism was, is, and always will be a form of anti-Semitism, that is, intrinsically composed of envy, jealousy, and fear.[183] This view is misguided. One cannot deny, as I hope to have demonstrated thus far, the sacramental, zealous quality of Arana's rhetoric and the violent imagery he used. However, Spanish nationalism, as an expression of state power, displayed its own secular ferocity.[184] This era of profound social and economic change challenged traditionally held identities, and it seems not inappropriate to speak in terms of an ontological struggle between both Basque and Spanish nationalism. However, while the former had to depend on an initial minority following and the use of symbolic constructions in its ideology, the latter had at its disposal the full force of state power. Once again, there is a pressing need to examine Basque nationalism in a dialogue with its Spanish counterpart, for as Joseba Gabilondo reminds us, "the inclusion of Spanish nationalism disrupts the self-objectifying effect of transparency between presentation and re-presentation. Thus, any politically engaged historical and critical account of Basque culture and nationalism must always be engaged in an active affirmation of another presence that is inherent to the re-presentation of the Basques, but which Spanish culture and theories deny: Spanish nationalism."[185]

As part of its universalizing (Spanish) project, the liberal state in Spain marginalized Basque culture, and it did so, in many cases, with the compliance of some (although not all) Basques themselves. Arana's sacramental, nativist reaction therefore appears less surprising, for as Frederik Barth observes, "ethnic distinctions do not depend on an absence of social interaction and acceptance, but are quite to the contrary often the very foundations on which embracing social systems are built. Interaction in such a social system does not lead to its liquidation through change and acculturation; cultural differences can persist despite inter-ethnic contact and interdependence."[186] There were a serious of overlapping cultural identities in both Spain and the Basque Country, but these did not imply a uniform nationality. It was, in fact, precisely the attempt to impose this uniformity that brought about the sacramental and exclusivist imagery of Arana.

In 1893, Arana took the first steps toward his conceptualization and articulation of a nationalist ideology that was, first and foremost, the product of the age and society into which it was born. The mentality conceived by Arana viewed the rise of the Spanish state as a threat to the indigenous culture of Bizkaia and the other Basque provinces. In contrast, Spanish cultural manipulation disregarded Basque traditional, rural, oral culture, instead promoting political and economic modernization, together with a sociocultural reliance on Castilian traditions. In part, this was due to the liberal vision of oral cultures as somehow "without" history. But as Hayden White reminds us, "the possibility of representing the development of certain cultures in a specifically historical discourse is not sufficient grounds for regarding cultures whose development cannot be similarly represented, because of their failure to produce these kinds of records, as continuing to persist in the condition of 'prehistory.'"[187] Arana's national project viewed Basque culture as lacking the necessary historical awareness to survive the tremendous upheaval that modernization had wrought,[188] and in his specific articulation of a nationalist discourse, he wove history into an existent bed of prehistorical (and mythical) consciousness.

The state (as Arana witnessed first hand) was not, moreover, beyond using force to implement its policies. Indeed, late nineteenth-century Spanish society seemed shrouded in an escalating fear of social and political violence, both at home and abroad. It was this attitude, however, that gave Bizkaian nationalism a certain momentum.[189] Having established the symbolic basis of Bizkaian nationalism, Arana, during the next four years, would set about articulating a more comprehensive ideology of Basque nationalism that would have ramifications well into the twentieth century.

CHAPTER THREE

Core Images in the Emergence of Basque Nationalism

Between 1894 and 1898, the major institutions of Basque nationalism were established by Sabino Arana: the institution of the Basque center, a meeting place for the nascent movement; a nationalist flag that subsequently became *the* Basque national flag; the Basque Nationalist Party itself; and an ideology framed by both religious imagery and the recovery of the *fueros*. These institutions would control nationalist ideology into the next century, forming the cornerstones of the Basque nationalist movement. During this period, the symbols invented by Arana during 1892–93 came to infuse Basque nationalism. Indeed, by the time Arana was elected to the provincial council of Bizkaia in September 1898, Basque nationalism had acquired and retained a symbolic discourse that it would find hard to relinquish. It was, moreover, a discourse that, on countless occasions, would challenge the necessary pragmatism of party politics in a stubborn resistance to compromise.

As I demonstrated in the previous chapter, this discourse relied on images of struggle and warfare and was frequently articulated in historical terms, implying Basque national liberation through symbolic resistance against a perceived occupying enemy. The subsequent period, after 1893, coincided with the fin-de-siècle crisis in Spain, a crisis that called into question the very nature of the country through literary protest and philosophical debate. Its most immediate cause was open insurrection in Cuba and the Philippines.

Struggle and Warfare in the Nationalist Consciousness, 1894–95

During the first few days of 1894, there was some hope that maybe the problems of the previous year had subsided. The dispute in Morocco had been settled, with the Rif tribesman capitulating to Spanish power,[1] producing a mood of cautious optimism in government circles. Yet this proved only temporary respite. Anarchist violence continued at an increasingly alarming rate,[2] and the foral protest that had swept the Basque provinces in the latter months of 1893 continued unabated. Indeed, the state's financial policy further confirmed Arana's opinion of Spain as an aggressive intruder in his native province.

Thus, an increasingly anti-Spanish rhetoric entered into his discourse.[3] Even the appointment of a new finance minister in March could not placate the protest, because to all intents and purposes Gamazo's policy remained intact.[4]

By the spring of 1894, it was clear that the initial promise of the new year had not been fulfilled for the Spanish government. A siege mentality gripped Madrid society, and people wearing large cloaks or heavy overcoats (the typical method of bomb concealment at the time) were regarded with great suspicion, especially when seen near official premises.[5] At the same time, the violence of Spanish society was spreading abroad.[6] That spring, Arana announced his intention of creating a society to promote nationalist interests, inspired by similar movements elsewhere in Europe.[7] It might well be that the inspiration to establish Basque nationalism in some sort of formal sense was the product of an increasing awareness of the concept of nationality. Interestingly, when Arana conceived the idea of a more formal organization to promote his Bizkaian ideology, he began to envisage a wider national context, a nationalism embracing the entire Basque Country.[8]

In July 1894, these ideas were realized at the inauguration of the Euskeldun Batzokija (Basque Center) in Bilbao.[9] At the formal inaugural ceremony, a flag was raised symbolizing Bizkaian nationalism. Termed the *ikurriña*, it was designed by Arana himself, and its colors represented the symbolism that had come to define the emergent ideology.[10] The flag was composed of two crosses, one white and the other green, superimposed on a red background. The white cross represented the importance of religion, while the green one represented the Bizkaian "race," its ancient laws (the *fueros*), and Euskara. The red background, according to Arana, symbolized the fact that Bizkaians were "ready to shed their blood in defense of the two crosses."[11]

In this age of nationalism, flags were central symbols in the construction of national consciousness. Bismarck devised the German flag, combining the black and white of Prussia with the black, red, and gold tricolor of the German Confederation (1815–66). In the United States, a daily homage to the national flag in the country's schools began in the 1880s, and even international socialism took a flag, the red banner, as its symbol.[12] National flags represented the visual articulation of differentiation, identification, hegemony, and power. They were cultural devices intended to cement a community's identity and to exclude unwanted outsiders.[13] As such, the flag remains one of the most powerful symbols in the modern human imagination, as was demonstrated in Gernika the previous year, when foral protesters attacked the Spanish banner as a symbol of state power in Bizkaia.

Although a symbol is an artifact or a "thing," its meaning can be grasped only by induction; one must observe how it is used and how it is perceived,[14] and in many respects, the entire fabric of human culture is woven by a web of symbols.[15] In designing the *ikurriña*, Arana produced much more than a piece of colored cloth. He created an icon that subsequently precipitated a collective memory among all those who felt united by their flag.[16] As such, the combination of red, green, and white demonstrated that symbolic organization was important. The sanguinary images of Arana's discourse were written into the red background. Green, another elemental color, was the "natural" choice to represent Bizkaian traditions as associated with the semimythical Tree of Gernika, moreover serving as a medium or natural balance between light and dark tones.[17] And both red and green were represented in submission to the purity of the white cross, with religion, of course, forming an integral part of Arana's sacramental nationalism.

These were also the principal themes occupying Arana during the fall of 1894, in the initial months of his nationalist organization.[18] Blood continued to be a central metaphor, and he used it to articulate his first thoughts concerning a potentially important revision of his historical argument. Up until that time, he had dated the loss of Bizkaian independence to 1876, but from the fall of 1894 onward, he began to view the real loss of sovereignty as inexorably linked to defeat in the First Carlist War in 1839.[19] In Arana's opinion, 1839 was yet "another date worthy of carving in letters of blood," for a "century in which so many Spanish colonies freed themselves from their mother country" also saw Bizkaia "conquered by that same nation."[20] He concluded with a desperate call to "the blood of our fathers!"[21] This focus on the First Carlist War proved to be a significant ideological shift, and Arana introduced the new interpretation not by an official act of policy within the organization, but through symbolic appropriation within the pages of *Bizkaitarra.*

The green cross also took the form of the cross of Saint Andrew, for it was on this saint's day that the battle of Arrigorriaga had been fought and won, an occasion on which, according to Arana, "our fathers shed their blood... to save Bizkaia from foreign domination, for the freedom of the race, [and] for national independence."[22] It thus implied a mixture of images, incorporating an homage to the Tree of Gernika with the celebration of the battle. As one would expect, Arana also used religious symbolism. It was the white cross that, above all else, took prominence on the flag, demonstrating once more that celestial omnipotence was a crucial aspect of his nationalist ideology.

If one heroic figure stood out for the nationalist leader, it was Saint Ignatius of Loyola, the Basque religious warrior par excellence. "The love of Ignatius for the sacred Christian religion grew day by day," recounted Arana on the feast day of Loyola, July 31, 1894, "and because he was a soldier, he lost no time in projecting himself to Christian society like a great army on the march, with the divine Redeemer as [his] captain."[23] Loyola is a seminal figure in the interpretation of the Basque cultural imagination, and his bellicose imagery would pervade the nationalist mentality from its very beginnings. Perhaps most important however, was Loyola's sacramental refusal to accept ambiguity. His personal view of the world was defined in terms of precise categories of right and wrong, truths and nontruths.[24] And this is itself intimately related to the centrality of a dynamic between negation and affirmation in Basque culture.[25] Arana took from Loyola a view of the world that saw a clear divide between right and wrong and a cosmology that demanded absolute precision and dedication. Ambiguity would not be tolerated.

Set against the background of a society plagued by social and political violence at home and insurrection abroad, these symbolic images came to influence political opinion in perhaps a more literal way than they might normally have done. For example, some members of the Conservative Party were convinced that the Carlists were once more preparing a military challenge to the state,[26] coinciding with a wave of violent rural protest in Navarre, the traditional home of Carlism: "Two regiments of soldiers were dispatched to restore order," reported *The Times* of London, "but the popular agitation continues ... the governor of the province has ordered all subordinate authorities to act with energy."[27]

Arana thus articulated Bizkaian nationalism in a very precise way, with a clear vision of the problems (as he saw them) facing the Basque Country. This articulation, however, drew more from metaphor and allegory than from political, economic, or even social discourse. So while many of the tenets of what was later to become Basque nationalism were rooted in the general European context of time and place (the importance of nationalism and race in late nineteenth-century Europe, for example), one must also look at the particularities of Basque culture as a location of the ideological foundations of Arana's discourse. Culture (in a Gramscian sense), like politics, is a site of power to be contested and negotiated,[28] and in the case of Basque nationalism, one individual laid the cultural foundations for an entire cultural program.[29] Arana conceived of Basque culture in such a way as to justify the appropriation of Loyola as a nationalist hero, for example. In doing so he revealed a highly personal interpretation of history that has caused critics to fault his historical discourse as mere invention, as if truth were the arbiter of cultural (and political) consciousness. His discourse *was* invention, of course, but culture is shaped by such invention. Indeed, fact and fiction inevitably become blurred in the evolution of a cultural consciousness. For a self-defined premodern individual such as Arana, historical accounts were employed to serve his truth, not necessarily to represent what actually happened in the past.[30]

The articulation of these images associated with Bizkaian nationalism coincided with a crisis for the Liberal government of Práxedes Sagasta. On October 30, 1894, the cabinet resigned, to be replaced by a more hawkish formation containing "two members representing the military element."[31] One reason for the increased military involvement in politics was the situation in Cuba. Ironically, the colonial issue came to prominence once more as Antonio Maura had entered the new cabinet, though this time as minister of justice.[32] Sagasta, however, calmed the fears of the military by pledging "that Spain would spend her last dollar and shed her last drop of blood to retain Cuba as a Spanish possession."[33] However, in February 1895, José Martí entered Cuba from United States and gave the order that sparked a widespread rebellion. A full-scale war ensued that proved the most direct challenge to Spain in the fin-de-siècle era. That same month, the Basque philosopher Miguel de Unamuno published the first in a series of essays entitled *En torno al casticismo*[34] (About traditionalism), the first literary inquiry into the "problem" of Spain and the liberal nationalism of the Restoration.[35]

In Madrid, Sagasta was faced with yet another resignation of the cabinet, this time precipitated by army pressure to censure the press.[36] It was a clear sign that the armed forces were increasingly involved in Restoration politics. Until the 1890s, the system generated by Cánovas and Sagasta was sufficiently strong to placate army interests within the two main political parties. With a growing rebellion in Cuba, however, the army began to flex its muscles at home. "The political barometer fluctuates almost hourly," reported *The Times* of London on March 22, "in a manner calculated to confuse the mind of even the most initiated."[37] On March 22, Cánovas returned to power "without any compromise with the military"[38] in an attempt to restore the Restoration system. His immediate concern was Cuba, where the war was going badly for Spain. His remedy was to send seven thousand troops as reinforcements to the island, demonstrating he would use "all necessary resources to insure the suppression of the insurrection."[39] At the end of March, Cánovas even remarked that if it was necessary, "we are prepared to send 100,000 men to Cuba. We must put an end to the struggle once and for all."[40]

By April, however, there was no improvement. Indeed, there were now an estimated twenty thousand Cuban insurgents, reinforced sporadically by Spanish defections.[41] On April 22, Cánovas, in accordance with earlier pressure from the army, approved a ban on what was termed "separatist propaganda," an offence that in effect constituted rebellion against the Spanish state.[42] The act was designed to suppress any act of popular support for the Cuban rebels, yet in this atmosphere, Arana's ideas were also highly suspect. Indeed, two of his articles in the April 24 edition of *Bizkaitarra* were judged to be in contravention of the recently passed law. In one of them, "Ellos y nosotros" (Them and us), he commented that "man is not known by his words, but by his deeds,"[43] a phrase regarded as inflammatory by the Spanish authorities.

"The worst pain a man can have," observed Herodotus, "is to know much and be impotent to act."[44] For Arana, this pain was emphasized by the Cuban rebellion. Action is a fundamental dynamic of human cultural activity, and as a general ideology, nationalism found its most expressive outlet in concrete deeds.[45] The power to act is also an important cultural value in traditional Basque society. *Ekintza* (action) enjoys a close relationship to the notion of *hitza* (the spoken word); *ekintza* implies commitment to "do" or to undertake a specific action, which may have been articulated initially through *hitza*.[46]

According to Joseba Zulaika, "the mentality of action is in itself indirectly but intimately related to the ideology of *hitza* and the meaning of acts of speech. Verbosity and double-talk irreparably devalue the worth of *hitza*, which has to fulfill a fundamental contractual function. Words 'do' things for people who 'do' them not only in speech but in their lives. The insistence on verbal economy turns into a one-sided appreciation of *ekintza*."[47] In calling for deeds to replace words, then, Arana invoked a call to action, for activities associated with the physical reality of "doing," instead of merely "saying."[48] Here once more, he was effectively following the sacramental model of Loyola in the ritual expression of political action for a specific cause.

Under the regulations of state censure, *Bizkaitarra* (through its editor) was fined. yet this did not deter him from launching an attack on his persecutors. In the May 12 issue of the newspaper (and coinciding with the Spanish municipal elections that same day), an article glorifying the Bizkaian defeat of Castile at Mungia in 1470 invoked what, by now, had become the standard images of struggle, warfare, and heroism for the leader of the nationalist cause. In bold letters the article began thus: "TO THE HEROES OF THE *PATRIA*. GENEROUS MARTYRS OF THEIR FREEDOM, EXALTED SONS OF BIZKAYA, THAT FOR HER SACRIFICED OR RISKED THEIR LIVES IN THE BLOODSTAINED BATTLE OF MUNGIA AND BY FORCE OF ARMS ACHIEVED A GLORIOUS VICTORY OVER THE SPANISH [*ESPAÑOL*] ARMY, REMAINING FREE FROM THE FOREIGN YOKE: GRATITUDE, PRAISE AND GLORY. BIZKAITARRA."[49] The rhetoric of struggle against an army of occupation could not be overlooked by the authorities. Arana had been fined once, but in the uncertain political climate of the time, he ran the risk of further sanctions.

In many respects, the summer of 1895 marked the end of the first chapter in the institutionalization of Basque nationalism. In an article entitled "Who Are We?" Arana completed his cosmological search for the essence of Basque identity: "Bizkaians are not Spanish by nature," he concluded, "although they are today de facto and by force."[50] Bizkaia was thus conceived as a natural and specific reality that owed its current status as a Spanish province only to the power of force. Blame lay with the "other" through historical discrimination. In other words, Bizkaia was the victim of an unjust Spanish violence.

The quest for a Bizkaian ontology recalled cosmic origins, invoking the themes of natural purity (good) broken by a pernicious foreign violence (evil). These creation myths, set in the age of industrial and social transformation, formed the initial nationalist consciousness and resulted in an ideology of right and wrong, an apex of sacramental passion transferred into an absolutist political ideology.[51] Such an ideology, conceptualized this way, cannot but help to create what one observer has termed a "logic of difference."[52] In "Who Are We?" Arana demonstrated how Bizkaia differed from Spain through race, language, government and laws, character and customs, and historical personality.[53] He further stressed this natural difference in the second part of the article: "the Bizkaian that lives in the mountains . . . the true Bizkaian, is through [his] natural character, religious," mused Arana, while "the Spaniard that lives far from the town . . . the true Spaniard, either knows no word of religion . . . is a fanatic, or is ungodly."[54] On July 31, 1895 (the feast day of Loyola, once more), the Bizkai Buru Batzar (the Bizkaian Council) was launched. A clearly political organization, it subsequently evolved into the Partido Nacionalista Vasco (the Basque Nationalist Party).[55] In the weeks leading up to its creation, the dominant images in *Bizkaitarra* included eulogies to Basque heroic figures and a plethora of warlike metaphors,[56] and this at a time when Spain was actively engaged in an increasingly problematic colonial war of its own.

In August, a disturbance of the peace complaint was filed against the Euskeldun Batzokija by a neighbor of the organization's premises. The individual who registered the complaint was subsequently vilified by *Bizkaitarra*, which provoked further legal action. Arana was tried and sentenced to an initial term of forty-one days. However, a further charge was placed against him: that of subversion. The accusation of subversion, or rebellion,[57] was related to the publication of two articles that appeared in a supplement edition of *Bizkaitarra* on July 21. Though not penned by Arana, he assumed the responsibility and therefore the consequences.[58] He was fined once more, but his refusal to pay, however, meant that he remained in jail a total of three months, from August 28, 1895 to January 13, 1896.[59] Arana consequently assumed the mantle of embattled martyr, and the discourse of nationalist ideology was reinforced in its sacramental vision. At the trial, his defense attorney, Daniel de Irujo, referred to the nationalist leader as "a hero" suffering persecution for no more than "feeling in his heart the sacred fire of love for his ancestors, for the home in which their lives ended [and] the mountains in which those homes [were] settled."[60]

A week later, Arana's newspaper was in further trouble. A case was brought against the entire edition for the offence of threatening the security of the state. Aranzadi recalled that the military authorities in Bilbao had taken particular offence at his description of the activities of certain soldiers in Donostia–San Sebastián: "soldiers that are filled with fear ... because they do not fit the [kind of] force required [to fight] Maceo [a Cuban rebel leader], but whose uniform and imposing, unused sabre look nice, if a little rusty."[61] The official reaction was uncompromising. On the orders of both civil and military authorities, the charge against *Bizkaitarra* was now one of threatening the state.[62] As a result, Arana had to go through both a civil trial and a military trial,[63] and on September 12, the governor of Bizkaia approved the forced closure of the Basque Center.[64] The political climate was tense. Spain, after all, was engaged in a full-scale war. Yet the involvement of the military authorities seems to indicate that Arana's use of symbolic insurrection in his political discourse had, indeed, had the desired effect.

This was the view held by Aranzadi, who wondered whether two or three hundred Bizkaian nationalists were truly a serious threat to the Spanish state in the latter months of 1895.[65] The physical threat of Basque nationalism to Spain, at this time, was purely symbolic. Nationalists had neither the numbers nor the resources to engage in direct confrontation with the state. However the state itself and its military took the symbolic threat of violence very seriously indeed, seriously enough to prosecute the nationalist leader, proscribe the nationalist newspaper, and close the nationalist center, all acts that themselves resonated with political symbolism. This also coincided with a renewed wave of Spanish nationalism. *The Times* of London reported that public opinion in the country would "unquestionably support" the government in its belief that "Cuba must not be lost to Spain, and any measures necessary to put an end even to the remote risk of such a contingency must be unhesitatingly and cheerfully accepted."[66] Moreover, it was noted that "for Spain retention of the island is regarded almost as a question of national existence ... [and] whatever defects the Spaniards may have they still possess in a very high degree the national virtue of patriotism."[67]

For whatever reason, both the civil and the military authorities saw fit to incarcerate Arana. Aranzadi had no doubt that they viewed him as a "resurrected Zumalakarregi"–Tomás de Zumalacárregui was the charismatic principal Gipuzkoan Carlist military leader during the First Carlist War–"and Cánovas del Castillo knew perfectly well that there are neither rifles nor cannons capable of keeping down or destroying a people elevated by their ideals."[68] As 1895 drew to a close, Arana could reflect from his prison cell on the advances that Bizkaian nationalism had made. From being an idea the previous year, it had grown to encompass a solid core of adherents. He created a radical, uncompromising ideology that invoked constant metaphorical references to war, heroism, and sacrifice. And the movement had evolved to the symbolic sacrifice of its leader as he awaited his fate in Bilbao's Larrinaga Prison.

The Consolidation of the Cause, 1896–98

Although released on January 13, 1896, Arana remained under house arrest. This obliged him to be at home every day between ten in the morning and one o'clock in the afternoon, and he was prohibited from leaving Bilbao for whatever reason.[69] Events, both on the peninsula and abroad, continued to worry the authorities, and this was probably the underlying motivation for keeping a close check on the nationalist leader.

On February 10, General Valeriano Weyler y Nicolau took control of military operations in Cuba, committed to meet the insurrection with ruthless determination. To this end, he created concentration camps on the island, a policy he saw as the only viable way to fight against a well-supported guerrilla army.[70] Meanwhile, on February 19, yet another anarchist bomb exploded, this time in the vicinity of the royal palace in Madrid.[71] Arana wrote soon after that Spain still kept him under strict observation and that his fellow nationalists should continue to organize clandestine meetings in order to maintain and develop the movement.[72] Arana obviously saw an opportunity, given the prevailing circumstances, not only for consolidating the movement as it was, but for actually extending its popularity.[73] He was probably also aided by a growing political mood of intolerance linked to events in Cuba and a surge in Spanish nationalism. That same March, for example, a university student in Bilbao was attacked for shouting "Death to Spain!" and thereafter was prevented from attending classes.[74]

By May, Arana had finally managed to secure his release from military observation, prompting him to remark that, "now is the time"[75] to reinforce the nationalist cause. Through the summer of 1896, there were repeated acts of political and social violence in Spain, including an anarchist bomb attack in Barcelona on June 7 and more rural protests at tax levies in Valencia the following August.[76] This outbreak of violence "created great uneasiness in Madrid… [for] the Government believed that the movement had been started by friends of the Cuban rebels."[77] To make matters even worse for the Spanish government, a rebellion also broke out in the Philippines, causing Cánovas to admit that "since the War of Independence Spain had never found herself confronted with an emergency so grave."[78] Such insurrections were especially infuriating for Spanish nationalists, for they challenged the very notion of Spanish identity championed throughout the nineteenth century. The novelist Juan Valera, for example, explicitly invoked race in his condemnation of the Cuban uprising: "The rebels are Spaniards [who] are now struggling to leave the metropolis [Spain], forsaking their race and loathing the blood that runs

Sabino Arana in Larrinaga Prison, Bilbao, 1895. Arana's imprisonment and images such as this were used by Basque nationalists to demonstrate the heavy-handed approach of the Spanish authorities to the movement. Subsequently, Arana would become a martyr for the nationalist cause. By permission of Abertzaletasunaren Agiritegia, Sabino Arana Kultur Elkargoa archives.

through their veins, undoubtedly perverted by the ferment of, and corruption by, mixing with African blood."[79] Meanwhile, in Bilbao, Luis Arana took up the case of a young "*bilbaino* nationalist" who, on refusing to join the Spanish Army and fight in Cuba, had crossed the Pyrenees into exile in the French Basque Country.[80] Although the level of popular Spanish patriotism was high, it was much less pronounced in areas targeted for forcible conscription. Such areas were commonly found in rural Spain.[81]

In 1897, the political map of Bizkaia changed. The Liberals had governed in Bilbao until the 1890s, when both Republican and Socialist challenges gained momentum through the application of universal male suffrage to the working-class districts of the city. In 1897, the Liberals reorganized municipal elections so as to protect their own political and economic interests–they were the party of Bilbao's important industrial families of the time. This marked the formal establishment of *caciquismo* in a city that until that time had been relatively free of its vices, certainly in comparison with the rest of the Spanish state.[82] It was against this background that Arana continued to develop his nationalist program. In addition, 1897 was the year in which two events would effectively seal the radical phase of Arana's ideological formation: the publication of his major doctrinal treatise,[83] *El Partido Carlista y los fueros Vasco-Nabarros* (The Carlist party and the Basque-Navarrese *fueros*), and the creation of a new propaganda journal, *Baseñtara* (The peasant).

El Partido Carlista y los fueros Vasco-Nabarros, published in separate articles through February and March of 1897, marked a significant change for Arana. Gone were the overtly allegorical tales of heroism, replaced instead by something approaching a standard political manifesto, although still framed in the historical terms he favored. The principal argument of the work can be summarized under four main points: the official change of policy in referring to 1839 (not 1876) as marking the loss of Bizkaian independence; a consequent distancing from the Euskalerriacos, whose agenda looked toward a revision of the 1876 settlement; an easier way of identifying independence with the *fueros*; and finally, a straightforward legal way to pursue this goal by revising the foral change of 1839, instead of the more problematic liberal constitution of 1876.[84]

That said, there remained some symbolic resonances in the work. Arana opened the discussion by alluding to the *fueros* as intrinsically Spanish. Even the word *fuero*, he argued, was Spanish. Arana called for an interpretation of the Basque-Navarrese *fueros* as basic laws of sovereign peoples, not as privileges granted by Spain.[85] Furthermore, he represented the Basque provinces (including Navarre) as independent sovereign states (*estado*), with the Basques as a whole constituting a people (*pueblo*), while he represented the Spanish as merely a nation (*nación*).[86] Arana lived in an age in which the word "nationalism" was very much in fashion, and he himself had used the word "nationalist" to describe his movement. Yet he apparently placed more importance on the concept of "people" as constituting a sovereign, primordial entity prior to the formation of any state.[87]

The tone of the work is more confident in its discourse than previous efforts. Arana now envisaged a political situation in which he could afford to distance himself from erstwhile bedfellows such as the Carlists and the Euskalerriacos. It seems likely that the

Cuban struggle and the misfortunes of Restoration Spain influenced a more aggressively optimistic conceptualization of Arana's nationalism. And if one considers the symbolism of warfare and heroic struggle within this conceptualization, then events in Cuba were especially important in contextualizing Basque nationalism.[88] In the spring of 1897, the triumph of the liberal state in Spain appeared more remote than ever as an already desperate situation worsened. In Cuba, the tactics of General Weyler were described, even by a generally pro-Spanish source, as creating a "system of terrorism."[89] On May 4, five anarchists were executed,[90] and later that same month, the Duke of Tetuan, Cánovas's minister of foreign affairs, resorted to "personal violence" in a public fracas with another senator in the Spanish Parliament.[91]

That same month, May 1897, Arana and his followers published the first edition of *Baseritara*. A weekly publication, its original aim was to attack Carlism, although it would soon focus the majority of its anger toward the Euskalerriacos. It was distinguished from its predecessor, *Bizkaitarra*, by two main developments: less of an emphasis on anti-Spanish propaganda,[92] and a more diverse staff of writers in terms of age, ideological leanings, and so on, including its editor, Teófilo Guiard. The publication of *Baseritara* undoubtedly marked an attempt to develop a specific political program for nationalism. Yet it is worth noting that an allegorical rhetoric continued within its pages, alongside the emergent formal party political ideology. In the very first edition, for example, Arana used the text of an article in a French hunting magazine as the occasion for a bitter attack on Spanish imperialism in Latin America. Given his previous experience and the continuing conflict in Cuba, this was an effective and safe way of satirizing Spain. The article in question talked of the historical role that the colonial planter's dog had played in the development of imperial power, especially in regard to controlling native populations. "The hunter is in this case the dog," it observed, "the game is man, the black man, the slave." Arana concluded that such savagery was not the fault of the dog, but "the Spanish, who had the savage and inhumane idea to use dogs in the extermination of the Indians in their conquests." His conclusion was damning: "Truly the ... glories of certain nations, examined and judged before morality and justice, prove to be horrendous crimes."[93]

Events both in Spain and in Cuba may well have influenced this outburst by Arana, for it was known that the Spanish authorities were employing large-scale torture in reacting to their domestic and colonial problems. World opinion was even aware of this, as was evident from correspondence received by *The Times* of London that summer. For example, one complaint called attention to the widespread torture of prisoners in Spain, Cuba, and the Philippines. "It is the inevitable effect of such punishments as the torture," argued the letter, "to compel pity and interest for the sufferer."[94] Arana was more than likely aware of this during his own stay in prison, although he apparently did not suffer any torture. Later that summer, a representative of the Spanish Atrocities Committee in London, Joseph Perry, called for the Spanish government to cease its policy of torture: "Unless she speaks, and speaks truly, the black cloud that now overhangs her will surely burst with terrible havoc."[95]

The institutionalization or even the culture of the practice in Spain served to highlight a basic component of political or state power: the extraction of truth and information through torture. Torture in this way can be viewed as a primary ritual act and expressive symbol of state power.[96] In the late nineteenth century, the liberal states of Europe distanced themselves from those countries (such as the Chinese Empire) where torture was still a part of the judicial process. However, those same liberal states, when confronted by their own social violence, were apt to employ the same methods.[97]

Losing no time to emphasize his argument against the injustice of occupation, Arana confronted the question of Bizkaian action in the face of that same Spanish occupation: "To die for the *Patria*... understood [as]... the society, people, nation, or great family that by nature one belongs to... is not to die for [any] trivial cause, but to die for God, the ultimate End of everything."[98] Self-denial, sacrifice, and death were, consequently, reinforced as central themes of Arana's thought when he warned his fellow Bizkaians that "the people that are slaves of the foreigner deserve the slavery they suffer."[99]

On August 8, 1897, *Baseritara* published a poem by the Philippine nationalist José Rizal as an obituary to his recent death and as inspiration for the Bizkaian movement.[100] The poem recalled many of the images and themes that had characterized the previous year's battles and provided a poignant ending to a summer in which Arana had envisioned for the first time a clear political path that his ideology would assume. Rizal's poem concluded thus:[101]

> Pray for all those who died without fortune,
> for those who suffered unequalled torture,
> for our poor mothers who [guard?] their bitterness,
> for orphans and widows, for tortured prisoners,
> and pray for yourself, as you face the final
> redemption.

The words were, strangely prophetic, because that same day, Antonio Cánovas del Castillo, the chief architect behind the construction of Restoration Spain and the liberal Spanish state, was assassinated in, of all places, the Basque Country.

That August Sunday, Cánovas, who had been spending the traditional vacation month in the Basque spa town of Santa Agueda (Gipuzkoa), was shot twice by an Italian anarchist, Michele Angiolillo. Cánovas died instantly. At the time, it was widely suspected that members of "colonial secret societies" had been involved in the assassination,[102] but it subsequently came to light that Angiolillo had acted solely on behalf of the anarchists. "We've just heard the auspicious news of the death of the Spanish pig," wrote Arana that same day in a private letter, "National Joy!"[103]

While there was a genuine reaction of shock throughout Spain, in the Basque Country (at least in rural areas), this was not the case. The residents of Bergara (Gipuzkoa), where Angiolillo was being held pending trial, were reported as being "indifferent" to the commotion.[104] And Joxe Manuel Lujanbio (popularly known as Txirrita), a *bertsolari*, or traditional Basque versifier, even composed a verse attacking Cánovas to record the event.[105] That same month, after a military trial, Angiolillo was garroted in the Bergara prison.[106] If anything, the whole event served to increase the mood of pessimism within Spain. Even more, it highlighted the fact that major public figures could not escape the social and political violence prevalent in the country for a number of years. As August drew to a close, Sagasta (who within a month returned as prime minister) revealed the fear which many ordinary Spaniards felt: "In his opinion the situation in Cuba was going from bad to worse and things remained serious in the Philippines"; further, he "declared that the Carlists were already prepared and that they were only waiting for a false step on the part of the Government or for some unforeseen incident to rise in armed revolt."[107]

Sagasta's warning about the Carlist threat was alarmist. Ever since the termination of the Second Carlist War, the Carlists had rarely seemed likely to mount the challenge necessary to overthrow the state. Spain was a changing country. In some cities, at least, there was now an industrial proletariat, and socialism was beginning to take root among its ranks. At the gates of the modern age, talk of a Carlist threat seemed anachronistic. Carlism survived as a political ideology, even continuing to exercise power at a local level (specifically, in the Basque Country), but a statewide threat as such was purely symbolic. Sagasta, however, took the threat seriously, from which one can only deduce that symbolism remained a strong factor in Spanish politics. One might speculate that Carlism survived as an ideological taboo within liberal Spain, representing a dangerous, yet sacred set of beliefs that struck at the very heart of Spanish political culture. Zulaika describes a contemporary taboo, the phenomenon of terrorism, as functioning

> largely as a device for identifying and localizing military danger. If with pollution we enter the realm of fear and terror, we could add that with terrorism we are at the center of political taboo, its true value residing more on ritual and a magical system which defines dirt as disorderly and out of place. Terrorism, likewise, appears as an anomaly within a national or international order. Uncleanliness must not be included if a pattern is to be maintained; like dirt, terrorism is a residual category.[108]

This definition could be equally applicable in Restoration Spain, where although anarchists were the most obvious target of such a state taboo, representing a new, secret, and unknown menace, Carlists also aroused state fear and suspicion as the traditional, open, and known threat. As 1897 drew to an end, then, there is evidence to suggest that the political mentality of those in control of Spain viewed a threefold possibility of revolution: from above (Carlism), from below (anarchism), and from outside (Cuba).

With Sagasta once more in office, an offer of autonomy was granted to Cuba that November, but it would ultimately prove too little and too late.[109] The Cuban failure apart, Luis Arana detected a mood of increased optimism in the country, leading to more support for the Spanish government. This caused him to reflect on the hatred he personally felt for Spain "as our conqueror."[110] As the year drew to a close, a renewed wave of Spanish nationalism, the result of a threat of direct U.S. involvement in the Cuban war, enveloped the country, confirming the suspicions of the elder Arana. In Madrid, following a victorious battle over Philippine insurgents, for example, it was recorded that "there was unusual excitement... the monuments were illuminated, and most of the houses were hung with flags." Furthermore, "groups of people paraded through the streets shouting, 'Long live the Spanish Army!'"[111] Quoting the Spanish newspaper, the *Imparcial*, *The Times* of London reported that, "of Spanish patriotism there is no need to speak."[112]

When the direct involvement of the United States did come, Spanish nationalism overtook the country in the early months of 1898,[113] yet such popular feeling could not completely avoid the existent social problems of the country.[114] On April 18, a joint resolution in Washington gave President William McKinley the impetus to declare a state of war with Spain. This only encouraged Spanish nationalists more, and they were coincidentally soon given a state occasion to demonstrate their loyalty. On April 20, the monarchs officially opened the new session of the Spanish Parliament, the Cortes. The event was reported in detail by *The Times* of London, which observed that "the audience in the Senate today displayed much loyal enthusiasm, though the expression of it was naturally tempered by the consciousness... that at this critical moment the Fatherland is menaced by the most serious dangers." The proceedings duly closed with communal shouts of "Long live the king!" "Long live the queen!" "Long live Spain!" and "Long live Spanish Cuba!"[115] The following Sunday, eight thousand people filled the streets of Bilbao in a prowar demonstration. That same day, the American fleet blockaded Cuba for the first time, implying a state of war whose official declaration would come the next day. With tension running high in the ranks of the demonstration, the crowd turned violent. On passing Arana's house, the mob began to shout "Long live Spain!" and "Death to separatism!" The house was then stoned in an act of very real violence that undoubtedly affected Arana.[116]

Throughout May and into the early summer of 1898, the nationalist leader withdrew from political activity. Elsewhere, while there was certainly a high degree of popular Spanish nationalism, this did not preclude sporadic rural protests at rapidly deteriorating conditions in the countryside. They were protests that, if anything, emphasized an undercurrent of crisis and dissatisfaction within rural Spain that ironically paralleled the apparent enthusiasm in its cities. In May 1898, for example, there were eighty-one disturbances, principally related to food prices, throughout the country.[117] Abroad, the official entry of the United States into the Cuban war turned the course of events in the colony. In particular, two decisive naval defeats of the Spanish (in May and July, respectively) effectively ended the conflict. At the same time, Basque nationalist activity during the summer was limited to clandestine meetings at which the "warlike glories of Spain"[118] were discussed and her defeats celebrated.

Defeat in 1898 was a traumatic experience for Spanish culture, leading to what Joseba Gabilondo terms Spain's "first nationalist hegemonic organization."[119] Although such cultural mobilization was already underway,[120] it is certainly true that 1898 served as a catalyst, through its symbolic emphasis on loss, in focusing the articulation of Spanish nationalism. José Álvarez Junco locates this as "a moment when an intense, even hectic, period of the nation-building process in Castilian-Spanish terms began. Nationalism linked to the cause of internal reform reappeared under the name of regenerationism."[121] Furthermore, as Gabilondo also points out, the loss of an international (imperial) dimension to Spanish culture led directly to a reworking of this culture in national terms. "As a result of the new Spanish nationalist hegemonic organization," he continues, "Spain became 'existentially different' from the outside and 'historically homogeneous' on the inside. Thus, ironically enough, the end of Spanish history (Spain in global history) also represents the beginning of Spanish history (Spain as the hegemonic national subject of its 'different' and internally 'homogeneous' history)."[122]

The major preoccupation for Luis Arana seems to have been a growing interest in nationalist propaganda among Bilbao's student body. He wrote that the nationalists should organize historical information for interested students so that they could defend themselves against the "stupid Spaniards and *españolistas*."[123] He even went so far as to call for Basque nationalists to imitate the North Americans in their struggle against Spain, with a plea for "Deeds, deeds!"[124] However, at the same time, Sabino Arana was beginning to distance himself from such rhetoric. The younger Arana realized that for his ideas to have any real mark on Basque politics, a degree of compromise was necessary with what in effect constituted the other branch of Basque nationalism: the Euskalerriacos and Ramón de la Sota. To this end, they agreed to an alliance in the forthcoming provincial elections. On September 11, 1898, Sabino Arana was duly elected as a nationalist representative for the district of Bilbao.

It is widely accepted that this marked the end of the initial or more radical phase of Basque nationalism.[125] With regard to Arana's day-to-day political activity, this is certainly the case. That fall, Arana found himself elected with a popular vote of nearly five thousand sympathizers, a level of support that he could not have imagined six months before. The principal reason for this success was the compromise agreed with the Euskalerriacos, but this should not detract from the importance of symbolic rhetoric that pervaded Arana's ideology. The Euskalerriaco group came to Arana, not the reverse, and was gradually integrated into the Basque Nationalist Party between 1898 and 1902. During this time, Arana's bellicose discourse was discreetly put to one side as the party sought to establish a nationalist ideology that emphasized reason, modernity, and progress. Yet the core images established by Sabino Arana were, in their own *prepolitical* way, too powerful to eradicate completely.

Arana's ideology was genuinely original, combining premodern mythical constructions in a modern dialectic in which the Basque Country began as naturally independent while it retained the *fueros*. The Spanish then conquered it by arms, colonized it through immigration, and abolished the *fueros*. In danger of dying, Basques could save themselves only through the redemption of independence.[126] The dialectic was sustained by a logic of differentiation that conceptualized the Spanish as an ancestral enemy, a secular oppressor, and an enthusiastic practitioner of genocide.[127] From its conception, this dialectic of loss and redemption relied on recourse to symbolic violence. From the publication of *Bizkaya por su independencia* in 1893 through the Cuban war of independence and even the attack on Arana's house, violence permeated the nascent ideology. It even recalled the Carlist background of the Arana family and the civil wars of the nineteenth century.

One cannot underestimate, then, the rhetorical force of violent imagery in the origins and inception of Basque nationalism.[128] The images that Arana established constituted the basis of nationalist discourse, but it was a discourse understood not in an abstract way. This was an expressive discourse that was essentially performative, and relied on imagery associated with action, heroism, and sacrifice for its rhetorical force. The same images would survive and surface at regular intervals throughout the twentieth century in an increasingly real and less symbolic form of nationalist cultural expression.

In the next four years after Arana was elected to Bizkaia's provincial council, he gradually amended his earlier rhetoric in the pragmatic approach that had sealed the alliance with the Euskalerriacos. However, in 1902, he was once again sent to prison after a telegram he had sent to President Theodore Roosevelt congratulating the United States on freeing Cuba from "slavery" was intercepted by the Spanish authorities. After this second spell in prison, Arana significantly modified his earlier strategy, viewing the still essentially Bizkaian movement as too weak in the face of state power. At the same time, his health deteriorated, and he contracted Addison's disease in 1902. A year later, on November 25, 1903, he died of the illness.[129]

Arana's Legacy for Basque Nationalism

William A. Douglass contends that "in many respects Sabino is a tragic figure. For most of his contemporaries his campaign must have seemed downright comical. Initially, his newspaper had miniscule circulation and his party but a tiny following."[130] While this was probably true prior to 1895, in the degenerating social and political atmosphere of Spain in the mid-1890s, Arana's ideas began to arouse the suspicion of the Spanish authorities as Arana began to generate unity in the Basque nationalist movement[131] as a direct result of the kind of symbolic discourse he developed regarding Basque history and culture. Indeed, the initial foundation of Basque nationalism relied more on such symbolic appeals than a specifically political program.

Basque nationalism emerged in an introspective social and cultural context, the age of Rodin's *The Thinker*, when self-interrogation was expressed not only through art, but in the new sciences of psychology, sociology, and anthropology. Such self-analysis, amid "the melancholic paralysis of *fin-de-siècle* culture,"[132] represented a quest for essential truths beyond the confines of rational discourse. It was an era in which Henri Bergson argued for an intuitive approach to the study of society with an emphasis on the power of sentiment and the spirit as a challenge to Cartesian rationalism.[133] It was a society in which symbolism, emotionalism, pessimism, and dependency were key themes.[134]

One must, then, place the discourse of Basque nationalism in its European context. The fact that this discourse owed much to an interpretation of Basque traditional culture perhaps tells us something of fin-de-siècle Europe: that despite extensive and seemingly confident strides toward the twentieth century, the past could not be easily obliterated. If

Basque nationalism was rooted in Arana's personal experience, this too was reflective of the age. The framework of Arana's discourse, envisaged in terms of violence, struggle, and warfare, implied a similar collective mentality for Basque nationalists in the twentieth century. In a profoundly elemental question such as the nature of identity, these images would come to resonate with some power. It was, after all, an age in which the very same images, warfare and struggle, and the very same concerns, basic human loyalties, would lead to the Great War. The power of Arana's discourse for the twentieth century cannot, therefore, be underestimated.

CHAPTER FOUR

The Age of Dissent: Basque Nationalism, 1903–23

During the first two decades of the twentieth century, Restoration Spain gradually succumbed to social pressures, including the challenges of socialism and anarchism, that influenced the post–Arana development of Basque nationalist ideology and the course of Basque nationalism during this period. This was an era in Europe characterized by a generational conflict between young and old and by an increasing division between political opinions favoring either moderate or radical policies. Both themes were germane to Basque nationalism in the aftermath of Arana's death. Furthermore, Basque nationalists increasingly looked to other national movements for inspiration. Specifically, in both Morocco and Ireland, they found symbolic examples to follow. In this general context, two specific themes stand out: the recognition and response of Basque nationalism to the increasingly important social question and a growing recourse to the symbolism of political violence within its discourse.

At the dawn of the new century, the triumph of the liberal state was far from assured in Spain. Defeat by the United States in 1898 and the loss of its last colonies had provoked a literary and philosophical protest in the country that questioned the very nature of the country, a crisis of identity that foreshadowed similar problems to come in Europe. In 1914, practically the whole of the continent, aside from Spain, was plunged into the Great War. It was a war fought on behalf of a metropolitan European civilization that was aggressively capitalist, constitutionally liberal, and culturally bourgeois.[1] The Great War in Europe echoed many of the tensions that, a generation previously in Spain, had led to the emergence of Basque nationalism. Arana had constructed the discourse of Basque nationalism around the suspicion of modernization. During the Great War, the glorification of science, technology, and progress were increasingly questioned as the conflict wrought a previously unknown mass destruction of human lives. Thus, Basque nationalism's reaction against the new placed it within a discourse in the West that might be thought of not just as "a desperate rejection of all things modern and a plunge into cherished memories,"[2] but also as a natural reticence toward uncritically accepting modernity.

After the war, through the peace settlement of Versailles, the moral right and legal principle of national self-determination became a founding principle of what was newly recognized as international relations. At least one of the multiple causes of the conflict had been the so-called nationalities question in Europe, a particularly troublesome issue for the Ottoman and Russian empires and the Austro-Hungarian monarchy, where throughout the previous century there had been an increasing demand for political autonomy or even independence on the part of constituent peoples or nationalities. While statesmanlike attempts to resolve the question in the aftermath of the war proved ultimately flawed,[3] the principle itself marked an important addition to the justification of nationalist causes.[4] A student at the time, future Basque nationalist leader Jesús María de Leizaola Sánchez, later recalled that "in reality, 1917–18 was the *requiescat in pace* of imperialism . . . there had already been nationalist wars, the first [of which] . . . was that of Belgium in 1830."[5] The growing concern in fin-de-siècle Spain over questions of identity, nationality, and community thus reflected more general European concerns that were ultimately tested in the conflict of 1914–18.

Within this European context, however, one crisis of nationality stood out from the rest: that between Britain and Ireland. In the nineteenth century, a peaceful, constitutional home-rule movement for the island had been narrowly defeated. In the early twentieth century, after an armed uprising, Ireland gained a limited independence. It was a remarkable achievement, given the symbolic power of Britain, the imperial power par excellence throughout the previous century. The emotional quality of the struggle for Irish independence had an obvious resonance for Basque nationalism, itself an ideology rooted in heroic tales of warfare and resistance against impossible odds. And the affective element of Irish independence, the morally just and noble victory of a small nation over a larger state, acted as a powerful agent in the affirmation of struggle as a central symbolic image in the rhetoric of Basque nationalism.

The pace of change in nineteenth-century Europe had been principally, although not exclusively dictated by the economic and social transformation of society. This transformation had clearly played an important role in Arana's original vision of Basque nationalism. In the twentieth century, rapid change assumed an increasingly political face, and this, too, figured into the course of Basque nationalism. Socialist revolutions held the world's attention in the aftermath of the Great War, but their importance for Basque nationalists was ambiguous. The propensity for a violent overthrow of the state was a charge that had been levied at socialists for some time in Spain, and ideological debate within Basque nationalism, for example about the events in Russia in 1917, was muted. That said, the Russian Revolution did make the outside world aware of the potential for violent political change in societies previously regarded as invincible.

Two other insurrections were also widely discussed in the Basque Country at this time: the long revolution in Mexico, which entered its most radical phase in 1917, and a student rebellion in Córdoba (Argentina) in 1918.[6] Interest in these events was due to the presence of large and influential Basque émigré populations in the two countries, themselves challenging Aranist notions of geographical location as a key marker of Basque identity. Throughout the nineteenth century, there had developed a "relatively small political diaspora-Basque consciousness" that found expression in several publications and cultural activities. However, "by the early 1900s, there were several Basque periodicals consistently published in the Americas that promoted the *fueros* and ethnonationalist ideas," and although these were "mostly disseminated to, and read by, educated elite, the imagining of an interconnected Basque diaspora had taken form."[7] Indeed, this sense of an interconnected Basque identity, spanning the Atlantic, had economic, as well as cultural repercussions: In one Basque province, "many returned emigrants and even successful Basque businessmen who had settled in other countries contributed financial resources to the industrial development of Vizcaya. The constant back-and-forth movement of people and capital along these networks instilled a certain cosmopolitanism, which helped keep the Bilbao entrepreneurial elite informed of new developments in the business world."[8]

The impending European crisis in the first decade of the twentieth century was even more pronounced in Spain, for the 1898 defeat was still current in the Spanish imagination as both a political and a psychological event. In many respects, a study of Spanish history in the period reveals later trends for the continent as a whole. The crisis of the liberal state had already gained momentum in the latter decades of the nineteenth century, and after 1898, the Restoration system had gradually broken down. Spain entered the twentieth century a conquered and demoralized country. Defeat was noticeable as thousands of maimed and diseased soldiers returned from Cuba without hope of finding work.[9] For them, and indeed for the country at large, thoughts of entering yet another war remained distant.

Thus, the first two decades of the twentieth century marked for Spain the culmination of the social and political crises of the late 1880s and 1890s. The Restoration system was grinding to a halt, symbolized most emphatically by the loss of empire in 1898. In the face of a corrupt political system, the continuation of traditional social tensions, and an erratic economy struggling to find its way after the imperial losses, a battle ensued for authority in the country. This was the immediate context in which Basque nationalism emerged after the death of its founder in 1903. It was, moreover, the context that sustained a radical discourse of redemption through struggle, and this despite the apparent victory of a pragmatic vision of the Basque cause that sought accommodation within modern Spain.

Basque Nationalism and the Fall of Restoration Spain, 1903–16

Práxedes Sagasta and Sabino Arana both died in 1903. The death of the former Liberal prime minister signaled the end of any hopes for the continued successful implementation of the Restoration system. Similarly, the death of Arana apparently seemed to end Basque nationalism's association with aggressive symbolism. The new guard of the Basque movement was attuned to the needs of the modern state. In Bilbao, the organizational center of Basque nationalism, these men saw around them an expanding metropolis that had been at the forefront of Spain's economic and political modernization.[10] Yet it was a deceptive picture.

After nearly a century of liberalism, much of Spanish society had still not assimilated liberal values. The power of the church remained intact,[11] and demographic trends had not significantly altered the occupational structure of the country as a whole. For example, census figures reveal that the industrial population of Spain only rose from about 850,000 (out of a total population of 15,673,000) in 1860 to just under 1,000,000 (out of a population of 18,617,956) in 1900, while those sectors of the Spanish populace engaged in agricultural employment remained relatively stable, rising from 4,250,000 in 1860 to 4,558,000 in 1900.[12] Furthermore, two-thirds of the population still lived in rural or semirural population centers relatively untouched by the changes of the Restoration system.[13] Spanish economic development had been slow and uneven throughout the nineteenth century. Thus, a layer of traditional power interests remained intact, despite any impetus to change, on the eve of the Spanish-American War. This was still the case after 1898, when the growing dissatisfaction of modern Spain blossomed into a widespread regenerative movement. As with most matters in Spain, however, there were vastly different competing views as to the form this regeneration should take.

A conservative traditionalist reaction was assured from those sectors of society, the landed oligarchy, dissatisfied military men, and the religious hierarchy, who viewed the experiment of liberal Spain as the root cause of the social and political crisis engulfing the country in the early twentieth century. For many of these sectors, the country's ills stemmed from importing foreign ideas, whether historically from the Habsburgs, Bourbons, or the Enlightenment or in more recent times those of the two-party political system of the Restoration monarchy. The only remedy was to look back to the historic *mission* of Spain: militant Catholicism and Castilian traditions of aggressive expansionism. A liberal modernist outlook, on the other hand, took the view that Spain's problems were the result of its failure to modernize sufficiently. The institutionalization of the *cacique* system had merely confirmed a traditional flow of power in the country toward vested interests. Therefore, a profound and widespread reform was necessary to drag Spain into the new century. This could not be left to the discredited politicians of the Restoration state; it should instead be the prerogative of the intellectual class. It was they, after all, who had foreseen the events of 1898.[14] Within this growing political divide, successive governments after 1898 attempted to recuperate the system that, at least until the 1890s, had functioned successfully. In this way, it was hoped, both conservative and liberal opinion could be successfully reintegrated into the system. However, the level of hostility from all sectors of society meant that the system itself was increasingly fragile.

While the figures for socioeconomic change in Spain as a whole reflected a society ambling toward modernization, this turned into a veritable sprint in the Basque Country. After 1900, the iron-ore trade on which Bizkaian wealth had been built began to decrease, but by that time, the Basque economy had already sufficiently diversified to make it much stronger than, for example, a Catalan counterpart heavily reliant on the textile industry.[15]

Spain's neutrality in the Great War further benefited the Basque economy through import substitution in the domestic market, an increased supply of materials to the belligerent countries, and filling the export vacuum left by their participation in the hostilities. In particular, the conflict provided the opportunity for massive profits to be made by the Basque financial and shipbuilding concerns of Bilbao.[16] Between 1900 and 1930, a further 480,000 people came to Bizkaia to reinforce the already rapidly changing demographic picture of the province.[17] Bilbao itself doubled its population between 1900 and 1936, from around 83,000 to just under 162,000, and the total population of the Basque Country increased by 50 percent in the same period.[18]

Meanwhile, Donostia–San Sebastián had established itself as the most popular resort in Spain. Sea bathing as an organized, commercially run activity in Spain actually began in the city in the late 1820s and early 1830s, and a combination of royal patronage and improved communications meant that by the 1870s, it was receiving tens of thousands of visitors annually.[19] When the monarchy established its summer residence in Donostia–San Sebastián to escape the heat of the Spanish capital, it brought in its wake every year the politicians, intellectuals, and upper classes of elite Madrid society. The city had successfully cultivated an image of peace, comfort, and relaxation, promoting a curious identity mixing bourgeois European tastes in its elegant hotels and casino with the physical proximity of the town's old quarter, a repository of Basque-speaking laborers, fishermen, craftsmen, and petty traders.[20] During the first two decades of the twentieth century, the tourist industry in the city managed to widen its social appeal, attracting middle-class sectors,[21] and at the same time, its population increased at the same rate as that of Bilbao, rising from 41,000 in 1900 to over 85,000 in 1936.[22] As with Bilbao, however, the economic boom of Donostia–San Sebastián was not based on one industry alone. Indeed, "tourism was a relatively insignificant male employer," and a 1915 survey of industrial workers in the city revealed that over one-third of them were employed in construction, a further one-third in food, drink, tobacco, and textiles, and 6 percent each in metalworking and paper manufacturing. As in Bilbao, too, this development attracted immigration, and the 1930 census recorded that one-third of the city's inhabitants had been born outside the Basque Country.[23]

There were changes in the rural Basque Country, as well, as the first decades of the twentieth century witnessed an increasing tendency toward market production in Bizkaia and Gipuzkoa, instead of the traditional self-sufficiency of the *baserri*.[24] This tendency was stimulated by improving communications, which also served increasingly to break down the social and cultural barriers between the relatively isolated rural world of Basque speakers and the Spanish-speaking towns and cities. From around 1910 onward, smaller industrial towns in the rural Basque Country such as Eibar, Gipuzkoa, with its expanding arms manufacturing industry due to a war-induced boom, began to expand. This led to a gradual migration away from the land and toward the new jobs in these towns, which in turn had a noticeably subversive effect on both the traditional Basque family structure and the use of Euskara.[25] Yet in 1930, there were still healthy numbers of

Basque speakers: 60 percent of the population in Gipuzkoa and 50 percent in Bizkaia, although only 10 percent in Araba[26] and around 20 percent in Navarre. These latter two provinces, in fact, experienced less socioeconomic and demographic change than their counterparts. In Araba, between 1900 and 1930, 80 percent of the population was born in the province itself,[27] with what little immigration there was probably coming from the similar rural environments of surrounding provinces. A similar pattern could be found in Navarre, where minimal population growth in the period 1900–1930 (when the population only rose from 307,210 to 345,467) was principally the result of greater emigration than immigration levels.[28]

Against the backdrop of these changes, the immediate concern of the Partido Nacionalista Vasco (PNV) in the aftermath of Arana's death was to consolidate the small advances it had made toward the close of the century. With this in mind, "Kondaño" (Ángel Zabala, Arana's chosen successor) opted for a cautious approach. Zabala was a realist who, while accepting the ideological base that Arana had established, also concurred with the original leader's final policy modification: working toward a moderate proposal for autonomy within the electoral system. He was probably influenced in the decision by events in Catalonia, where in 1901, the Lliga Regionalista (Regionalist League) was formed as an alliance of middle-class, business-oriented nationalists under the leadership of Enric Prat de la Riba and Francesc Cambó.[29] Prat and Cambó also influenced the Basque movement's principal ideologue, Engracio de Aranzadi ("Kizkitza"), yet he still also acknowledged the continuing influence of Arana. In a 1904 speech in the Bilbao Basque Center, for example, he remarked that the Basque Country "had suffered the consequences of slavery and hatred with which it had struggled within itself, spilling in torrents its own blood and spreading its arms in search of shelter towards certified enemies of the *Patria*."[30] Using the language of Arana, Aranzadi pleaded for a reconciliation of the different sectors of Basque society in a common front against their enemies, an appeal that implied that he was aware of the complex nature of Basque society. This complexity was also reflected in the Basque Nationalist Party itself, because Zabala had to contend with an increasingly apparent division between the former Euskalerriacos (under Ramón de la Sota), who favored a policy of autonomy within Spain, and the followers of Arana's original program (headed by the founder's brother, Luis), whose goal was independence.[31]

In the wake of Arana's death, Zabala sought to impose his authority on the party. Although he lacked Arana's personal charisma, he did manage to organize the PNV into a well-disciplined political party that was still capable of reverting to clandestine operations, if necessary.[32] For example, in 1904, a youth wing of the party was created, Juventud Vasca/Euzko Gaztedija (Basque Youth), which effectively became the focus for clandestine political activity and propaganda. Subsequently, splinter groups (in reality no more than small circles of friends) were created from Basque Youth that, in time, transformed into the *mendigoizaleak*; the mountaineers and future nationalist soldiers who defended the original ideas of Arana.

This potential rupture of the party, increasingly provoked by the watchful eye of the state authorities and by their sporadic repression of its activities, forced Zabala into conceding that a specific doctrinal program was necessary to identify clearly a unified party strategy. This came in 1906, when the PNV formally ratified its main objective as the restoration of the *fueros*, marking a clear compromise. While foral restoration recalled the original aim of the PNV at its creation, they party now also favored a policy of moderate advancement within the Spanish state, distancing the PNV yet more from Arana's original doctrine.[33]

Two important events coincided with the PNV's adoption of this new policy. In February 1906, as a consequence of a Spanish military attack on a Catalan satirical publication, a varied coalition of independent republicans, Catalan republicans, Lliga nationalists, and Carlists formed the Solidaritat Catalana (the Catalan Solidarity Front) in Barcelona. It represented a unified regional response to the increasing use of state force in official efforts to shore up the liberal system,[34] and in the 1907 elections, it enjoyed a spectacular victory in Catalonia. Also in 1906, the March Law of Military Jurisdictions was implemented by the government. This granted military courts the power to try political prisoners and represented a considerable infringement on the supposed civil rights established by the state in the 1880s.[35]Any offence subsequently perpetrated against the army, police, or *patria* could theoretically be tried as a court martial. As has been noted, this development had a precedent during the 1890s, when Arana had been subject to the jurisdiction of the military authorities for what the state viewed as his political crimes.

With this in mind, in the aftermath of the 1906 decision, clandestine activity remained an important feature of the Basque nationalist program. Indeed, the Aranist faction (experts in such clandestine activity) enjoyed a significant victory within the party in 1908 when Luis Arana beat Ramón de la Sota in a vote over who would lead the Bizkai Buru Batzar (the Bizkaian Council of the PNV), the party's center of power. Thereafter, Luis remained faithful to the separatist demands that characterized his brother's (and Basque nationalism's) formative years. Furthermore, a still more important development of the era was the emergence of the aforementioned *mendigoizaleak*, or mountaineers, for they became the new young militants espousing Arana's symbolic values within the PNV. The organization came to embody the formative values of youth, action, and the sacramental importance of mountains. Within its ranks were groups of friends who organized excursions both to scale mountains and to spread the nationalist gospel into the rural Basque Country. In 1908, they united to form the Mendigoizale Bazkuna (Mountaineers' Assembly), which in turn became the Mendigoizale Aberri (Fatherland Mountaineers) in 1913. Their propaganda work involved a mixture of political and cultural endeavors, and as the foot soldiers of Basque nationalism, they were its most idealistic and zealous exponents. At this time, they were still intimately linked to the youth section of the party and its newspaper, *Aberri* (Fatherland). In 1921, the Mendigoizale Batza was formed, combining eighteen groups in Bizkaia, ten in Gipuzkoa, and one in Araba, later becoming the party's official youth wing. However, when the party itself split that same year, most of the *mendigoizaleak* joined the more radical and youth-oriented faction.[36]

After 1906, the fragmentation of Spanish society became progressively more obvious. In fact, this played into politics to such an extent that a major sociopolitical confrontation was increasingly expected by wide sectors of the public. With an expanding nationalist movement and increasing anarchist activity, Barcelona was very much the focus of attention for such a confrontation, and it duly came in 1909. In July of that year, a minor expedition in Morocco called for troops to defend Spanish mining concessions (allegedly owned by the Jesuits) beyond Spain's garrison town of Melilla, and the War Office duly looked to Catalonia for the reserves necessary to complete the operation. It was a deliberately provocative act, given not only the delicate situation in Catalonia, but a general popular feeling in Spain against military adventures. Scenes of starving, injured, and malaria-ridden troops returning to their towns and villages from Cuba were still fresh in people's minds, and it would be fair to say that the country was largely against any such military intervention.[37] On July 26, a strike was called by a group of Barcelona anarchists in protest at the conscription, and it subsequently spread throughout the city. In the ensuing violence, five days of rioting that was–curiously, in the eyes of some observers–directed against the church, forty-two churches and convents were burned, monks were killed, and tombs were desecrated. It came to be known as the *semana trágica*, the tragic week.

The power of the church in Spain, while not inconsiderable in both political and financial terms, has often been overestimated in terms of its popular appeal. While it retained a strong degree of control over Spanish education, in a largely undereducated society, this power was limited. At the turn of the century, perhaps as much as 60 percent of the Spanish population was unschooled and unchurched, particularly in the vast expanses of the south and the inner cities, the power bases of Spanish anarchism.[38] When the events of 1909 erupted, bizarre scenes swept the streets of Barcelona that week, when, in acts of pure symbolism, anarchist workers danced with the corpses of disinterred nuns.[39] Indeed, these riots recall Robert Darnton's well-known discussion of another act of symbolic political violence in eighteenth-century France, when workers found a way of turning the tables on their bourgeois masters through the ceremonious slaughter of cats.[40]

The rebellion was eventually put down by the authorities with an equal amount of violence: 175 workers were shot immediately afterward in the streets, and later trials led to a number of executions.[41] This was a classic reflection of state control, the "theater" of violence about which E. P. Thompson remarks that "the rulers act out the theatre of majesty, superstition, power, wealth, sublime justice; the poor enact their counter-theatre, occupying the stages of the streets for markets and employing the symbolism of ridicule or protest."[42] Indeed, following both Max Weber and David Held, it would seem that this very "control of the means of violence" demonstrated a fundamental legitimizing factor in defining the modern Spanish state itself. In Held's words, "the claim to hold a monopoly on force and the means of coercion (sustained by a standing army and the police) became possible only with the 'pacification' of peoples–the breaking down of rival centers of power and authority–in the nation-state."[43]

However, although the Spanish state managed to quell this confrontation, it could not overlook the seriousness of the incident. It was a riot unlike any other in the recent history of Spain, and its brutality recalled scenes of the Carlist Wars more than the social protests of the 1890s: a bitter civil confrontation marked by ruthless acts of violence. Sensing this was their moment, in 1911, the Catalan Solidarity Front sought legislation to devolve administrative power in the region. This, in turn, unleashed many of the tensions that had accumulated within Spain's two main political parties, the Conservatives and Liberals, since the late 1880s, and in the period 1912–13, they disintegrated amid bitter party infighting. This effectively ended the two-party system, and in 1913, the Mancomunitat, a chamber of limited administrative devolution, was ceded to Catalonia.[44]

In 1913, there was widespread mistrust of the Spanish political system from all sides of the political spectrum. Many PNV members, sensitive to the gains made by Catalan nationalists and their evolutionary (as opposed to revolutionary) platform, informally began to term their organization the Comunión Nacionalista Vasca (CNV, the Basque Nationalist Communion) in an attempt to widen the base of its support by disassociating itself from Arana's original nomenclature. They felt that the party should reach out to all sections of Basque society, and thus the implications of a nationalist *party* (with its connotations of separatism) would be too exclusivist.[45]

At the same time, a daily newspaper, *Euzkadi* (Arana's term for the Basque Country), was also founded to promote the ideology of the party. Edited by Aranzadi and Luis de Eleizalde ("Axe"), it was originally fairly orthodox in its support of Arana's traditional claims, but it gradually evolved a more independent line, encompassing what might be termed a more social than strictly political vision of Basque nationalism. In other words, it sought to make nationalism a movement that transcended formal party politics.[46] It therefore represented a conscious effort to imagine the Basque nationalist community in a different way from that originally envisaged by Arana.

Euzkadi's editorial line increasingly influenced the direction of the party itself, which did indeed gradually evolve into a social movement, or what José Luis de la Granja describes as a "nationalist community" with the party at its center.[47] It thus evolved into an "ethnic" party,[48] or *sammelpartei*: a layered social movement crystallized around the central focus of the party and more specifically around a central council within the party. In the case of the PNV, this was the Bizkai Buru Batzar, the party's Bizkaian provincial council.[49] With this idea in mind, the party created its own labor union in 1911, (ELA/SOV) Eusko Langileen Alkartasuna/Solidaridad de Obreros Vascos (Basque Workers' Solidarity), which later changed its Spanish title to Solidaridad de Trabajadores Vascos (STV). It was envisaged as a Christian labor organization dedicated to challenging the power of the Spanish socialist General Workers Union, the Unión General de Trabajadores (UGT) and to safeguarding the small-scale rural industries of the Basque Country.[50] The creation of this labor union addressed two crucial questions for Basque nationalism: the advance of socialism among the Basque Country's working-class population and the need to separate Basque workers from their immigrant Spanish counterparts.[51]

In the years leading up to the outbreak of war in Europe, the PNV continued to seek political gains within the system, combining remnants of Arana's mythical foundational discourse with a pragmatic approach designed to achieve such advances. Yet while the official party line increasingly emphasized the latter approach, Arana's cultural projection of symbolic warfare and violence continued to permeate the party's social base. For example, in the summer of 1913, *Euzkadi* published an article that both captured the mood of the time in Spain and foresaw impending events in Europe while also reflecting a direct line of thought stretching back to Arana's conceptualization of history. José Mª de Ojarbide wrote that it was not "an exclusive position of Basque writers, but of many historians ... [to] reduce history ... to battles and the battlefield: it seems as if war is history." He continued: "ask Basques which illustrious sons have stood out in their country; straightaway they will propose the names of warriors, not of scholars, proficient inventors, [or] outstanding artists."[52]

This reference to history as war in a 1913 article reveals the deeply rooted image of warfare in the Basque nationalist imagination. The nineteenth century was an age marked by civil war and revolution in Spain. These conflicts, while played out throughout the country, were particularly sanguine in the Basque provinces, a reflection, perhaps, of the complex historical legacy pitting Basque against Basque. Basque nationalism itself was born during an era of social protest and political violence, and these influences continued to capture the nationalist imagination well into the twentieth century.[53] Warfare thus became a standard measure of Basque history, and it comes as little surprise to find an argument in 1913 stressing that Basque heroes were more likely to be warriors than, say, artists.

The most receptive audience for such articulations of Basque identity was drawn from members of nationalist youth organizations such as the *mendigoizaleak*. They themselves celebrated and articulated their role within the nationalist movement as guardians of Arana's purist doctrine, that is, as authentic representatives of the struggle and prophets of the future. Even *Euzkadi*, the official journal of the party, reinforced this idea: "On the pinnacles of our high mountains," eulogized one article, "they [the mountaineers] appear raised in order to live closer to the Lord Creator."[54] These activists were in this way seen as blessed with a sort of divine quality, a sacramental justification for the propaganda work they undertook as symbolic warriors of the Basque nation. This was important work for the party, and the message they spread in rural areas was a crucial element in the growth of Basque nationalism during the period. In the years immediately prior to the outbreak of the Great War, although serious efforts were being made to the contrary, the rural Basque Country (as in rural areas elsewhere) was yet to experience the communications revolution of the press, roads, and railroads.[55]

Spain, still suffering the emotional consequences of a bitter colonial struggle two decades earlier, remained neutral throughout the course of World War I. As noted above, this allowed the country to benefit economically, as profits rose at a spectacular rate, particularly in Catalonia, the Basque Country, and Asturias. While many of these profits represented only short-term growth in much of the country, there was some consolidation in the Basque Country through investment for the future. For example, a business school was opened at the University of Deusto, in Bilbao, in 1916 with money made out of the war.[56]

At the same time, the PNV continued to grow. In 1909, it had 380 members in Bilbao. This figure rose to 1,000 in 1915, and the number of local chapters rose from twenty-five in 1904 to seventy-two in 1911.[57] Yet this growth was also problematic. Between 1914 and 1916, divisions (principally as a result of the marginalization of non-Bizkaian interests) led to a split in the party. Specifically, members from the other provinces rebelled against Bizkaian domination, forcing out Luis Arana, the president of the party and representative par excellence of nationalist orthodoxy.[58] From 1916 onward, the reconstituted party would officially be known by its "more vague and less exclusive name," the Basque Nationalist Communion (CNV).[59] Thereafter, the CNV would follow a strictly moderate program, distancing itself from Arana's original radical vision. A member of the CNV at the time described these ideological differences within the party, describing the its position as one of "convenience" in its relations with Madrid or whatever government might cede concessions to the Basque Country: "There were really no great differences between them [the moderates and extremists] in the ideological sense. I regard them all as patriots."[60]

Yet these events coincided with the 1916 Easter Rising in Ireland, which captured the political imagination of younger, more radical Basque nationalists. The CNV "was a party of the *conciertos ecónomicos*, autonomy, and the statute [of autonomy]," recalled one such dissatisfied young activist; "it was not nationalist [or] separatist." Indeed, the CNV "was born at the speech given by Sabino at Larrazábal" among those present who rejected Arana's original ideas.[61] Such attitudes demonstrate the beginnings of a youth-inspired collective challenge to what was perceived (from such circles) as a discredited older generation, a sentiment that would reverberate in future generations of radical young nationalists. Importantly, then, in its transition, the CNV failed to incorporate its youth sector, a faction that, through its enthusiastic rural recruitment campaign, had been crucial in expanding the social base of the party. Yet this group felt more and more out of place in a party dedicated to what it saw as half-hearted measures, such as gaining a statute of limited administrative self-government like that of the Catalans, although even smaller in scope.

This policy of "convenience" had, in all probability, been decided on by the Basque delegation to the third Conference of Nationalities held in Lausanne in June 1916, at which the Basque representatives (from the CNV) saw the need of cooperation with other nationalities (both within and outside Spain) as a means of achieving their political goals.[62] The report of this delegation provides a good insight into the general political atmosphere in the Basque Country at the time, although obviously from the perspective of the CNV. According to the delegation, official government persecution had assumed an increasingly violent dimension in the preceding years, compounded by the de facto proscription of universal suffrage, a policy enforced by the civil governors (the official representatives of central government in the provinces) and the Civil Guard. The Spanish Constitution was suspended in 1914, and the country was in effect placed under a state of martial law, although unlike in 1898, the conflict was domestic in origin. Furthermore, the delegation argued that it was noticeable that young nationalists were especially singled out for persecution at the hands of the Civil Guard. Even an officially elected nationalist representative to the provincial council of Bizkaia had been suspended for writing "Gora Euzkadi Azkatuta!"–"Long live the free Basque Country!"–in his private journal. Furthermore, the delegation argued, the Madrid press was especially hostile to Basque nationalism. For example, newspapers such as *La Acción*, *ABC*, and *El Ejército Español* argued that any display of Basque nationalism should be countered by withdrawing citizenship from the perpetrators, thereby denying them recourse to basic civil rights. These actions, concluded the report, would lead only to a more radical form of nationalism, a separatist nationalism that, it believed, would be increasingly popular within the Basque Country. Indeed, it concluded that such a nationalism was already evident and gaining popularity.[63]

That same summer, Santiago Alba, the minister of finance in the Liberal government of the Conde de Romanones, announced his intention to levy an extra tax on all profits made from the war by industry and trade. Raising money in this way, he hoped, would finance an ambitious scheme of public works that would help alleviate the social conflict engulfing the country.[64] The plan was bitterly opposed by Catalan and Basque regional interests, and opposition to it was driven by the Lliga Regionalista of Catalonia and its leader, Fransesc Cambó. He found support from both Basque nationalists and, encouragingly for the CNV, the major Bizkaian industrial families. They had remained distant from the cause of Basque nationalism up to that point, retaining strong economic and political ties with Madrid. However, toward the end of 1916, it seemed that an alliance was possible between these disparate sectors.

In January 1917, the Catalan leader visited Bilbao at the invitation of the *fuerzas vivas* (literally "live forces" but meaning the business and political elites) of Bizkaia to explain his plans for reorganizing the structure of the Spanish state. Yet while his rhetoric served to stimulate the cause of Basque nationalism, it could not draw the full support of the non-Basque nationalist oligarchy. "You should not believe in the fruitfulness of any movement that makes a painless appearance," argued Cambó; "you should not believe in the renovative fruitfulness of any ideal that, once it appears, does not clash with the status quo, for if it does not clash, it is because it has no renovative force. . . . We feel the necessity of action, total action, in transforming a raw ideal with all its pain and imperfection [into reality]."[65]

Ironically, Cambó's visit served both to strengthen the CNV and to highlight its limitations. On the one hand, the dominant moderate nationalist faction within the party found an expressive articulation of its own sentiments. Yet Cambó's rhetoric appealed to neither the industrial leaders or the radical youth faction. His worship of money had little influence on the youth faction's social vision of nationalism.[66] However, the success of Cambó's speech (from the perspective of the CNV) convinced the moderate nationalists of the value of cooperation. Yet this cooperation was the cause of a twofold criticism, from both the conservative *mauristas* (followers of Antonio Maura's party) and the nationalists loyal to the ideals of Arana. The CNV continued, however, in the face of this criticism, to broaden its appeal. Indeed, in the March 1917 provincial elections, it gained more support than any other party in Bizkaia: 39.6 percent of the vote. From a combined total of fifty-nine seats in the four Basque provincial councils, the CNV held thirteen places, making it the joint leading party with the Carlists.[67] These gains were, indeed, important, but were also achieved in the context of a rapidly deteriorating Spanish political system.

The Fall of Restoration Spain,, 1917–23

Spain in 1917 could hardly be described as a model of stability. Since the 1890s, wave after wave of social protest, compounded by an increasingly corrupt political system that divided the country along class and national lines, gradually had been bringing the country to its knees. The economic boom enjoyed during the early years of the war in Europe had faltered, and the whole country was suffering the consequences. From the politically radicalized masses of Catalonia to the army's junior officers, there was widespread discontent. It was, in fact, the extensive nature of the discontent that propelled the country into a six-year crisis, marking the end of the Restoration system.

One of the key elements to the success of Restoration Spain in its early years was the integration of the army into the political system. This had been due to the accommodation of army interests within the two main political parties. Gradually, however, the military had grown dissatisfied with what it saw as indecision and inefficiency within the country. The disastrous 1898 war only compounded this growing distrust, and by 1913, with the two-party system already in disarray, the first stirrings in four decades of serious discontent within the armed forces were heard. Later, in the period from 1919 to 1923, Spain's parliamentary monarchy was plagued by a greater military intervention in political affairs than at any time since its creation in 1876.[68] In the spring of 1917, elements within the army set up the *juntas de defensa*. These were councils composed of junior officers below the rank of colonel, provisionally created to protest the escalating corruption in both the political system and the higher ranks of the army. Their initial dissent concerned the low pay and poor conditions they had endured since the Cuban war. It also reflected the general wish to create a more modern and more efficient army.[69] Yet there was another dimension to their complaints. These junior officers were principally composed of recruits from traditionalist sectors in Castile and Andalusia and were therefore strongly centralist. They viewed events in Catalonia, especially the creation of the Mancomunitat and the growth of the Lliga as the region's main political party, with a great deal of suspicion and hostility. After all, it was separatist Cuba that had nearly destroyed both the *patria* and the army in 1898.[70]

That same summer of 1917, a coalition was formed as a kind of lobby to recapture the spirit of liberal renovation in the country: the Assembly Movement. Interestingly, this represented a cross-party spectrum of political thought: Bilbao and Barcelona industrialists, socialists, republicans, and the more progressive elements of Spain's middle classes. In July, members of the Spanish Parliament close to the movement met in Barcelona and called for genuinely free and fair elections. The March provincial elections had also given the CNV a new confidence, and that summer, they worked out a specific plan for Basque autonomy. In July, the party voted to petition the government for restoration of the foral system.[71] The Assembly Movement represented, for the first time, a large body of opinion that sought to rid Spain of the last vestiges of the ancien régime and truly bring about a modern, efficient society. That capitalists and socialists, together with monarchists and republicans, had united only demonstrated the fundamental importance of the issue. At this critical moment in the country's history, the military *juntas de defensa* also seriously considered joining the Assembly Movement. This would have given it a solid base of army support and may perhaps have saved Spain from the spiraling social conflict dominating the country with a depressing regularity.

However, that August, the government's response to what was, in effect, a minor railroad strike provoked a larger confrontation between the army and the socialists and anarchists. A general strike was called for August 12, and government opposition to the Assembly Movement's call for restraint seemed to reflect the forces of traditional Spain within the Restoration system. They refused to entertain any notion of the movement's calls for reform. After three days of violence, including a brutal response by the army, there were seven dead and two thousand prisoners. From this time on, there could be no alliance between the socialists and the army.[72] In November 1917, a new coalition government led by a Liberal, Manuel García Prieto, sought to placate both the army and the Assembly Movement, but the cause was a hopeless one. García Prieto resigned in March of the following the year, and Antonio Maura formed a national government. It was fundamentally conservative in tone, yet it, too, was unable to placate the diverse sources of discontent, falling in 1919. These crises left political control to yet another patchwork government without the mandate of an operational party system.

In the Bilbao municipal elections of November 1917, the CNV triumphed with just under half the vote, confirming its power base in the principal Basque city.[73] As a result, at the close of the year, the party decided to use its electoral strength to promote a plan for autonomy. A general assembly of the party met in December to ratify its moderate aims and to silence any internal dissent. In the 1918 general elections the following February, the CNV won seven of the twenty seats available in the four provinces.[74] That victory, however, marked the pinnacle of nationalist parliamentary success. Sweeping social protest and its resultant violence tarred the image of all marginal groups in the Restoration system. The state perceived all such groups as collective threats to national unity and did all it could to mobilize its forces against them, including a propaganda campaign against such ideas. In 1919, the CNV lost its majority in Bizkaia, and a year later had its Madrid representation seriously weakened.[75] Although an autonomy commission was established in 1920, events on the streets of Spain were bringing the country to the brink of revolution, and all other issues were put aside.[76]

The failure of the CNV's cautious program probably helped to radicalize many of its members.[77] A radical vision of Basque nationalism had, of course, been a salient factor in the party's youth wing for a number of years, and a more liberal precedent, of sorts, existed in the (ultimately unsuccessful) lay nationalism of Francisco de Ulacia, one of the PNV's first councilmen in Bilbao, who had founded two breakaway parties: the Partido Nacionalista Vasco Liberal (the Liberal Basque Nationalist Party) in 1910 and the Partido Republicano Nacionalista Vasco (the Basque Nationalist Republican Party) the following year.[78] And while the CNV disseminated its moderate reformist program during the years from 1914 to 1918 in the pages of *Euzkadi*, the young radical nationalists had responded with their own weekly, *Aberri* , in 1916. According to José María Lorenzo Espinosa, radical Basque nationalism dates from this time.[79]

Radical Basque nationalism certainly gained momentum from 1916 onward, principally due to a common opposition among various groups within the CNV to the official party line of autonomy.[80] A number of incidents then served to alienate the radical faction more: the 1916 Easter Rising in Ireland, which found unequivocal support from the nationalist youth organization; the visit of Cambó in January 1917, which sealed the importance of a capitalist economic base for the CNV's nationalist program; the party's general assembly in December 1917, which effectively stifled any potential internal dissent; the increasing street violence after 1920; and, finally, the Spanish war in Morocco.

Youth, of course, had been a powerful category and symbol for nationalism since the 1830 revolution in France that overthrew the Bourbon monarchy. Aided by Romanticism's insistence on youth as the metaphor for eternal creativity, as well as for the future, European nationalist movements through the nineteenth century embraced this symbolism, beginning with the Europe-wide youth movements founded or inspired by Giuseppe Mazzini after 1830 (Young Italy, Young Poland, Young Switzerland, Young Germany, and Young France, in the period from 1831 to 1836), through Young Ireland in the 1840s, to the Young Wales movement and the Young Turks in the late nineteenth and early twentieth centuries.[81] There even emerged in Spain, after 1914, a young intellectual nationalist movement aimed at contesting the predominance of its 1898 counterpart. The so-called Generation of 1914, composed of individuals such as José Ortega y Gasset, Salvador de Madariaga, Luis de Zulueta, and Luis Araquistain, challenged the older intellectuals with a more specific emphasis on the dynamism of youth and a special attention to what it viewed as Spain's *national* mission: to further scientific inquiry in the country and to transform society through direct political action.[82] And related ideas, combining youthful energy with an emphasis on direct action and a worship of the new, swept across Europe prior to and during the Great War; from Filipo Tommaso Marinetti's Futurism (embracing the full force of speed and technological change) to Hitler's brooding, dark vision of a new order rooted in cultural tradition, but open to technological innovation.

Youth activism offered nationalist movements a dynamic and zealous devotion that captured the frequent need for deeds, rather than just words. This was clear for Jesús de Sarría, a nationalist intellectual and editor of the influential cultural review *Hermes*. "Our nationality," wrote Sarría in 1918, "is youth, renovation; everlasting brilliant youth... sometimes audacious, others anxious, frequently timid." He continued: "In nationalism youth is not, as in all organizations, the vanguard. In nationalism, which is the struggle of an eternally young nationality for full nationhood, youth is at the same time redoubt and tabernacle; combatant redoubt and a tabernacle of inflamed passions." For Sarría, the eternally young Basque nation should view its nationality, in words recalling Arana's, as "tradition and anguish."[83] He saw young nationalists as the purest expression of the original conception of Arana's creed and in 1919 came out in favor of the radical direction being taken by the Juventud Vasca de Bilbao.[84]

In 1919, Elías de Gallastegui was elected head of the Juventud Vasca. A charismatic young man, "Gudari" (meaning warrior), as he was known, brought the organization into open confrontation with the party elders. Specifically, he fostered, together with other *aberrianos*, a vision of nationalism that owed its ideological foundations to Arana's original discourse. This time, however, it contained an additional element gleaned from the domestic problems of the age: social reform.[85] In July 1921, this radicalism became too much for the CNV. The *aberrianos* were expelled from the party, breaking its vision of a broad-based nationalist "community." That September, the expelled members reconstituted themselves into a political party, taking the original title of the Partido Nacionalista Vasco, the PNV, as a radical alternative to the CNV, with Luis Arana as their leader and Ángel Zabala among their ranks.

Two events were especially important in influencing their decision to found a new party. As we have noted, since 1918, Spain had been swept up in escalating domestic protests that found their only expression in acts of violence. These protests came later to the Basque Country, although with equal vehemence. Then, a disastrous colonial war in Morocco convinced the *aberrianos* of the fruitless nature of Spanish imperial expansion.[86] "It is well known that the rights of the less powerful are at the mercy of those more powerful," wrote a PNV sympathizer in 1922, and the radical turn called for a twofold program of action: "in reclaiming from illegality what the state itself has committed... and... the simple action of separation." These were the ideals that constituted the basic program of the reformed Basque Nationalist Party.[87]

After 1918, Spain experienced the most widespread domestic protests against the entire Restoration system. In the impoverished agricultural southern region of Andalusia, this took the shape of a pronounced form of traditional rural rioting that lasted two years and brought the region to the brink of revolution. Inspired in part by events in Russia, the protests took on a more organized dimension. Indeed, the successful organization of the movement's propaganda encouraged protests in other regions, such as the Levante and Valencia, to the southeast. The government was eventually forced to send in a large number of troops, almost the equivalent of a war campaign, and the protests were defeated in the spring of 1919. Meanwhile, in Barcelona, labor protests over increased unemployment led to a form of gang warfare in the streets as rival groups of anarchists and assorted leftists fought it out, both among themselves and with the authorities, for control of the *barrios* (neighborhoods). Conditions there were exacerbated by a breakdown in communications between the civil and military authorities, and between 1920 and 1922, the protesting groups effectively controlled the inner city while the leaders of the anarchist movement's labor union, the CNT (the Confederación Nacional de Trabajo, the National Work Confederation) were in prison. Yet these groups were still able to maintain an effective network of cooperation with other anarchists in Bilbao and Valencia.[88]

In the Basque Country, the domestic violence that had affected Spain since 1917 finally arrived in 1920. There were a number of shootings in conflicts related to industrial protests in the iron and steel sector, and socialist action groups fought street battles with their young nationalist counterparts from the *aberri* faction of the party.[89] Jesús de Sarría observed at the beginning of 1920 that Basque nationalism had "an enormous mass of laborers, workers, and employees of all categories and industries. Non-Basque organizations have influence with them. It would be regrettable if they could give them what we cannot ourselves."[90] The only solution, in the face of violent confrontation between the forces of capital and labor, according to Sarría, was a socializing imperative, and "in the socializing imperative, as in anything else, action, and intelligent and swift action"[91] was required. It was, for the CNV, a radical view and earned Sarría official condemnation from the party.[92]

At the end of May 1920, a local general strike was called in Errenteria (Rentería), an industrial town near Donostia–San Sebastián, after a minor traffic incident sparked off labor problems. The violent response of the police only incensed the protesters, who were supported by the Basque nationalists in their demonstrations. The problems were still simmering (particularly a unified call for the removal of Gipuzkoa's civil governor) when a summer railroad strike began to incorporate the use of incendiary devices in its protest. Finally, in the tourist capital of Spain, a waiters' strike broke out on August 16, 1920.[93] The strike resorted in part to the traditional tactic, used before and subsequently, of protesting in the town's main fashionable concourse and then retreating to the comparative safety of the old quarter's narrow streets, an area of the city that was known for both its preservation of traditional Basque culture and its radicalism.[94] In Bilbao, the picture was equally violent, with a wave of bombings culminating in the burning of a new transatlantic ship, the *Alfonso XIII*, as it was being completed in one of the city shipyards. However, given that Bilbao was one of *the* industrial centers of Spain, the level of violence was actually lower than that of similar cities such as Barcelona, Valencia, and Zaragoza,[95] due most likely to the weaker level of anarchist organization within the city.

To compound matters, Spain embarked on a disastrous colonial adventure in North Africa. With the war in Europe at its height, Spain attempted to bypass international opinion and extend its influence in Morocco in the vague hope of fulfilling its African "mission" and, no doubt, deflecting Spanish public opinion away from domestic problems.

Beginning in 1914, an increasing number of expeditions were undertaken by the Spanish Army, departing from the relative safety of the garrison towns of Ceuta and Melilla and striking into the forbidding interior. As with previous encounters, however, the campaign proved more difficult than expected. Local tribes rebelled against the Spanish encroachment, and a fierce colonial war broke out. From 1919 on, official Spanish policy was geared to establishing a land-based link between Ceuta and Melilla. If achieved, this would have constituted a not inconsiderable foothold in North Africa.

In late 1920, Spain's version of the French Foreign Legion (the Tercio de Extranjeros) was formed to counter the attacks on Spanish expeditions out of Ceuta and Melilla. "The Legion," as it was popularly known, would gain infamy for the grim cruelty of its actions in Morocco. Composed of common criminals, Great War veterans from all over Europe, and Barcelona gunmen, it also listed among its ranks a physically unassuming twenty-eight-year-old major, Francisco Franco. Under Franco, there was ruthless discipline and no quarter offered in the offensive. Within a week of arriving in Morocco, the Legion was posted to the major battle zone, where it regularly attacked local villages, making little distinction between innocent bystanders and insurgents. Franco regularly ordered the decapitation of prisoners and the parading of their heads in public, seeking to terrorize the local population into submission. This gave the force a notoriety that "taught [him] much about the exemplary function of terror."[96]

In 1921, however, Spanish advances came to a halt as twenty thousand soldiers were driven back to Melilla by the Rif tribesmen, newly united under an able and aggressive leader, Abd-el-Krim. Known by the name of the village where the counteroffensive started, Annual, it was actually a rout that, in three weeks, wiped away a decade of territorial gains by Spain. It was a disastrous psychological blow, comparable to the one suffered by the Spanish Navy at the hands of the United States in 1898. A rearguard offense by the Spanish offered temporary relief to the situation (including publicity for the bravery of Franco himself), but the stigma of defeat was hard to ignore. If the government would not be accountable for its military policy, then the army would have to take matters into its own hands in order to salvage Spain's battered pride. Between 1921 and 1923, the cry from the military thus was one of responsibility, as a popular base within the armed forces sought political accountability for the country's disastrous military policy.[97] Whereas Spain's domestic problems upset and angered the army, defeat in Morocco involved it, and the loss of prestige suffered by the military compounded its growing anxiety within the country. With events in Barcelona racing out of control, the military organized a classic *pronunciamiento*: on September 23, 1923 General Miguel Primo de Rivera, the captain general of Barcelona, assumed the leadership of Spain in the name of God, *patria*, and the army.

The first three decades of the twentieth century had proved a momentous period of change for European society. Total war, national self-determination, and socialism entered the vocabulary. Empires crumbled and revolutions erupted. In Spain, as elsewhere, there was widespread discontent among all sectors of society that manifested itself in a variety of reactions. During the same period, Basque nationalism ceased to be a singular, unified movement. The more cautious approach of the CNV opted for integration within the system–a moderate, conservative, and capitalist economic nationalism linked to the Basque economic boom during and after the Great War.[98] The PNV blended both radical and traditionalist concerns, incorporating a progressive policy of social change that separated them from Arana's ideology. Despite a trend toward accommodation and moderation, there thus remained elements of Arana's original thought that continued to pervade the nationalist imagination. In the broader social context, where society was obsessed by images of struggle and confrontation, the original symbols employed by Arana could not fail to have some effect, and it is to these symbols and their impact that I will turn my attention in the following chapter.

There, I will examine the discourse, opinion, and mentality of both moderate and radical Basque nationalism in an attempt to discover how far and to what extent Arana's original production of images continued to play a decisive role within the nationalist movement. The founder's influence remained sufficiently strong within both factions of Basque nationalism that one can, indeed, speak of a collective Basque nationalist mentality, a particular way of seeing the world and its events that recalls the original concerns of Arana and confirms Roland Barthes' maxim that "it is language that speaks, not the author."[99] Arana's discourse of Basque nationalism survived in a specific outlook that constantly referred to an ideology of struggle and that reserved a sacred place for the symbolic role of warfare. The vague and provisional prototypes established by Arana gradually acquired more specificity as accepted nationalist dogma, particularly when posed against contemporaneous events.[100]

CHAPTER FIVE

Core Images in Basque Nationalism, 1916–23: The Saint, the Prophet, the Peasant, and the Warrior

Despite the moderate turn of the PNV toward the end of Arana's life and its transformation into the CNV during the crisis-torn final years of the Restoration system, a more orthodox Aranist line continued to function within the movement's discourse. This internal war of words surrounding Arana's original discourse actually served to maintain those original symbols–of violence, struggle, and warfare–within the Basque nationalist imagination. This discourse was most evident in the realm of symbolic appropriation, although it also surfaced in regard to policy, particularly in relation to external events such as the Great War and the Easter Rising in Ireland. Events in Ireland exerted an especially important influence on the course of Basque nationalism during this period, and this has not been fully appreciated in the relevant historiography of Basque nationalism. There was, moreover, an emerging cult surrounding the figure of Arana, itself a point of contention between the two factions of Basque nationalism.

"No nobler feeling than this of admiration for one higher than himself dwells in the breast of man."[1] Thomas Carlyle's assessment of the nature of heroism has a profound resonance within the litany of agonistic images that together made up the cultural imagination of Basque nationalism. Arana nurtured the idea that heroism is an essential component of nationalism. He saw it as both an example of the kind of conduct expected of the nationalists themselves and a means of revering those who had gone before them in the struggle that made them heroes. It served, in this way, to link the themes of war, history, and heroism to the present. In other words, one could live the past more easily through the heroic celebrations of its great men, a highly sacramental discourse. It also reflects the search for a relationship with a divine or superior being that may ultimately prove fruitless, imparting a fatalistic tendency among its adherents.[2] Yet it is the search itself, the obeying of sacramental vows, that remains the essential component of this strategy, in effect revealing adherence to one's cause.

This Aranist discourse continued to play a critical role in the consolidation of Basque nationalism in the years from 1916 to 1923, especially through the use of heroic images that might be categorized as the saint, the prophet, the peasant, and the warrior. In effect, the use of such figures at this time came to represent the symbolic ties between old and new, the representative bonds of the Basque historical imagination.

A recurrently seminal date in the history of Basque nationalism is July 31, the feast day of Saint Ignatius of Loyola. In 1916, it represented, for the Basque nationalist community, at least, the most important day of shared values and the authentic symbolic expression of a collective mentality. This mentality had been shaped by Arana's original doctrine, which had appropriated the figure of Loyola to represent a set of values to which all Basque nationalists should aspire. And this mentality actively continued long after Arana's death. To celebrate the saint's feast day in 1916, *Euzkadi* published an article establishing two aspects of "the great Basque's" character that, it urged, should serve as an inspiration to the cause of Basque nationalism: Loyola's prudence "in planning, conceiving, designing, and above all, resolving" and fortitude "in putting into effect and arriving at the end, crushing [all] obstacles." By following these examples, the article contended, an "omnipotent fortitude will be with us, infusing us with the security of victory."[3] While a continued association with Loyola was emphasized, this appropriation was different from that originally conceived by Arana. He saw in the saint sacramental precision (his distinction between good and evil) and physical force (the religious warrior). While the official journal of the CNV preferred to emphasize his moral fortitude, however, there was also an element of precise or absolute moral definitions. By following Loyola's example, *Euzkadi* argued, one would have "right" on one's side.

In the figure of Arana, of course, a latter-day Loyola could be celebrated, and he duly became the sacred national prophet of Basque nationalism in the twentieth century.[4] Arana sacrificed his life for the cause, and thus the mantle of heroic martyr passed into the Basque nationalist imagination. On the fourteenth anniversary of his "sacred death," it was recorded that the "savior of the race" had dedicated his short life to "national redemption." Its remembrance was thus to serve to create a feeling of "venerable spiritual community" within the ranks of Basque nationalism. At the service to commemorate the death, these nationalists asked for perpetual light to bless their prophet, who had been on Earth for the sole purpose of serving God and his *patria*.[5] The true inheritors of Arana's legacy, however, (at least in their own opinion) were the radical *aberrianos*. For one *aberriano*, the growth of the CNV during the second decade of the new century owed its success to people "who were neither nationalists nor participants in the ideas of Sabino."[6] As a result, radical nationalists created alternative ways to mythologize the dead leader, such as ceremonies of homage at his grave.[7]

A different kind of hero was also celebrated by Basque nationalists during the same period. Not the saintly warrior or national prophet, but rather the noble peasant, and especially the peasant-poet, the individual capable of expressing the sentiments of rural culture held to be the true essence of the Basque soul: the *bertsolari*, or versifier. *Bertsolaritza*, the art of extemporaneous versifying, was one of the central cultural expressions of traditional Basque society. The versifying art is reflective of an oral literature executed by and for the people, an intimate expression of rural popular culture.[8] *Bertsolaritza* involves spontaneous versifying in song and is conducted as a contest between two or more *bertsolariak* (versifiers). Its artistic quality rests in the nature of improvisation, which infuses it with a temporary essence common to all artistic expressions of oral cultures. The text of the *bertsolariak* is not fixed in the sense that poets fix their texts through the act of writing. However, within the spontaneous setting, there are fixed rules, rules of rhyme and rhythm, that control the verses themselves. Given the nature of Euskara, the words that express the ending of a versifier's idea actually appear first in the strophe, recalling the Basque refrain "amaia da hasiera," "the end is the beginning."[9] It has been argued that the rhymes and rhythms of the verses stem from the rural work patterns of traditional Basque culture out of which the art emerged. These work patterns were, similarly, appropriated by Arana to compound his emphasis on the value of *ekintza* (action), rather than the mere words of written text.[10] In this way, the figure of the *bertsolari* became seminal to Basque nationalism, combining not only an image of the noble peasant, but also the figure of the political activist.[11]

The most politicized *bertsolari* of this age was Kepa Enbeita ("Urretxindorra," The Nightingale). He was an active participant in nationalist activities, the spokesman of the rural imagination, and a living hero.[12] Born in Bizkaia in 1878, Enbeita joined the PNV and dedicated a great part of his work to the nationalist cause. He especially wanted to transform *bertsolaritza* into a source of culture for all Basques. To this end, he was the first *bertsolari* to take the art form out of the tavern and into the public space of squares and theaters, and he wrote poems such as "'Abesti abertzalia" (Patriotic song), "Aberrijaren ziñopea" (Patriotic oath), and "Il zan Aberrija biztuteko" (To revive the dead homeland). Enbeita, then, not only represented an expressive component of the still-existent and vibrant rural Basque culture, but was also an active transmitter of that culture. This transmission was also political: After speaking to some nationalist groups, the listeners "hoisted him onto their shoulders like a victorious bullfighter."[13] This would seem to bear out James W. Fernandez's argument that folklore is an integral component of nationalism.[14]

Engracio de Aranzadi lauded Enbeita as a "flawless patriot" who was capable (in metaphorically ascending terms) of "one day raising all Euzkadi [the Basque Country] to place it on the throne of its rights." He perhaps also served as a metaphorical representation of the nationalist cause itself: "Enbeita should be known and loved by the entire Basque population." He "should be glorified." If he did represent the nationalist cause in this way, then his personal qualities reflected the inherent qualities of that cause, for Enbeita was "a Basque of admirable moral integrity, superior intelligence, a patriot formed in the stoicism of self-denial, and an artist, a wonderful improviser who, through vocal rhythm, knows how to put together in a lightning instant torrents of ideas and feelings of an ever noble and upright ancestry."[15]

This expressive encomium, which immediately drew attention to the collective nationalist mentality, regarded Enbeita as not only an individual of moral integrity (a required virtue of the nationalist cadre since the times of Arana), but also as possessing superior intelligence. The rural *bertsolariak* were often illiterate and, as such, stigmatized by the bourgeois metropolitan culture of the Basque Country. Yet as Joseba Zulaika maintains, they remained "the genuine generator[s] of expressive culture . . . rendering into speech collective sentiments of solidarity and proposing solutions to conflictive aspects of social life."[16] This was celebrated by nationalist discourse as both a facet of intelligence and an authentic artistic representation of Basque traditional culture. Enbeita's self-denial was also praised, for he had sacrificed himself to the higher cause of nationalism, instead of seeking (admittedly limited) earthly rewards for his art. And finally, the nature of improvisation itself was celebrated. *Bertsolaritza* is a spontaneous performance, a momentary response to a situation or problem. Its lessons, by implication, were crucial for Basque nationalists.

The last canon of mythical Basque heroism was that of the warrior. Tomás de Zumalacárregui was a Basque Carlist commander during the First Carlist War who was able to rally a broad base of popular support in Navarre in 1834, a warrior combining political acumen and inspired military leadership. However, against his own judgment, he was forced into a strategy that ultimately cost his life,[17] and his death gave Carlism its first martyr. Once again, it was Aranzadi who articulated the importance of the warrior for the nationalist cause, for the "idealism and spirit of sacrifice of the Basque Carlists," had to be recognized by their descendants, the nationalists. "In all the great historical events there appears a key man," argued Aranzadi; "everything rests with him, he explains everything." Zumalacárregui "defeated in a hundred battles the enemies of Basque freedom," and it was his memory that, without doubt, "contributed principally to the successes of the second war." Aranzadi continued:

> Zumalakarregi is the hero of armed Basque insurgents. Of those who raise up and arm themselves for God and the *Patria*. He is the representative hero of the Race, for his dignity, for his spirit of organization, for his shrewdness and his silent bravery. . . . Nobody has extolled the military virtues of the Basque like he . . . and nobody has crushed the enemy's pride like Zumalakarregi, not with explosive words, but with the sword. . . . [He was] surely the Basque most respected and exalted by his brothers.

Furthermore, although Zumalacárregui was a Carlist, it was "a genuinely nationalist sentiment that took the Basque Carlist population into war . . . [and when] threatened by the impiety and ambition of Spanish imperialism, the Basque took up arms."[18]

Aranzadi's mythologizing of Zumalacárregui recalled Arana's original discourse. Not only did he establish a link between contemporary Basque nationalism and Carlism, he especially emphasized those elements of the Carlist creed that celebrated military endeavor. This was not the Carlism of monarchical loyalty or even of legal protest at the loss of regional rights. It was the Carlism of political violence: insurrection or rebellion in the face of foreign occupation. And it fed the hungry myth of a Basque recourse to arms in the face of tyranny and oppression.[19]

Furthermore, and crucially in the context of the time during which Aranzadi was writing, his words did not reflect the ambiguity and compromise characteristic of the CNV, but instead echoed the more sacramental doctrine of Arana. One can only speculate about the reasons behind this, but it likely that events in Spain (the precipitous nature of the system and open revolt in many parts of the country) and the challenge of the reconstituted PNV as a more radical alternative to its aged counterpart influenced moderate nationalism's principal ideologue.

History as War

While a discourse surrounding heroic figures personified the individual in the imagination of Basque nationalists, the collective theme that united the roles played by such individuals was a recurring reference to history as warfare, a constant and necessary struggle between good and bad to save the nation from foreign excess. This is, of course, a universal theme, for human history is marked by military dominance and its celebration as a noble endeavor.[20] In the Basque case, the belief in history as war took multifarious forms, reflecting the theme's pervasive quality in the nationalist construction of identity.

In 1921, for example, *Euzkadi* celebrated the decision by the Navarrese Commission of Historic and Artistic Monuments to erect a monument in honor of the battle of Maya/Amayur at which the Navarrese had defended their independent kingdom against Castile in 1522.[21] The monument itself was completed the following year, four hundred years after the original battle. Its inscription read: "To the men who, in the castle of Maya [Amayur], fought for the independence of Navarre. Perpetual light. 1522."[22] *Euzkadi* emphasized that this should serve as a lesson for all Basque nationalists: "Look at [the monument of] Amayur and learn to be heroes ... look at history and follow its golden examples. Give the *Patria* your entire being."[23]

This notion of history as a narrative of warfare and struggle involved not only Basques within their own territory, but those beyond, as well. Indeed, as if to emphasize the emergent transatlantic nature of Basque identity, a natural location for emphasizing the heroic qualities of the warrior was to be found in Latin America, the focus of centuries of Basque migration. During the second decade of the nineteenth century, when several new countries emerged in Latin America as a result of fighting for their independence against the Spanish Empire, Basques (according to *Euzkadi*) were prominent in the struggle. Particular attention was reserved for Simón Bolívar; the liberator of the northern part of Latin America and the descendant of Bizkaian emigrants. *Euzkadi* emphasized that his struggle incorporated black and indigenous peoples, as well as the Creole population. Furthermore, the historical role of Basques in Latin America was exonerated from violence toward the indigenous population: "As assistants in the work of conquest, Basques distinguished themselves through, and by preference engaged themselves in, peaceful works."[24] Although far from the truth,[25] this was an important image for moderate Basque nationalism to present. Warfare was a just and noble endeavor when employed against tyranny, but in the case of the conquest of the Americas, the Basques were passive participants–secondary assistants, at best, within (by implication) *Spanish* imperial expansion. Thus, history as war was an idea that could be refined into the notion of history as just warfare and struggle. It is interesting, however, to contrast the views of the moderate CNV with their more radical counterparts in the reconstituted PNV. According to *Aberri*, there was no consistent tradition of militarism, but rather, Basques historically took up arms only as a defensive recourse. Furthermore, *Aberri* openly criticized Basque participation in the Spanish colonization of the Americas:

> If history records some Basque names sadly celebrated for their banditlike military exploits, they are only isolated individuals who, not being able to come to terms with an honorable, peaceful life in which our people have always intimately gathered, left and, placing their military endeavor at the service of Spain, collaborated, to disgrace their race ... in that work of conquest and extermination of the indigenous American races.[26]

Those Basques who did take part in the conquest of the Americas were, by implication, isolated individuals outside the collective. They were not "good" Basques, like the nationalists. Indeed, the very fact that they were not nationalists, it was argued, meant that they served (without complaint) the Spanish Empire. The warlike qualities of Basques then, were generally viewed as defensive, except when placed at the service of Spain.

History continued to be a principal focus of Basque nationalist propaganda, and this propaganda continued to frame its historical references in warlike imagery. "Space and time are two major elements of forgetfulness," *Aberri* observed, "and because forgetting is a human condition, we forget ... when distance or years move us away and separate us from the generating cause of a passion." What was needed, continued the author, was regeneration, a rebirth of past ideals and passions:

> Euzkadi was a grave, its sons indifferent to the national cause. See now how the "dry bones of that grave are coming to life again." Do you know what that movement means? That after so many years, Euzkadi wants to restore its own life, its manner of being, its *national personality*, and accelerate toward the day when it can say to itself: I AM; to Europe: I AM WORTH SOMETHING; and to the oppressor: I AM ABLE; because I have lifted myself and, by force, my sons up.[27]

It is difficult to avoid the direct, ontological quest implied by these words, framed in what is almost ethnographic discourse. In many ways, this is a retroactive text–a twentieth-century text expressing Arana's nineteenth-century doctrine–as well as a discourse both anticipating existentialism and reflective of the agonizing self-reflection of modernism.

War in Europe and Nationalist Imagery, 1916–17

Following an official party policy of support for the Entente powers during World War I, the CNV, through *Euzkadi*, stressed the moral justification of their cause. The nationalist daily had a correspondent in London who regularly sent back reports about the front. Indeed, these reports were highly influential in shaping the opinion of CNV nationalists toward the conflict. "The soldier wastes heroism," wrote *Euzkadi* in 1916, "in proportion to the hope that encourages him ... and that hope is a very powerful weapon in every war, and is the strength that comforts the warrior in the middle of battle."[28] There were questions, however, as the same correspondent looked toward the eventual implications of the conflict: "There is . . . something fundamental in war, that its effects . . . imply a change in the future course of societies and even in the future progress of the spirit. The present struggle is a competition of principles. Ascendancy now is not simply superiority; it is future action, it is the political and moral future."[29] While there was ambiguity in his words, they still reflected the importance of the struggle. It seems likely that, at the close of 1917, a widely shared belief held that the outcome of the war would change the world, thus making the conflict seem a just one.

The Great War entered the Basque nationalist imagination in another, different, although no less important way. While Spain was not involved in the conflict, France was, and this meant that French Basques were at the front. There was a sense, then, that the imagined Basque nation was indeed involved in the war. Consequently, tales of bravery and heroism concerning French Basques were reported in full. Moreover, these stories were reported in Euskara, rather than in the more typical Spanish, probably as much an emotional decision as anything else. When discussing the greater Basque nation, nationalists would use their timeless language, thus serving to connect Basques by a common frame of reference while at the same time distancing them from both Spain and France. Articles about French Basque soldiers were short by comparison with the main stories in the paper, but they resonated with symbolic value. At the same time, however, more than any other subject, they brought home a reality to the theme of history as war, celebrating the just nature of the cause and individual acts of heroism while mourning losses and defeats. Moreover, eulogies to these Basque warriors were written in the style of Arana, with titles such as "Strong Basque Soldiers" and "Our Brother Soldiers." For example, at the beginning of 1916, it was reported that Captain Jon Laferrere, a "Zuberoan [Souletine] soldier," had been awarded the Croix de Guerre for outstanding bravery in battle.[30]

The External Influence: Ireland and Morocco

Meanwhile, the example of the nationalist movement in Ireland continued to influence Basque nationalists. After the failure of Gladstone's 1892 Home Rule Bill, the Irish question in Great Britain took another course. Moderate Irish nationalists reorganized the Irish Parliamentary Party (IPP) under the leadership of John Redmond after 1900 and, with a base of eighty members of parliament in London, effectively controlled the balance between the Conservative and Liberal Parties there. With the passing of the 1911 Parliament Act curtailing the veto power of the House of Lords, the influence of the Conservative power base there, which had blocked the 1892 bill, was limited to vetoes in two consecutive years, after which, if passed by the Commons in a third year, the bill would become law. The Conservatives in the House of Lords nevertheless still threatened to veto any change in Ireland, while, when a third Home Rule bill was introduced in 1912, Irish unionists (especially in Ulster) formed militias, anticipating the need to resist the constitutional change. Their mobilization coincided with a wave of strikes and demonstrations in

Dublin to rival the events in Barcelona, and the British authorities were faced with a potentially bloody scenario.

There were three expressions of Irish nationalism (also known as republicanism) in the second decade of the twentieth century: the moderate and constitutionalist approach of the IPP, led by Redmond, favoring home rule or limited autonomy and (prior to 1916) supported by the majority of the Irish Catholic population; the more radical Fenian tradition, favoring separation from Britain and represented principally by the Irish Republican Brotherhood (IRB), by the Irish Volunteers (a nationalist militia that later became the Irish Republican Army or IRA),[31] and by a new political party, Sínn Féin, which advocated the use of force in this struggle; and the socially conscious nationalism of James Connolly's Irish Citizen's Army (ICA). With protestant militias marching in the streets of Ulster, and representing, of course, another variant of nationalism in Ireland–unionism or loyalism–the years from 1913 to 1914 were marked by an increasing belief that the island would soon be plunged into civil war.

The outbreak of war in Europe actually managed to avert the expected conflict in Ireland, with the newly approved 1914 Home Rule Bill suspended until the end of continental hostilities, but it was only a temporary respite. On Easter Day in 1916, in the center of Dublin, a collection of different individuals, drawn principally from the IRB, the Irish Volunteers, and the ICA, carried out an attempted rebellion against British rule. The rising did not enjoy the majority support of the population. Indeed, most residents of the city probably viewed the events with a mixture of curiosity and detachment. For example, the majority IPP had backed Britain in the war, confident that home rule would be granted after the cessation of hostilities abroad. However, British repression, following a week of fighting, turned events in favor of the radical nationalists.

There is no doubt that radical Irish nationalism attached a symbolic importance to the events of 1916, particularly through the representation of thematic imagery such as chivalry, sacrifice, heroism, history, joy, and agony,[32] the same symbols used to similar effect by Basque nationalists. The leaders of the Irish rebellion were immediately executed, and this led to a growing feeling that the force of arms was necessary to gain Irish independence. Indeed, in his influential study of the IRA, Richard English observes that "The dead rebels became martyrs. Masses, postcards and badges all honoured them in period after the rising. A cult had come into existence, with a quasi-sacred quality quickly attaching itself to the rebel leaders after the rising had entered the popular imagination. Catholic Ireland had found new heroes, and their celebration–unsurprisingly–possessed a markedly religious flavour."[33] The aftermath of the 1916 rising, rather than the actual even itself, and the profound impact of the executions hardly resolved the situation. Between 1919 and 1921, Irish nationalists (in the main led by the Volunteers/IRA) fought a bitter war against the British, and in 1921, twenty-six of Ireland's thirty-two counties gained a de facto independence with the creation of the Irish Free State.

The 1916 Easter Rising marked a critical watershed in Irish nationalist (or republican) political thought, most obviously the key notion that parliamentary politics had failed.

"Indeed," English argues, "1916 was as much about the battle between competing Irish political traditions as it was about Ireland's struggle against Britain," and subsequently, for example, "between 1916 and 1921 the Volunteers/IRA changed from a body of largely non-violent protest to one of extremely violent anti-state activity."[34]

The symbolic resonance of 1916 was also felt across the Bay of Biscay, with an important effect on competing varieties of Basque nationalism, for Ireland continued to be an issue of symbolic importance for the Basque nationalist movement. In the 1880s, Arana had been supportive of Charles Stewart Parnell's home-rule movement, ironically while at the same time remaining resolutely Anglophile. This attitude continued under the CNV, which broadly supported the aims and aspirations of Redmond's Irish Parliamentary Party, rather than those of Sínn Féin.[35] In Aranzadi's opinion, the Easter Rebellion was a "foolish Fenian uprising," for while he recognized that the Irish people had been conquered by force, this did not justify insurrection: "it is not fair," he continued, "to provoke or support an insurrection that, according to all reasonable calculations, had to end in failure."[36] Reflecting the party line of the CNV, he concluded that "it is not enough that, if in any oppressed nation a revolutionary liberation movement should appear, we should see ourselves obliged to go to help of the insurgents," because "'stamping one's convictions with blood' does not legitimize any insurrection."[37]

Given the conservative and religious nature of the CNV, it was, moreover, not surprising that someone like Connolly would be looked on with suspicion as an "anarchist patriot."[38] *Aberri*, however, was naturally more sympathetic to the uprising. It later recalled that 1916 was a noteworthy year in which "*Sinn Fein* was launched on [its] heroic path."[39] And Gallastegui wrote in similar terms that "the Irish Republican Army [IRA] astonished the world for a week with its heroism [and] bravery in defense of the independence of its *Patria*, for which it surrendered its blood."[40] The Easter Rising provided radical Basque nationalism with a symbolic aim to pursue, if not with a specifically concrete example to follow, uniting at the same time the spatial relationship between "occupied" Ireland and the Basque Country with temporal or historical images of struggle and warfare.[41]

From 1916 onward, Ireland was used as a symbolic prism through which events in the Basque Country were refracted. For example, while the CNV was not exactly sympathetic toward the radical nationalism of Sínn Féin, it was even more hostile to the (Protestant) loyalist movement in Ulster. And it used Ulster in a guarded attack on what it saw as a traitorous element within the Basque Country: the Spanish liberal parties. "Our Ulster," *Euzkadi* argued, "is not, like the Irish one, localized within a given region, [but instead is] scattered throughout the Basque Country." Furthermore, Basque "Ulstermen" were believed to "impede and exasperate the prospect of an autonomous resurgence of Basque territory."[42] Indeed, as Ulster became a key factor within the Irish situation, CNV policy (in line with that of the moderate Irish nationalists themselves) was increasingly sympathetic to the more radical elements within Ireland.[43] In the aftermath of the Great War and with a confrontation threatening civil war in Ireland, the CNV actually began to sympathize more with Sínn Féin. "There is a blind and weak British government," *Euzkadi* reported in 1920, "and a fanatical and oppressive Ulster, before which the London politicians habitually capitulate . . . the Irish cannot put up with it."[44] The solution, according to *Euzkadi*, was to support the more radical vision of Irish nationalism: "Sinn Fein will bring independence to Ireland. When, I do not know, because it is God's secret; what I do know is that Sinn Fein represents the exasperated will of an entire people to resist oppression and death, whatever the cost, and I also know that there is no historical example of a people who, placed in such a situation, have not ended up victorious."[45] Thus, when assessing CNV attitudes toward Ireland, it is important to note that a significant change took place between 1916 and 1920.[46] *Euzkadi* even mourned the death of Michael Collins in 1922, referring to him as a "distinguished Irishman who risked his life hundreds of times for his country and to whom his *patria* owes, in large part, the liberty that it enjoys today."[47]

Aberri reflected on Irish independence in glowing terms: "Never in the history of peoples," it argued, "has such an exemplary case as this, of the titanic struggle of seven centuries for the independence of the *patria*, occurred . . . we Basques should learn. *GORA IRLANDA AZKATUTA*!" ["Long Live Free Ireland!]"[48] This admiration for the Irish nationalist movement was, moreover, emphasized in terms inherited from Arana, such as its "spirit of . . . sacrifice in the most stoic disdain of suffering and death."[49] On the seventh anniversary of the Easter Rising, Elías de Gallastegui (Gudari) recalled the event as an inspiration to the Basque cause. Those who lost their lives in the rebellion had "died gloriously . . . for their honor," and an example had been set for Basque youth: "Patriotic youth! This Easter, in which the Communion vainly wants to show off [its] spent force, let your spirit raise up for the integrity of the free, independent, and separatist *Patria*! Long live the 'rebel' army!"[50]

Eugenio Ibarzábal argues that the Irish question did not effect the direction of the CNV during the period, particularly in regard to the possibility of an armed nationalist struggle.[51] While this may be correct in terms of the party's official policy, there is evidence to suggest that at a more popular level within the nationalist community (especially its youth section), there emerged a symbolic identification with the tactic of political violence employed in the Irish case. For example, on recalling two possible examples to follow as a young man, those of Ghandi and Sínn Féin, the future activist Lezo de Urreztieta was always more inclined toward the latter: "I have never been a *Ghandista*; it was fine, but the Irish way was a lot better."[52]

The other external issue that fed into the Basque nationalist imagination during the era of the Great War and beyond was Spain's imperial adventure in Morocco. As we have seen, Arana's attitude toward the anticolonial struggles of the Rif tribesmen was one of unconditional support. According to his notion of national rights, they deserved independence, for they were the autochthonous inhabitants of the territory, and this continued to be the policy of the CNV, which, in its discussion of the resurrected Moroccan issue in 1921, came increasingly close to the more radical position adopted by the PNV.

Elías de Gallastegui, better known as Gudari. A charismatic and prominent leader of a more radical vision of Basque nationalism in the 1920s and 1930s, Gudari remained loyal to the original separatist ideas of Arana. He also incorporated an important social dimension to his ideology, and was strongly influenced by the struggle for independence in Ireland. By permission of Abertzaletasunaren Agiritegia, Sabino Arana Kultur Elkargoa archives.

Even before the battle of Annual (July 1921), *Euzkadi* had published an article in favor of African independence. Entitled "Africa for the Africans," it addressed the wider issue of European imperialism. African soldiers, it argued, had served the European cause during the Great War and therefore deserved the same rights as their white counterparts. Through the moral justice of national self-determination and the shedding of blood for Europe, Africa deserved its independence. If this was not granted, *Euzkadi* predicted, the continent would rise up against the Europeans.[53] In the case of Spain, this would spread insurrection to the peninsula itself. And, given the worsening social conflict within the country, it would not take much, *Euzkadi* implied, for an African revolt to spread to the peninsula: "Events in Melilla," it argued, "demonstrate one more time the weak constitution of the Spanish state,"[54] a weakness that would not be able to halt impending revolution on its own territory.

The most immediately pressing concern for Basque nationalists, however, was the conscription of soldiers to fight in Morocco. Not only was the war an unjust conflict, but the conscripts were subject to an infamous litany of atrocious conditions, both in and out of battle. The issue, according to *Euzkadi*, symbolized the rotten presence of the Spanish state in the Basque Country. After all, it was the Constitution of 1876, scarcely forty years previously, that had, for the first time, compelled Basques to undertake military service in the Spanish army.[55] The Moroccan troubles of the early 1920s were thus remembered as unjust imperialist conflicts, and even the justification (from some quarters) of the war as a crusade had little impact for the CNV. Aranzadi himself argued that "for us, Catholic Basque nationalists, no evangelization justifies conquest of any sort," and "to declare that one can legally impose the Gospel by the thrust of a bayonet... is, in our opinion, hideous blasphemy."[56] Any moral basis of the war, Aranzadi opined, resided with the Moslem population, rather than the "Catholic Spanish imperialists."[57] *Aberri*, meanwhile, also viewed the war as a struggle between good and evil. Good was represented by the troops of Abd-el-Krim and "a people who want to be free like us." This made the conscription of Basque recruits a supreme injustice, for they would be "defending a nation [*patria*] that was not their own."[58] There was, though, a message for those soldiers who returned alive: "Now work in peace to free your country [*patria*], for only in this way will you see that your son... will not have to suffer what you suffered and that his mother will not have to cry as your mother cried."[59]

Events in both Ireland and Morocco thus had a direct influence in the development of Basque nationalist discourse, both within the CNV and the PNV, in the period between 1921 and 1923. In the past, that influence has been undervalued by, among others, Daniele Conversi.[60] Conversi argues that, in a general sense, international influence on the internal developments of Basque nationalism have been limited and (in the period under study here) were restricted in the main to minor organizational changes.[61] However, particularly in the case of Ireland, an external event did indeed exercise (and continues to exercise) a profound influence on the internal development of Basque nationalism. There is evidence, in the pages of both *Euzkadi* and *Aberri*, not to mention in subsequent developments such as Gallastegui's exile in Ireland, that the Irish example supported and amplified adherence to the potential strategy of violence in the Basque nationalist imagination.

Consider the image of Britain during the early twentieth century, not least among Basque nationalists themselves. It was still regarded as the premier world power, with an empire encircling the globe. Ireland, on the other hand, for all the Romantic mysticism surrounding its cultural identity, was a marginal nation: a "First World country, but with a Third World memory," as Luke Gibbons terms it.[62] Ireland was somewhere spatially outside the international corridors of power and completely incapable of mounting a real military challenge to a great power such as Britain. Yet it did confront Britain, just as Morocco also fought back against Spain. In a nationalist culture imbued with a notion of *ekintza*, such challenges could not fail to go unnoticed. This may, once more, have been a case of symbolic importance, like that of Arana's ideas concerning the need to deoccupy the Basque Country,[63] but this should not detract from acknowledging the power and influence of such symbolism. Especially in the case of Ireland, external events did play a significant role in the symbolic discourse of Basque nationalism.

Conflict, Repression, and Basque Nationalism, 1917–23

The disintegration of the Restoration system and the accompanying violent protest were the key themes for Basque nationalists in the period between 1917 and 1923. Indeed, with the consistent reporting of events abroad (nationalist rebellion in Ireland, a peasant uprising in Mexico, and the Bolshevik Revolution in Russia) and at home, violent upheaval was a constant and normal feature of everyday life. Although the violence suffocating Barcelona was not seen to the same extent in the Basque Country, it did affect society there. As early as April 1917, *Euzkadi*, reacting to the possibility that the civil governor of Bizkaia might send the Civil Guard out to suppress a Basque nationalist demonstration, remarked that "it is not we who put public order in danger; it is the usual trouble makers who force ... weak peoples into serving their interests."[64]

By 1920, however, social protest and its concomitant violence had arrived in Bilbao. *Euzkadi* did not hesitate in referring to the events as "the Spanish revolution"[65] and pinned the blame squarely on the system itself: "The modern state, atheist and amoral, born of revolution, developed through revolution, cannot generate anything but revolution ... all the history that the State teaches in schools and universities is a hymn to revolutions ... consequently ... the conduct, inclination, and tendency of the modern generation is ... radically revolutionary ... in its intellectual and moral education."[66] The violence in the Basque Country was not, then, the product of Basque society, but rather the consequence of Spanish state influence: "In Bizkaia and all Euzkadi, we have a thousand institutions of all social, political, economic, and cultural types, some imposed [on us] by the Spanish [*hispánico*] state."[67]

One of the most prominent of these state institutions was increasingly apparent in Basque society: military service. As already mentioned, the conflict in Morocco called for a level of conscription unknown since the disaster of 1898, and the CNV viewed the

Moroccan war as a redundant exercise. Furthermore, it protested obligatory military service:

> We live in times in which the state confiscates, from the age of twenty and for many years, all robust lives to teach them technically the craft of killing and dying. It does not matter that among these confiscated lives there are many who are completely unsuited to the aforementioned craft and others endowed with ingenuity, culture, and sometimes a talent whose social value is almost infinite and whose inevitable deformation or premature end would be a true disaster for the human race.[68]

Without the just cause of a war, the CNV appeared almost pacifist.

Another important state institution was the Civil Guard. The CNV reserved much of its criticism for the force as a principal cause of the domestic unrest sweeping the Basque Country. In May 1920, *Euzkadi* responded to an article in *La Gaceta del Norte* in which it was stated that the Civil Guard was always right in the actions it took.[69] "The people of Donostia [San Sebastián]," the nationalist journal argued, "feel a profound aversion to the Civil Guard. They do not believe that the Civil Guard is always right."[70]

Under such a regime, the increasing social violence came as no surprise to *Euzkadi*. It was the natural outcome, after all, of "Alphonsine capitalism." Ironically however,

> the strange, incomprehensible, ignoble, monstrous thing is that Bizkaia and the Basque people are calmly witnessing how Basque workers are bloodily attacked by force of arms, [and] how the constituent authorities go against them, and how on every occasion public force [the Civil Guard] looms up before these heroic self-sacrificing masses, who defend public order, the pockets of wealthy Basques, the security of their sons, and the honor of their daughters, with their [the masses'] blood.[71]

After specific incidents in Azkoitia (Gipuzkoa) and Erandio (Bizkaia) in October 1920 in which demonstrators were fired upon by the Civil Guard, one of the strikers, Marcelino de Txarterina, died in the latter incident. The nationalist labor union (ELA/SOV) then sent the following telegram to the civil authorities: "We angrily protest that a sergeant of the Civil Guard... caused the death, in an unspeakable form, of a Basque sympathizer. ... At the same time, we protest the conduct of governmental authority [and] ask that a purge of responsibilities be made, applying the deserved punishment."[72] The killing of Txarterina in Erandio served as a powerful reminder of state force. It also served to create another nationalist martyr, "a brother sacrificed to race hatred."[73] Recalling the atmosphere in Bilbao, an active *aberriano*, Lezo de Urreztieta, remembered that most of the movement's organization was clandestine:

> In those times, being a nationalist was not exactly comfortable. In the *pueblo* [Portugalete, a town on Greater Bilbao's left bank] there was a bad atmosphere against us, and the *caciques* harassed and did any kind of harm that they could toward us. ... We got into fights with the socialists and even worse, with the monarchist "*piña*" [the Unión Liberal group that supported the Basque industrial oligarchy]. The parish priest, although a traditionalist [*integrista*], was decent.[74]

When Arana conceived his vision of Basque nationalism in the 1890s, he did so against a background of an increasingly violent society, although at the time, such violence was more customary elsewhere in Spain (in Barcelona and in rural Andalusia), coming only sporadically to the Basque Country, too. However, actual physical violence had become a reality of life in Spain by the second decade of the twentieth century, when it became the most common form of popular protest at the failures of a crumbling state. This was more than evident in the Basque Country, where the street battles of industrial workers against the state security forces (most typically the Civil Guard) were compounded by a nationalist dimension.

Although it was the official policy of the moderate CNV to eschew violence, this did not prevent the party from criticizing the brutality of the Civil Guard in combative terms. Furthermore, the creation of a nationalist labor union directly involved the party in the confrontation between the industrial proletariat and the state. The CNV's more radical youth wing, which subsequently formed its own party, was directly involved in much of the confrontation, and in the era of the 1916 Easter Rising, the PNV probably took more than a symbolic inspiration from events across the Bay of Biscay. There was a strand of thought common to both moderate and radical Basque nationalism that united their causes, both at that time and for the future: the legacy of Arana's discourse, relying on a metaphorical recourse to themes of struggle, warfare, and heroism, and redemption, as well as the sacramental agony of defeat and occupation. The latter sentiments, in fact, were just as important to the allegorical allusions of warfare in the discourse of Basque nationalism, for they provided the reason behind the call to action, *ekintza*, that would be increasingly heard as the century wore on.

One of the best expressions of this blend of idealism and catastrophe in Basque nationalism during the early twentieth century is a book written in 1920 by Jesús de Sarría: *Patria vasca.* Its closing pages are worth considering, both for the expressive sentiment of the time and for the thoughts and emotions that linked past ideas to future developments. Entitled "The Rhythm of Pain and Joy," they were dedicated to "all those who suffer for the *Patria*," and read:

> And while you are in pain, which will be forever, you will have, also forever, solace... Do not fear pain, Basque brothers. Do not fear it as men or patriots. Do not run away from the *Patria* through a fear that, [both] threatening and serving it, increases your human pain. The Cross of pain should not threaten you. And, in Apotheosis or Calvary, surrender yourselves with all your heart to the *Patria* that, after having given you [your] blood and soul, opened up its heart, so that you might save it, to the loyalty of your love.[75]

It was a clear expression of the same sentiment espoused by Arana: a bond of soul and body to the fortunes of the *patria* that implied constant suffering and sporadic joy. It also, by implication, tied the individual to the collective. If the *patria* suffered, there was individual pain, and redemption of the nation would come only through individual action, action that ultimately called for personal sacrifice.

These general ideas were given more specific context when, on July 20, 1923, *Aberri* reflected on the current situation in Spain: "If we do not prepare ourselves, if we remain indifferent, we will not be able to draw aside when the moment comes, but will sink with Spain into the precipice that opens at its feet."[76] With much caution (it is questionable whether a sufficient collective mentality of armed resistance existed at the time), Basque nationalists had taken an important ideological step from Arana's pure imagining to a clear *aberriano* rhetoric of actual future struggle.

I do not believe that Arana's discourse (and even less his program) presupposed an argument necessarily invoking images of violence. The original articulation of Basque nationalism was, in fact, couched in such terms as to render it a cultural power through prepolitical images. However, it was not simply this cultural force that allowed for the persistence of those images in the Basque nationalist rhetoric of the early twentieth century. It was also the context of wider events (in Spain and Europe) and ideas (war, imperialism, and revolution) that shaped a mentality of struggle within Basque nationalism. However, this should not detract from the power of continuity within the ideology itself, because the classification of the world through categories has a certain staying power that is hard to relinquish.[77] And a sufficient body of Arana's categories was evident within the ideological transformation of Basque nationalism (both moderate and radical) in the first decades of the twentieth century. A nascent ideology of recourse to arms thus emerged within the greater ideology of Basque nationalism in the early twentieth century.

This ideology of political violence owed its origins to the philosophical and political thought of Arana, the cultural framework of Basque society, and the political, social, and economic structural changes in society at the dawn of the new century. It remained largely theoretical, but it did stimulate its own rhetorical power, a power that found expression in a temporal dimension: "To 'know the future,'" Terry Eagleton argues, "can only mean to grasp the present under the sign of its internal contradictions, in the alienation of its desire, in its persistent inability ever quite to coincide with itself."[78] The emerging symbolism of political violence within the Basque nationalist movement represented both a link to the past and a means of confronting the present in a combined effort to look ahead, or know the future. At the close of 1923, a generation after Arana had introduced his sacramental vision of Basque nationalism, a cultural identity infused with images of struggle and warfare continued to pervade the nationalist imagination. It would find a degree of concrete expression less than a generation later.

CHAPTER SIX

An Opportunity Missed? Basque Nationalism, 1930–36

By the 1930s, the conservative attempt (in the guise of a military dictatorship) at resolving the ills of the Restoration system failed under the ineffective leadership of Primo de Rivera, and with the proclamation of Spain's Second Republic in 1931, the country changed its political system dramatically once more. The Republic had its ideological origins in three traditions: the new liberalism of the Restoration's early years, which placed great emphasis on political and legal institutions, the value of education, and the responsibilities of both state and individual in a common cause; a republican tradition and culture that affirmed a secular ethic over the power of the church; and the growing strength of Spanish socialism, with its commitment to social reform.[1] In the 1930s, while Europe drifted into a sectarian divide between the forces of the right and the left, Spain, as an ideological battleground for over a century between reactionary and progressive forces, increasingly reflected this trend. Furthermore, in an age of when nationalism continued to dominate European politics, both the Catalan and Basque national movements competed with a Spanish nationalism in both liberal republican and conservative reactionary forms.

The task of the Second Republic can be condensed to three main aims: instituting a progressive and democratic state; limiting the traditional power and influence of church, army, and landed interests; and accommodating Catalan and Basque nationalist aspirations.[2] This simple description, however, belies a complex situation. While the Second Republic's aims were clear, their implementation was more complicated. Spain was a fragmented country, beset by class, regional, and religious differences. For example, by the 1930s, sufficient modernization had taken place for both industrialists and workers (mutually antagonistic themselves) to present a real threat to the hegemony of traditional landed oligarchs. Furthermore, the working classes were internally divided between adherence to socialism and to anarchism. The peasantry, depending on geographical location and cultural tradition, could be classified as reactionary Carlists (Navarre), rebellious anarchists (Andalusia), or revolutionary socialists (Extremadura).[3]

The fortunes of the Second Republic, inexorably tied to events in Europe, would assume center stage on the continent in 1936, when the accumulated tensions of the previous hundred years, coupled with a failure to resolve the fractious nature of Spanish society under an increasingly fragile Republic, erupted in civil war. The Basque case is one of the best examples of the complex nature of the war, for there it was a conflict fought on different levels: Basques fought either other Basques or Spaniards, according to political affiliation (Basque nationalist, socialist, or Carlist) and regional location (Bizkaia and Gipuzkoa fought with the Republic against Araba and Navarre, which sided with the insurgents). Furthermore, the conflict physically introduced the world into Spain and the Basque Country, with the participation of Nazi Germany, Fascist Italy, the Soviet Union, and the multinational International Brigades, and it is also worth noting that during and after the Civil War, some of the first foreign assessments of Basque nationalism would be made.[4]

Revolutionary Reform: The Second Spanish Republic, 1931–33

In April 1931, the Spanish monarchy was peacefully overthrown. The discredited Alfonso XIII (who had tacitly supported the dictatorship of Primo de Rivera) went into exile, and the Second Republic was proclaimed. The first ministry of the new regime, headed by Manuel Azaña, had at its disposal all the constitutional instruments of radical reform, including a single parliamentary chamber. These were used in the early years of the Republic to attempt the creation of a new society in Spain.

Although raised and schooled in a religious atmosphere, Azaña, as befitting the future leader of the Spanish Republican Party, rebelled at what he saw as the shallow dogma of religious authority. He became a politician of action, dedicated to introducing a comprehensive body of legislation that, he believed, would plant republican values in Spanish society. He was not an ambitious politician in the sense of seeking high office for its power and prestige. Rather, his ambition was projected through the Republic itself. For that reason, he desperately wanted it to succeed.[5] To this end, Azaña's radical government presented a program of regional reform in Catalonia, together with social legislation in religious matters, labor relations, and the so-called agrarian question,[6] and between 1931 and 1933, the government introduced legislative measures designed to bring about the proposed changes.

One of the self-declared aims of the new regime was the laicization-secularization of the country, a policy that found much support from both the rural community and the industrial masses, who, regardless of their personal religiosity, viewed the church suspiciously as an ally of the rich.[7] With this in mind, Azaña's government gradually withdrew state support for the church and in December 1931 passed the most anticlerical constitution in Spain's history. More ominous for the church, however, was the government's failure to protect church property and personnel from the not infrequent attacks of anticlerical radicals during the formative years of the Republic.[8]

Another of the new republic's goals was to resolve the regional question through the constructive assimilation of nationalist sentiment. A settlement was quickly arrived at for Catalonia, prompted by an abortive military coup led by General José Sanjurjo,[9] and the

Generalitat (the Catalan autonomous government) came into effect in September 1932. Azaña's government, as befitting the heirs of Restoration liberalism's most enlightened members, also introduced an educational policy that recalled the philosophy of Francisco Giner de los Ríos and the nineteenth-century Institución Libre de Enseñanza. This philosophy equated state education with national obligation and implied a unitary vision of Spain as a historical and cultural entity.[10] After the government initiated a policy of educational expansion, on average, about two thousand state schools were created annually throughout the course of the Republic. While this marked a steady development of Spanish educational facilities, it never reached the original aspirations of those who initiated the policy.[11]

Despite the autonomy statute for Catalonia, there was, then, a state policy of Spanish nationalism projected through education. At the center of this system was an insistence on the use of Spanish, and in the Basque Country, Euskara continued to suffer official stigmatization: "It was considered vulgar, peasant-like to be caught speaking Basque by the majority of Spanish nuns at my school," recalled Asunción Caro, "we couldn't speak our own language in our own country."[12] The state also introduced the Misiones Pedagógicas (Pedagogical Missions), a form of direct civic education for the undereducated masses of Spain through theatrical and musical performances. Here, the government recognized the value of culture in the state-building process, and the artistic performances were supported by a determined program of library construction to bring culture into Spanish village life. By 1935, five thousand libraries had been established in villages of fewer than 200 inhabitants, and the state had truly made inroads into previously isolated rural life.[13]

In the initial period of the Republic, then, between 1931 and 1933, a progressive and at times radical program of reform was pursued by Azaña's government. In many ways–the granting of a statute of autonomy to Catalonia, for example–it was a program that attracted Basque nationalists. In others, such as the vigorous policy of state building (with its concomitant Spanish nationalism) and an open hostility to the church, it did not.

Confrontation and Accommodation: The Course of Basque Nationalism, 1930–33

After the fall of the Primo de Rivera dictatorship, the immediate concern of Basque nationalists was resolving the differences that had split the party in 1921. This reunification allowed for the growth of Basque nationalism during the Second Republic, but it was an expansion challenged by a continuing crisis within the party and by an equally ascendant foe in the guise of Basque socialism. The rise of both political forces owed much to the particularities of Basque society, which displayed an ever greater diversity and complexity.[14]

In the early 1930s, Basque industrial output had reached a fragile juncture in its history. During the 1920s, the Basque economy had enjoyed a period of consolidated growth and prosperity,[15] although the long-term decline of the mining sector had been a steady feature since the turn of the century. With the fall of the dictatorship, a small, but noteworthy economic decline began to set in. For example, in 1933, the important Basque cement industry was working at only 42 percent of its full capacity; in 1934, Bizkaian production of iron rails (used in railroad construction) fell to 12 percent of its 1929 level; and by 1935, one-quarter of Bizkaia's industrial labor force was out of work. While this figure was above the national average, it was still better than those of Andalusia or Extremadura, where levels of unemployment ran at twice the national average.[16]

Partly as a result of this rising unemployment level, although also as the result of a longer-term historical tendency, socialism grew at an extraordinary rate in the Basque Country during the twentieth century. In the early 1930s, there were a reported thirty thousand members of the Basque wing of the PSOE (the Partido Socialista Obrero de España, the Spanish Socialist Workers' Party). There were also nine thousand Basque Communists, with whom there had been sporadic, yet violent confrontations since the turn of the century, principally in Bilbao. By the coming of the Second Republic, these differences had not been resolved, so the Basque left (like its nationalist counterpart) was internally divided.[17] The dominant figure of Basque socialism and *the* representative of the moderate, evolutionary left in Spain was Indalecio Prieto. After election to the Spanish Parliament in 1919, the Bilbao PSOE leader had been considered the house's most eloquent speaker. By the 1930s, he rose to the position of chief representative of the flexible, Republic-friendly wing of Spanish socialism.[18] That decade, his main battles would be fought not only with the Basque nationalists, but also with the more radical, revolutionary socialism of Francisco Largo Caballero.

Spanish agricultural production, while undergoing sustained growth in the period from 1900 to 1931, still lagged behind that of France, the nearest comparable agricultural economy.[19] There was a cautious move toward modernization within the Spanish agricultural sector as a whole, although, as with industry, the change was more pronounced in the Basque Country. Since the turn of the century, the traditional *baserri* organization of rural Basque society had undergone a gradual transformation, so that by 1930, many *baserritarak*, or Basque peasants, had not only bought their (previously leased) farmsteads, but were also beginning to enjoy surplus profits from the sales of dairy and garden produce. For example, one study has shown how such modernization in the village of Elgeta (Gipuzkoa) affected daily life for the Basque peasantry there. From 1910 onward, there was a considerable rise in the number of *baserritarak* buying their farmsteads in the municipality, which increased their economic independence. This in turn meant that the farmers came to rely less on their (Carlist) landlords and began to exercise a greater political freedom, with a resultant benefit for both Basque nationalists and socialists. Growth, however, was tempered by increased mobility and the continued attraction of large urban centers. Consequently, the village's youth were progressively either going to the industrial cities and towns of the Basque Country or, after taking advantage of increased educational opportunities to learn new skills, opening small businesses in the village itself. The result was that there were fewer young people to take over the actual farmsteads, thus breaking the traditional rhythm of rural inheritance patterns.[20]

After a successful strategy of clandestine cultural propaganda during the years of Primo de Rivera's dictatorship,[21] Basque nationalism had begun to enjoy the reputation of a serious political ideology that offered a complete structural program for the defense of Basque interests. However, Basque nationalists still needed to convince potential sympathizers that their party was a solid political force with real prospects of attaining power. This would be best achieved, it was proposed, through the reunification of its two factions. With this in mind, representatives of the two wings met in Bergara (Gipuzkoa) in November 1930 to arrange such a reconciliation. Throughout the 1920s, there had been contact between the groups, and in the early 1930s, it seemed a sound compromise to marry the youth, energy, and dynamism of the radicals to the broader appeal of the moderates. Through the Bergara Assembly (as it came to be known), the party was reunited under the original PNV title, recognizing the two groups' common legacy through the influence of Sabino Arana. The official homage to Arana, cementing his slogan of "Jaungoikua eta legi-zarra"–God and the Old Laws–within the PNV's manifesto, thus became an ideological milestone that would remain in place for the next forty-five years.[22]

Leading a new generation of young moderates and the individual chiefly responsible for holding Basque nationalism to its centrist course during the 1930s was a young lawyer named José Antonio de Aguirre y Lecube. His father, also a lawyer, had acted as assistant to Arana's defense attorney, Daniel de Irujo, in the famous 1895 trial. Although from a solidly traditional nationalist background, Aguirre displayed a willingness to adapt Basque nationalism to the twentieth century, and it is to him, perhaps more than to any other individual, that one must look for the ideological roots of Basque nationalism's evolutionary move toward the politics of European Christian Democracy. Later, in 1936, he would be elected the first president of the autonomous Basque government.[23]

Despite official reunification in 1930, however, Basque nationalism remained divided. Within the party itself, radicals (composed in the main by former *aberrianos*) continued to veto any compromise that would result in moves toward mere autonomy, instead of independence.[24] Furthermore, a breakaway faction, unable to accept the continued adherence to Arana's orthodox foundations by both moderates and radicals, formed another party almost immediately: Acción Nacionalista Vasca (ANV, Basque Nationalist Action) in November 1930.[25] It was a liberal and nondenominational republican party that rejected the PNV's reactionary traditionalism and sought a complete modernization of Basque nationalist ideology.[26] For the ANV, the Second Spanish Republic heralded an opportunity to achieve twin goals: the possibility of attracting those sectors of Basque society traditionally sympathetic to the left into the nationalist fold[27] and an opportunity for the Basque Country to realize fully its right of national self-determination.[28] "It was fine," recalled an ANV sympathizer. "We were the troublemakers, and they [the PNV] were the well-behaved ones."[29]

Then there was a second split within the party. Composed of former *aberrianos* and led by Gudari (Elías de Gallastegui), a pro-independence faction of the party rallied behind *Jagi Jagi* (Arise, arise), the weekly publication of the Federación Vizcaína de Mendigoizales (Bizkaian Mountaineers Federation), an official group within the PNV.[30] Yet in their own opinion, the PNV was ruled "by half a dozen *caciques*, with the best intention[s] perhaps, but half a dozen *caciques*, collaborating with the Spanish; that was the party."[31] In 1934, a small group of activists broke away to form its own party, because, in the opinion of one of its ranks, the PNV was "too concerned with Spanish politics."[32] The group took the name of the weekly through which its members had originally discussed their ideas, and the new party, Jagi Jagi, refused any idea of compromise or cooperation with Madrid. Instead, taking their inspiration directly from Arana, they sought outright independence in place of the official PNV goal of limited autonomy and proposed a more direct form of political action: personal sacrifice through civil disobedience. Jagi Jagi was, to a certain extent, anticapitalist. However, it could not be described as socialist. Rather, it proposed a limited capitalist economy based on small-scale business and industry, and its social policy depended more on the principles of social Catholicism than on socialism. The tactic of direct political action had already appeared within the pages of the mountaineers' paper in 1933: "We nationalists, all of us who feel a yearning for liberation and justice, should refuse to pay any tax, whatever it may be, whether of the Spanish state or the [provincial] council or municipal authority, while those posts that today engage in antidemocratic duties against the people are not withdrawn."[33]

It was a classic piece of Aranist dogma, framed in the terms of sacrifice and confrontation, and it established a pattern that radical nationalists would follow throughout the course of the Republic. For moderate members of the PNV, it was also extremely fatalist.[34] This was emphasized when the breakaway group failed to attract the support for which it had hoped. A close collaborator of Gallastegui's noted his dwindling spirit after he had formed the new party: At the time of the split in 1934, there were "exactly thirty-three [of us], including Eli and myself. From then on, Gallastegui never got involved in anything and dealt only with me. He stopped writing. He was totally disillusioned."[35]

The initial signs, however, were better for the moderate Basque nationalists who controlled the party. In the 1931 parliamentary elections, the PNV, in alliance with the Carlist Party and Catholic Independents, enjoyed impressive results, gaining over 60 percent of the vote in Bizkaia, for example, and seven of twenty-four Basque seats available, the Carlists taking five and the Independents three.[36] The importance of reunification at the Bergara Assembly, together with the electoral alliance forged with the traditionalist right of the movement, has prompted one commentator to define the PNV in the early years of the Second Republic as a moderate Catholic populist party.[37] However, this is only partly true, because the separatist influence was still a key factor within the party structure. In 1931, the PNV still embraced a number of competing ideologies within its ranks, and one can speak only of the *beginnings* of an evolution toward Christian Democracy in the period from 1934 to 1936.[38]

The question calls to mind, however, the important role that religion continued to play in the affairs of Basque nationalism. Arana constructed an austere ideology inspired by the twin religious symbols of service and salvation.[39] Yet the leading figure of the PNV in the 1930s, Aguirre, had also been active in Christian social action during the previous decade as head of the Catholic Youth, an activist church association, and his was an altogether more liberal interpretation of religious duty compared with that of Arana. There were, then, intimate links between nationalism and religion, although these were facilitated by the religiosity of Basque society as a whole,[40] ultimately confirming what one observer has defined (although for a later period) as the role of religion in "the social definition of the political and symbolic conflict which exists between the Basque Country and central government."[41] Thus, when considering the relationship between religion and nationalism, it is worth bearing in mind that there were both strongly orthodox and liberal tendencies within the PNV that only compounded its general complexity, emphasizing the view that the party was a central focus of Basque nationalism's plural community. When considering the future development of the PNV, one cannot underestimate the bonds between its apparently disparate elements.

During the early years of the Republic, official PNV policy sought a statute of autonomy similar to that already granted to Catalonia, the contentious issue over which the pro-independence Jagi Jagi seceded from the party in 1934. Despite official reunification, then, the PNV remained split. At an official or doctrinal level, it followed much of Arana's original orthodoxy. However, it also practiced more moderate politics in the de facto pursuit of the statute.[42] Despite the appearance of Jagi Jagi, however, pro-independence nationalists (composed mainly, although not exclusively, of the youth wing of the party) worked side by side their pro-autonomy counterparts in propaganda work during the early 1930s.[43] This initial period of the Republic was by no means tranquil, and such propaganda endeavors often brought young nationalists into confrontation with both the state authorities and other political factions.

Although a pro-independence nationalist, Lezo de Urreztieta (a former *aberriano* and future member of the Jagi Jagi breakaway) carried out propaganda work for the PNV in favor of a statute of autonomy. "I doubt if anyone had more stones thrown at them than me," he recalled, and "in Santa Cruz de Campezo I was shot at several times."[44] A similar fate awaited Teodoro Hernandorena, the president of the PNV's youth section in Gipuzkoa during the period from 1931 to 1932. In both Arrasate–Mondragón (Gipuzkoa) and Bilbao, he and other activists were attacked by the Assault Guards (a corps formed by the Republic and composed of sympathizers of the new political regime)—a fact that gave him a particular satisfaction, because it signified that the nationalist propaganda was having the desired effect.[45] However, Juan Beistegui, who undertook propaganda work for the PNV in Eibar (Gipuzkoa), noted that on an outing to the neighboring town of Azpeitia with the intention of putting up propaganda posters, "not even the Civil Guards" said anything, even though they had seen the young nationalists at work.[46]

Street confrontations, however, could start randomly and not infrequently led to violent clashes with shootings and deaths. Even the cry of "Gora Euskadi!" –"Long live the Basque Country!"–was enough to spark such confrontations, as a member of the Basque branch of the socialist labor union, the UGT (the Unión General de Trabajadores, the General Workers' Union), Ramón Rubial, later recalled: "When the new republican constitution incorporated the idea of regional autonomy, we accepted it. But our hostility toward the PNV as a party did not cease. The Socialist Party then, it should be remembered, was resolutely anticlerical. A member could be expelled from his branch for getting married in church or baptizing his children."[47] There was similar hostility from the Communist ranks: "The foreman and supervisors were Basques, [and] the majority of the miners were from other parts of Spain," remembered a young Communist, Saturnino Calvo; "the PNV supporters had their own insulting word to describe us non-Basques: *maketo*. But the Communist Party's attitude toward the nationalists was, admittedly, pretty sectarian in the first years of the Republic."[48] To complicate matters, some of ANV's more radical members were affiliated with the anarchist CNT (the Confederación Nacional de Trabajo, the National Work Confederation) and took part in street confrontations on its behalf.[49]

The early 1930s witnessed a revival in the cult of Arana's personality, with a number of reprinted Basque nationalist books complementing a growing industry in Aranist hagiography. The tone of the works was more radical than the official line of the PNV at the time, for they apparently served a more youthful market.[50] The reissued edition of *Bizkaya por su independencia* (1932) is a case in point. To the reprint were added sketches portraying many of the heroic deeds described in Arana's work. Many of the sketches invoked the hunting imagery and personal sacrifice central to Arana's late nineteenth-century articulation of Basque nationalism.

Juan Beistegui read *Bizkaya por su independencia* and recalled with pride the victory of the Basques in sending the Castilians "back" to their country. Yet he also felt in part like one of the "last of the Mohicans," a noble, but small group of people threatened by distinction. He therefore agreed with Arana's idea that knowing one's history was vital if one were to preserve the traditions of a people. And of particular importance and interest to him was the example of the Carlist struggle. Among his friends, tales circulated of their fathers' and grandfathers' exploits during the nineteenth-century wars.[51] Similarly, Lezo de Urreztieta took from Arana's example a fourfold ideology: idealism, purity, toughness, and sacrifice.[52]

Reverence for Arana was also promoted through the official nationalist propaganda of the PNV. Miguel de Ergabia, for example, wrote of Arana as the "great martyr of Euzkadi" who had died in poverty as a result of the repression and imprisonment suffered at the hands of the state authorities.[53] In similar fashion, one of the principal ideologues of Basque nationalism during the 1930s, Manuel Eguileor, remarked before a gathering of the PNV's youth section in Bilbao that "the appearance of Basque nationalism was a clearly providential fact, and . . . . for that reason, Providence was served by Arana-Goiri, just him and no other Basque."[54]

Together with this propaganda, radical nationalists continued to organize their own network of communication, which included clandestine meetings, political discussions, and celebrations. However, only on certain occasions–such as the first Aberri Eguna (Day of the Fatherland) in 1932–did their activism coincide with that of the official party line. Juan Beistegui remembered that thousands of young people took part that day, dressed in the clothes of the *mendigoizaleak* (nationalist mountaineers), in a march from the Bilbao soccer team's stadium to the Sabin Etxea, the family house of Arana and seat of the party.[55]

By this time, Azaña's administration was coming under increasing pressure from the Spanish right, alarmed at what it saw as the radical nature of the Second Republic's first government. In the Basque Country, there was increasing tension as nationalists (principally the *mendigoizaleak*) engaged in physical confrontation with rival groups, whether republicans or socialists, in Bizkaia between the fall of 1932 and the summer of 1933. In response, the civil governors of the Basque provinces engaged in a repressive policy toward the PNV, which in turn encouraged claims for outright independence.[56] Yet violence was no new phenomenon, having already come to Bilbao earlier in 1932, when, after a meeting celebrated by the traditionalist Carlists, a riot broke out that left four dead and a number of injuries.[57]

The official line of the PNV during this time continued to be a moderate call for autonomy. Historically, there had been an accommodation, of sorts, toward more pro-independence interests within the nationalist "community," and the PNV was still able to pursue the statute of autonomy through the legal means of the Republic.[58] However, the fault lines within the community remained. One PNV member, Juan Manuel Epalza, likened his party to a harlequin's costume: "It covered everything: upper class, middle class, workers, peasants. United by a deep sense of religion, Basque patriotism, and democracy. It had its left and right wings; it was like a resistance movement. When the oppressor had been got rid of and freedom won, the party would almost certainly split into its constituent parts." [59]

During the first two years of the Republic, then, while the PNV campaigned for a statute of autonomy, a splinter group (Jagi Jagi) was already emerging. At root were basic ideological and operational policies, and in the mood of 1933, an increasing tension highlighted the differences. The mountaineering journal *Jagi Jagi*, for example, was becoming more virulent in its attitude toward the authorities and the action to be taken. "The Civil Guard," one article argued, "exists . . . with the same viciousness and defects of an earlier age" and noted one particular member of the force: "in the figure of the sergeant, there was an evil and cowardliness of someone who hurls abuse aided by the force of a rifle."[60] In the face of such persecution, specific action, in the opinion of Elías de Gallastegui, was the only recourse: "I do not know how the patriot can live in peace without devoting great effort and sacrifice, calmly floating in the dead water of this agreeable and comfortable, although humiliating legal normality."[61] The language was telling: A just cause took precedence over legal constraints.

Until this time, the PNV had been solidly affiliated with a Catholic traditionalist bloc in the Basque Country, gaining some electoral ground through an alliance with Navarrese Carlists. However, this was to prove increasingly frustrating for the party in its attempts to achieve a statute of autonomy. Beyond the fact that the PNV found it difficult to achieve institutional power in the electorally important province of Navarre,[62] the party also found itself in a doubly difficult ideological position. Arana's original legacy emphasized Spain as an oppressor of the Basque Country and implied as little collaboration as possible with the state. However, such cooperation was the key to gaining the moderate goal of a statute of autonomy, a fact demonstrated by Catalan statute in 1932. Therefore, such a policy implied greater cooperation, not only with nonnationalist parties within the Basque Country (principally the ascendant PSOE), but also with the government and parliament in Madrid.[63] Cooperation with the Basque socialists was hindered by the PNV's conservative and traditionalist leanings and by the alliance with the Carlists. There were problems from the PSOE, as well, not the least of which were the numerous incidents of street confrontations between the two groups throughout the early years of the Republic, a point made by one of the PNV's leaders in Gipuzkoa, Manuel de Irujo y Ollo. He later recalled that in the Basque Country during this time, especially in Bizkaia, nationalists and socialists were *the* enemies par excellence. When the PNV leader, José Antonio de Aguirre, went to see his PSOE counterpart, Indalecio Prieto, in 1933, in the hope of negotiating a settlement, Prieto responded by saying that the struggle between the two groups had been so brutal that he could conceive of no possible way of forming such an alliance.[64]

Gradually, however, throughout the course of the Second Republic, the PNV successfully sought greater accommodation with the forces of the Basque left and Spanish republicans in Madrid, at the same time sacrificing its alliance with the Carlists. For some observers, this was not much of a sacrifice, given the PNV's failure to make significant inroads in Navarre.[65] However, others view this failure more as a result of the electoral system (and its irregularities), than of lack of popular support per se.[66] The move to the left in the PNV served only to accentuate party divisions, as its more radical members, embittered through physical confrontation with Basque socialists, moved still further away from the official party line of autonomy. From a party of the right in 1931, the PNV thus evolved into one of the center parties during the period from 1933 to 1934.[67] Interestingly, during the first months of the Republic, ANV had proposed a pragmatic autonomy policy, anticipating the path taken by the PNV later on.[68]

Reaction on the Right, Revolution on the Left: Spain, 1933–36

In November 1933, the fragile government of Azaña lost the general election to an electoral confederation of Catholic parties known as the CEDA, the Confederación Española de Derechas Autónomas, or Spanish Confederation of Right-Wing Groups, under the leadership of José María Gil Robles. While hostile to the secular tendencies of the Azaña government, it professed a commitment to social activism based on Catholic principles. It was thus able to concede leadership of a new coalition government to a figure of the moderate tendency within the Radical Republican Party (with whom the CEDA had agreed local electoral pacts), Alejandro Lerroux. Still, there had been a swing to the right during the elections, reflected above all in the coalition's antisocialist form of republicanism. The subsequent period in Spanish politics (until the victory of the Popular Front in February 1936) became known to the Spanish left as *el bienio negro*, "the two black years." Lerroux actually aspired to incorporate the Catholic right into the Republican fold, but in plotting a middle course, he only alienated his own party's left wing and ultimately failed to make sufficient concessions to involve the CEDA in the Second Republic's state-building process.[69]

In 1934, a number of problems coincided to present the first serious challenge to the existence of the new state. In April, Lerroux resigned, to be replaced by another Radical Republican Party member, Ricardo Samper. However, Gil Robles and the CEDA (still the largest single party in the Spanish Parliament) gradually withdrew their support of Samper's administration, and in October, the incumbent leader was himself forced to resign. Lerroux then returned, although this time under more control by the CEDA. As a consequence, he was forced to admit three CEDA members into the cabinet. This sparked an outburst of popular protest from the radical Spanish left, culminating in the October Revolution of 1934. Under the impression that Europe was gearing itself for a violent confrontation between right and left, revolutionary organizations saw the increasing importance of the CEDA as a threat to the very existence of the Republic. With this in mind, they conceived of a revolution to challenge the power of the right.

The events, sporadic and haphazardly organized, failed to assume the desired "national" character, however, and the uprising only had any real impact in the northern coal-mining province of Asturias, parts of Catalonia, and the industrial towns of the Basque Country. That said, the violent confrontations (bordering on civil war in Asturias) served to accentuate the bitter divisions within Spanish society as a whole. The Asturian rebels held out for two weeks, but in the end, the uprising was brutally suppressed by Spain's armed forces, including the Foreign Legion and the Spanish Moroccan Army, led by Franco. At the end of the confrontation, there were four thousand casualties and a level of physical destruction that presaged the Civil War to come. Even more than the physical damage, however, was the scar this incident left revealing the division of opinion in Spain, a division that assumed the dimensions of an either/or mentality regarding the existence of the Republic itself.[70]

The electoral strength of the CEDA also reflected an ideological watershed in the development of Spanish nationalism. It was an increasingly identifiable ideology, constructed on a unitary vision of Spain that saw little benefit in ceding power to the regions. Although it was an ideology most obviously of the right and was evident more than ever within the ranks of the armed forces, it should be remembered that it drew much strength from the Spanish constitution itself, which conceived of Spain as an integral, unitary state in both a legal and cultural sense.[71] This institutional basis ingrained Spanish nationalism within the system, so while Azaña's reformist government was careful not to affirm its Spanish nationalist character openly (because of the authoritarian connections this might have implied), it was effectively an administration dedicated to the ideology.[72] Even Ortega y Gasset, Spain's principal liberal philosopher of the twentieth century, while recognizing the country's regional diversity, was a fierce defender of the historical and cultural reality of a unitary Spain.[73]

Juan Pablo Fusi argues that this period in the history of republican Spain was noteworthy for the "appearance . . . of a unitary, antiregionalist Spanish nationalism that conditioned Spanish politics insofar as it had an ample dissemination in an institution as fundamental as the army."[74] While it is true that Spanish nationalism was a feature of the period from 1933 to 1936, it was not its first appearance. Spanish nationalism had been a dominant policy of both Restoration Spain and the dictatorship of Primo de Rivera, as well as forming an ideological underpinning to the Second Republic. Thus, as we have seen, the phenomenon stretched back into the previous century and was especially evident (at both institutional and popular levels) during periods of military endeavor such as the wars in Cuba or Morocco or as a response to growing ethnonationalist movements within the state itself.

Toward the end of 1935, with the support of the Basque Socialist Indalecio Prieto, a rejuvenated Azaña made repeated calls for a Popular Front (based on the French example) as a coalition to counter the power of the CEDA. As the left gradually united, the right began to disintegrate. Gil Robles, the leader of the CEDA, was accused by the coalition's more radical members of failing to seize power for the right. Furthermore, the Radical Republican Party of Lerroux, which had formed the alliance keeping the right in power for nearly three years, was divided and discredited.[75] Elections were called for February 1936, and in the resultant poll, the Popular Front recorded a narrow victory over the right to herald a left-of-center republican administration.

Shifting Alliances: Basque Nationalism, 1934–36

The events of 1934 and 1935 convinced the PNV of the need for a new political strategy. With this in mind, and under the increasing threat of attack from the right-wing government in Madrid, conciliatory moves were made toward the Basque Socialists, who coincidentally found it expedient to play the regionalist card at that moment, in order to confront the CEDA-supported government in Madrid.[76] On the eve of the 1934 October uprising, the PNV celebrated a congress at which, one commentator observes, a coherent social and economic program was conspicuous by its absence.[77] This effectively had left the matter in the hands of Jagi Jagi (with their superior local organization and dedication to social activism) during the previous four years. By 1934, the level of street confrontation had given the radical wing of the party a better perspective on urban socioeconomic conditions. Thereafter, despite an alliance with the PSOE, the confrontation continued. One activist of the time recalled frequent clashes with political opponents of all dimensions, resulting, for example, in the death of two PNV members during elections in Donostia–San Sebastián.[78]

When the 1934 insurrection broke out, then, the party found itself unable to form a unified policy in response. However, isolated incidents forced its members into action. For example, at the outbreak of the uprising, a number of PNV members were put in prison on dubious charges under orders of the Socialist authorities of Bilbao. In response, the Emakume Abertzale Batza (Women's Patriotic Section) of the PNV mobilized in a demonstration outside city hall. They were then attacked by the Assault Guards, and when news of this reached the headquarters of the party youth section, they quickly went to the scene. However, before arriving, they were met in the street by a group of armed Socialists. The Assault Guards soon arrived and detained the nationalists.[79]

At this point, it is worth examining the opinion of the PNV and the nationalist labor union, ELA/STV, with regard to the rebellion, for these attitudes reflected social policy within the Basque nationalist community. In the Basque Country, there was an uprising, though of less impact than that of Asturias. It was organized by the Socialists and their union, the UGT, and counted the support of Communists and (in places) anarchists, *aenuvistas* (members of ANV), and the nationalist *mendigoizaleak* (mountaineers). Although the official policy of the PNV and its union (ELA/STV) was one of neutrality, it seems as if in some places (such as the industrial towns of Eibar and Arrasate–Mondragón in Gipuzkoa, as well as the mining area west of Bilbao in Bizkaia), there was both PNV and ELA/STV participation in the uprising.[80]

Whatever the official policy of the party, the labor union was always more likely to be involved in areas of maximum activity: the industrial towns of the Basque Country. Furthermore, as Manuel Robles-Aranguiz, one of the union's founders and a Basque nationalist councilman in the 1930s, recalled, the STV remained relatively independent from the orders of the central party organization.[81] "We couldn't believe that the history of the world should be reduced to two classes," recalled Robles later. "Certainly, it was the capitalists who were responsible for imposing a system opposed to the workers. But we always remembered Basque history, the time before we lost our freedom, in which class struggle did not exist." To this end, Robles and the STV proposed an idea of "communitarianism," a third way between Marxist socialism and capitalism.[82]

Nationalist participation in the 1934 uprising was confirmed by the radical activist Lezo de Urreztieta, who took an active part in the events with the compliance of the party. It was the actual PNV leadership, he contends, who asked him to get involved in the insurrection, and he himself had no qualms about participating: "We wanted to rise up against the dictatorship of Gil Robles, Lerroux, and team, [because] they were even worse than the left [had been] during the first two years."[83] A symbolic resort to physical action, of course, had been one of the central legacies of Arana's original articulation of Basque nationalism, and this idea was continuously promoted throughout the 1930s.[84] Violent incidents, although confined to these areas, were nevertheless brutal: sixteen people were killed in Bilbao, six in Eibar, and four in Arrasate–Mondragón.[85] A participant in the fighting in Eibar remembered that the death toll could have been even higher had the insurgents gained full access to the town's many weapons (it was an arms-manufacturing center). As it was, the number of deaths was comparatively small, although hundreds of men were later incarcerated.[86]

Throughout 1935, the general atmosphere in Spain remained tense, with the various political forces realigning in attempts to gain popular support for their programs, and as the country prepared itself for the February elections of 1936, there was an increasing uneasiness at the fragile nature of the young democracy. All the while, the PNV continued to hesitate, nervous at the idea of allying itself with political parties with whom it had little in common.

Basque Nationalism and the Popular Front

Part of the electoral strategy formulated by the Popular Front in 1936 was a promise of autonomy for the Basque Country. This was as much the idea of Prieto as of anyone else. Indeed, he saw this policy as the only means of integrating Basque nationalism into the constitutional framework of the Second Republic.[87] As a consequence, the PNV remained neutral in the February elections, gaining a (somewhat disappointing) 35 percent of the vote in Bizkaia, Gipuzkoa, and Araba, a decline of 10 percent from the 1933 elections.[88] However, the PNV secured 130,000 votes, independent of either left-wing or right-wing blocs (the Popular Front achieved its victory by a relatively slender majority of 700,000) and remained the strongest single party in the Basque Country.

Victory for the Popular Front in February 1936 assured another period of left-wing republicanism in the Spanish government. Azaña assumed office once more on a left-republican ticket, although he would take up the presidency in May, leaving the responsibility of running the government to Santiago Casares Quiroga. Governing was made difficult, however, by a divisive and increasingly violent political confrontation outside the formal political institutions, and within six months, the short-lived Republic would dissolve under internal pressure. As in the right-wing coalitions before it, there was an increasing internal argument within the left: *among* members of the PSOE themselves; *between* the PSOE and its affiliated union, the UGT; and *between* the UGT and the both the anarchist CNT and the Basque nationalist union, ELA/STV. To complicate matters further, the forces of the radical right, upset at Gil Robles's failure to become their *caudillo*, had been training their own militias for the previous two years. In the spring of 1936, Spain erupted in street battles on a level previously unseen, between left and right, centrist and regionalist, and moderates and radicals of all factions.

In this escalating violence, Basque participation was most noticeable in the activities of the Navarrese Carlists. Even before the left-inspired revolutionary uprising of 1934, they had formed their own militia, the *Requetés*, composed of around six thousand men. They were organized at the local level in a framework of communication between neighboring villages, often counting on the support of the clergy.[89] After the events of October

1934, the military wing of Carlism was even more effectively organized. During the winter of 1935–36, for example, a military committee was established to coordinate the transport of arms and men across the border from the French Basque Country into Navarre.[90] On the eve of the uprising and amid a heady atmosphere of plotting and insurrection in Pamplona–Iruñea, it was reported to the military conspirators that seven thousand volunteers would be at their disposal if and when the revolution came.[91]

The attitude of the PNV resembled that during the October 1934 uprising. The party, bereft of any specific program of support for either left or right, vacillated between the two. Although the PNV's leaders may have been naturally more sympathetic toward the forces of tradition, it was the left that had promised autonomy. Political violence was the dominant feature of everyday life in the country as a whole, and the Basque nationalists followed the example of the Carlists in preparing for a military confrontation. During the 1934 left-wing insurrection, the PNV had been severely lacking in arms.[92] It could not afford to make the same mistake again.

Juan Beistegui later remembered that after the February 1936 election, he had expected a revolt to come any day. He worked for his family's arms manufacturing company (one of Eibar's principal industries) and received a letter that spring advertising Belgian warplanes. "I wanted that letter to send to my party," he remembered, "so that they would have [the] information," and he duly sent it on. The mood of the town was particularly tense, with a number of German visitors prompting speculation of intrigue and espionage. His father had already dealt with two inquiries for arms to use against the Republic, one from France and the other from one of Eibar's Carlist leaders. Both requests were turned down. "We were against the Germans, against the Carlists, against anybody that we thought was preparing a revolution," continued Beistegui; "we did not want a war." However, if a confrontation was coming, then he obviously wanted the nationalists to be prepared for battle: "I thought if a revolution were to come, [the 16-gauge Remington] would be a good weapon in street fighting," because he and his friends had used it on frequent hunting trips.[93] There is some debate over the extent to which the PNV had made military preparations before the outbreak of the Civil War. There may have been arms negotiations as early as the beginning of April, and certainly, by the late spring, it seems as if the Basque nationalists had made some degree of formal military preparation.[94] That said, at the outbreak of hostilities, the PNV would find itself woefully bereft of arms in comparison with other political factions.[95]

However, radical Basque nationalists were in no doubt as to both their political goals and their tactics. Following a general call for international solidarity among the oppressed peoples of the world–including a rallying call of "Gora Etiopía Azkatuta!" "Long Live Free Ethiopia!"–*Jagi Jagi* informed its readers of the lessons to be learned from a radical wing of the Breton nationalist group in France: Gwen ha Du. It included among its tactics a form of direct confrontation: political violence in the nationalist cause. In May 1936, with society more sharply divided than ever and acutely aware of escalating and uncontrollable domestic violence, the radical weekly reprinted a political statement by the Breton group (originally dated April 13, 1936) with the intention of fomenting similar opinions among radical Basque nationalists:

> All our blood for Brittany; not a drop for France.... Understand that Brittany would not have been resurrected but for the force of men who possess a Celtic spirit and sturdy arms, men that can put military force at the service of Brittany, men that could be Breton soldiers. Your lifelong goal should be that of the Breton soldier. You should undertake collective and disciplined action as the most efficient means of achieving our goal... Prepare... to be with us [as] the soldiers that Brittany needs, and rest assured: We will meet again when the right moment comes.[96]

The article not only recalled the imagery used by Arana, but also implied its contemporary relevance to the use of force in the nationalist struggle. It is also interesting to note the importance afforded to international nationalist movements, a role traditionally fulfilled for Basque nationalism by the Irish case.

Indeed, the Irish example continued to exert a strong influence on the Basque nationalist imagination throughout the course of the Republic. Teodoro Hernandorena (president of the Gipuzkoan youth section of the PNV) visited Ireland in 1932 on a propaganda mission to publicize the Basque cause, taking with him the gift of a commemorative tray donated by the women's section of the PNV, Emakume Abertzale Batza, who owed their existence to an Irish model: Cumann man nBan, in the IRA.[97] Furthermore, the IRA even contemplated sending military advisers to help Basque nationalists during the Civil War, although this support never materialized, and the PNV maintained contact with the Irish president, Eamon De Valera, into the late 1930s.[98]

The attitude of the *Jagi Jagi* journal had an immediate precursor in the work of Manuel Eguileor Orueta. A founding member of the radical *aberriano* group before the dictatorship of Primo de Rivera, though curiously not of Jagi Jagi, Eguileor nevertheless had continued his labor for radical Basque nationalism throughout the 1930s as president of the PNV's propaganda section. In 1936, he published a pamphlet entitled *Nacionalismo vasco* (Basque nationalism), perhaps the most radical public doctrinal statement of Basque nationalism to that date. The book argued, in a standard line of thought dating from Arana, that the Basque Country had been occupied by the force of both the Spanish and French states and that independence should remain the ultimate goal of Basque nationalism. Eguileor then went on to defend the use of force as a potential means of securing that independence. It was the most forthright statement yet of its kind, proposed by one of the principal leaders of the PNV in the 1930s and openly alluding to political violence as a means of achieving the goal of Basque nationalism.[99] By the 1930s, the symbolic foundations laid by Arana were becoming reality.

In keeping with the times, Eguileor's language was careful, yet it left no doubt as to the message, and is worth repeating:

> If, then, through "legal" means we have not achieved our freedom, if Spain and France have not consented to recognize our right to independence, and if Euzkadi cannot, by any

> other means, keep going in its endeavor of emancipation, there remains no doubt that "extralegal" methods for the ruler, legal for us, means *of force*, will be the only ones that allow us . . . to achieve our freedom, as they have allowed other oppressed nations to achieve theirs.[100]

According to Eguileor's argument, this appeal to the use of force was perfectly congruent with the line of thought established by Arana himself. The legitimacy of the use of force was a "fact" as signaled by "our Master," and if freedom were to be achieved, it would won "*only by force*." Eguileor continued: "Sabino, who in his wonderful vision surveyed the entire range and consequences of the Basque problem, thus established [in] our code of conduct an ultimate means to follow unavoidably [in order] to shake the foreign yoke: force." Finally, and in keeping with the tradition of Aranist nationalism, this force, according to Eguileor, would signify a willingness to sacrifice oneself: "there is no greater recourse than to redeem the *Patria* with our sacrifice."[101]

It is impossible to judge the effect that these words had. Soon after writing them, Spain was plunged into a bitter civil war. There are, however, some clues that were provided much later by those present at this time. After contemplating a hypothetical question about the use of force in a political struggle, former Jagi Jagi activist Lezo de Urreztieta responded in the following manner: "If they come to fight with you, you are obliged to face them. If they choose force, then you [must], too. . . . I think persuasion is better than force, but . . . if some day we have sufficient force, we will win."[102] The words would resonate for a later generation.

During the spring of 1936, the principal official concern of the PNV, however, was the statute of autonomy. Plans for the statute were drafted and ready for implementation before July, although its final approval was temporarily blocked by the summer recess of Spain's congress. In a final twist of fate, the Basque statute of autonomy, so doggedly sought by the PNV during the course of the Republic, yet so divisive for the party itself, would be delayed until after a reactionary uprising that would bring the Republic down. On July 18, 1936 a military revolt took place in different parts of Spain that launched the entire country into civil war. Quiroga's government immediately resigned as towns, cities, and entire provinces geared themselves for a confrontation that, given the events of the past four years and the prevailing mood of the previous five months, was not entirely unexpected. Between July 19 and 24, the military demarcation of the conflict was set in place. From that moment on, there was little chance for compromise or peace.

The immediate response of the PNV was one of hesitation. As Juan Ajuriaguerra, the head of the party in Bizkaia at the time, later recalled, "we had fought the recent elections alone, joining neither right- nor left-wing blocs. The right had been attacking us violently, the left was dragging its feet over getting our autonomy statute through parliament; we were quite alone."[103] It was the culmination of a period when the party could not accommodate itself easily to either the right or the left in Spain, and this forced it to maintain a cautious neutrality during the first twenty-four hours of the conflict. However, events overtook the party as the Basque Country split along provincial lines according to the complex affiliations of Basque society. In Navarre and Araba, the military insurrection enjoyed sufficient support to take immediate control of the provinces. However, Bizkaia and Gipuzkoa remained loyal to the Republic, as well-organized workers' and nationalist associations took to the streets to avert any possible military advances. In Bilbao, for example, thousands of miners from the industrial hinterland of the Bizkaian capital converged to avert any advances from the city's Garellano military barracks.

For the PNV, it became increasingly apparent that nationalist fortunes, by default, lay with the left: "The military rising was the work of the right-wing oligarchy whose slogan was unity–an aggressive Spanish unity that was aimed at us. The right was ferociously hostile to any statute for the Basque country."[104] At 6 A.M. on July 19, the PNV officially declared its loyalty to the Second Republic.[105] As Stanley G. Payne astutely observes, the Spanish Civil War would be not just a conflict between Spaniards, but also among Basques,[106] and it is this that will be examined in the next chapter through an interpretation of Basque war stories.

CHAPTER SEVEN

Basque War Stories

The Civil War in the Basque Country forced a qualitative leap in the Basque nationalist collective imagination. Where previously Basque nationalism conceptualized its cause in terms of a symbolic recourse to resistance and heroism, during the Civil War, Basque nationalists experienced firsthand many of the thoughts and emotions that, until that time, had remained limited to metaphor and allusion. It marked an important moment when Aranist images and actual experience came together.

A comprehensive discussion about the events of 1936–37 during the course of the Spanish Civil War in the Basque Country would be a volume in and of itself. Here, I will present a basic summary of the war, viewed from a Basque nationalist perspective, then I will introduce a more detailed analysis of events, based on of eyewitness accounts of the fighting, destruction, and horror of war and its effect on both the individual and collective nationalist imagination.

The Spanish Civil War was a complex and multifarious conflict involving the entire country across class, gender, national, social, and political lines. Here, I seek only to understand how certain people (predominantly Basque nationalists) conceptualized and articulated their everyday experiences during the conflict, how the violence surrounding their daily lives entered their imaginations, and, given the ideological foundations of the Basque nationalist worldview, how they perceived this bloodshed. It is this clash of emotions, ideas, and thoughts that prepared the immediate context for later social, political, and cultural developments within Basque nationalism. During the Civil War, ordinary people were suddenly faced with terrifying experiences. Normal mental constructs could not help them to overcome these experiences, and they consequently sought different conceptual frameworks to understand the destruction of war around them. A significant part of their collective, imaginative response came from images already established four decades previously by Arana.

Anthropologist Joseba Zulaika refers to the war, in the context of his home village of Itziar (Gipuzkoa), as "the great divide." "Before" and "after" the war refer to distinct periods with different historical realities.[1] This is a commonly shared view of history among those who experienced the conflict. It is the trauma that unites the village, regardless of social position or political affiliation. This same trauma, judged from the perspective of the Basque nationalist community, later served to crystallize a common ideology of struggle and warfare into reality.

Such a transformation did not necessarily depend on heroic experience (as related by Arana for example) or even on the all too frequent experience of death and destruction suffered by Basque nationalists. As Iwona Irwin-Zarecka remarks,

> what these tragic experiences share may be found in a variety of events devoid of the ultimate encounters with death and evil, but still carrying enough "formative force" to become the basis for collective self-definition. There is an element of great adversity, both to the human spirit and human ingenuity; there are moral choices to be made, challenges to traditional ways, often fear of the unknown. There is, in short, the intensity of human drama in its many dimensions, the out-of-ordinary experience.[2]

As will emerge from the personal testimonies below, wherever what is normal is transgressed, emotions rise to the surface in an unusually evocative manner.[3] In such a situation, ideology can give meaning to an otherwise confusing or even terrifying situation. Indeed, it is perhaps the very irrationality of war, its trancelike quality, that serves as a productive tool for historical investigation.[4]

These emotions reflect a synthesis of past experience (the ideological inheritance of Arana) with actual reality (the violence of war) to provide a contextual framework for the emergence of ETA in the 1950s. By the 1930s, of course, the emotional discourse of tragedy and defeat was already present in Basque nationalist ideology. Indeed, since the time of Arana, this had occupied a central position within the nationalist imagination. Together with a vague and mythological concept of heroism, such a discourse, in fact, had helped conceptualize and shape this imagination. And in 1936–37, the symbolic discourse assumed a reality unknown in the Basque Country since the Second Carlist War ended in the 1870s.

The Basque Civil War, 1936–37

There was a divided response to the outbreak of war within each Basque province, highlighting the complex and often mutually exclusive nature of the allegiances, interests, and inclinations of the groups and individuals in Basque society. For the most part (although with some exceptions), Navarre quickly proved to be one of the bastions of Franco's insurgent cause. Araba's response to the uprising was one of gradual and widespread support. Gipuzkoa managed to resist the rebel advance briefly through a fragile alliance of its disparate pro-Republic elements, and Bizkaia remained the most solidly opposed of the four to Franco's revolution.

In the Navarrese capital, Pamplona–Iruñea, a warlike zeal rapidly engulfed the city, demonstrating an unequaled popular enthusiasm for the uprising.[5] Antonio Izu was a Navarrse peasant from Etxauri (Echauri), just over eight miles from Pamplona–Iruñea. Like the majority of people from his village, he was a Carlist and had been raised listening to his grandfather's tales of the nineteenth-century wars. Now, in the July uprising of 1936 he, like thousands of other Carlists, saw a means of revenge, a final struggle against the Liberals: "Carrying the need in our hearts and souls, waiting for the opportunity," he later recalled, "when it came, we grabbed a rifle and shouted, 'Let's get on with it.'"[6]

At the head of the Pamplona–Iruñea insurrection was General Emilio Mola Vidal.[7] Together with Franco, he had been central to the planning of the uprising and would consequently command the first wave of advances into Gipuzkoa. He also had been acutely aware of Carlist preparations in the preceding years and regarded Carlism as a force that required harnessing.[8] Its zealous call to action recalled a feeling that went beyond a mere ideology. Indeed, one of the Carlists' rallying calls was a traditional song that expressed the sacramental quality that war, conceived as both revenge and crusade, could assume:

No llores, madre, no llores	Don't cry mother, don't cry
Porque a la guerra tus hijos van,	Because your sons are going to war,
¡Qué importa que el cuerpo muera	What matter the body perish
Si al fin el alma triunfará	When the soul triumphs at last
en la Eternidad!	in Eternity.[9]

The fanatical qualities expressed in the song would soon be put to use by Mola.

Although the uprising in Navarre enjoyed widespread popular support, the insurgent leader found it expedient from the outset to let it be known that any opposition would be violently swept away. To this end, he issued a decree on July 19 calling for a regime of terror to be created in order to prevent any disturbance to the contrary.[10] And in the Carlist peasantry, he found willing foot soldiers to enforce his wishes. On July 20, the Navarrese PNV, a minority faction isolated and under threat, issued a statement disavowing support of the Republic in an attempt to remain neutral from the unfolding events.[11] It did them few favors, however. That same day, July 20, both the head of the Navarrese section of the PNV, José Agerre, and the charismatic Basque nationalist mayor of Lizarra–Estella (an important town twenty-seven miles southwest of Pamplona–Iruñea), Fortunato Aguirre, were arrested, and the latter was executed several months later. The subsequent repression in Lizarra–Estella (a town broadly sympathetic to Basque nationalism during the 1930s) was telling. There, by military order, "all objects or garments (including articles of clothing) of a separatist nature, books, newspapers, maps, and portraits of that man known as Sabino Arana [together with] books and similar material in the former Basque school, documents, objects, emblems and funds of nationalist associations," were to be confiscated.[12] In other words, all semblance of Basque nationalism was to be physically erased–including people.

In the capital of Araba, Vitoria–Gasteiz, the situation was less straightforward. The head of the PNV in the province, Julián Aguirre y Basterra, had been in Donostia–San Sebastián (Gipuzkoa) on July 18 for a meeting of the party's central council. He returned that night to confirm Basque nationalist loyalty to the Republic, but the next few days were marked by total confusion,[13] and he was arrested, together with other nationalist leaders.[14] The local army garrison, led by General Ángel García Benítez, quickly seized control of the capital on July 19 with the swift and effective support of the Civil Guard, groups of *Requetés* (the Carlist militias most commonly associated with Navarre), and the Assault Guards.[15] There was an instant repression of pro-Republic sympathizers: Groups of *Requetés* and Assault Guards roamed the streets, encouraging people to join in with shouts of "*¡Viva España!*" Men who did not comply were immediately rounded up for not joining in a "demonstration of joy," while women who were accused of "disseminating false information" had their heads shaved.

The new civil governor appointed by the military, Fernández Ichaso, then set about creating what one observer has termed a "bureaucracy of terror" that politicized the policing duties of the various militias at work in favor of the uprising to such an extent that they believed they were at the vanguard of an authentic social and political revolution. Within twenty-four hours of the insurrection, 60 arrests had been made, rising to 224 ten days later.[16] Among those arrested, a number were executed, including the Republican mayor of the city, Teodoro González de Zárate, and several other members of left-wing or progressive republican parties. However, the violence never reached the levels of that experienced elsewhere in the peninsula.[17] Indeed, throughout the first few weeks of the uprising, the PNV was left relatively unharmed (compared with the Socialists, Communists, anarchists, and pro-Republic sympathizers), because Catholic traditionalists and Carlists thought an alliance might be possible with their Basque nationalist counterparts.[18] However, by the end of July, all city halls in the province with Basque nationalist majorities had been closed down, together with all nationalist centers and meeting places. By August, the authorities began to arrest PNV members and sympathizers, and in September 1936, with no agreement with the traditionalists and Carlists forthcoming, the PNV was also subject to the repressive measures of the provincial authorities.[19]

In Bilbao, there had been no army revolt to challenge the solidly pro-Republic province. The military commander, Colonel Piñeiroa, refused Mola's request to support the insurgency, and the local garrison battalion was eventually incorporated into the anti-insurgent defense.[20] As mentioned previously, any possible thoughts of assisting in the uprising were probably extinguished by the rapid mobilization of Socialist and anarchist action groups. Amid great confusion through a lack of coordination, they had taken to the streets of the Bizkaian capital within hours of the insurrection, to be reinforced during the next few days by industrial workers from elsewhere in the province.

At the headquarters of the PNV, there was a hesitant reaction to the uprising. The vice president of the Bilbao *mendigoizaleak* (nationalist mountaineers), Juan Manuel Epalza, later revealed the extent of this hesitation: "Until the evening before, *our* real enemy had been the left.... We vacillated for two weeks or more, hesitating to ally ourselves with our former enemies.... It was absurd, tragic–we had more in common with the Carlists who were attacking us than with the people we suddenly found ourselves in alliance with."[21] Two factors finally convinced the party of its commitment to the Republic: the promise of a stronger statute of autonomy ceding virtual self-rule to the Basque Country and emerging news from both Navarre and Gipuzkoa of atrocities committed against Basque nationalists.[22]

In Gipuzkoa, the situation was more complicated, because it bordered the insurgent provinces of both Araba and Navarre, with the latter, particularly, providing the immediate threat for Gipuzkoans. In their provincial capital, Donostia–San Sebastián, a confused situation brought rival political factions (including those Civil and Assault Guards who remained loyal to the Republic) into the streets to fight among themselves and against an attempted revolt by soldiers stationed at the Loyola barracks.[23] Amid greater disorder than any other of the provincial capitals, the anarchist CNT assumed an important street presence. As clashes between insurgents and those loyal to the Republic continued to take place into August, the CNT reinforced its position by taking possession of most of the arms confiscated in their street encounters.[24]

The PNV found itself unprepared for the violence of the street fighting. Lacking arms to enforce its position, it attempted to broker a peaceful course of events, although it could not prevent a number of atrocities being committed against insurgent sympathizers. Matters were complicated by Mola's advances into eastern Gipuzkoa with the Navarrese Carlists. This meant that the Gipuzkoan PNV found itself, from the outset, fighting a twofold battle: an urban struggle in the provincial capital and open warfare on the eastern front. The latter, José Manuel Irardi remembered, "was the principal task," although it was also important to demonstrate to the city (and supposedly to the other political factions) that "we were not shrinking at all from the struggle and that we knew how to fight as much as they did."[25]

By the middle of August 1936, the PNV militias had begun to take some control back from the left-wing factions, although events would soon conspire to render their actions obsolete. On August 26, an assault on Irun (the town bordering France in northeastern Gipuzkoa) brought the Navarrese Carlists into direct confrontation with Basque nationalists. The Basque nationalist army, Euzko Gudarostea, was still in the formative days of its mobilization and could offer no effective defense. Although smaller in number, the insurgent forces demonstrated greater organizational skill, and the town fell on September 2. It was a crucial strategic victory for Mola, for it meant that the northern pro-Republic zone was now cut off from a possible escape route across the French border.[26]

With the pro-Republic forces now on the retreat, Donostia–San Sebastián fell eleven days later. By now, the Basque nationalists had organized their militias to such an extent that they were able to prevent reprisals (principally by their pro-Republic allies, the anarchists) against people sympathetic to the uprising. This was the case in the defense of Ondarreta jail, which housed insurgent sympathizers. Andrés Plazaola, a member of Euzko Gaztedi (EG, the PNV youth wing), which was guarding the jail, later recalled that a number of people arrived one day to undertake reprisals, but Basque nationalists successfully repelled their assault.[27] Unfortunately for the nationalists, there was no such defense in their favor. The Navarrese Carlists, swept up in the crusade of their cause, charged across Gipuzkoa with sanguinary efficiency. On September 13, the same day the insurgents entered the Gipuzkoan capital, they captured five members of Euzko Gaztedi in the town of Orio (west of Donostia–San Sebastián). "The oldest was no more than eighteen," José Manuel Irardi remembered; "they were shot immediately."[28] Two days later, after resting and regrouping, Mola's troops continued their advance into western Gipuzkoa, reaching the River Deba on September 22. The advance would have continued further for actual distances but for the successful counteroffensive of the Basque nationalist troops, the *gudariak*, toward the end of the month. At the same time, the military leaders of the rebellion decided to concentrate their manpower on the capture of the Spanish capital, Madrid.

The culmination of this initial phase of the Civil War in the Basque Country coincided with the decision by the insurgents to direct their attention southward. In an effort to relieve the pressure on the beleaguered Republican forces in Madrid and in an attempt to take advantage of the thinly defended front to the south of Bizkaia, the Euzko Gudarostea launched an offensive into northern Araba. Known as the Villareal (Legutio) offensive (after the town on which it was centered), the attack proved to be a disaster. During the first two weeks of November 1936, a series of uncoordinated assaults on the rebel positions failed to capture the town, inducing severe losses on the Basque nationalist side. This prompted its military leaders to suspend the offensive on December 12.

The second phase of the war in the Basque Country, during the winter of 1936–37, was largely a time of consolidation in the nationalist camp. The rebel offensive had been suspended to concentrate its efforts on Madrid, with fronts established at the southern extent of Bizkaia and the westernmost limit of Gipuzkoa. At this point, two important developments took place: the ratification of the Basque statute of autonomy and the development of the nationalist army into an effective fighting force.

On September 4, 1936 the first wholly Popular Front government came into being under the leadership of the revolutionary Socialist, Largo Caballero. With insurgent forces sweeping into Gipuzkoa from Navarre and the Basque nationalists still hesitant about officially committing themselves to the cause of the Republic, the Madrid government decided that autonomy should be granted as soon as possible to the Basques, mainly due to the necessity of bringing Basque nationalists into the pro-Republic camp. Therefore, on October 1, after a particularly brave defensive battle against the insurgents near the village of Elgeta in western Gipuzkoa, Basques were granted a statute of autonomy.[29] From October 1936 on, then, an autonomous Basque government (controlled principally by the PNV) officially dictated policy in the southern Basque Country (or, more accurately, in Bizkaia, for that amounted to the only province outside the control of the rebels).

On October 7, the PNV leader, José Antonio de Aguirre, went to Gernika to swear the traditional oath of loyalty before the town's oak tree, the symbol of Basque foral rights. Yet this agreement did not please all members of the Basque nationalist community. "It was nothing," thought Urreztieta, musing on the strategic location of the Basque Country in relation to besieged Madrid, "and we had the statute only thanks to geography."[30] According to Jagi Jagi member Trifón Echeberria, the statute was "a maneuver by

Front cover of *Gudari*, the weekly magazine of Euzko Gudarostea during the Spanish Civil War, celebrating the sixth Aberri Eguna or Day of the Fatherland in March 1937. Within days of its publication, Franco's forces began a renewed push that culminated in the bombing of Gernika and the fall of Bilbao. Note the image of the *gudari* (Basque soldier) holding the Basque flag with the crest of the Basque provinces on his beret and poised to defend the preeminent symbol of Basque culture: the *baserri* or traditional farmstead. By permission of Abertzaletasunaren Agiritegia, Sabino Arana Kultur Elkargoa archives.

the Madrid government, which ceded a semblance of autonomy in order to assure our support in the war."[31] At the celebration in Gernika, Aguirre, on exclaiming to the gathered crowd "Gora Euskadi! ("Long Live the Basque Country!") was jeered with the response, "askatuta" (free),[32] together with cries of "¡Estatuto, no! ¡Independencia, sí!" ("No to the statute! Yes to independence!") by young and already battle-experienced *gudariak*.[33] As another young nationalist observed, "we had guns in our hands now; we didn't need anyone granting us our autonomy."[34]

The incident was important as one of the first political demonstrations by a new group within the Basque nationalist community: the *gudariak*. At the outbreak of the war, there were limited military resources in the pro-Republic provinces of Bizkaia and Gipuzkoa. Therefore, in October 1936, the Basque government introduced conscription, and by the beginning of November, a general staff had been created for a future Basque military force, Euzko Gudarostia, and its soldiers, the *gudariak*. By that same November, the army was composed of twenty-seven infantry battalions of approximately seven hundred and fifty men each, a total of twenty-five thousand men, plus a further twelve to fifteen thousand volunteers, organized in militias, who were defending the temporarily inactive front.[35] The battalions themselves were organized along party lines, and those of the nationalists revealed a strong connection with the mythological construction of Basque nationalism. For example, they bore the names of heroes such as Loyola, Arana Goiri, and Simón Bolíbar; historical references such as Gordexola, Amayur, Otxandio, Mungia, Larrazábal (the speech of 1893), and Rebelión de la Sal (commemorative of a bloody Basque peasant uprising in protest at the paying of a salt tax in the seventeenth century); natural images such as Itxas-Alde (By the Shoreline) and Ibaizabal (a river in Bizkaia). Furthermore, two of the three Jagi Jagi battalions took their names from songs written by Arana himself: "Lenago Il" (Death before Surrender) and "Zergaitik Ez" (Why Not?).[36]

Robert P. Clark recounts the story of a conversation he had with a former member of the Basque army: The old soldier told him that he first felt truly Basque when standing with his battalion in Bilbao, listening to José Antonio de Aguirre urge on his troops in the war. A decade of propaganda and a generation of Basque nationalism, Clark argues, had failed to achieve such a powerful collective bonding mechanism of Basque national consciousness.[37] War now provided the catalyst for the mythical construction of Basque identity to bear fruit. It might even be argued that a wider Basque identity was born into war.[38] While war in the Basque Country certainly emphasized the role of Basque nationalism and the importance of Basque identity, it also effectively crystallized a previously established mythology. Certainly, the spirit of the Basque army was its most notable asset, and youth was especially celebrated within the ranks. "The youth then was brave," recalled the chief administrative officer of the Basque Army, Luis Ruiz de Aguirre, "and answered the call to war with enthusiasm."[39] In the opinion of ANV member Gonzalo Nardiz, "the truly exceptional [aspect of the army] was the endurance of our men, proving with their courage the special quality that would bestow our war with the knowledge that it was defending one's own territory."[40]

In the early spring of 1937, rebel forces, unable to take Madrid in the winter offensive, redoubled their efforts in the north of the peninsula. General Mola, with four newly formed Navarrese brigades (totaling twenty-eight thousand troops) and ten battalions of recruits (both voluntary and forced) from Gipuzkoa and Araba, directed an offensive specifically aimed at Bizkaia. It was then to be a true civil war among Basques.[41] The *Requetés* (Navarrese Carlists), in particular, assumed the mantle of standard-bearers of Franco's crusade. Indeed, the U.S. ambassador to Spain, Claude G. Bowers, reported to Washington at the time that "the Carlists, who have a prominent part... in the Basque offensive, are fighting with the fanaticism of their hate."[42]

As if to demonstrate this, on March 31, 1937, Mola issued the following proclamation: "I have decided to end the war rapidly in the north. The lives and property of those who surrender with their arms and who are not guilty of murder will be respected. But if the surrender is not immediate, I shall raze Vizcaya to its very foundations, beginning with the war industry. I have the means to do so."[43] The tactics employed by Mola included heavy aerial bombardment, followed by the swift ground action of men who had undergone eight months of intensive and highly effective military training. Basque nationalists could not respond with anything like the air power of the insurgents. Furthermore, they were hampered by a lack of coordination and communication with the left-wing battalions. Their only advantages were the heavy rainfall of a Basque spring (which hampered aerial bombing) and the mountainous terrain that, as Napoleon's troops had discovered before them, made offensive actions by regular infantry difficult.[44]

On March 31, Durango, a Bizkaian town of ten thousand inhabitants well behind the front, was the first target of a strategic bombing campaign carried out by the Nazi Condor Legion in support of the rebels. In the attack, over one hundred twenty civilians were killed, including several priests and nuns.[45] At the same time, a southern offensive by Franco's forces advanced from Legutio–Villareal (Araba) to Otxandio (Bizkaia), so that by early April, the insurgent forces were closing in on their target: Bilbao. Bad weather then delayed the advance and allowed the pro-Republic forces to regroup. A renewed offensive, however, began on April 20, when Mola's troops attacked the last line of defense in Gipuzkoa: an area of the province bordering on Bizkaia centered on the hilltop village of Elgeta. The attack was undertaken by the First Navarrese Brigade and a battalion of Franco's Army of Africa, a mixture of the Spanish Foreign Legion and Moroccan recruits.[46] The Basque *gudariak* defending the area lacked coordination and were often left in isolated groups entrenched into hillsides. In the offensive, a panic thus ensued that sent them fleeing the overwhelming attack,[47] and victory for the insurgents ensured a relatively easy passage into Bizkaia.

The effects of the offensive for Elgeta would prove hard to forget.[48] George L. Steer later recalled the image of the Navarrese troops sweeping down from the Gipuzkoan village to the first town across the border in Bizkaia, Elorrio:

> It was eight o'clock when the heavy moths... were fluttering around our orchard where our trenches lay.... [We] saw a movement on the ridge of Memaya–a movement down-

> wards, in orderly fashion. At the head of the men ... went the red and yellow flag [of Spain]. It was bold; it printed on us a great impression of daring and mastery; it was the spirit of victory that had led them on. Then they burst into song, the jaunty "*Viva el Rey*" [Long live the King] of the Requetés.[49]

The power of the image was obviously enforced by the fact that the triumphant soldiers were fellow Basques. Yet it must have been equally powerful for the Carlist *Requetés*. A Gipuzkoan recruit to the Carlist ranks later observed that "the war against another country is a beautiful one. But that war against one another ... that is a hard thing. Nobody who hasn't experienced it knows what it's like."[50]

On April 26, with the experience of Durango fresh in people's minds, a similar raid took place on Gernika, the historic foral capital of Bizkaia and a place of tremendous symbolic importance to Basque nationalists. With a nominal population of seven thousand people, Gernika was, in reality, a sleepy market town of little strategic importance. After all, it lay on a flat plain at the mouth of a wide creek leading to the small, but strategically more important, port of Bermeo. The town itself lay less than twenty miles to the northeast of Bilbao and ten miles from the front.[51]

Monday was the traditional market day, and the town's population had been temporarily swelled by visitors, as well as by a number of refugees and retreating soldiers from the eastern front. On April 26, 1937, at 4:40 in the afternoon, a bombing raid began that continued until 7:45 that evening. In those three hours, a combination of incendiary, high-explosive, and shrapnel bombs, together weighing one hundred thousand pounds, were dropped by several waves of aircraft, destroying the town. The people who managed to flee were machine-gunned down as they escaped the devastated and burning center. The final casualty count, according to one observer, reached 1,654 killed and 899 wounded.[52] The town had been used as a testing ground for the Luftwaffe. The principal test had been of German incendiary bombs, designed to set fire to the targets they hit. The effect of the raid was to set Gernika on fire, as well as destroying the town. However, clearly, people were also the target: "The fighters dived down and machine-gunned people trying to flee across the plain," remembered one eyewitness; "the bombers were flying so low you could see the crewmen."[53]

The following Wednesday, *The Times* of London, through its correspondent, George Steer, printed an editorial about "the tragic story [of] the pitiless bombardment of a country town" in which "the planning of the attack was murderously logical and efficient. Its aim was unquestionably to terrorize the Basque Government into surrender."[54] Steer himself later recalled his overriding impression as one of terror and fear: "Gernika's face was turning to ashes, everybody's face in Gernika was ash-grey, but terror had reached a condition of submissive stubbornness not seen before in Vizcaya," the surrounding *baserriak* "aflame in the hills made candles," and for "the people within Gernika it was not a question of figures, but of inquantitative and immeasurable terror."[55] Similarly, the following Friday, U.S. ambassador Bowers sent a telegram to Washington: "Guernica 'holy city of the Basques' totally destroyed though an open country town with unarmed population by huge bombs dropped from insurgent planes of German origin and pilotage. Population fleeing to the country attacked with hand grenades and machine guns in planes.... The extermination of town in line with Mola's threat to exterminate every town in province unless Bilbao surrenders."[56] Bowers later wrote that "when the revolting news reached Saint-Jean-de-Luz, I was horrified, most of all by the heartless complacency with which the bestial crime was accepted by many."[57]

Juan Pablo Fusi rightly argues that the destruction of Gernika almost immediately became the symbol of international Nazi aggression against a small and distinct people,[58] presaging future events across both the European continent and throughout the world. However, there is another dimension to the destruction of Gernika that often is overlooked by historiographical debate. Gernika is testament not only to Basque suffering and international persecution, but to Spanish complicity–at least, to the complicity of the Spanish insurgents. Addressing the issue of whether the attack was a specifically orchestrated test on the part of the Condor Legion, Paul Preston concludes that it was not principally the work of the Nazis and that it was Salamanca (Franco's headquarters at the time), rather than Berlin, that approved the action.[59] This would seem to indicate that Gernika was attacked as much for its symbolic as for its strategic value. And this symbolic importance *was* recognized by Salamanca. Therefore, one cannot discount political symbolism as a pertinent factor in the struggle between Basque and Spanish nationalism, even when this symbolism assumed the tragically real proportions of the destruction of Gernika.

Thereafter, Mola's troops, now consisting of the Navarrese division, two Italian divisions, and the North African soldiers, began their advance toward Bilbao. Elgeta had been taken on April 24, and Durango and Gernika soon followed on April 28. By early May, the *gudariak* had withdrawn to the defensive position around Bilbao known as the *cinturón de hierro* (ring of iron), a sort of Bizkaian Maginot Line.[60] For seven more weeks, five divisions of Euzko Gudarostea defended the twenty miles of terrain to Bilbao. Bad weather continued to hamper the advance, but the weather was not severe enough to halt totally the aerial support of Mola's ground troops. Bilbao itself, during this time, was suffering from the effects of a naval blockade supported by considerable aerial bombing, which further served to demoralize both the army and the civilian population.[61] On June 2, 1937, the final assault on Bilbao began, and after piercing the ring of iron with ease on June 11, the insurgent forces were only six miles away from the Bizkaian capital.

Gonzalo Nardiz, an ANV member of the Basque government, later recalled that from this moment on, it was generally accepted that the war was lost.[62] A similar view was held by Jesús Solaun, a member of the PNV's central council. From the temporary party headquarters located in the center of the city, he could actually see the fighting taking place on the surrounding hills; "there was not the least doubt that the end was near," he later admitted.[63] President Aguirre then met with his cabinet to plan a general evacuation of both the Basque government and its army. However, a force would remain to ensure civilian safety and prevent a possible scorched-earth policy by the left.[64]

On June 17, twenty thousand shells dropped on Bilbao, and at dusk on the following day, the remaining Basque units in the city were ordered to evacuate. Two days later, at noon on June 19, rebel tanks entered Bilbao, to be followed later that same afternoon by the Fifth Navarrese Brigade, which raised the monarchist flag at the city hall.[65] Most of the Basque Country was now under insurgent control, and for the Basque nationalists, the war was all but over. They had seen their country occupied by a force of their own people, and this trauma would dictate future events in the Basque Country.[66]

Shortly before being executed on June 25, the Basque poet and nationalist sympathizer Esteban Urquiaga (known by the pseudonym Lauaxeta), wrote the following note to his friend Iñaki Garmendia:

> In a few hours I am to be executed. I die happy because I feel Jesus close to me and I love as never before the only homeland of the Basques. . . . When you think of me, who has loved you like a father, love Christ, be pure and chaste, love Euzkadi as your parents have done. Visit my poor mother and kiss her forehead. Farewell until heaven. I bless you a thousand times.[67]

The words he used expressed ideas that had been developed through nearly half a century of Basque nationalism. Lauaxeta became, in 1937, what Loyola and Arana had been before in the canon of Basque national identity: a martyr to the cause.[68]

The remnants of Euzko Gudarostea retreated westward into the neighboring province of Santander. In all, approximately thirty thousand troops were added to pro-Republic forces in the province, although much of the spirit had been drained from the Basque soldiers. On August 14, the insurgents (still with a heavy presence of six Navarrese brigades) then began their Santander campaign, which in less than ten days resulted in victory. Between August 18 and 22, most of the Basque government was evacuated by sea to France. Basque troops, who (as Hugh Thomas observes) had fought better for Santander than their *santanderino* counterparts had done for Bilbao, then refused orders to retreat farther westward into Asturias. Instead, they remained in the port of Santoña, awaiting surrender to the advancing Italians and hoping to evacuate as many of their number as possible.[69]

On August 24, Basque representatives began a negotiation with General Sandro Piazzoni of the Italian Freccie Nere, the Black Arrows, over the surrender of the *gudariak*, yet the ultimate decision lay with the overall commander of the Italian forces in Spain, General Mario Roatta ("Mancini"). The formal unconditional surrender delivered a total of sixty thousand prisoners (Basque and non-Basque) into rebel hands, the largest single victory of the Civil War.[70] By August 26, the surrender was complete, with Basque forces releasing insurgent prisoners in return for Italian guarantees that the lives of the *gudariak* would be spared. Furthermore, a condition was added that allowed all who were able to do so to flee to France on two British vessels waiting in Santoña harbor. However, on September 4, a Spanish unit replaced the Italian forces, establishing its authority in the province of Santander and preventing the ships from leaving Santoña. Furthermore, this unit quickly rounded up any remaining Basque nationalist leaders and took the Basque troops prisoner. Some managed to escape by hiding in the ships' machinery, but most of these men were then subject to reprisals.

They were first imprisoned and then put in the Dueso jail. After a number of show trials, many were instantly sentenced to death. Moreover, while all the time awaiting the call that would actually take them to the firing squad, they had to put up with brutal treatment in the jail. Luis Sansinenea, an ANV member and *gudari* from the Eusko Indarra battalion sentenced to death in Dueso, remembered this particular period: "The new period ... was characterized ... by a brutality with which our guards behaved ... that forced us to witness scenes that it's better to forget. They repeatedly beat and punished [us] for any triviality ... at the same time as hunger, applied systematically as another means of repression, began to sink in."[71] On October 15, the first prisoners were carefully selected for execution: two PNV political leaders, two PNV army leaders, two ELA/STV leaders, two Socialists, two Communists, two anarchists, and two republicans.[72] American ambassador Bowers wrote to Washington at the time that "I know nothing during the war so atrocious and contemptuous of the laws of war and the common instincts of humanity as the treatment of the Basques after the surrender on the terms agreed to in the capitulation. ... The Basques are now afraid to give publicity to these executions lest the lives of hundreds of Basque prisoners be imperiled."[73] "It was an amazing story of treachery and military dishonor," Bowers recalled later.[74] It was also a story that predicted much of the conduct of Franco's regime.

The Civil War remains a key moment in the history of Basque nationalism, whether in local or national, individual or collective terms. At a basic ideological level, the war served finally to confirm the PNV as a liberal Christian Democratic party, leaving its confessional Catholic past as a minority tendency within the party structure.[75] Of further importance, a new military tradition was established. Like its Carlist counterpart of the nineteenth century, it was now swathed in fatalist tales of heroism in the face of adversity. It was also the party of a defeated and destroyed people with little opportunity for hope or optimism.

Basque War Stories

Because the trauma of war served to bond the Basque nationalist community's social memory,[76] there is a great deal to be learned from individual experience, however small or seemingly insignificant with respect to the context of wider events surrounding it. Indeed, as Zulaika maintains in his study of the Gipuzkoan village of Itziar, "the civil war was an event that originated and was decided outside village boundaries [yet] it belongs to village life as a reflection and indicator of larger processes that transcend local society."[77] First-person accounts of reactions to the war, from those who survived two of its most traumatic events, the battle of Legutio–Villareal and the destruction of Gernika, exemplify the thoughts, feelings, and emotions produced as a result of seeing and experiencing the conflict firsthand.[78] To analyze these thoughts, feelings, and emotions, we need to employ a blend what James Clifford defines as the traditional distinction between historical (documentary, archival) and ethnographic (oral, experiential) practices.[79] As such, the analysis will involve what Clifford Geertz describes as "guessing at meanings, assessing the guesses, and drawing explanatory conclusions from the latter."[80]

Legutio–Villareal: The Lost Battle

The town of Legutio–Villareal (Araba) marked the southern front of the Basque campaign for most of the war, at a distance of approximately thirty miles due south of Bilbao. In late November 1936, pro-Republic Basque forces launched what proved to be their only offensive action of the conflict. Its limited failure, together with its horrendous casualties, ultimately combined to bring the full impact of war to the Basque populace.[81]

Luis Ruiz de Aguirre Urkijo was born in 1908 in the town of Barakaldo, Bizkaia. In the 1920s, he had become an active member of the youth wing of Basque nationalism as a member of Juventud Vasca. Like its counterpart in Bilbao during the previous decade, the Barakaldo section gradually gained a reputation within the nationalist community for its more radical position vis-à-vis the moderate line of the party as a whole, and it later provided the breakaway ANV (including Ruiz de Aguirre himself) with some of its principal figures. Barakaldo was later enveloped by the industrialization of greater Bilbao, becoming one of the most important industrial towns in the region, but during his youth, it still retained a rural heritage, and it is from this background that the young activist hailed.[82]

In the 1930s, as an active member of the ANV, Ruiz de Aguirre rose to become secretary of the party and its president in Barakaldo, its strongest constituency. At the outbreak of the war in 1936, the ANV created its own battalions to fight alongside those of the pro-autonomy PNV and the pro-independence Jagi Jagi. Ruiz de Aguirre initially became a captain in the first ANV battalion, rising in 1937 to the position of chief administrative officer in the Basque army. In November and December 1936, he took part in the initial Legutio–Villareal offensive, and his testimony provides an unusually vivid account of the conflict.

On November 30, Ruiz de Aguirre and his battalion arrived in the southern Bizkaian town of Otxandio (celebrated by Arana in *Bizkaya por su independencia*) and that night set off on a hike into the mountainous terrain dividing Bizkaia from Araba. Although the night sky was clear, the previous day's rain had made the mountain trails practically impassable. After hiking over ten miles uphill, their uniforms, dampened by the moist night air, were beginning to weigh them down. They also began to feel the effects of the heavy equipment they were carrying, although their spirit, according to Ruiz de Aguirre, remained positive.[83] Soon after, they set up camp in a ravine near Mount Albertia, just to the north west of Legutio–Villareal itself: "The night was spent in the pine grove, getting ready and stationing the companies in the hollows and trenches of the last Carlist war," recalled Ruiz de Aguirre.[84] Clearly, he was aware of the historical precedent of war and, probably, like the Carlists of Navarre, had been raised on the tales of his forebears' exploits during the nineteenth-century conflicts.

At dawn the next day, the offensive began. From the outset, however, it was clear that a good fighting spirit would not be enough. Their opponents were equally determined, better organized, and well entrenched in and behind the town. Further, they were receiving both troop and artillery reinforcements from Vitoria–Gasteiz, as well as effective (and unchallenged) aerial support. The *gudariak* advanced close enough to see their opponents in the town, but had great difficulty making out their own men among the thickness of pine trees, an abundant undergrowth, and heavy morning mist. Combat proceeded with "a tremendous violence," and toward midday, most of the battalion's officers lay dead or wounded. "The number of casualties was very high," lamented Ruiz de Aguirre, "as well as those dead who [could not] be removed, and it was distressing to see faces one knew."[85] In fact, physical conditions, together with the strength of the insurgent forces, ultimately conspired against the *gudariak*:

> The *gudariak* sweat nervously.... There was not one bit of news. Only rage and anger. Shots, shots and death to shouts of Gora Euzkadi [Long live the Basque Country]. It was hopeless.... The combat continued in savage fashion. Nine hours had passed. Everything had been destroyed.... The casualties were almost total.... Night came and the silence was frightening. The pine trees still burned gently, and the place was a tomb full of Basque blood. Within that silence there was a serenity that hurt, because nobody complained, nobody protested. Just looking out into the darkness, *gudariak* found themselves crying because they had lost their brothers, cousins, or best friends in the struggle.... Prisoners taken by the enemy were shot immediately during combat, in the pine grove.[86]

A retreat was called, and the decimated battalion made its way slowly back to Otxandio, accompanied by several local *baserritarrak* as guides.

The images conveyed by Ruiz de Aguirre's testimony are clear and concise in their description of the reality of war for the Basque nationalist imagination. In many ways, they maintain a strong attachment (even from ANV member Ruiz de Aguirre) to the original articulation of Basque nationalism by Arana. Furthermore, one can see how the testimony of the individual bears witness to the collective dynamic of the Basque nationalist community.[87] Ruiz de Aguirre's testimony thus serves as a text (a reflection on a lived practice or experience) to be read, yet in doing so (and bearing in mind the subject of the text), one must remember that lived practices have material effects on human beings that transcend metaphorical analysis.[88] The reality of war, explicitly expressed in the testimony, was weariness, cold, hunger, and, ultimately, death. And the overriding symbolism, in the case of Legutio–Villareal, was one of defeat and despair. This testimony thus serves as a narrative reflective of wider cultural forms.

To any of the *gudariak* who had read the 1932 reprint edition of *Bizkaya por su independencia*, for example, the terrain they encountered in this offensive would resonate with importance. The town of Otxandio marked the site of one of the battles chosen by Arana to symbolize the defense of Bizkaia against Castile. It lay within sight of Gorbea, the most

Gudariak (Basque soldiers) at the Legutio–Villareal front, December 1936. The inhospitable terrain, harsh winter conditions and superiority of the opposing forces made this offensive–the only advance of Euzko Gudarostea during the Spanish Civil War–a lost cause. By permission of Abertzaletasunaren Agiritegia, Sabino Arana Kultur Elkargoa archives.

commanding mountain in the province and part of a range dominating the central area of the Basque Country. The images used by Arana (mountains, trees, ravines, and mist) were encountered in their starkest reality by the advancing soldiers. Yet as Ruiz de Aguirre noted, these natural symbols acted as more of a hindrance than a help to an uncoordinated and undertrained battalion. The battle was conducted to the nationalist war cry of "'Gora Euzkadi," and Ruiz de Aguirre describes the losses as bathing the battlefield in Basque blood. His interpretation of events seems to be projected through a collective dimension: He felt the losses (the faces of dead soldiers known to him, for example) as part of a communal grief.

How, then, does the description reflect the local experience of war? Zulaika refers to a polarized structure in which two sides are represented by two sets of pronouns: "their side"/"them"/"they" and "our side"/"us"/"we." This is reinforced by an either/or dichotomy that claims an antagonistic perfection: There can be no ambiguity–you are on one side or the other.[89] Ruiz de Aguirre quickly establishes this dichotomy: "They" could be seen in the town itself, in a defensive position behind the town, coming with reinforcements from Vitoria–Gasteiz, and even overhead. His side, the "we" in the distinction, were left amid the pine trees, observing the faces of dead comrades "known to us." Furthermore, and to prevent any ambiguity, no mention is made of the fact that the enemy was also Basque, only that their material and aerial support (no doubt through the non-Basque aid of Franco, Hitler, or Mussolini) had been decisive.

In the local experience of war, Zulaika argues, there is a lack of personal choice. One is bound by the rules and obligations of one's side, and therefore individuality is sacrificed in favor of group solidarity. Further, the totality of the dichotomy is reinforced by the totality of life and death itself, the starkest reality of war.[90] In Ruiz de Aguirre's account, nobody complained or protested. If there was blame, it was directed ambiguously: The fault rested with faraway decision makers, or the lack of resources, or fate, or even the elements. No one individual is ascribed responsibility by this testimony. The totality of life and death is most apparent in the losses described (brothers, cousins, best friends) and in the very act of survival itself, Ruiz de Aguirre being one of the survivors.

Gernika: The Basque Holocaust

Of the many personal accounts describing the bombing of Gernika, that of Joseba Elosegi remains one of the most pertinent, especially given subsequent events in the life of this PNV activist. In 1970, while (the then Spanish leader) General Franco was attending a sporting event in Donostia–San Sebastián, Elosegi, a witness to the destruction of Gernika, in an act of self-immolation,set his own body on fire and threw himself before the dictator, shouting "Gora Euskadi Askatuta!" He survived, however, and later recalled that the incident represented the last desperate act of a former *gudari* who had obsessively remembered the scenes he saw in Gernika for over thirty years before feeling the compulsion to repeat in his protest the flames he had witnessed in the town that day. "Death does not frighten me," he later wrote, employing the sacramental language of Arana; "it is an obligatory end. When one is born, the journey toward death has begun."[91] In throwing himself before Franco, he had "symbolically wanted to convey to him the fire of Gernika,"[92] for its destruction, a Holocaust-like offering to the technological advances of Nazi Germany, represented for many Basques an attack on their very existence.

Born in 1916, Elosegi had been due to undertake his compulsory military service when the war broke out. He immediately enlisted in Euzko Gudarostea and saw active service in his native province of Gipuzkoa on the eastern front, subsequently forming part of the great retreat that brought thousands of Gipuzkoans into Bizkaia in September 1936. He continued to serve throughout the winter of 1936–37 and witnessed the full horrors of conventional fighting at the front. However, there was a good spirit within his battalion, and he readily took to the kind of guerrilla fighting that had stabilized the front at Eibar in western Gipuzkoa: "We were a great group of friends," he observed of his unit, "where a perfect camaraderie, great combative spirit, and cheerful optimism prevailed.... There was no hate in our actions. We hadn't wanted the war; we didn't want to kill or destroy."[93]

In the spring of 1937, however, such thoughts would change. Elosegi's unit, the Saseta Battalion, was withdrawn from the front to spend a period of recuperation in Gernika. They were the only active soldiers in the town at the time, arriving on April 25, the day before the attack: "When we arrived in Gernika, it was a totally normal town," he observed.[94] The following day, after lunching with his unit, he went to visit some wounded colleagues in the Augustine monastery on the outskirts of the town. From inside the monastery, he then heard the ringing of the church bell signifying an air raid and went outside to see smoke rising from the town.

Elosegi rushed to the town center and was confronted by the destruction. Although it was a fine day, many of the streets had been covered with canvas sheets to protect the market traders from any potential rain. Under the saturation bombing, this had impeded evacuation. Many people perished then and there under the sheets, covered by falling rubble and then burned by the incendiary bombing.[95] "I then took part in a scene that left a profound imprint on me for a long time," recalled Elosegi:

> I came across a good woman, covered in dust and with disheveled hair, who couldn't find anything to say but "My son, my son." I crawled among a mountain of debris that had been her house. I began to work like a madman, removing stones and heavy wooden rafters. I scraped until I broke my nails. The bombs kept falling, but I didn't pay any attention; I just felt the presence of that woman behind me, which forced me to take no rest. Unfortunately, everything was hopeless. When I came to touch the clothing of that small child, who was no more than three years old, I stained my hands with his still-warm blood. I gathered that destroyed and lifeless body and carried it to his mother. The spectacle was atrocious, and I have seen that mother's eyes for many years. She took her son, let out a piercing yell, and disappeared.[96]

The impression left on Elosegi changed the course of his life. His immediate reaction was one of rage toward the perpetrators, as he thought to himself: "God's wrath will fall on you! I swear to undertake an obligation to burn the conscience of those responsible!"[97]

The bombing continued as the "evil birds" persevered with their attack: "I had by that time lost my will to live," confessed Elosegi; "at the end of the day it was an honor to be buried in the revered Basque town." His family, and especially his mother, came to mind as he felt his sticky hands: "I looked at them, and they were stained with blood, a blood now darkened, the blood of that child who would no longer call out to his mother."[98] As the evening came, he looked out over the destroyed town. "Fire doesn't kill," he later observed, "it destroys and makes people flee. In those last moments [of the raid], I felt that the town had been destroyed and there was nothing to do. Most of the people [there] thought that way, in a logical fatalism."[99]

Elosegi's final thoughts on the destruction of Gernika are perhaps the most telling of all, for they recall the common trauma of the Basque nationalist community and its response to the defeat of war:

> The Basque ... could not easily forgive, and certainly not forget the serious wrong inflicted on his people.... We understand that there is always slaughter in war, but genocide, the methodical destruction of an entire people, fully enters the realm of crime and barbarism. Violence engenders violence, especially when it is promoted by the masses, and we know the consequences that bring with them the infection of rage among the people ... the civil population suffered severe consequences and ... those bombs produced a depressing effect in the morale of resistance ... it was not difficult to see ... changes in disposition and vigor among the *gudariak*, after suffering the bombardment of Gernika; some reported depression and disinclination, others rage and desperation that made them more fearsome in the struggle.[100]

George Steer recalled seeing a group of men from Elosegi's battalion after the bombing had ceased: "We saw a dazed score of militiamen, Battalion Saseta, standing by the roadside, half waiting for, half incapable of understanding, their orders. The fire of the houses lit up their spent, open faces."[101]

Elosegi's testimony calls to mind some of Arana's concepts from the 1890s. Although his experience at the front had brought him personal danger and he had obviously witnessed the scenes of battle that every active soldier must face, he still remembers the joy of camaraderie and the optimism bred from group solidarity in the service of what was collectively perceived as a just cause. However, all such feeling is drained away by the destruction of Gernika, an unjust and unexplainable sacrifice. At one point, he actually loses his will to live, taking on a fatalism induced by the sight of the mother's eyes and his own blood-stained hands. Elosegi's closing comments on the different reactions of individual *gudariak* to the event reflect his own concerns as he felt both rage and despair.[102] The contrast of images is particularly expressive. On arriving in Gernika, he is struck by its absolute normality, however relative that might have been in the context of a war situation. Compared with life at the front, there is peace and safety. Yet the next day, the

Gernika after the bombing, 1937. "Gernika's face was turning to ashes, everybody's face in Gernika was ash-grey, but terror had reached a condition of submissive stubbornness not seen before," George Steer, *The Tree of Gernika* (1938). By permission of Luis Mª Jiménez de Aberasturi Corta, *Crónica de la guerra en el Norte (1936-1937)* (San Sebastián: Editorial Txertoa, 2003), 197.

overriding image for Elosegi is fire: the fire of incendiary bombs that raze the town to the ground. It is fire that fills the afternoon sky with smoke and in the evening lights up the countryside where the town had once been. In the space of twenty-four hours, normality is replaced by an almost surreal scene in which even night could not fully fall.

The catalyst for Elosegi, the moment when he ceases to be the joyful *gudari* among his youthful comrades at the front, is the incident with the mother and her child. According to Zulaika's characteristic features of a war situation, the collective defense of one's own side during the struggle is equivalent to defending individual lives. It is this that sustains group identity or even biological survival in its basic form.[103] The death of the child symbolizes not only defeat and demoralization, but an attack on his group existence. The child represents the future, yet there could be no future after this.

Both stories reflect individual projections of the collective mentality of the Basque nationalist community during the Civil War and are part of the war experience that shaped the development of Basque nationalism. These testimonies stand as evidence to what Clifford describes as the ongoing process of a collective culture's reinvention, a process in which periodic encounters (in this case, war) are essential to its continuity and survival.[104] One cannot, then, judge subsequent events in the course of Basque nationalism without taking account of the emotions and feelings expressed (in these particular cases) by Ruiz de Aguirre and Elosegi. "For the people who actually experienced it, war was the source of dreadful memories to be turned into 'stories' that are meant to embody the essence of the antisociety's complete lack of ordinary rules and values," contends Zulaika; "for them, from the present perspective, the meaning of war is the projection of a past history replete with tragedy and defeat."[105] War, therefore, in this sense, can be regarded as a work of memory for the Basque nationalist community, that is, as an event conceived of in such a way as to serve the future needs of that community. Indeed, its representation would serve as witness to "the times" (both present and past) while serving to construct the basis of the future.[106]

Moreover, while the Civil War stands as a testament to the defeat, agony, sacrifice, or heroism of the Basque nationalist community, it also serves as a projection of internal and individual contexts.[107] This process of individual interpretation came to change the face of Basque nationalism in the postwar era. In the following decades, the Civil War experience matured in a number of competing ways. The war would be forgotten, or remembered solely in terms of past heroic deeds to be celebrated, rather than repeated, or specifically used to articulate a revised definition of Basque nationalism. A new generation of Basque nationalists used the Civil War to articulate their own collective cultural identity. In particular, the ideology of violent political struggle, framed mythically by Arana and tested unsuccessfully by Basque nationalists during the war, would take another turn two decades later. The Civil War crystallized many of Arana's symbolic arguments into a collectively experienced traumatic event. War also provided the catalyst for the emergence of a more virulent generation of Basque nationalists. The experience of the Civil

War, then, suggests a link between the mythical constructions of Arana and the appearance of ETA in the 1950s.

CHAPTER EIGHT

Franco and the Basque Country, 1937–51

The implementation of the Francoist state marked a new stage in Spanish history for Basque nationalism. Sabino Arana articulated his original theory amid the throes of a nineteenth-century liberal monarchy. The nationalist movement then enjoyed a period of sustained growth during the disintegration of the liberal state and the weak dictatorship of Primo de Rivera. Basque nationalism vacillated during the Second Republic, and now it faced the uncompromising challenge of Franco's so-called new state.

The Sword and the Cross: Franco's "New State"

General Franco's triumph in 1939 marked a victory for violence as a central instrument of political action. In other words, violence came to define the functioning of everyday society.[1] Francoist mythology sought a regeneration of Spain along the lines of Castilian expansionism, through aggression, power, and Spanish nationalism expressed as self-sufficiency.[2] It was a call for a new *Reconquista*, Counter-Reformation, and empire that invoked repression and force as the basis of state authority.[3] The immediate aim of the new regime was to consolidate its power, which, throughout the war, had been exercised by the threat and use of violence. By the retroactive Law of Political Responsibilities in 1939, anyone who had supported the Republic or had hindered the triumph of Franco's forces since October 1934 would be subject to prosecution, and this legislation formed the basis of a massive wave of persecution after the war was over. It has been estimated that as many as two hundred thousand people were executed and a further four hundred thousand were imprisoned.[4] It was, as one commentator has suggested, a physical repression based on metaphysical concerns: Franco sought a systematic means to repress and eradicate *ideas*, above all else.[5] It was also, of course, a new variant of Spanish nationalism.[6]

Politically, Franco faced a dilemma over his control of the state. Both the Carlists and the Falangists, the members of Falange Española, the Spanish Fascist Party,[7] had been at the forefront of the struggle during the Civil War, yet the new leader realized that traditionalist monarchists and the neofascists would always make uneasy bedfellows. As such, he needed to temper their influence by replacing those loyalties. Therefore, with the war still in progress, he ordered the amalgamation of the two forces into the state's official party, Falange Española Tradicionalista y de las Juntas de Ofensiva Nacional Sindicalista (FET y de las JONS) in April 1937. According to Javier Tusell, the creation of the FET y de las JONS came reasonably close to replicating an authentic fascist institution in Spain, although its ultimate failure fully to dominate the military precluded the emergence of a truly fascist Spanish state.[8]

Despite the merger of the two groups, however, they continued to retain their individual identities. Indeed, during the early years of the dictatorship, there was a power struggle between the military and the Falange, with Carlist monarchists waiting to capitalize on any disruption of the political order. To compound Franco's problems, he had to contend with a small, but persistent clandestine opposition movement within Spain and later (after the defeat of the Axis powers in 1945) a brief period of international isolation after 1946, when the Allied powers withdrew diplomatic relations from the country and barred it from entering the United Nations. FET y de las JONS came to be popularly known as the Movimiento Nacional (National Movement) or just Movimiento, and implemented the proclamations of Franco in regard to the creation of a "new state."[9] By a law of 1943, the party and state were combined in what Stanley G. Payne terms a "controlled corporative parliamentary system"[10] whereby the Spanish Parliament was composed of various syndicates and corporate bodies.[11] However, ultimate power rested with Franco, and with hindsight, one can see that Franco's political rise was based on the elimination not only of his outright enemies at the opposite end of the political spectrum, but also of any allies who might potentially become too powerful.[12]

During 1946–47, the regime was perhaps at its most fragile moment since victory in 1939. However, Franco emerged from the period unscathed through a combination of changes in his religious, political, and diplomatic policies: a closer relationship with the church to cement a new ideology, national Catholicism, that attracted a sufficiently broad-based (if not yet exactly popular) support; the appointment of a deputy leader the *caudillo*[13] could trust (Admiral Luis Carrero Blanco), along with an accommodation with the monarchists; and beginning in 1949, the receipt of a series of financial aid payments from the United States , a policy that would eventually translate into both military and economic agreements.[14]

U.S. aid, in particular, was decisive in allowing the future integration of Spain into a postwar international community that had initially shunned Franco. In the international atmosphere of the emerging Cold War, the United States increasingly viewed Spain as a strategic bulwark against Communism and to this end sought closer cooperation with Franco. The Truman Doctrine, committing U.S. foreign policy to aid anti-Communist regimes, was proclaimed in 1947, and in 1949, the year of the first official American aid to the Franco's Spain, the United States ratified a new policy toward the country. Official sources record that "the Department of State reached the conclusion in October, 1947 that the national interest required a modification of US policy toward Spain with a view to early normalization of US-Spanish relations. This decision was confirmed in January 1948 by the National Security Council and approved by the President."[15] This subsequently allowed for Spain's acceptance into the World Health Organization (1951) and then into UNESCO (1952) and the International Labor Organization (1953), culminating in full membership of the United Nations in December 1955.[16] By the end of the 1950s, "probably the largest and certainly the most modern defence installation outside the United States" had been constructed for the American military at Rota in the Andalusian province of Cádiz,[17] and $1 billion in U.S. aid had filtered into the country.[18] In return, together with the land for the U.S. Army, General Franco sent General Eisenhower a donkey.[19]

Under the new regime,[20] Franco's authoritarian state could thus proceed with its primary goal: the economic modernization of Spain. "Franco," as the American chargé d'affaires, Paul T. Culbertson, observed in 1950, "is the kind of Spaniard who likes to get into a movie without buying a ticket,"[21] and this personal austerity translated into his vision for the country as a whole. This was to be achieved through a state-controlled policy of autarchy or self-sufficiency, that is, a policy of industrialization that relied on import substitution through recourse to cheap domestic labor. It was, moreover, a vision in which the lower classes of Spanish society would bear the brunt of enforced economic hardship in the name of progress.[22] Yet autarchy ultimately proved limited. In 1948, industrial production had only just caught up to 1929 levels, and by 1951, it remained at the level of production prior to the outbreak of the Civil War.[23]

Agriculture was also subject to strict state control, principally through fixed pricing and marketing boards.[24] This led to an even harsher standard of living in the countryside, where, in real terms, agricultural wages fell by 40 percent between 1941 and 1951. In the Basque village of Elgeta, for example, the *baserritarrak* had to register their annual production with the local city hall. These figures would then be checked in frequent visits by local Carlist elites. From this annual figure, each member of the *baserri* household would be allotted a certain amount, with the remainder being sold to the local authorities at a fixed rate of roughly half the market value.[25] Furthermore, the state had to contend with a growing rural exodus to urban centers, a particularly acute phenomenon in the poorer, rural expanses of Andalusia, Extremadura, Galicia, and the Castilian plains, although it was a feature, too, of Basque rural society.[26] Therefore, fearful of the social and economic effects this might have, the state subjected the rural poor to strict controls on movement. In effect, Franco's regime secretly hoped to maintain a large body of surplus labor in the countryside and consequently state propaganda eulogized rural Spain, in its own version of *Volksgemeinschaft*, as the repository of Christian piety, morality, and purity.[27]

Throughout the 1940s, then, Franco's economic policy made his country a poor and desperate state. Unlike as in World War I, Spain did not benefit from its neutrality during the conflict in Europe between 1939 and 1945.[28] Work and food were hard to come by. Official rationing (in force between 1939 and 1952, although its effects would last until the beginning of the 1960s) was inadequate,[29] and starvation and disease (principally malaria and typhoid) were common. The people who suffered the most were those most alienated from the centers of power such as the party or from traditionally powerful social groups such as landowners.[30]

By the 1950s, one foreign observer could remark that "fear and uneasiness characterize the Spaniard today. Economically he is in bad shape, so much so that he is more concerned over the pure necessities of living than he is over existing political disabilities."[31] In fact, official state policy purposely deprived the Spanish people of adequate resources, and Franco viewed the shortages as part of the necessary purge that Spain should undergo on the road to rejuvenation and modernization. Moreover, he had no hesitation in forcing the burden of hardship on those least able to cope with its effects, and in many respects, one could define his policies as real state terrorism, a means of forcing the people to acquiesce before Franco's supreme power.[32] While the machinery of state kept close guard on political and economic developments, the regime also recognized the value of cultural control.[33] At the root of Franco's Spanish cultural nationalism was a religious interpretation of Spanish destiny. What in times of war was considered a crusade became in the postwar epoch a new Inquisition, with religion used to justify the extreme violence of the state. Furthermore, this use of violence was sanctioned and justified by the church as a means of exterminating the enemies of the faith[34] and of leading ultimately to the re-Spanishification and re-Catholicization of society.[35] Any "tendency toward freer social life" in the aftermath of war, then, as one foreign correspondent noted, was "countered by an even stronger Catholic reaction."[36] Indeed, after a 1941 agreement and 1953 concordat between Franco and the Vatican, Spain became a confessional state: In other words, all laws were subject to Catholic moral orthodoxy.[37]

This cultural nationalism followed a two-stage process. Initially, there would be a moral purge of society through a wide-ranging policy of censorship. Thereafter, the state, working closely with the church, would promote its own cultural vision, the basis of which was a negation of those who had lost the war and all they stood for,[38] meaning, in effect, that Spanish society was divided into winners and losers.[39] However, as Ander Gurruchaga demonstrates, in bifurcating Spanish society in this way, the winners would never be able to attract the losers into their one-nation project. Francoist Spain was a state divided between a public space (defined by members of the Movimiento, business and landed interests, the church, and the military) that openly articulated the myth of a unified nation and a private sphere, the preserve of the vast majority of the population, who were never fully integrated into the state.[40] Indeed, as Alfonso Pérez-Agote puts it, "the Franco regime was not capable . . . of setting in motion the social mechanisms . . . necessary to socially disseminate the idea of Spain as a community."[41]

Franco's cultural nationalism was imposed in a variety of ways. Perhaps most importantly, education (adopting many pedagogical aspects of the nineteenth-century liberal state builders) served to underpin his vision of the new Spain. Taking as their model the principles of sixteenth-century and seventeenth-century Spanish institutions and traditional Catholic educational theory, Francoist educational policies emphasized the natural inequality of humankind and the inherently sinful nature of human beings, thereby justifying the socioeconomic disparities of Spanish society in the 1940s.[42] Remembering his education during the early years of the new regime, a future ETA activist recalled that resistance to his *españolista* schoolmaster was futile, resulting only in severe public humiliation. If he spoke Basque, he was punished, and until he could speak acceptable Spanish, he was laughed at. There was, he remembered, a complete ridicule of Basque culture and language. He therefore kept quiet, studied Spanish history, and did not speak Basque, although he never wholeheartedly believed in what he was doing. Rather, there developed, from this childhood experience onward, an attitude of quiet refusal to accept what he was taught in school.[43]

Language, of course, was a key battleground for the state. By a 1941 decree, the use of "dialects" (such as Catalan and Basque), "barbarisms" (foreign borrowings), and foreign languages themselves was proscribed (although Franco himself continued to study English in private). Furthermore, all place and first names had to be Castilianized in an effort to realize Franco's one-nation vision.[44] As early as 1938, with the war still in progress, one observer remembered reading a sign in a hotel restaurant in Hondarribia (Gipuzkoa) that read: "If you are Spanish, speak Spanish," meaning in no uncertain terms that speaking Basque was prohibited.[45]

The regime also promoted its policy of cultural indoctrination through artistic media such as film and music. In the 1940s and 1950s, Spaniards flocked to the movies as their only means (except other cheap entertainment such as sports) of escaping the harsh economic realities of their everyday existence. Indeed, at the time, there were more cinema seats per capita in Spain than in any other European country.[46] The state film company, Cifesa (Compañía Industrial Film Español) promoted an ideology emphasizing God, nation, and family through a mixture of heroic war films, historical epics, and carefully selected elements of Spanish folklore.[47] Even Franco himself had a book that he had written made into a movie.[48] During the 1940s, the regime also discouraged both innovation and the expression of regionalist sentiment in music. Instead, it promoted a traditionalist return to authentic Spanish roots with a special emphasis on the heroic tradition of Castile and what Julian White terms a "superficial folkloric Andalusianism."[49] Even architecture was used by the state as an instrument to promote what might be termed a "return to history" through Franco's vision of Spanishness.[50]

Basque Society: Defeat, Repression, Stigmatization, and Suffering

The Civil War in the Basque Country ended in 1937, but would continue for another two years in the remaining parts of the peninsula loyal to the Republic. In those two years, however, the political system promoted an uncoordinated, although efficient state of terror in the region. It was this initial period of violence in the immediate aftermath of a brutal war that effectively heralded a period of widespread and severe repression in the Basque Country, the abiding theme of Franco's new state in its formative phase.

Any discussion of Franco's political inheritance, however, must be preceded by an examination of the effects (both physical and psychological) of war, defeat, and repression on Basque society. The demographic effects of the war are hard to calculate, although one study estimates a death toll of just under twenty-five thousand in the Basque Country.[51] Yet the killing did not stop with the termination of the war. After the fall of Bilbao, a two-month period of terror reigned when no known Basque nationalist was safe from reprisals. At the very least, property was confiscated and businesses closed down. For hundreds of individuals thought to be sympathetic to the nationalist cause, their fate was even worse. Teams of Falangists, members of the Movimiento brought in from outside the Basque Country, summarily rounded up Basque nationalist suspects and executed them.[52] It actually reached the point that Carlists, who had been at the forefront of the bitterest fighting in the Basque Country *against* Basque nationalists, intervened to stop the slaughter.[53]

The death toll of the war and the immediate aftermath of state-endorsed terrorism were further compounded by the losses suffered in Franco's jails. One estimate places the number of Basque political prisoners throughout this time as anywhere between four and seven thousand.[54] Recalling his time in the Dueso jail, Joseba Elosegi remembered that the overriding feeling of the prisoners was one of hunger and that the atmosphere was one of hatred and vengeance on the part of the authorities.[55] As another inmate observed:

> To be a prisoner is the last thing... when you are in the battlefield you are defending what is yours, and you have the weapon with you, you have the bullets for the gun, you will have the pistol, hand grenade, and friends, too. You are there defending your side... But when you are a prisoner you have nothing. They tell you everything, they scorn you, you have to put up with everything, always under someone else–that is what is worthless. To be a prisoner is the worst thing.[56]

Furthermore, out of the half a million people who fled Spain in the aftermath of war, approximately one hundred to one hundred and fifty thousand were Basque.[57] As a result, there was a very real human loss that demoralized the remaining Basque population.

The material damage of the war was varied. Traveling through the Basque Country shortly after his arrival in Spain in August 1939, *New York Times* correspondent Thomas J. Hamilton observed "only a few sagging walls ... standing in the business district" of Irun, the Gipuzkoan border town, while "the hundreds of junked automobiles and trucks which were rusting in a military area just outside contributed to a scene of utter desolation."[58] By contrast, "except for an acute shortage of hotel space, there were no signs of war in San Sebastián," and Hamilton was struck by "the lightness of the destruction of Bilbao."[59] Gernika, however, was a different story: "Scarcely a building had a wall left standing more than waist-high, and most were piles of rubble, so completely demolished that it was difficult to tell where the streets had once run," while "to stand inside the roofless buildings and look up at the blue sky was even more poignant than walking among the other ruins." Later that day, he wrote in his journal that Gernika "would be a perfect illustration of the Biblical story of the Cities of the Plain."[60]

The complete and overpowering sense of loss was emphasized even more by Franco's official branding of Bizkaia and Gipuzkoa as traitorous provinces. While the physical suffering of war, as recounted, for example, by Luis Ruiz de Aguirre and Joseba Elosegi, was the most obvious root of a collective trauma among the Basque population, the psychological effects of Franco's stigmatization of Bizkaia and Gipuzkoa cannot be underestimated. Collective suffering is practically impossible to measure, yet if it is conceived of as a variety of components forming a general negative social status, one might argue that, from the very inception of the Franco regime, Bizkaia and Gipuzkoa suffered a stigmatization unlike any other province of Spain.[61] Once again, there was a historical precedent for this stigmatization. Since the gradual rise of the liberal state in the nineteenth century, specific sectors of Basque society (namely, those rural and coastal Basque-speaking communities) had been progressively isolated from the Spanish national project.[62] This isolation, however, was the result of a vague and haphazard policy that explains much of Arana's need to articulate his program through myth and metaphor. By the late 1930s, after the reality of a bitter civil war and the ascendancy of Franco, this collective Basque (nationalist) stigma was an officially recognized fact, codified under Spanish law.

Following the fall of Bilbao in 1937, the new state abolished the Basque *conciertos económicos* when it officially declared Bizkaia and Gipuzkoa as traitorous provinces. The two provinces had not only declared themselves against Franco from the outset, but they had also fiercely defended their territory. To emphasize their hostility (in Franco's opinion), this resistance was underpinned by a strong nationalist fervor that rejected the *caudillo*'s vision of a unitary Spain. Franco's reaction to Basque nationalism was, in many ways, ironic, given that most Basque nationalists were generally religious and socially conservative. In other words, they represented the very values that Franco claimed as his–and Spain's–moral destiny. Yet this was never mentioned, and the legislation against Bizkaia and Gipuzkoa in effect prolonged the state of war in the Basque Country, legitimizing a policy of terror.[63] This was not an attempt to castigate a specific group of perceived traitors (those people known to have been sympathetic to the Republic), as in the rest of the state. Rather, the state wanted to punish publicly the provinces themselves as territorial symbols of attempts to deny their Spanish national identity. From the outset of the new state, then, there was an attempt to separate these two provinces from the policy of national integration practiced elsewhere, at the same time allowing for a sustained period of repression, persecution, and discrimination.[64] This was the imposed mark of the Spanish state, which immediately relegated Basque culture in general to the position of the stigmatized.[65] The more Basque an individual was in the new state (through the use of Euskara for example), the more that individual would be stigmatized.

Therefore, when considering the arguments of Juan Aranzadi, Jon Juaristi, and Patxo Unzueta (paralleling Eric Hobsbawm and Terence Ranger's "invention of tradition" thesis) that Basque nationalism effectively invented and mythologized a picture of traditional Basque culture,[66] it is also worth bearing in mind that the Spanish state itself embraced these inventions, constructions, and myths. Indeed, this imposed otherness, a central policy of Spanish nationalism since the previous century (and antedating Basque nationalism), also revealed the continuity of a state-building policy in Spain between nineteenth-century liberalism and twentieth-century dictatorship.

Take the destruction of Gernika, for example, an act of brutality beyond a mere tactic of war that resonated with symbolic importance, being directed against a *mythically* (rather than strategically) important Basque town, or the postwar repression of Basque culture that sought to eliminate the Basque language through the enforced use of Spanish. If the symbol of Gernika was *merely* an invented tradition, why did Franco's forces attack it? Furthermore, if traditional Basque culture was dying out in a natural fashion, why invest so much time and effort in its destruction? The answers to these questions might actually have more to do with constructing Spanish identity than with destroying Basque culture. Similarly, the assertion that state repression was no worse in the Basque Country than in, for example, Asturias or Madrid, is misleading.[67] Individual *asturianos* and *madrileños* may have suffered persecution as a result of their political affiliation, but in addition to *political* stigmatization, state persecution in the Basque Country also involved *ethnic* differentiation.[68]

With a military defeat emphasized by tremendous human, physical, and material loss, the common theme of postwar Basque society was that of collective suffering and terror, and its most public manifestation (as in the rest of the state) was hunger.[69] Between 1937 and 1944, the cost of living rose fourfold, although wages stagnated at their 1936 levels.[70] For some Basques, smuggling contraband goods into Spain offered some alleviation to the suffering, but this was obviously restricted to those villages bordering France.[71] In 1939, it was reported that victory meant little in the aftermath of war, for the country had been economically crippled.[72] Furthermore, with Franco having officially closed all means of public expression to Basque nationalism (and Basque culture in general), such feelings became part of a more intimate, personal, and private world. Increasingly, Basque identity was expressed only through the family, the local (Basque) church, and the *cuadrilla*, or social group. It was through these social institutions that a publicly silent and collective Basque suffering was painfully experienced during the 1940s and 1950s.[73] Indeed, there was a very real sense, throughout the early years of Franco's new regime, that all public space was automatically subject to the closest possible supervision by the state in its obsession with controlling and influencing people's lives.[74]

As a social institution, the family is the principal transmitter of social and cultural values.[75] In another sense, it also defines and promotes political identification. In the wake of the economic boom in the Basque Country following World War I that brought new prosperity to rural Basque society, the PNV began to extend its influence among the Basque peasantry so that, by the 1930s, it was the principal party of rural Bizkaia and Gipuzkoa.[76] Families thus became "PNV families," and party values were typically transmitted through subsequent generations. In the 1940s and 1950s, however, with the Basque population as a whole deprived of any public space in which to discuss politics, the family became an intimate location of political education. Yet the traumatic effect of the war and its aftermath tended to divide familial relations and led to generational conflicts. Although individual adults who had experienced the war might discuss politics among themselves, there was an overriding silence when it came to articulating such matters in front of the children. Silence and defeat, then, were common themes in most postwar nationalist households.[77]

That said, different families reacted in different ways regarding the political and cultural education of their children. Many Basque-speaking parents, for example, refused to teach their children Euskara out of fear, while others maintained the language, but only as the most intimate means of expression.[78] Generational conflict therefore was also commonplace in postwar Basque homes. And when those children who had not known the war began to take an active interest in politics, they typically viewed their parents' generation as weak, passive, and silent. "The frustration of parents, a denial of their culture and language and their own ambivalence in the transmission of the [nationalist] code, the culture and the language, would be perceived and profoundly experienced by some in terms of a necessity to do something, radicalizing their political attitude and the means by which politics was conducted."[79] Thus, traditional Basque nationalism, whose values (associated with the PNV) were still transmitted by nationalist parents, became associated with defeat, passivity, and humiliation.[80]

It does seem incongruous, though, that this conflict-ridden reproduction process of nationalist values could have taken place without these same families transmitting at least some sense of appreciation for Basque cultural values to their children, values that many in the younger generation increasingly wished to defend. However, at least some of these youths also began to rebel against some of those values, especially the traditional interpretation of Basque nationalism, thus focusing their protest in two ways: against both the Spanish state and their own culture's perceived capitulation to Spanish authority and cultural domination, a dual focus that underpinned their social and political rebellion.[81]

From the outbreak of hostilities in 1936 on, the Spanish church hierarchy had been closely associated with Franco's rebels. By contrast, many Basque parish priests supported Basque nationalism. Any attempt on the part of the state authorities to justify war in the Basque Country as a religious crusade therefore would struggle to find acceptance. In the course and aftermath of the war, those priests supportive of Basque nationalism suffered a repression concomitant with their status as traitors in Franco's Spain. Indeed, over four hundred priests and monks were imprisoned, and sixteen were executed. Furthermore, Spanish priests were routinely sent to replace those suspected of sympathizing with the nationalists.[82] However, the repression was not absolute, and many priests, even if they were not outright supporters of Basque nationalism, at least continued to preserve and use Euskara wherever possible. Indeed, as in the family, the Basque language during the dictatorship also found refuge within the local church.[83]

At another level, the Basque church also served to preserve and extend Basque culture (and nationalism) through its many associations or cultural groups. As part of the Movimiento, the church in Spain had its own militant organization, Acción Católica (Catholic Action). In the rural Basque Country, this took the form of Baserri Gaztedi

(Baserri Youth), while in urban areas, there was the more working-class organization Juventudes Obreras Católicas (JOC, Catholic Workers' Youths). Some of these organizations, departing considerably from the propagandizing intentions of their foundation, promoted a localized militancy based on the effectiveness of small cellular groups tackling pressing social problems.[84] According to Jesús Azcona, "these movements ... adopted the famous Christian method of action: 'See, judge, act' ... in contrast to the traditional maxim 'See, listen, be silent' ... and were soon transformed into Basque social movements."[85] At the same time, they relied on the enthusiasm of young people to organize parish groups, cultural and folkloric societies, and mountaineering expeditions. Sympathetic priests often encouraged the use of Euskara, especially in the rural associations, and even, where possible, the promotion of Basque nationalism. In the latter case, this social reproduction of Basque nationalist values took place amid a dynamic and militant atmosphere dominated by young people.[86]

The power of cultural associations was emphasized in Basque society by the importance of the *cuadrilla*: "a social group that, in the Basque Country, vertebrates and organizes the activities of public space. In this imaginary place, it exchanges information and interacts at the base level of everyday life."[87] Typically composed of between eight and twenty individuals of similar age, sex, and lifestyle, the *cuadrilla* is a group bonded by a common outlook on life. Membership is fixed, as are its activities (most often revolving around socializing), and the group is sustained by active membership. The *cuadrilla* is also sustained by balanced reciprocity, and although it commonly has an acknowledged central figure, great care is paid not to overemphasize that person's role, for in theory, the groups are based on communal equality. *Cuadrillas* thus tend to be closed and exclusive, supportive, and, when occasion calls, easily mobilized.[88] In the 1940s and 1950s, the *cuadrilla* both provided an outlet for expression in the closed public world of Basque culture and nationalism and fed the grassroots militancy of the Basque church. The *cuadrilla* was defined by strict rules and regulations that served to bond its members and to exclude outsiders. In postwar Basque society, it thus became *the* vehicle for articulating collective responses to defeat in the war and possible responses for the future. When allowed a certain freedom from state scrutiny (on hikes to the mountains, for example), its members could also openly discuss politics.

According to Marianne Heiberg's study of the Basque village Elgeta, the *cuadrilla* served to replace traditional neighborhood relations, because people felt they could trust their fellow *cuadrilla* members more than their neighbors, who might have been potential *chivatos* (informers). "Public politics no longer existed," Heiberg maintains, and "all political activity–both official and clandestine–was organized behind the protective shield of the closed *cuadrillas*."[89] The *cuadrilla* derived its strength from a less conflictive or generational division than that of the family, and unlike other youth groups, from a certain independence from the church. Consequently, while its original purpose was socializing, it actually served as the basis for a new brand of militant Basque nationalism in the 1950s and 1960s.

Basque Nationalism and the Response to Franco

Despite a number of ideological divisions, the course of Basque nationalism through to the outbreak of the Civil War had been marked by consistent growth and expansion. In the aftermath of the war and under the auspices of a hostile state, Basque nationalism suffered a decline in its fortunes. By the 1950s, the PNV had become associated with defeat and capitulation in some sectors of Basque society, particularly among a new generation of nationalists eager to atone for their parents' defeat in the war.

After the war, the PNV went into foreign exile and domestic clandestinity. In the immediate aftermath of the conflict (1939–45), the repressive nature of the Spanish state against internal dissent and the human and material losses suffered by Basque society in general combined to divert nationalist political strategy abroad. An international network of Basque nationalist representatives was thus gradually established in France, Britain, and the United States, together with the support of Basque diaspora communities in Argentina, Uruguay, and Mexico.[90] During World War II, however, attempts to involve the international community in the Basque issue were limited. For the PNV leadership, the best policy was to support the Allied war effort in Europe in the hope of eventually dethroning the Axis-friendly (although officially neutral) Franco.

In 1941, after negotiations with Charles De Gaulle's Free French in London, a Basque military unit was established. However, Winston Churchill's reluctance to test Franco's neutrality forced the disbanding of the unit the following year. More importantly for the Allies, a spy network was created within the Basque Country itself in 1942, supported by the Allied countries as a check on Franco's friendship with the Axis powers.[91] Since the outbreak of the war, and particularly after the German occupation of France and the creation of the Vichy regime there, there had been unofficial clandestine activity on the French-Spanish border, with a number of Basques involved in anti-Nazi actions and the transport of refugees into neutral Spain. These activities were coordinated by the Unión Nacional de Guerrilleros Españoles (National Union of Spanish Guerrillas), an organization composed of many different exiled political groups, but led in the main by Spanish Communists and coordinated within the general framework of the French Resistance.

There is some debate over the extent of Basque involvement in the French rural resistance, the Maquis. Robert P. Clark claims that at least several hundred Basques must have been among the fourteen thousand Civil War veterans in the Maquis.[92] However, Emilio López Adán maintains that there was no official PNV participation in such activities, although a former ANV *gudari*, Pedro Ordoki, was prominent.[93] Ordoki was indeed involved in the activities of the French Resistance, although without official sanction from the exiled Basque government. However, in 1943, he was contacted by exiled PNV representatives with the idea of forming a specifically Basque battalion, and he later led around two hundred men in offensives against the Germans in occupied France. The battalion, though, was still officially linked to the National Union of Spanish Guerrillas, and Ordoki was ordered to move to the Spanish frontier in October 1944, with the intention of mounting an offensive into Spain. The Basque government warned against such a move, however, and Ordoki, with the exception of seven individuals, withdrew his unit from the National Union.[94]

With the war turning in favor of the Allies in 1944, a more formal military unit, the Gernikako Batalloa (Gernika Battalion) was formed and began training under Ordoki with the official approval of the PNV. Composed of just under two hundred men (predominantly, although not exclusively members of the PNV), it was integrated into the Eighth Mixed Moroccan-Foreign Regiment of the French Army and entered the war in late 1944 in the Atlantic offensive. It saw active service in 1945 against the last remnants of German resistance around Bordeaux and particularly distinguished itself in the battle of Pointe-de-Grave. For its combat in the battle, the battalion was decorated by De Gaulle with the Croix de Guerre, and after the liberation of France, it was accorded a triumphant welcome in the French Basque city of Baiona (Bayonne). Thereafter, the unit continued to serve until March 1946, when it was finally disbanded.[95] One observer views the PNV's (late) sanction of the battalion's formation as an attempt to gain political influence among the Allied countries.[96]

With the war in Europe over in 1945, there was good reason on the part of the PNV to feel optimistic about the prospect of international pressure forcing Franco out of power. Within Spain itself, Basque nationalists had been stigmatized as part of the losing faction of the Civil War, yet the PNV had successfully established an international alliance with the victorious powers of World War II. Furthermore, the party had an operational spy network in place, and at least some of its members had seen battle, either in open warfare or in guerrilla activity, during the course of the war. It has even been argued that the PNV in the 1940s was a paramilitary organization[97] and that during 1945 and 1946 there was a serious debate within the party over whether an armed insurrection against Franco's fragile regime at that time might have been effective.[98] As López Adán outlines, there were three possible tactical moves that the party might have made at this moment: an armed struggle, capitalizing on the Basque experience within the Maquis; a popular struggle from within the Spanish state using the power and numbers of the working classes and their clandestine organizations; and advancing the Basque nationalist cause through the context of international politics. Ultimately, the PNV, after its experience during the war and attracted by the idea of becoming part of the European Christian Democratic movement, opted for the third possibility.[99]

In 1945, the Basque government in exile met in plenary session for the first time since the Civil War. A subsequent agreement reaffirmed the legality of the Republic and the 1936 Basque statute of autonomy. However, amid changed circumstances prompted by events during World War II, the role of the PNV within the Basque government (a coalition of several parties representing a cross section of Basque politics) had altered. By 1945, the nationalists had assumed a leading role and began to campaign on an independent platform, with José Antonio Aguirre (the party leader and Basque president) adopting the mantle of international statesman.[100] Therefore, with a renewed confidence gained from the Allied victory in 1945, the PNV began to organize a system of resistance within the Basque Country itself, something that had been impossible just a few years earlier. However, logistics and the continued need to appear moderate within the context of Western diplomacy meant that an armed struggle remained low on the agenda for the PNV. Instead, a series of symbolic acts of sabotage were carried out between 1945 and 1947 in an attempt to unsettle Franco's regime. The Basque flag (*ikurriña*) was planted on public locations such as church steeples and monuments; nationalist slogans and the prohibited word "Euzkadi" were daubed on walls; and a statue of General Mola in Bilbao was blown up in 1946. The following year, the Basque Resistance managed to interrupt the regular broadcast of a Donostia–San Sebastián radio station with a few words in Euskara proclaiming freedom for the Basque Country. That same day (the Aberri Eguna, or Day of the Fatherland), twelve thousand people peacefully congregated in the four Basque capitals, and a few days later, two bombs exploded in Gernika on the tenth anniversary of the town's destruction.[101]

The repression in response to these acts was severe. Noting a rising dissatisfaction among the general populace, Franco's Spain was at a critical juncture in its brief history. It was at this time imperative to extinguish any insurgent activities, for unrest was gradually spreading to the workers. Between 1946 and 1947, a number of arrests were made in the Basque Country, leading to the detention and even execution of many nationalists.[102] At about the same time, Francisco Letamendia Belzunce claims, a military unit had been formed out of the ashes of the disbanded Gernikako Batalloa, and about one hundred and fifty U.S.-trained men were subsequently positioned on the French-Spanish border with the intention of carrying out a number of resistance-style operations in Spain.[103] There were, indeed, one hundred fifty men being trained in France by an American colonel, Pedro Ordoki maintains, but they came directly from the southern Basque Country (not the Gernika Battalion) and were destined to be the future officials of a proposed Basque army. This idea, however, was never realized.[104]

Amid the growing Cold War atmosphere, however, the French authorities became progressively more sensitive to military activity on their southern border. Accordingly, the Basque armed group was officially disbanded, although this did not preclude individual participation in the sporadic guerrilla activity taking place within the Spanish state. According to a former Spanish guerrilla, while most of the activity in the Basque Country was anarchist-led, some nationalists did take part in clandestine operations. During late 1944 and early 1945, "Bakunin," an anarchist guerrilla operating with his unit in an area of northeastern Gipuzkoa and northwestern Navarre (between the towns of Hernani, Oiartzun, and Endarlatsa) met both ex-members of the Gernikako Batalloa and about one hundred Basques led by a figure named Elustondo. "What I always respected most about the Basques," an older "Bakunin" recalled: "is their discretion." He continued: "This did not mean that they were not proud. It seems like one does not go with the other, doesn't it? But as they had a great sense of responsibility and were not partial to organizing things in a hurry and running, I told myself that whatever might happen, the

Basques were going to be very hard in combat. Well, you are seeing it now"–a reference to ETA.[105]

In 1947, Pedro Ordoki and Joseba Elosegi were entrusted with the organization of an official resistance group within Spain. It was subsequently organized into two units and spent three months waiting for orders to strike, although the orders never came.[106] At the same time, the spy network developed between the PNV and the Western powers during the war continued to operate successfully. Elosegi, a Basque nationalist who carried out a number of clandestine operations during the war and in its aftermath (principally the transportation of material and information across the French-Spanish border) recalled one contact in particular, "an American who lived in Bilbao,"[107] to whom he delivered packages on frequent occasions.

This initial period of resistance culminated in the spring of 1947 with a general strike in the Basque Country, an event that marked the first direct and popular challenge to Franco's new state.[108] In April 1947, on the occasion of the Aberri Eguna, a number of leaflets were circulated calling for a general strike at the beginning of May. The strike began among the mining and metallurgical workers of Bizkaia and quickly gained support. According to reports reaching *The Times* of London, "the strikes in the Bilbao industrial area of Spain now affect nearly three-quarters of the workers there, and are spreading from Vizcaya to the neighbouring province of Giupuzcoa. In spite of the ban imposed by the Spanish Government, nearly 50,000 Bilbao workers observed May Day."[109] However, despite a similar reaction among fifteen thousand workers in Madrid, the strike failed to extend through the country as a whole. With three-quarters of the Bizkaian workforce out, the army was sent into the province to patrol the streets, but by the second week of May, the challenge was over.[110]

Between 1947 and 1951, a further wave of strikes followed in an attempt to unsettle the state, fostered in no small way by worsening economic conditions, and culminated in another general strike, this time called for late April 1951 in order to avoid any preemptive measures by the state authorities during the traditional strike month of May. On April 23, 1951, a quarter of a million workers, representing nearly the total labor force of Bizkaia and Gipuzkoa, walked out in the proposed two-day strike. It was a peaceful stoppage, with *The Times* of London reporting that "order does not appear to have been disturbed anywhere."[111] However the repression was harsh. By April 25, some of the Bilbao workers were already returning to work, although in Gipuzkoa, the strikers stayed out in protest at the arrest of many workers. The strike then took a more violent turn, with police forcibly breaking up a demonstration by women in the Gipuzkoan town of Tolosa.[112] The following day, there were several clashes between strikers and police in Donostia–San Sebastián, although calm prevailed in Bilbao.[113] Then, with the last efforts of resistance wilting in Gipuzkoa, spontaneous sympathy strikes broke out in the other Basque capitals of Pamplona–Iruñea and Vitoria–Gasteiz. On May 8, thirty-five thousand workers went on strike in Pamplona–Iruñea, leading to violent clashes between protesters and police in the Navarrese capital. In Vitoria–Gasteiz, three thousand working women went on a twenty-one-hour strike,[114] leading to a complete stoppage in the city. The response of the authorities was, once again, severe: "Shots were fired over the heads of the crowd and, earlier, two men and two women were injured in a clash between strikers and others. In more than one instance employers and priests in the north have given the strikers moral support."[115] However, as in the case of the 1947 general strike, there was insufficient support in the rest of the state for the Basque protest.[116]

Yet the events of 1951 confirmed that the Basque nationalists (in cooperation with left-wing workers' organizations) could mobilize a significant portion of the working population in protest. It also demonstrated to the new generation of Basque nationalists the effectiveness (if only the moral effectiveness) of this mobilization,[117] a fact also recognized by the Spanish authorities, who saw behind the disturbances the influence of the exiled Basque government.[118] While some of the popular Spanish responses to the Basque social protest recalled the atmosphere of the Civil War,[119] Franco remained calm. He placed blame for the economic crisis squarely at the door of the historical legacy of Spanish liberalism, traitorous elements within Spain, and foreign intervention against Spanish development. The remedy, according to the *caudillo*, was a recourse to self-sacrifice and national pride.[120]

The words of Michael Richards eloquently capture the complete sense of despair that enveloped those large sectors of society associated with the losing side after the Spanish Civil War:

> Any account of the Franco years in Spain has to be concerned, in some measure, with the issues of memory, war, violence, Catholicism and economy. The memories of those who suffered defeat and repression in the Spanish post–war years are shrouded in darkness and silence. A sense of fear, absence and insecurity cast an oppressive shadow over lives. . . . The history of countless individuals and the story of families was of entrapment, hunger, blood: the fearful mysteries of parents' and grandparents' tears. . . . Existence was shaped by an often indefinable sensation of loss and isolation.[121]

This is the society into which a new generation of Basque nationalists were born, and the stark nature of Franco's Spain explains, to some extent at least, why some members of this generation felt the need to embrace Arana's mythological and sacramental vision in a more literal way. From a Basque nationalist perspective, although there were many positive results to emerge from the 1951 strike, there remained a feeling that, in many respects, the 1947 stoppage represented the best opportunity for mass insurgency against Franco. In 1946, the United States, France, and Britain had jointly condemned the Spanish dictatorship, and Franco had remained isolated internationally. However, 1947 marked the beginning of a change in U.S. foreign policy that would eventually conclude in an economic and military pact with the Spanish dictator. Although they could have no knowledge of this pact at the time, the PNV leadership continued to reaffirm its faith in the Western democracies as the best source of favorably changing the political climate in Spain. In March 1950, for example, the PNV leader and Basque president in exile, José Antonio Aguirre, met with State Department officials in Washington to discuss U.S. policy in regard to Spain. Aguirre asked that a further international agreement, along the lines of the 1946 statement, be signed. The previous accord had failed to spark any changes in Spain, he argued, because the exiled pro-Republic factions had not been sufficiently united to build on the resolution. Now, however, they were (minus the Communists), and he felt that if a new agreement was forthcoming, there was "a good chance that top-level Army officers would force Franco to step down."[122]

Yet U.S. policy was heading for a complete about-face. In his annual Christmas message in 1950, broadcast to the Basque Country from Radio Euzkadi's exiled Venezuelan location, Aguirre reaffirmed the PNV's commitment to change through Western diplomacy.[123] This reliance on the Western powers in general and the United States in particular is a matter of some debate. According to López Adán, the PNV's alliance with the United States was counterproductive and was based more on middle-class conservative political interests than on any general preoccupation for the Basque cause. Furthermore, López Adán claims, the PNV failure to comprehend the magnitude of U.S. foreign interests and the relative insignificance of the Basque case for the American government resulted in a weak and conciliatory policy.[124] Clark, on the other hand, criticizes this opinion, asking what a more aggressive Basque policy could have hoped to achieve in the same period.[125] Such a policy would probably have achieved very little in terms of short-term political gains, but, as will be seen, the subsequent emergence of a more militant Basque nationalism restored moral confidence to many Basques in the 1940s and 1950s.

That the PNV failed to recognize and respond to the changes of postwar Basque society is, perhaps, understandable. Its leadership was, after all, composed of an older generation who had witnessed the war and its terrible effects firsthand. However, from their position of exile in the aftermath of the conflict, they could never fully appreciate the sense of grieving within the Basque Country itself. By the 1950s, the PNV was unable to adapt its general policy to such changing times, instead stagnating in the face of the significant social and economic changes now affecting the Basque Country.

Furthermore, whereas one might applaud Aguirre's statesmanlike efforts to secure minimal losses for Basque nationalists (and others) during the Civil War and his bold attempt to involve the Western powers on behalf of the Basque case in the postwar era, we should equally fault his lack of vision regarding the change in U.S. policy toward the end of the 1940s. By the 1950s, the foreign policy of the United States openly favored supporting Franco's dictatorship, and Juan Ajuriaguerra, the major PNV leader within the Spanish state itself, was perfectly aware of this. Since 1945, Ajuriaguerra had been responsible for the three wings of the party (political, military, and espionage) in its clandestine organization in the Basque Country. However, he split with the exiled leaders in 1953 over their insistence on following the Western lead, and from that time on, he began independently organizing the PNV's affairs within the Spanish state.[126] Aguirre, on the other hand, through a personal affinity for the United States that blinded him to a more pragmatic change of policy, continued to pursue the same line as before, thereby delaying a new strategy of extending PNV interests within the Basque Country. Both the 1947 and 1951 strikes had demonstrated the willingness of Basque nationalists and Socialists to work together, yet the PNV did not immediately capitalize on this unity. Of course, historically these two groups had been the traditional political opponents within the Basque Country, and it could be argued that their mutual enmity had precluded the possibility of both sides fulfilling their aspirations.

Instead, during the 1950s, it was a new generation of Basque nationalists who realized, ahead of the traditional leadership of the PNV, that a more socially progressive policy was the key to establishing a grassroots movement in the Basque Country. The PNV, too, came to recognize this, but by then it was competing with a new rival. This new generation of Basque nationalists, who had known neither war nor (for the most part) the clandestine activity of the 1940s, were more than just a product of Spain's Civil War and postwar era; they were also a post–World War II, post-Holocaust, and postimperial generation keenly aware of postwar European intellectual and political trends. As a result, they came to combine these ideas with a return to Arana's original articulation of Basque nationalism: an adaptation of Aranist thought to the changed circumstances of the 1950s, something that had been lost in Basque nationalism amid the throes of the PNV's postwar policy of international diplomacy.

CHAPTER NINE

From Ekin to ETA: The New Struggle?

In "The First Love: A Comedy in One Act by Scribe" (1843), Søren Kierkegaard describes the relationship between inspiration, "the great one, the exalted," and "an agile little person" named "occasion":

> Without the occasion, nothing at all actually occurs, and yet the occasion has no part at all in what occurs. The occasion is the final category, the essential category of transition from the sphere of the idea to actuality.... The occasion is a finite category, and it is impossible for immanental thinking to grasp it; it is too much paradox for that.... The occasion, then, is nothing in and by itself and is something only in relation to that which it occasions, and in relation to that it is actually nothing.[1]

Kierkegaard, one of the principle influences on the new postwar generation of Basque nationalist youth, ably expresses here the acute irony in the interplay between inspiration and occasion. There has been a continual discourse within the history of Basque nationalism surrounding the question of armed resistance: an ideology, however symbolic, metaphorical, or conceptual, of struggle and warfare in the Basque nationalist imagination. If this reflects (in an ideological sense) a potential for Kierkegaard's "inspiration," then one must at the same time point to the historical absence of the agile "occasion"–until the 1950s, when just such an occasion surfaced in the historical trajectory of Basque nationalism. And to a certain extent, with this, a missing part of Arana's essentialist ideology, the actual recourse to arms, was fulfilled by the new postwar generation.

The present chapter will focus on a description of the circumstances that gave rise to Ekin, a group of young men who rejected what they saw as the passive and indifferent policy of the PNV in the 1950s and who, in 1959, formed ETA. The creation of Ekin and its transformation into ETA has been described by several authors, who typically use these origins as a prelude to later developments.[2] Instead, I will concentrate on the formation of ETA as the *culmination* of a particular sequence of events in the historical evolution of Basque nationalism, specifically in the period from 1952 to 1959.[3] Following a consideration here of the principal events in ETA's formation, in the next chapter, I will examine the influences that challenged these young men's minds during the 1950s. It is an analysis whose effectiveness rests upon a willingness to deduce the importance of political and intellectual currents on certain individuals.

Previous historical investigation of the period has tended to shy away from a detailed analysis of this kind. This may be because ETA did not begin to use violence until the late 1960s, after a period of intense ideological debate that led to an ideological reorganization of the group. In other words, perhaps understandably, what has most interested academic investigation of ETA has been its violence. Yet one cannot fully understand the ideological debates within the group in the mid-1960s or the resultant recourse to political violence without viewing ETA's emergence as the culmination of a historical process. And the appearance of ETA in 1959 was also reflective of a wider historical evolution that must be situated in postwar European society and politics. The present chapter, then, seeks to chart the rise of Ekin, the group that would eventually become ETA, placing it within the more general development of Basque nationalism as a whole. Indeed, one cannot separate the two, insofar as the formation of ETA marked an explicit projection of the historical juncture at which Basque nationalism had arrived in 1959.

The Formation of Ekin, 1951–53

One of the persistent reasons given for the emergence of the Ekin group is its members' dissatisfaction with what they perceived as a failed and weakened PNV. This was principally manifest in the general failure of the party to gain a satisfactory outcome from its alliance with the Western powers, but there was a more immediate and very striking context that signaled the weakness of Basque nationalism within Franco's authoritarian state: the large-scale repression of Basque nationalists in the period from 1947 to 1951, a repression that physically defeated the movement through the imprisonment of most known activists.

In 1947, numerous suspects were jailed for their involvement in the general strike. That same year, José Luis Alvarez Enparantza (more commonly known later by the nom de guerre Txillardegi) began working for Euzko Ikasle Alkartasuna (EIA), the Society of Basque Students.[4] During the next two years, Txillardegi took part in the group's clandestine actions, including the publication and distribution of magazines such as *Erne* (Be Alert) in Gipuzkoa and *Ikasle* (Student) in Bizkaia. At the same time, another young activist, Iulen de Madariaga, began distributing the same propaganda.[5] Both would subsequently form part of the Ekin group, from which ETA eventually emerged.

EIA however, was not versed in the ways of secure clandestine organization, and in 1950, virtually its entire leadership was arrested and sent to jail or exiled. Among those arrested were the future ETA founders José Mari Benito del Valle, Iñaki Gaintzarain, and Iñaki Larramendi. When the police came to arrest Txillardegi, they accused him of belonging to Jagi Jagi, and he was imprisoned for one month. As Txillardegi later recalled, he was sent to the same prison (Martutene, just outside his hometown of Donostia–San Sebastián) where José de Ariztimuño (Aitzol), the best-known of the sixteen Basque priests killed by Franco's forces, had been sent and tortured prior to his execution during the

Civil War.[6] The experience of arrest and incarceration taught the young activist the value of secrecy in any future organization.[7]

The second event that had an immediate effect on the events leading to the creation of Ekin was the almost total destruction of the PNV's network of clandestine cells in the wake of the failed 1951 strike, leaving the younger generation to organize their own activities.[8] One case in particular was that of seventeen Basque nationalists arrested immediately after the strike, later released, and then rearrested three years later prior to trial. It was a case taken up internationally by a group of British Labour MPs who described the affair as an "inhuman and unjust action,"[9] and the final sentences ranged from acquittal and heavy fines to eleven and fourteen years in prison.[10]

Furthermore, the early 1950s coincided with an intense policy debate within the PNV that left the party internally divided and weakened.[11] In general terms, as Eugenio Ibarzábal rightly points out, a general weariness had overcome the older nationalist leaders in relation to continuing the struggle in the way that they had done through a bitter civil war and over a decade of Francoism.[12] As a consequence, Basque nationalism suffered a temporarily divided organizational structure during this time. Indeed, this would partly serve to provide the opportunity by which, gradually and coincidentally, a new type of Basque nationalism emerged within a small cadre of individuals: "The atmosphere of the era was truly sad from the Basque point of view," recalled one of their number, and "people had lost hope."[13]

During the academic year 1951–52, a group of students at the Engineering School of La Casilla in Bilbao's Deusto University began meeting secretly on an informal basis to discuss their common interest in Euskara and Basque culture.[14] They were predominantly members of upper-middle-class Basque society, Spanish-speaking and urban, and in their spare time away from their studies, they shared a common inquisitive intellectual desire to know more about Basque history and culture. As such, they read whatever little remained in the Bizkaian provincial government's library in Bilbao about Basque culture.[15] These were generally older books examining medieval Basque history and the question of the *fueros*, predominantly in relation to Navarre. They also read whatever books they could on the new intellectual currents sweeping Europe, especially existentialism. The consequence of this reading and the subsequent debates that took place among the group was that they began to see their efforts as a kind of communal labor.[16]

During this time, there were around eleven members of the group, and if any one figure stood out from the rest, it was the introverted and, as Txillardegi remembers, "the philosopher of our *cuadrilla*," Iñaki Gaintzarain. He had already been in jail twice, after the 1947 strike and in the EIA detentions of 1950, and being slightly older than his friends, served to direct the younger individuals in their intellectual curiosity.[17] Gradually, the group began to take on a more formal organization, with each individual member dedicating his spare time to studying a particular interest in Basque history or culture. "There came a moment," recalled Madariaga, "when the objectively mature–if not all, [then] some of us that were there–began to tell ourselves that we could not continue as we had been doing before the state of submission of our people."[18]

They decided that they would publish the results of their individual research in an internal newsletter titled *Ekin*, which in Euskara means "to do."[19] It was a name that resonated with symbolic significance, embracing the call to action (*ekintza*) of Arana's early activism. The common goal of this new group was a desire for real political change at the root level through direct activism or action–something that, in its opinion, had been lost in the existing Basque nationalist movement.[20] Between 1951 and 1953, the group, gradually adopting the name of the internal newsletter, dedicated its initial *ekintza* to raising its members' own political consciousness. It also gradually conceived, as founding member Iulen de Madariaga later recalled, a specific vision of nationalism that saw outright independence as the natural and moral outcome of Basque destiny, a policy that, the group believed, was more faithful to the original conception of Basque nationalism by Arana, compared with the vaguer insistence at the time (on the part of the PNV) on self-determination.[21]

Ekin was rooted in a twin ideological foundation: first, the group's own view that it reflected a return to the roots of Basque nationalism and in this way simply represented a continuation of what it perceived to be the authentic historical development of the movement,[22] and second, its incorporation of both existentialism as a means of explaining a Basque cosmology and the rhetoric of anticolonial national liberation struggles, as opposed to the tactic of international diplomacy favored by the PNV. Ekin's members were very conscious of the historical development of Basque nationalism and their role in that development.[23] Txillardegi, for example, understood the importance of meeting historic nationalists such as Manu Eguileor, Manu Robles-Aranguiz, and Manu Sota,[24] although age separated the different generations to such an extent that he could do no more than feel respect for their previous labor.[25] However, given the repressive and closed nature of Francoist Spain, any symbolic link to the past (especially to a past marked by the more radical vision of Basque nationalism) was of immeasurable importance to the members of Ekin.

In October 1961, on the twenty-fifth anniversary of the formation of the autonomous Basque government, Txillardegi gave a speech in Paris that recalled these influences:

> I think that the first word that comes to my lips is this: respect. For all of us, the young patriots who did not know the war of 1936, but only Francoism: Consequently, for the generation of those born in the 1930s and even 1940s, the campaign for the statute [of autonomy], the *Aberri Egunas*, the election of Aguirre, the Basque battalions, the ring of iron, the executions to the notes of "Euzko gudariak gara" [the hymn of the Basque warrior, the Basque army's battle song], et cetera are amazing events that inflame us, that move and later destroy us in the deepest sadness.

After an emotive description of the effects that seeing, among other things, pictures of masses of people carrying *ikurriñas* (Basque flags), he continued:

> We are alive thanks to that gigantic effort worthy of the eternal gratitude of every generation of Basques. Because it is GIGANTIC what those men did in five years: gather a people in a state of general unconsciousness and take them in five years to autonomy [the period 1931–36], even faced with a holocaust [Gernika and the Spanish Civil War], [their work] was definitive when it comes to judging a generation. And we, those of the 1930s and 1940s, even when we complain and protest, complain and protest thanks to them.... A few weeks ago... reading *Gudaris de Gartxot* by the late Tellagorri, I felt again the chill of that afternoon on October 7, 1936; I even almost clearly heard the hymns of the *gudariak* who broke away toward the front. The date that we are commemorating represents all of that. And we are filled with respect and nostalgia. Everyone of my generation believes [and] would endorse that.[26]

In these words we can see an almost reverential respect for those "warriors" (*gudariak*) who fought in the war, although their ultimate destiny was that of defeat and "holocaust." Txillardegi even confessed that he had almost "lived" these experiences himself, thus connecting his struggle to what came before him.

There is also, unquestionably, a mythical construction in the discourse. Perhaps it is not quite so pronounced as that of Arana in *Bizkaya por su independencia*, but it does feed the discursive element of Ekin's ideology. At a crucial time in Basque history, the PNV was able to seize an opportunity in forming the autonomous government, and it was willing to defend this by force of arms. According to Ekin, the contrast could not be starker with the inactive PNV of the 1950s. However, while such a discourse was designed to criticize the policy of the hegemonic party, it also acted as a kind of self-affirmation for Ekin, a means of binding their cause to the historical legacy, as they perceived it, of Basque nationalism.[27]

The Consolidation of Ekin, 1953–56

In 1953, the members of Ekin began to operate as a formal activist organization dedicated specifically to their vision of Basque nationalism. "Ekin declared itself a nonconfessional organization," distancing itself from ties to the church, Madariaga remembered, and "taking this position... seemed at the time revolutionary... [because] the classic [Basque] nationalism was confessional and bourgeois." However, at its creation, Ekin had no social program. In fact, Madariaga confessed, Ekin's ideology at its creation was essentially marked by a profound opposition to the classical nationalism of the PNV.[28] This position was itself a classic dialectic of negation, much like the original Aranist conception of Basque nationalism as opposed to Carlism. It also served as a mechanism by which a certain feeling of collectivity could be generated among the individual members of the group.[29]

In 1953, its members edited the original discussions they had undertaken during the previous two years into seven themes. The seven publications, today known as the "Ekin notebooks," formed the ideological basis of the group, and its subsequent propaganda work would be entirely based on their conclusions. The notebooks also formed the basis of the future ETA publication, the so-called White Book, which served as the organization's first ideological statement.[30] Among the most important ideas to emerge from these notebooks was an affirmation of a radical policy: a return to the roots of Basque nationalism. "Only the return to natural sources," argued Ekin, "can save those who, on losing something or other, have been converted into an inert and defeatist mass, [the] dead weight of our people." The solution could be sought only by those who were "conscious of the Basque 'being'" and who were willing to "be Basques in more than [just] name." Refusing to fight in the defense of this was considered "cowardliness and suicide," and the central aim of Ekin was "a struggle for life that should overcome the destructive politics of occupation."[31]

According to Robert P. Clark, there were at least two basic ideological differences between Ekin and the PNV in the 1950s: the use of Euskara, which Ekin defined as fundamental to the cause of Basque nationalism and to the creation of an independent Basque republic,[32] and the creation of this republic, which Ekin saw as possible only by a complete separation from Spain. On the other hand, the PNV believed in working within a future system with the former parties of the Second Republic toward a degree of self-determination.[33] "Euzkadi cannot be at the mercy of a Spanish political card," argued Txillardegi later, and "we refuse to create another Carlist experience."[34]

In his seminal investigation of the origins of ETA, Eugenio Ibarzábal argues that the group's emergence and subsequent ideology should be placed in a certain historical context, contending specifically that Ekin represented a way of avoiding the desperate realities of everyday life in the Basque Country during the 1950s. Indeed, Ibarzábal accuses Ekin of being "more sentimental than rational ... [and] charging responsibility with excessive ease on the backs of the previous generation's resistance."[35] Four of the founding members of Ekin responded themselves to this accusation. In their own words, "the mentality of the instigators of ETA (first Ekin) was always inspired by an unquestionably *activist project* [emphasis added]. To confuse the planning that an efficient and innovative activism would require with cultural escapism supposes a crass error."[36]

It indeed seems, in retrospect, somewhat shallow criticism to accuse the founders of Ekin with an overt sentimentalism. There was, to be sure, a sentimentalist and even irrational dimension to their project, but surely this recalled the very inception of Basque nationalism itself. Both cultural sentimentalism and irrationality is often the spark that ignites a political and/or cultural movement. This is more than evident throughout the history of Basque nationalism. Furthermore, such sentimentality as did exist was promoted in tandem with objective political aims. For example, Ekin argued that "the principal source of Basque law is *custom*, tradition," so that, "the value of these [historic Basque] laws ... is due to the fact that *they represent the spirit of a people that knew how to live democratically*, in the true sense of this word, throughout their entire existence."[37] On the eve of ETA's creation, a leading PNV member echoed these words, referring to the three bases of the PNV's doctrine in vague and sentimental terms as Christian morality (the divergent point), sociopolitical democracy, and Basque sovereignty.[38] Thus, to detach the sentimentalism (usually framed in historical terms) from the wider nationalist movement as a whole appears misguided.

As to the second charge, that the members of Ekin relied too heavily on apportioning the blame on the older generation, this was clearly not the case. One only need read Txillardegi's 1961 speech to see the emotion felt by the younger generation toward their parents' bravery and honor. In fact, Ekin acknowledged its historical debt to former Basque nationalists and represented no more than another branch of Basque nationalism, a contemporary version of the varieties of Basque nationalism that had emerged through the course of its history (the *aberrianos*, ANV, and Jagi Jagi for example) and testimony to a plurality of opinion within the plurality of the movement.

A third charge is made against Ekin that merits some consideration. According to Robert Clark, "it was clear that the Ekin youth stood for the creation of a Basque state that would be more intransigent and more demanding than any envisioned by the PNV."[39] During the early 1950s, no movement of national liberation in recent history had achieved its goals through negotiation. Therefore, the rhetoric of Ekin, judged in the context of the era and coupled with its idealism, may have appeared more intransigent than it actually was. However, such intransigence was directed toward facing the everyday reality of existence in Franco's Spain, a fact that the exiled leadership of the PNV did not have to face. They may have known the war, but the Ekin members (together with those of the PNV, such as Ajuriaguerra, who also differed from the exiled leadership over party policy) faced an altogether different reality than the older party leaders. Moreover, the PNV (indeed, Basque nationalism in general) had its own history of intransigence, not the least of which was its confessional nature. Whether this was an appropriate ideology for the Basque Country in the 1950s is open to question. What, after all, would the growing working classes in Bizkaia and Gipuzkoa make of a party devoted to religious dogma of this kind?

Furthermore, the question arises as to whether Ekin really stood for a much more radical vision of Basque nationalism than the PNV. Much has been made (and indeed was at the time) of the PNV's gradual evolution toward Christian Democracy and its strong links with Europe. Yet Ekin, too, envisaged a federal Europe as a means toward Basque national liberation. In a remarkably moderate and visionary policy statement (one of the notebooks, *La Federación Europea*), it was concluded that an "individual step toward Europe [should occur] through a series of balanced and flexible relations, through the council (Basque municipalities), the region (Basque provinces) and the nation Euzkadi. Nowadays, the European Community is the greatest hope of the Basque patriot. We should not spare any force, therefore, in supporting it."[40] This does not read like the policy of an intransigent group, but like a sensible appreciation of the role that a federated Europe might play in a possible future independent Basque state.

Ekin did not offer a complete solution to the problems of Basque nationalism in the early 1950s. Furthermore, the group made little effort at compromise when attempting to forge common ground with the PNV, particularly with the party's more dynamic youth activists. Moreover, there were indeed elements in the organization's foundation that recalled a degree of obvious sentimentalism or Romanticism. However, the group's ideas were always framed by an enthusiasm and genuine commitment that even the staunchest of PNV adherents could not match at the time. For example, while several authors might highlight Ekin's irrational concentration on the defense of Euskara, this remains one of the group's most important contributions to the nationalist movement. Indeed, one only need view the subsequent surge in interest in the language a decade later to comprehend this importance. There were, perhaps, more similarities between the two groups than either subsequently wished to admit.[41] Yet this idea is refuted by two of Ekin's members, who argue that "it is more than evident the EKIN group . . . had a political, even patriotic, as well as strategic and tactical conception certainly different from those of the PNV."[42] Indeed, the two factions could not maintain a successful relationship, and ultimately, Basque nationalism was once again divided.

In 1953, Ekin, having lost four members of the original group that used to meet outside of their university studies, counted two cells, representing Bizkaia and Gipuzkoa. José Mari Benito del Valle, Alfonso Irigoien, Iñaki Gaintzarain, José Manuel Agirre, and Iulen de Madariaga formed the Bizkaian cell, while the Gipuzkoan counterpart was composed of Txillardegi (José Luis Alvarez Enparantza), together with a close family friend, Rafael Albisu, and his relative, Iñaki Larramendi. The latter three members had also been activists together in EIA and, as Txillardegi records, they first conceived of the idea that they were part of a resistance in a 1948 meeting that Gaintzarain also attended.[43] The organization of the group served a dual purpose. Its first intention was to educate its members in Euskara, Basque history and culture, contemporary intellectual developments, and political strategy. Secondly, it was supposed to create the basis of a truly clandestine Basque nationalist movement.[44] Indeed, Ekin's members swore not to tell anyone about the existence of their group: "This oath, which later became an indispensable condition of having access to Ekin, did not obey–as some people have later commented–a supposed extremist or obscurantist nature on the part of its members, but only the desire to not fall into the hands of the police, an experience that some of us were well experienced in."[45] Yet this also served as the springboard from which Ekin began to court outside interest in 1953.

A natural contact was obviously the PNV, and informal links were quickly established between the two organizations through information supplied by Madariaga, who continued to be a member of the nationalist student organization (EIA), which had more or less been incorporated by the PNV in the early 1950s, while at the same time he was helping to found Ekin. However, the first attempt to establish a working dialogue between the two groups occurred in mid-1953, when José Mari Benito del Valle, on a private initiative, asked to meet a representative of the PNV in Paris. He subsequently met with an ex-member of EIA, Juan José Rekondo, and thus became aware that the PNV had known not only of Ekin's existence, but also its internal organization and structure. It was from this moment on that an atmosphere of suspicion grew between Ekin and the PNV.[46] For its part, Ekin was wary of the power of the PNV's espionage network and began to work

La France expulse !

— Le 16 octobre 1962, la France expulse quatre jeunes démocrates basques que le régime franquiste avait déjà chassé de leurs provinces natales.

— Le 5 mai 1964, la France expulse un académicien basque.

— Le mardi 17 novembre dernier, la France expulse quatre autres patriotes basques appartenant au Mouvement ETA :

MM. Julian Madariaga, 32 ans, avocat, père de 5 enfants ;
Eneko Irigarai, 28 ans, étudiant en médecine, père de 1 enfant ;
José-Luis Alvarez-Enparantza, 35 ans, ingénieur, père de 4 enfants ;
José-Mari Benito del Valle, 37 ans, ingénieur, père de 4 enfants ;

Cette mesure a suscité tant d'interventions et de commentaires les plus divers que nous devons à nos lecteurs d'en retracer ici la genèse.

LE mardi 17 novembre, donc, un arrêté d'éloignement de 12 départements, dont celui des Basses-Pyrénées, signé de M. Frey, Ministre de l'Intérieur du gouvernement de Paris, était signifié aux quatre personnes citées plus avant. Cet arrêté est signé du 26 octobre, retenez bien cette date, elle a son importance dans le déroulement de l'affaire. Pour nous, éloignement veut dire expulsion dès qu'il s'agit pour un Basque de quitter le Pays Basque. Quelle différence y a-t-il pour un Bizkayen, en effet, à s'installer à Limoges ou à Bruxelles ? Ces quatre Basques, réfugiés avec leurs familles en Euzkadi nord, depuis trois ans, s'y étaient totalement adaptés. Eskualdun, ils s'étaient pleinement intégrés à la vie culturelle et économique de nos provinces du nord.

Deux d'entre eux, ingénieurs, avaient investi leurs capitaux et leur savoir dans une nouvelle industrie métallique à Hasparren (la seule usine nouvelle depuis 10 ans à Hasparren qui vit le marasme que l'on sait) qui emploie aujourd'hui vingt salariés. Deux autres, animaient une entreprise d'artisanat basque, une société d'import-export et une maison d'édition. De plus, pour compléter leurs revenus, MM. Alvarez-Enparantza et Irigaray assuraient depuis cette année des cours aux collèges St-Joseph de Hasparren et St-Louis-de-Gonzague à Bayonne. Ces quatre Bas-

Les autonomistes basques espagnols de Biarritz cherchaient aussi à rançonner de riches compatriotes

L'information judiciaire ouverte par le parquet de Bayonne à la suite de la découverte, au siège de la société import-export Ikar, dirigée 6 rue Paul-Déroulède, à Biarritz, par Julien Madariaga et Ignace Irigaray, d'une dizaine de cartes grises volées l'été dernier sur la Côte Basque, se double d'une un revolver, est du 28 du même mois, c'est-à-dire deux jours plus tard. D'ailleurs, indépendamment des mesures administratives, une information judiciaire a été ouverte, ayant amené l'inculpation à ce jour du seul Madariaga qui a reconnu que le revolver, trouvé à son bureau, lui appartenait. Julien Madariaga a passé deux séjours dans les geôles franquistes dont un de six mois à la fameuse prison de Carabanchel de Madrid.

Il a été affreusement torturé et a

Les quatre patriotes basques expulsés par la France, de gauche à droite : J.L. Alvarez-Enparantza, J. Madariaga, E. Irigarai, J.M. Benito del Valle.

Top (left to right): José Luis Alvarez Enparantza, "Txillardegi," Iulen de Madariaga, Eneko Irigarai, and José Mari Benito del Valle.
Left: Rafael Albisu. With the exception of Irigarai, all the others were part of the original two cells that made up the Ekin group. By permission of Enbata and Koldo Mitxelena Kulturunea archives.

toward even stricter secrecy. For example, it is no coincidence that at this stage, Madariaga definitively broke off his relations with the PNV to concentrate on his work in Ekin. Yet the PNV also suspected Ekin of infiltrating it, even to the extent of regarding Rekondo (without foundation) as a possible member of the more radical group. Despite this, still in 1953 and particularly in Gipuzkoa, Ekin made contact with the official youth wing of the PNV, Euzko Gaztedi (EG).[47]

The PNV had relaunched its youth wing, Euzko Gaztedi–Juventud Vasca (Basque Youth), in December 1945. In the 1950s, it was also reorganized clandestinely within the Basque Country itself and took the suffix "I" (standing for *del Interior*, literally "of the interior," meaning within the Spanish state) on its amalgamation with Ekin in 1956.[48] The original membership of the EG thus served as the principal bridge between the PNV and the young men of Ekin.[49] The EG's Gipuzkoan branch was sufficiently oriented toward direct activism for negotiation to begin talks with Ekin about the merging of the two groups in 1953. As a consequence, during the next three years, the EG allowed members of Ekin to give lectures and lead discussions with the PNV's young militants, a labor that was realized with the full knowledge and support of the party.[50] At the time, Txillardegi recalled, "the PNV considered that all nationalist youth who wanted to work for the [Basque] Country necessarily had to join the organization, which we did not dispute." However, Ekin did not officially consider joining the party, because more members of the EG were joining them than the reverse. Moreover, the PNV was attempting to exert more control, attempting, for example, to ascertain a full list of Ekin's leadership, which the new group refused to submit.[51]

Negotiations between Ekin and the EG continued through 1956 and, particularly in Gipuzkoa, the activism of the PNV's youth wing surprised their more intellectual counterparts.[52] Txillardegi even writes that the differences between the PNV and the EG recalled, to some extent, the earlier division of the party (in the period 1916–21) between its Comunión and Partido factions.[53] The initial period of Ekin's existence culminated in 1956, when the group gave in to the PNV's wishes and officially amalgamated with the EG (to form EGI) at the World Basque Conference (see below). That same year, two events coincided to cement Ekin's involvement with EGI and at the same time to signal the beginning of the end for the success of any future collaboration.

In 1956, many of the tensions of the previous two decades began to come to the fore in Spain, especially through the activities of a new generation of Spanish youth who had not known the war.[54] "There are signs," reported *The Times* of London in 1956, "that the [Spanish] political machine which started with so much force may be suffering from fatigue."[55] Furthermore, in the spring of 1956, Basque workers once more walked out in protest at the rising cost of living and the refusal of the state to sanction wage increases. In April, three thousand workers began a strike in Pamplona–Iruñea, which spread quickly to Gipuzkoa.[56] While unrest then subsided in Navarre and Gipuzkoa, it broke out in Bilbao. By late April, an estimated forty thousand workers were out in the Bizkaian capital, and the protest then spread to Vitoria–Gasteiz.[57] Franco's response was a call for national unity, "but the winning of active political support throughout the country," remarked *The Times* of London, "particularly in the more developed and articulate regions of the north, is another and harder matter."[58]

The year 1956 also marked a critical moment in the history of Basque nationalism. In Paris, one of the PNV's principal ideologues, Francisco Javier de Landáburu, wrote a book that seemed to touch a chord in the younger generation of Basque nationalists. In the first chapter of *La causa del pueblo vasco* (The cause of the Basque people), entitled "A Request of Basque Youth," Landáburu launched into a brief interpretation of the fortunes of Basque nationalism during the postwar era. The analysis included a heated attack on both the United Nations and the United States for their failure to keep their word about ostracizing Franco.[59] He then went on to explain that the book had been written for "the young people, children in 1936 . . . to whom we might explain the reasons for our posture that they intuitively share." After twenty years of Francoism, "many of those young people are approaching us to ask for some of the idealism" that their parents' generation had previously known.[60] Landáburu further believed that "totalitarianism has done much damage to today's youth" and that "if that regime continues any longer, Basque youth would lose its Basqueness."[61] Then he concluded:

> The world is living a period of revolutionizing many things. In that universal revolution, Basques, principally young Basques, must not be satisfied with the role of spectator. The Basque . . . must act, arousing the patriotic and the humane and reconciling the two terms. . . . This book . . . is like an open letter to those [Basque nationalist] young people, written and signed by a man for whom, like others, too, it has been very many years since he perceived Euzkadi through more than just other writings, who sees only what he can make out by coming to the coast or the mountains of Laburdi [the province of Labourd in the north or French Basque Country], that every day, while the present dual foreign occupation lasts, has to physically stop himself from not responding to the eternal call of: "Ator, ator, mutil etxera" [The song "Come, come home, boy"].[62]

Landáburu's book has been analyzed elsewhere,[63] but some points are worth underscoring. While he did not make an outright statement to the effect, there is evidence in the above lines to suggest that Landáburu not only perceived a certain discontent among some sections of the Basque nationalist youth movement, but also foresaw (and maybe even sympathized with) its desire for action. Skeptical of the recent PNV policy of seeking progress vicariously through international means, Landáburu believed it was the task of young Basques to "act" for themselves, not to resign themselves to the mere role of "spectator."

This was doubly important because they were potentially in danger of losing their Basqueness. He himself, in the summary to the first chapter of the work, alluded to both the emotional and physical power that the Basque Country exerted as he gazed upon his homeland from exile in France. It was powerful rhetoric that recalled Arana's legacy. A call to such ontological concerns had been a powerful and consistent theme throughout the course of Basque nationalism, and in the mid-1950s, amid the degradations of a repressive and hostile regime, it was even more apparent. When faced with such elemental questions, individuals often feel moved to resort to more radical measures than they might normally contemplate. The threat, after all, like the dead child's blood on Joseba Elosegi's hands, recalled a communal attack on the existence of Basque culture through the persecution of its youth. During the 1950s the publication of *La causa del pueblo vasco* had a profound effect on all the young people involved in Basque nationalism, whether of Ekin or EGI.

In September 1956, the World Basque Conference took place in Paris as an attempt to combine cultural and political developments within the exiled Basque community. It was attended by representatives of all the Basque political parties and unions, although the PNV remained the dominant political presence. Two members of Ekin, José Manu Agirre and José Mari Benito del Valle, went to the meeting in order to present their views to the party. A glance at the official publication of the PNV, *Alderdi* (Party), is revealing as to the extent to which party unity (or perhaps more accurately, unity in the nationalist community) was sought at the conference: "The Party leaders need," lectured *Alderdi*, "now more than ever, to feel supported by the members." For "in order to conquer our freedom, the effort of everyone is required; we should contribute to this effort . . . fully convinced that the conquest of our freedom is our work, and our work alone."[64] If there was any doubt as to whom the words were addressed, it was later emphasized that "the young people, the new generation present at the conference, have seen in the example of unity given by the seniors a guide for their own conduct."[65]

It was in this atmosphere that the two Ekin members duly spoke with PNV leader Aguirre, and the outcome was an agreement whereby their more radical group would be officially incorporated into the party's youth wing, which henceforth would be known as the EGI.[66] However, one incident at the conference would, at the very moment when Ekin formally agreed to join the PNV, introduce a note of discord between the two groups. Federico Krutwig Sagredo, an independent Basque nationalist ideologue and former secretary of the Basque Language Academy, gave a speech that shocked the proceedings. In the speech, he called for an armed uprising to form the central basis of a Basque insurrection of national liberation.[67] This insurrection, Krutwig contended, would be principally carried out by commando-style actions. His speech, at the time, was publicly ridiculed.[68] Indeed, one of the official conclusions of the conference manifested its "satisfaction with the activity of the Basque Resistance." The conference further recommended "not to exacerbate passions that could cloud the friendship of democratic Basques and loosen their ties."[69]

The Irreversible Divide: Ekin and the PNV, 1956–59

The fusion of Ekin into EGI theoretically benefited both sides. EGI received a group of activists with a much higher intellectual and political awareness, and this was more than evident in the courses imparted by Ekin members to the more folkloric EG activists. At the same time, Ekin received access to many more operatives and through them the beginnings of a communication with the world outside the university.[70] In particular, the EG's network of village activism in the rural Basque Country was especially attractive to the former Ekin members.[71] To Itziar's village youth in Gipuzkoa (where the nationalist youth were at the time more active than Bizkaia), the activism of EGI seemed *benetakoagoa* (more genuine) than, for example, that of the Catholic Baserri Gaztedi organization. One of the young people, "Martín," Zulaika records, was attracted to EGI because of the risk involved and the clandestine nature of the activities.[72]

However, an atmosphere of suspicion also marked the two groups' alliance. From Ekin's point of view, the PNV exerted far too much influence on the youth movement, for example, in its censorship of some of EGI's more radical publications. There was even some hostility toward the former members of Ekin (now officially incorporated into EGI) on the part of Juan Ajuriaguerra, the leader of the PNV within the Spanish state itself. As Ajuriaguerra later commented, they "tried to have self-autonomy within the haven of Euzko Gaztedi and refused to pass us information about their groups and membership ... they continued working outside the directives set by the Party."[73] Initial attempts to resolve the conflict between Ekin and the PNV were, naturally, carried out by EGI itself. In 1957, three members of EGI traveled to Paris in an attempt to resolve the conflict through a meeting with the exiled PNV leadership. They met with the PNV vice president, Jesús María de Leizaola, but their efforts to secure a solution to the problem of Ekin's incorporation into the party ended in disaster. They were especially shocked by the distance of Leizaola from the everyday realities of the Basque Country in the late 1950s and saw in his continued justification of international negotiation (through the auspices of the exiled Spanish republican parties) a relic of the past that did not serve pressing contemporary problems. As a result, the members of EGI came back from Paris convinced in their determination to follow the course directed by Ekin, not the PNV.[74]

In April 1957, the Gipuzkoan section of EGI presented a complaint against the Gipuzkoan branch of the PNV directed against what the young nationalists perceived as the party's failure to support their activism adequately and against the PNV's overall lethargy. The Gipuzkoan PNV then demanded to know what individual or individuals had penned the criticism, but EGI refused to divulge their names. While no action was officially taken, the gradual rupture between the party and its youth wing had been set in motion.[75]

It was during this period (1957–58) that, according to Txillardegi, the strongest clashes between Ekin and the PNV actually occurred in Bizkaia, with a continual argument between Ajuriaguerra and Ekin's Madariaga and Benito del Valle.[76] "I remember a phrase by Ajuriaguerra," Madariaga recalled, "that said ... that what they had to do with us was first crush and then assimilate us one by one of those that could be of service."[77] There was, certainly, activism by the newly fused Ekin-EGI members of Bizkaia that went beyond the stipulations of the party regarding political strategy and EGI activity: ideological formation, dissemination of information, legal activity, propaganda, and the studying of Euskara. Madariaga remembered that, "around 1957 the first measures leading to direct action were taken: the first, crudely painted graffiti... [and] also the first *ikurriñas*–small ones made of paper and large ones of cloth–appeared in '58."[78] However, on his incorporation into EGI, former Ekin member Madariaga proposed the creation of another wing that would be even more clandestine in nature and especially directed toward the possibility of strategically placing bombs and firecrackers in a form of direct action. It was subsequently decided to create this wing, although nobody wanted to assume responsibility for it. Finally, a lottery was held, and it was decided that it would be led by Benito del Valle and Patxi Amezaga, together with the voluntary cooperation of Madariaga. Ultimately, they never carried out any of their original plans, although the official sanction of activism of this type marked an important step.[79]

Ajuriaguerra saw as the only solution to the problems surfacing between the two groups as the complete dissolution of Ekin and its membership's incorporation officially into the PNV.[80] The tension culminated, according to Ajuriaguerra, with a threat on the part of Ekin to denounce the leadership of the PNV in Bizkaia should Ekin's members fall into the hands of the authorities. This was divulged to the PNV by EGI member Mikel Isasi, who disagreed with the directive proposed by his colleagues Txillardegi, Benito del Valle, and José Murua. The PNV's Bizkaian branch responded in early 1958 by proposing the expulsion of Benito del Valle from the organization and an official apology from EGI for its actions.[81] However, EGI refused to apologize, and at the end of April 1958, José Manu Agirre and Txillardegi traveled to Paris and met the PNV leader José Antonio de Aguirre. "Aguirre received us," Txillardegi recalled, "with great kindness, facilitating a number of meetings, to many of which came Landáburu, Leizaola, and Irujo, all of them behaving with an admirable propriety." He further remembered that:

> José Antonio understood perfectly our anxiety, as did the rest of our speakers.... Manuel de Irujo, the most effusive of them all, told me that they, too, saw the crisis of which we were speaking.... At the end of the those conversations, José Antonio was disposed to intervene in reaching a possible agreement, to which end he gave us a signed letter to be handed in to the PNV leaders in the interior. That document had not the least effect.[82]

The response of the PNV in Bizkaia was that before Benito del Valle could be reinstated, EGI should recognize the supreme authority of the party. As Ajuriaguerra commented later, "Aguirre judged the reality of the interior from the free country in which he lived and with the view, logically, of the president of the Basque Government, and we, on the contrary, [behaved] as the Basque Nationalist Party working in the strictest secrecy. Differences were inevitable."[83] As a consequence, EGI gradually began to split into two factions, and those individuals most closely associated with Ekin (together with a number of new recruits) in effect began to form their own independent organization.[84]

From the spring of 1958 onward, there was, as a consequence, a struggle between the two factions of EGI. In Bizkaia, the majority of EGI's membership remained in the faction still allied with the PNV. However, the breakaway Ekin-inspired group took with it the majority of the Gipuzkoan membership. In total, half of EGI's members joined the ex-Ekin leaders.[85] Throughout this time, both factions were using the title "EGI," but it was clear that they would have to demarcate their respective political activities.[86] For Gurutz Jáuregui Bereciartu, the 1958 split benefited Ekin more than the PNV and served to highlight the hegemonic party's distance from the everyday realities in the Spanish Basque Country under Franco's regime.[87] Therefore, a year later, Txillardegi proposed the name ATA (Aberri ta Askatasuna, or Homeland and Freedom), but because it resembled too closely the word for "duck" in Bizkaian Euskara, the name was changed to Euzkadi ta Askatasuna (Euzkadi and Freedom): ETA.[88] The new organization was officially constituted on July 31, 1959–the patron saint's day of Loyola and the anniversary of the foundation of the PNV.[89] And Iulen de Madariaga remarked on the occasion that ETA "will soon be more famous than the abbreviation EOKA."[90]

"If we felt the need to break with what was before us," concluded Txillardegi, "it was because there was a particular vision... and [our] own definition[s] that we did not see represented in the Basque Nationalist Party." It was the same, he reasoned, "as Sabino Arana breaking away from the Carlist Party."[91] Arana conceived of a particular vision that he subsequently molded into his own definition of political activism on behalf of the Basque Country. The creation of ETA in 1959 must also be seen as a product of this vision. To some extent at least, this is how the founders of the new organization viewed it. Txillardegi's interpretation differs, however, from that of his former Ekin colleague Madariaga, who frames the break from the PNV in more dialectical terms as a reaction to the hegemonic party's general intransigence and, in particular, to the attitude of Ajuriaguerra.[92] Furthermore, Madariaga remembered, "at the moment we embarked on a determined action of a politico-cultural sort, we had as an objective the awakening of the national conscience of our people."[93]

It may well be, then, that Kierkegaard's occasion surfaced in large part through a basic question of individual differences. Ajuriaguerra, the leader of the PNV within the Spanish Basque Country, considered the members of Ekin arrogant, particularly in regard to what he perceived as their dismissal of the party's record of struggle against Franco.[94] However, as was evident in Txillardegi's words in 1961 (at the time as an ETA leader), the members of the Ekin group were fully aware of the past record of the PNV. Their criticism of the party referred more to its activities in the 1950s than to what it had done the previous two decades. Ajuriaguerra, on the contrary, probably judged this as lacking sufficient respect for the PNV's elder statesman. Judging by Basque president José Antonio de Aguirre's efforts to broker a solution to the problem of Ekin's integration, he was perhaps more aware of the damaging effects that a split might have.

Past experience really should have convinced the party of the need to keep the youth group within the nationalist fold. Ironically, however, the PNV, in its own inflexibility (their basic charge against Ekin) could not compromise with the young intellectuals. As Jáuregui Bereciartu argues, given the circumstances, the PNV could not have found itself in a better position to be in during the late 1950s: It had a sound ideological base that was more than sufficient to feed a hungry young generation (including Ekin, whose members viewed themselves as part of the Basque nationalist legacy), and it had fifty years of experience in building up the party structure and the nationalist community. Furthermore, it had at its disposal a new generation of active, intelligent young activists who were willing to continue with its previous labors. However, the PNV leadership remained anchored in the past, unable to move beyond the rupture that war and defeat had caused. Perhaps more than any other single factor, this marked the chance for occasion to fashion the formation of ETA.[95]

CHAPTER TEN

Cultural Representation and Political Violence: The *Creative* Legacy of Ekin

Seen in terms of the cultural atmosphere in which the group developed, Ekin was reflective of longer historical processes and specifically Basque cultural formations, as well as of more general intellectual and political trends of postwar European society. In much of the contemporary literature concerning ETA, which focuses on the groups *destructive* history and defines it according to the politically and academically derived coordinates of international terrorism, much has been overlooked in the early, *creative* legacy of Ekin.[1]

In what follows, I will first discuss the intellectual atmosphere of existentialism surrounding the young men who formed Ekin, which perhaps more than any other external philosophical influence, had a tremendous impact on the collective thought process of Ekin. In fact, in many respects, it defined Ekin's intellectual formation, a formation that lay at the heart of its subsequent transformation into ETA.

The focus then shifts to two figures who enter only sporadically into the academic discourse surrounding ETA: writer Marc Légasse and sculptor Jorge Oteiza. Neither had any direct contact with the emergence and development of Ekin, but through their work, one can discern something of the intellectual preoccupation of Basque society in the 1950s. It should be stressed here that neither figure has been directly linked with the activities of ETA, although both, in different degrees and at different times, influenced the intellectual discourse of the organization.

In addition to the political and cultural legacy of Légasse and Oteiza, I will examine the contemporaneous political influences and historical nationalist legacy to which the founding members of Ekin lay claim. Ekin took as its principle tactical example the insurgent Israeli nationalist movement. Bearing this in mind, I will evaluate the extent to which one can ascribe the ideology of that movement with the nascent Basque insurgents. Finally, I will analyze several historical nationalist texts that Ekin members were still able to access during the censorship of Franco's Spain.

Existentialism

"I am a nationalist existentialist; and an involved intellectual, *engagé* in French."[2] Txillardegi's comment is the most direct affirmation of Ekin's debt to postwar Europe's new intellectual currents. Among the philosophical mentors of Ekin were the great names of the existential tradition: Miguel de Unamuno, Søren Kierkegaard, Martin Heidegger, Michele Sciacca, Jean-Paul Sartre, Albert Camus, and Gabriel Marcel. If one overriding intellectual principle exemplified what members of Ekin found compelling in existentialist thought, according to Txillardegi, it was Sartre's search for *authenticité*.[3] But how can one measure the relationship between existentialism and the emergence of ETA? Initially, one must define existentialism itself. Jean-Paul Sartre, the *doyen* of the existential movement, characterized the idea in the following way:

> In philosophical terminology, every object has an essence and an existence. An essence is an intelligible and unchanging unity of properties; an existence is a certain actual presence in the world. Many people think that the essence comes first and then the existence.... This idea originated in religious thought.... Existentialism, on the contrary, maintains that in man–and in man alone–existence precedes essence.... This simply means that man first *is*, and only subsequently is this or that. In a word, man must create his own essence: it is in throwing himself into the world, suffering there, struggling there, that he gradually defines himself.[4]

There is immediately a striking distinction to be drawn between the original conception of Basque nationalism, as defined by Arana, and the new nationalism of Ekin. Although Arana displayed a degree of self-reflexivity, he accepted the Basque "being" as a given: It was an essence imparted by God. However, to the members of Ekin, following Sartre's definition, the Basque essence had to be created. Like Arana's ideology, however, this creation was part of a greater struggle–against the Spanish state, for example, in its efforts to impose a Spanish essence, a struggle that (in the terms of Sartre's argument) would necessarily involve suffering. As a means of understanding Ekin's interpretation of existentialism, then, one might thus refine Sartre's definition into three distinct parts: the question of being, or of a Basque essence; the struggle, anguish, and suffering involved in striving for this essence; and the negation or even deoccupation ultimately required to achieve these goals.

As to the first point, the nature of the Basque essence, Ekin's philosophical heritage gave it some immediate directions. According to Martin Heidegger,

> thinking accomplishes the relation of Being to the essence of man. It does not make or cause the relation. Thinking brings this relation to Being solely as something handed over to it from Being. Such offering consists in the fact that in thinking Being comes to language. Language is the home of being. In its home dwells man. Those who think and those who create with words are the guardians of this home.... Thinking acts insofar as it thinks. Such action is presumably the simplest and at the same time the highest because it concerns the relation of Being to man.[5]

From Heidegger, then, two points emerge: the importance of thinking and the primacy of language. Ekin valued thought as part of their action. One might say that ETA was born as a more thoughtful and questioning response to the religious acceptance of PNV ideology by many of its adherents. For example, Txillardegi remembers that a common bond between the members of Ekin was that their actions had to mean something in an almost philosophical sense.[6] Second, language was seen as the primary vehicle of existence and, indeed, the defense of Euskara was paramount among the founders of ETA.

Action was also a central theme of existentialist thought. In Sartre's opinion, "existentialism defines man by action."[7] This action could initially be carried out, according to Heidegger, through thinking and contemplation, although a key defining moment of that action would also be accomplishment.[8] And similarly, for Gabriel Marcel, "the man who is most autonomous is, in a certain sense, most fully involved."[9] For the young members of Ekin, there was, as a consequence, a justification for what they termed the intellectual formation of the group, and this formation was indeed part of their action, their own very existence.

However, existentialism emphasized that such action would necessarily involve suffering, anguish, and sacrifice. For Sartre, "*anguish, far from being an obstacle to action, is the very condition for it, and is identical with the sense of that crushing responsibility of all before all which is the source of both our torment and our grandeur.*"[10] Furthermore, there was a certain optimism in despair, "the optimism of the man who has nothing, who knows he has no rights and nothing coming to him."[11] In the same way, Kierkegaard celebrated what he viewed as the inherent tragedy of action: "Tragic action always contains an element of suffering, and tragic suffering an element of action; the esthetic lies in their relativity."[12] The founders of Ekin thus inherited a dual heritage of the notion of heroic suffering, from both Arana and from existentialist thought.

From Kierkegaard, moreover, there was even an explanation for the connection between the new generation of Basque nationalists and their parents who had lost the war, via the existential concept of guilt: "the element of guilt that remains is not subjectively reflected, and this makes the sorrow profound. In other words, tragic guilt is more than just subjective guilt–it is hereditary guilt; but hereditary guilt, like hereditary sin, is a substantial category, and it is precisely this substantiality that makes the sorrow more profound."[13] Thus, existentialism could provide both an explanation of the frustration experienced by the new generation of Basque nationalists and a means by which this frustration or anguish could be tempered through action–through *ekin* and hence through Ekin.

There remained the need for an exact definition of strategy for the group, however, and once more, existential thought provided a clue to how this might be formulated. Following the historical legacy of both Nietzsche and Arana, the answer to how this strategy might be defined was to be found in the concept of will. According to Sartre, "man cannot will unless he has first understood that he can count on nothing but himself: that he is alone, left alone on earth in the middle of his infinite responsibilities, with neither help nor succor, with no other goal but the one he will set for himself, with no other destiny but the one he will forge on this earth."[14] Such words would seem to bear out the argument of former Ekin members that from the outset, they conceived of their group as autonomous and independent from the other wings of the Basque nationalist movement.[15]

Furthermore, as to the strategy that Ekin (and later ETA) adopted, there is an intellectual point at which certain elements of Basque culture and existential thought meet: in negation and Oteiza's concept of the deoccupation of space, which I will discuss in more detail later. For the existentialist Gabriel Marcel, "having is more often apt to reduce itself to the fact of containing. But . . . the containing itself cannot be defined in purely spatial terms. It seems to me always to imply the idea of potentiality. To contain is to enclose; but to enclose is to prevent, to resist, and to oppose the tendency of the content towards spreading, spilling out, and escaping."[16] The members of Ekin sought to will a *spilling out* of the container (Spanish rule or occupation), the deoccupation of that containment, thus breaking their perceived political and cultural enclosure. And this would be achieved through the denial or negation of that enclosure. "It is essential to note," Marcel argued, "that autonomy is above all the negation of heteronomy presupposed and rejected."[17] And further, as Sartre maintained, such denial, negation, and rejection was intimately involved with the founding theme of Ekin (and with Arana's original vision of Basque nationalism), heroic action: "Heroism, greatness, generosity, abnegation; I agree that there is nothing better and that in the end they are what make sense out of human action."[18]

Such words might be interpreted as epigraphs inscribed at ETA's creation, involving a curious mixture of Arana's original founding myths established in the late nineteenth century linked through time to the post–World War II European existential movement. The words also imply a dialectical relationship between nationalism and existentialism that sought to resolve the problem of individual and group identity. And this dialectic formed a constituent part of Ekin's new vision of Basque nationalism, a vision that reproduced the ethos of Arana's original conceptualization whereby heroic individual experience established identity through action.

Marc Légasse: An Existential Basque Anarchist Nationalist

"La politique, c'est du caca remué par des gens sans nez"—"Politics is shit stirred up by people without noses."[19] Marc Légasse's use of the absurd, ironic, and provocative meant that he would never truly be accepted as an intellectual of Basque nationalism.[20] Yet within his early work, dating from the mid and late 1940s, there emerged a remarkable vision of Basque nationalism that managed both to capture a timeless homage to Basque culture and history and to chart a truly revolutionary course that nationalism might potentially have taken. Légasse, however, remained distanced both in time (although only just so) and space from the young men who formed Ekin, with whom he otherwise had much in common. At the same time, the conservative Basque nationalist movement in France offered him little hope of advancing his ideas within its official framework. It is therefore problematic to discuss Légasse in direct connection to Ekin. However, his early work is highly prescient thematically, because it more or less directly points to the ideological underpinnings of Ekin.

Marc Légasse Celaya was born in Paris in 1918. His father, a wealthy French Basque shipbuilder from Donibane Lohizune (Saint-Jean-de-Luz) in Lapurdi (Labourd), had become president of the French shipbuilders association, and the family had thus relocated to the capital. His mother, a Spanish Basque from Errenteria in Gipuzkoa, came from a family with historical connections to the nationalist movement. As a young man, Légasse returned to his familial roots in the French Basque Country to take part in the work of the Spanish Civil War Relief Commission. The work involved helping with the reception of (mostly Basque) refugees from the conflict on the other side of the border, and it confirmed the young Légasse's commitment to the cause of Basque nationalism.

He took an early interest in the promotion of Basque culture and in 1942, together with other young French Basques such as Eugène Goyheneche, took part in the reestablishment of the cultural review *Aintzina*. Constrained by the confessional basis of the review, however, he established his own satirical magazine, *Hordago*, in 1944, which would remain in publication until 1978. After the liberation of France, he unsuccessfully ran for political office, and in one later campaign, he was imprisoned for the crime of "relative separatism" for encouraging Basques not to vote in a French election. It was during this period that he began to formulate his own vision of Basque nationalism, including a plan for a single Basque *département*. The plan was presented in the National Assembly by deputy Jean Etcheverry-Ainchart in 1945, but was rejected.[21]

Légasse's letter to the Basque president, José Antonio de Aguirre, in March 1946, was perhaps more reflective of the young French Basque's distance from the traditional policies of the PNV. In the letter, one can begin to see a reaction to the perceived inertia on the part of the dominant nationalist party. This was the same complaint that initially drew the members of Ekin together six years later.[22] Légasse complained in the letter that what he viewed as the truly authentic roots of Basque nationalism were being increasingly disregarded in the PNV's ideological evolution. He mentioned the imperialism of France among the Arab countries of North Africa and Arana's Larrazábal Address, which had called for the unity of all Basques, before concluding his protest:[23]

> In truth, Mr. president, I think that the reasons that you pushed the Basque Nationalist Party to adopt a hostile attitude toward us are quite other than those alleged and come in reality from a low and very sad spiritual and moral evolution. The party of Sabino, also ferociously separatist... has lost in growing up and... has forgotten a little, in ageing and working, of the very heart of its doctrine.[24]

For the first time since the war, the hegemonic party, and Aguirre in particular, had been criticized. It was an important event, although Légasse's distance from any real power within the nationalist movement meant that he would remain even more isolated thereafter. As a result of this isolation, he began to develop an independent form of Basque nationalism that blended an original conception of Arana's ideology with the new intellectual currents of thought sweeping France and Europe at the time. As a consequence, Légasse became what he termed an "existential Basque anarchist nationalist," thus quite clearly confirming his distance from the confessional Christian Democracy of the PNV.

In 1948, he published *Paroles d'un anarchiste basque* (Words of a Basque anarchist), a pamphlet that printed on its back cover a parody of the PNV's central slogan. Instead of the ubiquitous "Jaun goikua eta lege zarra," "God and the Old Laws," Légasse wrote "Jaun gabe eta lege'rik ez," "No God or Laws Either." Judged in the context of its time, this was a stunning indictment of the PNV, which was, after all, a party still spoken of in reverential terms for its conduct during the Civil War. Yet Légasse, in an early indication of his subsequent evolution to a more radical vision of Basque nationalism, had no qualms about printing such an attack.

The text itself, a rambling, often confusing, and at times nonsensical dissemination of Légasse's philosophy, nevertheless manages at times to allude to deeper concerns. Indeed, it raises questions that, with the benefit of hindsight, seem remarkably ahead of their time. And on more than one occasion, Légasse might be construed to be directly voicing the concerns of Ekin: "Even the Germans and the Japanese, several times over war criminals, have been accorded the right to form an independent nation," Légasse complained, "and Article I of the Declaration of the Rights of Man and of the Citizen says: '*Men* are born and live free and *equal* in law.' *Deduction*: Basques are not *men*."[25]

The root cause of the problem for Légasse (the anarchist) was the state, and Légasse (the nationalist) pointed in particular to the growth of the French and Spanish states as a historical development that denied Basques their independence. Part of the argument thus involved an attack on French and Spanish nationalism. In retrospect, this reference stands as apart from the Basque nationalist discourse of the time, a discourse that made no mention of statist nationalism. Thus, "French and Spanish nationalists, in wanting to Gallicize or Hispanicize the Basque Country, compelled the Basque to become nationalist in order to re-Basquize."[26] Légasse (the existentialist) later refined this argument so that "Spanish and French nationalists ... want to nationalize the Basque being."[27]

Therefore re-Basquization, argued Légasse (the existentialist), was concomitant with addressing the Basque cosmology itself. "Do the Basques exist?" he asked rhetorically. "Yes," he answered, they exist through their actions.[28] The question was a crucial one, for as Légasse argued, "an existential Basque will necessarily be a member of the political resistance in the face of the Latin spiritual and material occupation."[29] Here one can identify the beginnings of an ideology of resistance in the work of Légasse that, although resembling the later ideas of Ekin, has been overlooked by most observers, possibly due to its parody of Basque history, culture, and the nationalist movement itself.[30] "One must struggle to keep alive Basque culture and civilization," Légasse argued, in a resistance "through Basque existentialism to this [French cultural] evolution."[31] The underlying principle of this resistance, moreover, would be *negation*. In fact, negation of what was outside the Basque "being," according to Légasse, was *the* leitmotif of existential Basque nationalism.[32] There is, then, a unity between the power of negation in Basque culture, Arana's original conception of Basque nationalism as denying the Spanish the right to be in the Basque Country, and Légasse's use of existentialism to justify the importance of preserving Basqueness.

Many of the basic arguments used by Légasse tended to be framed in terms of parody. In one article, for example, he drew a parallel between the contraband industry and the spirit of Basque resistance to the encroachment of Spanish and French nationalism. "The Basque language," mused Légasse, "survives in contraband. It has no legal existence. It was, from two slopes of the border, struck by the hardest blow that could befall a language: It was struck by uselessness." However, the language, and indeed culture in general, "is transmitted from generation to generation, passed from one century to another century, *through contraband*."[33] However, while this might have been enough to resist or negate the pressure of French and Spanish culture, there remained, in Légasse's opinion, an ultimate irony: the failure of Kierkegaard's occasion to appear. In typically ironic fashion, he observed that "the greatest misfortune of the Basque people is not being situated in the Balkans. In fact, each war instigated by whatever Balkan tribe gives them the right to resort to slaughter."[34] Although parodic in style, the message was clear. Later, Légasse concluded that "if it is true that each soldier carries in his pouch his marshal's staff, it is yet more true that every Basque carries beneath his jacket [*chamar*] his anarchist's dynamite."[35]

Jorge Oteiza and the "Deoccupation" of Basque Space

Like Légasse, the Gipuzkoan sculptor Jorge Oteiza had no direct affiliation with the founding members of Ekin/ETA. However, this has not precluded one observer from labeling him the "spiritual mentor of ETA,"[36] and it is true that he was in contact with later ETA leaders.[37] Oteiza's life and work is interesting in relation to the atmosphere of the 1950s, for it was during that decade, in 1957, to be precise, that he relinquished a full-time devotion to sculpture in favor of the investigation of Basque culture. He subsequently began publishing philosophical works in the 1960s that, combining artistic, historical, and linguistic investigations, served to underpin much of the contemporary intellectual discourse of both Basque culture and nationalism.[38]

Jorge de Oteiza Embil was born in the Gipuzkoan town of Orio in 1908. His parents were hoteliers in Donostia–San Sebastián, Spanish-speaking, and reasonably wealthy. The young Oteiza was raised in a solid bourgeois atmosphere, unaware of his Basque cultural heritage. He left the Basque Country to study medicine in Madrid, although he gradually took to artistic endeavors, foregoing his medical studies and becoming a full-time artist. After winning several prizes for his art, he left Spain for Latin America in 1935. He would spend eleven years there, concentrating on sculpture as his primary cultural expression.[39] While in Latin America, and particularly after studying indigenous art forms, Oteiza underwent a profound personal change that was inspired by a new interest in Basque culture. On his return to the Basque Country in the late 1940s (and aware of the current trends in existential thought), he began searching for the differential quality that defined the Basques. This was not, however, what one might describe a political search. Oteiza was not involved in the politics of Basque nationalism, although, as Jesús Azcona observes, it is difficult in retrospect to separate his thought and work from the Basque nationalist movement.[40] According to Joseba Zulaika,

> Oteiza's aesthetic theories, interpretive speculations, and shamanic pathologies are not intended as "Basque" per se, nor are they elaborated for the sake of the Basque public.... His "Basque" interpretations provide primary content for discursive strategies that will openly and simultaneously adopt the most local and the most transnational of positions. Hence, there is contemporary relevance of Oteiza's oeuvre as the forerunner of present postmodern and postcolonial discourses.[41]

Oteiza's sculpture owed much to the impact of both Formalism and Constructivism. He conceived of art as a skeptical observer of society and emphasized the importance of parody. In particular, Oteiza was fascinated by concepts of space, and throughout the 1940s and 1950s, his work attempted to transform standard interpretations of the spatial imagination. He continued to gain prestige, designing a statue of Felipe IV for Donostia–San Sebastián and forming an artistic association of four Spanish abstract sculptors which traveled the country exhibiting its collective work.[42] In 1950, he won a Vatican-funded competition to design the sculpture for a new basilica in the holy town of Arantzazu (Aránzazu) in Gipuzkoa, and this project commanded his attention for much of the next decade. As a vanguard project, however, its construction ran into difficulties and was suspended by the Vatican after complaints by the local Franciscan monks.[43]

The Arantzazu project, in the opinion of one of its collaborators, reflected the cultural atmosphere of the Basque Country during the 1950s. Life for Basque artists during the decade was unlike that of their forebears. Consequently, they tended to concentrate less on traditional bucolic themes such as the peace and tranquility of the Basque countryside. Instead, they tended to rebel against overly harmonious artistic portrayals, taking instead Picasso's *Guernica* to be the most important work of art of the twentieth century. They also rebelled against what they saw as the PNV's archaic cultural policy, reflected in the "incredibly ugly" *batzokis*, the traditional PNV centers.[44] The construction of the Arantzazu basilica served, in effect, as both a cultural and a political statement for Oteiza as he drew closer to an all-embracing vision of Basque difference from Spanish culture. In 1957, he won the fourth biennial São Paolo International Prize for Sculpture, and two years later, after an exhibition in Washington, D.C., he officially retired from sculpting to concentrate on developing his philosophical inquiries into Basque culture and history.[45]

Crucial to Oteiza's subsequent philosophy was a spiritual revelation he experienced on Mount Aguiña upon encountering one of the many cromlechs, the stone circles that dot the Basque Country. Within the Paleolithic cromlech, Oteiza saw a circle encompassing a central and empty center. It was, in his opinion, a metaphor for the prehistoric and free Basque, whose ultimate expression was nothingness. Everything therefore should be reduced to zero to reflect the authentic Basque space, a philosophy that saw the Basque Country itself as a cromlech whose outer circle had been pierced and whose center was now occupied. Spanish culture, accordingly, had progressively occupied that space, and Oteiza viewed Basques as a defeated people, prevented from creative expression and in effect in a cultural death trance. Indo-European culture (as represented by Spain) had eaten away at the void and had spiritually colonized the Basque people. Consequently, the dual cultural layering of Basque history, with dominant and imperialist Spain triumphing over the defeated and subservient Basque Country, had caused the remnants of true Basque culture to develop inside this colonized Basque being. In order, then, to find once more the true essence of Basque culture, Oteiza believed, there would first have to be an existential questioning of the (Basque) self.[46]

According to Oteiza, the battle between life and death is a constant one, carved in both time and space. Theoretically, for Basque culture to win its battle for life, the space of time needs to be disassembled, thus creating a peaceful, balanced, and existentially isolated central void. Only that way would the nothing that was everything be attained.[47] Deoccupation was thus a cleansing or curing experience for Oteiza, leading to the empty and true Basque space.

While Oteiza's emergent theories were conceived of in abstract terms, the ideas he set forth resonated with importance for Basque nationalism, for his ideas demanded both negation (of Spanish cultural existence within the Basque Country) and action (to free the Basque Country from this occupation).[48] Further, as Zulaika argues, there was a bond between Oteiza's theories and Basque nationalism. In traditional Basque mythology, there existed the concept of a container or *aska* (also implying emptiness), forming part of words such as *seaska* (cradle), *arraska* (sink), and *aberaska* (honeycomb). The word *aske* (free) comes from the same root as *aska* and forms words such as *askatu* (to free, untie) and *askatasunez* (freely, spontaneously), and *askatasuna* (freedom). Freedom, in the political terms of Basque nationalism, thus bears an intimate association with Oteiza's deoccupation.[49] Finally, Zulaika contends,

> Oteiza provides a grand example of "strategic essentialism." He shamelessly exploited the subaltern condition of the Basques to compensate with art, mythology, and the linguistic imagination [what] history and politics had denied them. . . . In his writings Oteiza in fact devised a narrative plot in which aesthetic progression was inverse to historical progression. . . . This is also "The End of History" Basque style, or, in Oteiza's words: "I write backwards. I look forward, but I progress by regressing, by walking backwards."[50]

This appears to be the critical link between artistic theory and political reality in the work of Oteiza. Moreover, it is a theory that is central to the history of Basque nationalism and the original articulation of Arana's ideology. In Oteiza's opinion, Arana was noteworthy for awakening the Basque conscience and coordinating political thought with action: "Sabino . . . Saint Ignatius and Lope de Aguirre, are models of behavior of the first order within a typology of our behavior and great men."[51] Interestingly, Oteiza saw in Franco's demolition of the PNV headquarters, the Sabin Etxea (Sabino Arana's home in Bilbao) as a physical articulation of his theory. In his own words, "the very enemy had built, through a perfect spatial deoccupation, our sacred empty space, a cromlech–emptiness, the aesthetic perpetuation of the memory that it wanted to erase, in the monumental and commemorative character of our most remote and sacred tradition."[52] As with Légasse, parody was never far from Oteiza's mind, and he even concluded that "the only things that were any good in our [Basque] history were done by fools."[53]

Also like Légasse, Oteiza came to develop his theories only in the 1960s. However, given that he was the most charismatic and influential Basque artistic figure of the 1940s and 1950s,[54] there is a case for his inclusion as a seminal influence on the founders of ETA. His ideas and work, particularly those involving an existential questioning of the self, the parody of traditional forms, and deoccupation as a liberating principle, can be viewed as central to the nationalist project of Ekin during the 1950s. If art does indeed work with signs that are part of a greater semiotic system, then Oteiza's work must be viewed as an intimate expression of Basque nationalism.

The Direct Influences of Ekin

In addition to these indications of the broad cultural themes that were influential among Basque intellectuals in the 1950s and 1960s, a number of specific texts were influential in shaping the political ideas of the original founders of Ekin/ETA, according to the personal testimonies of those involved. While these texts have been cited in accounts of the rise of ETA, no analysis has been made of them in relation to the strategic or tactical influences they may have exerted on the organization. However, such analysis is crucial to understanding the transformation of Ekin into ETA in the 1950s.

The emergence of Ekin marked an evolutionary step within Basque nationalism. Just as the historical evolution of human consciousness incorporates more attention to the articulation and reflexivity of the self, distancing the individual from the communal structures in which each person is involved,[55] so Ekin emerged as a group intimately devoted to self-examination. Originally, Arana also devoted much time to introspective reflection, but the subsequent intellectual development of Basque nationalism owed more to a questioning of the communal ontology of the Basque people. With the emergence of Ekin, the ideology of Basque nationalism once more took an introspective turn.

This introspection took place through reading, and in the following examination of the works consulted, I ask some basic theoretical questions: What did the members of Ekin read? How did they make sense of what they read? What were the social and political effects of their experience of reading? What did the books mean for them?[56] As Robert Darnton observes, "reading has a history. It was not always and everywhere the same... information must be sifted, sorted, and interpreted. Interpretive schemes belong to cultural configurations, which have varied enormously over time... in different mental worlds.... It is an activity involving a peculiar relation–on the one hand the reader, on the other the text."[57] The following analysis is interpretative, and although "the interpretative act may be 'irrational' in the sense that it requires inspired guessing... it is 'rational' in the sense that our hypotheses must be able to withstand critical scrutiny."[58]

The young men of Ekin lived in a closed public society, and therefore the activity of reading, especially considering the subject matter that interested them, was a highly personal and secretive affair. They shared their thoughts in meetings, but the actual reading itself remained an intimate endeavor. Furthermore, they did not have the same access to books that previous generations of Basque nationalists had enjoyed. Of the four periods under consideration in the present study, the 1950s was the most restricted era in terms of access to written nationalist ideology, closely followed by the 1890s. Consider, for example, the difference during the Second Republic in the 1930s, when one can point to a boom in the publication of nationalist works.

Revolt and National Liberation: The Case of Israel

While the general precepts of existentialism served to provide a philosophical guideline for Ekin's belief in action, there were more specific examples that the group also employed. Just as Ireland had served as an example for the *aberrianos* of the early 1920s, the recent creation of Israel out of a bitter campaign of political violence aimed at an occupying force helped to inspire the young members of Ekin. According to two original members, José Mari Benito del Valle and José Manu Agirre, Ekin's security measures "were essentially an ... adaptation ... made from the experiences of the Jewish National Liberation Movement, 'Irgun,' headed at the time by the 'terrorist' Menachem Begin."[59]

Even a cursory reading of Begin's work *The Revolt* (1951) provides ample evidence of ETA's origins.[60] In particular, in the chapter entitled "We Fight, Therefore We Are," Begin stresses, with an almost primordial fervor, the importance of blood:

> Blood ... brought the revolt to life. The blood of our people cried out to us from the foreign soil on which it had been shed, fired revolt in our hearts and gave the rebels strength.... When we launched our revolt against the yoke of oppression and against the wanton shedding of Jewish blood we were convinced that our people truly had nothing to lose except the prospect of extermination. This was not a mere phrase or hyperbole. It was the truth; and it strengthened immeasurably the rebels' capacity for sacrifice. Capacity for sacrifice is the measure of revolt and the father of victory.... In short, in all history there is no greater force than the readiness for self-sacrifice, just as there is no greater love than the love of freedom. The soil of their country and the blood of their murdered people infused the Hebrew rebels with both that force and that love.[61]

This rich imagery, highly resonant of Arana's discourse, is worth some consideration. For Begin, the shedding of blood stood as a testament to the worth of his cause. Furthermore, in an echo of Sartre's optimism of "the man who has nothing," there was "nothing to lose" when faced with extermination. The capacity for self-sacrifice, in the opinion of the Irgun leader, underpinned the success of any revolt, as did the mixture of "force" and "love" in the struggle for freedom. These powerful words must have had affected the nascent ideology of Ekin. Once again, there seems an accommodation of sorts, philosophically speaking, between Aranist dogma, existentialism, and what might be considered as

Begin's political theory. Furthermore, Begin looked favorably on thought as an activity intimately linked to action,[62] thereby justifying even Ekin's own creation.

The Historical Discourse of Basque Nationalism

As mentioned in the previous chapter, part of Ekin's initial intellectual formation involved reading whatever books survived Franco's purges concerning Basque history and culture. Txillardegi, Madariaga and Agirre recalled consulting, among others, the works of Hermilio Oloriz, Arturo Campión, Padre Bernadino de Estella, and Engracio de Aranzadi.[63]

In *La cuestión foral* (1894), Oloriz raised the foral issue as a problem between the individualism of Navarre and the centralizing tendencies of the Spanish liberal state. In his discourse, the *fueros* thus become a symbolic domain of Navarrese difference and individualism. It is easy to see how the young men of Ekin might have inferred from this that the Spanish state of the late nineteenth century had an interest in attacking Navarrese (and by definition Basque) uniqueness. Furthermore the language employed by Oloriz justifies, to some extent at least, a particularist reaction against the state. For example, in his opinion, the state's threat to withdraw the Navarrese *fueros* "was the tremendous awakening of a noble people," and "civic virtue had discovered a reservoir in the heart of the Navarrese, and everyone wanted to embrace with yearning the cross of sacrifice."[64] This sacrifice, Oloriz argued, might take the form of direct confrontation: "Our right is indisputable ... and if by force they strip us of what we legitimately possess, there should not be a single Navarrese ... who does not respond to our pure history. *Hunger and death*, before contributing to the loss of our venerable institutions!"[65] The tone of the book recalled his Carlist sympathies, but there were also obvious parallels to be drawn for the young Ekin members reading such works. In particular, the allusion to sacrifice, the "hunger and death" of Oloriz's argument, must have had a profound effect on those readers.

Arturo Campión remained one of the most important literary figures in the Basque Country. Although he wrote in Spanish, he displayed an acute sensitivity to the importance of Basque culture. "Basque individualism, in its most perfect phase, in its highest expression," Campión argued in 1901, "is a familial individualism, the respect, to put it that way, of the *social cell*. This individualism transcends, imparts character on the historical evolution of the people."[66] Campión's ideas would seem to suggest that the existential emphasis on intimate and individual contemplation could o take place only within the framework of the collectivity. That was, after all, the collectively created Basque essence or being that Ekin proposed both to create for themselves and to defend against encroachment from Spanishness.

Through the work of Padre Bernadino de Estella it would have been possible to read about Arana and the first steps of Basque nationalism. In *Historia vasca* (1931), Padre Estella spoke at length about Arana and the foundation of Basque nationalism: "Sabino de Arana-Goiri founded the Basque Nationalist Party ... whose social goal was to preserve, strengthen and resurrect all expressions of the Basque spirit. ... Basque nationalism has continually progressed in spite of ferocious resistance [from] the king, governments, liberals and conservatives, republicans and socialists, who have opposed it."[67] Were there any argument to be made for the oppressed, yet ultimately triumphant nature of Basque nationalism, here it was. Furthermore, through the reading of *Historia vasca*, the members of Ekin were able to appreciate the role that Arana played in the conceptualization of Basque nationalism.

Aranzadi had been a noteworthy colleague of Arana's, and his *La nación vasca* (1931) was quite possibly the most openly nationalist published discourse that the Ekin group was able to read in the early 1950s. Within its pages, there were a number of both philosophical and tactical ideas that Ekin would employ. For example, Aranzadi anticipated much of existentialism's contribution to the cause of Basque nationalism by stating that "the basic nationalist idea is national existence." And this existence could be safeguarded only by Basque nationalism: "freedom can be death, and nationalism is first of all, above all else and in every way, the life of the national character."[68] An attack on this national character, in Aranzadi's opinion, could constitute an attack on the very existence of the Basque people. "There is no legislative power, however rudimentary, that does not exact from its subjects the contribution of money [and] the costliest contribution of blood. Living and defending oneself; that is where the state begins . . . the universality with which the duty of defending one's own territory by arms was extended [has been] an honorable, permanent, and just custom since antiquity."[69] Action, then, to any member of Ekin reading Aranzadi, might come to imply the force of arms, especially when framed in defensive terms.

Ekin and the Cultural Atmosphere of the 1950s

There were a number of tributary ideas flowing into the ideological stream that emerged among the founders of ETA. It is impossible to say with certainty that ETA was the product more of external than internal influences. Rather the creation of ETA represented both a culmination of Basque nationalist historical development and the specific circumstances of postwar Basque society. What is of particular interest, however, is the relative ease with which so modern a form of thought as existentialism was adapted to traditional Basque cultural and political ideas.[70]

Only hindsight affords us the luxury of examining figures such as Légasse and Oteiza in relation to the emergence of ETA. However, there is good reason to examine their ideas. For whatever the immediate consequences (or lack thereof) of their thoughts and deeds, there is a sense in which their ideas serve to generalize the atmosphere of the late 1940s and 1950s beyond the factional clandestine politics in which Ekin emerged and developed. I have attempted to place the emergence of ETA in a specific historical context. Ideas of armed resistance, however symbolic or purely theoretical, were never very far from the Basque nationalist conscience. However, in the work of Légasse and Oteiza, there emerged the most specific philosophical or cultural justification for such action. If this was, indeed, the case, then their ideas should not be taken lightly, for cultural representations are perhaps more important to the discourse of Basque nationalism than formal political strategy.

There were a number of ways in which the young nationalists made sense of what they read in the 1950s. At root, one might say that they read existentialism as almost a personal explanation of their own individual experiences. When this explanation extended to a communal basis through the formation of the group, a significant change had taken place in Basque nationalism. Even more than the *aberrianos* in the 1920s or the members of Jagi Jagi in the 1930s, Ekin emerged from a confluence of individual thought and action. This was represented in the different perspectives between, for example, the cerebral Txillardegi and the more dogmatic Madariaga.

A number of themes united traditional Basque nationalist ideology as envisaged by Arana and the founders of ETA: anguish, negation, action, and sacrifice, for example. Even religion had its place, although this would probably have been denied at the time. Indeed, for Alfonso Pérez-Agote, "religion permeated the ideological configuration of the new nationalist generations and of ETA in particular."[71] A link between all these themes is a tragic vision of Basque destiny that, in the context of the 1950s under a dictatorship attempting to erase many facets of Basque culture, took on a form that went beyond Arana's symbolic violence. Although I would emphasize that, at its creation, ETA remained a group that was only theoretically dedicated to an armed struggle, and in many ways it was much more concerned with intellectual and cultural questions relating to its political agenda.[72]

During the 1940s and 1950s, there was a systematic attempt by the Franco regime to erase Basque culture. Such cultural forms were, by official implication, seen to be inferior, antiquated, and even weak (the latter being somewhat ironic, given that both Basque and non-Basque observers often tended to highlight the culture's emphasis on brute strength). The state effectively constructed a system of social relations based on a specific vision of hierarchy, with Basque culture firmly rooted in the lower reaches of this pecking order.[73] However, as a general means of control, the state fostered a symbolically violent perpetual threat against Basque culture, and as Beate Krais observes, "symbolic violence is a subtle, euphemized, invisible mode of domination that prevents domination from being recognized as such and, therefore, as misrecognized domination, is socially recognized."[74] As a response, "the very term *Basque* became synonymous with resistance and, what was worse for the regime, opposition to the unity of the Spanish nation and state. The Basque cultural self-affirmation was transformed automatically into the work of an enemy essential to destroy ... the sacred, indivisible unity of one, great and free Spain, as was the standard shout after singing the Spanish national anthem."[75]

However, there is also evidence to believe that with a certain degree of complicity from the Civil War generation of Basque society, there was an atmosphere of resigned defeat in the Basque Country during the early 1950s. To the young members of Ekin, this represented the slow death of the Basque essence, and as a result, they sought to maintain or even to re-create this essence through their own (initially individual) endeavors.[76] It was, in their opinion (the product of their reading) a life-or-death struggle for existence. Indeed, as Zulaika argues, "the agonic perception of the imminent death of the Basque language, the demise of the very 'document' that grants history and identity to the Basques, is a fundamental factor justifying the decision by . . . ETA to promote the use of violence."[77] Furthermore, because these young men were aware of their own inferior physical and numerical strength, there was from the outset a tragic dimension to their struggle.[78]

CONCLUSION

Past Imperfect: The Historical and Cultural Dimensions of Basque Political Violence before ETA

As the work of (among others) Ernest Gellner and Eric Hobsbawm has demonstrated, there is little substance to any purely national claims, whether of the state or stateless variety.[1] Distinct peoples or cultures may exist, but they do not exist in either temporal or spatial isolation, and if there is an explanation for the political conflict in the Basque Country, it has derived probably from a mirrorlike insistence on maintaining a false sense of purity–on the part of all sides.[2] In fact, the preceding narrative, while focused on the Basque Country, has invariably had to incorporate into its plot people, events, and ideas from Europe, Africa, the Middle East, Asia, and the Americas.

"Cultural representations do not simply come after the event," Luke Gibbons observes, "'reflecting' experience or embellishing it with aesthetic form, but significantly alter and shape the ways we make sense of our lives."[3] Like nationalist movements elsewhere, the Basque case has historically appropriated a variety of cultural forms to sustain its momentum. Indeed, Basque nationalism has consistently used both culture and history to sustain its struggle against the Spanish state–and vice versa. At the core of this competition is the issue of cultural identity, or more specifically, a cultural identity for Basque nationalism. Historically, this has been the site of a contest for authority, both between competing factions within Basque nationalism and between the wider forces of the Spanish state. The struggle for cultural authority has itself consistently involved competing claims for representation. Moreover, it has been marked by an ever-changing pattern of development, allowing Basque nationalism to assume a number of differing guises throughout its history.

I have argued here that, from the very inception of the movement itself, the fluid nature of Basque nationalist cultural identity has allowed for the emergence of a potential strategy of political violence. Indeed, it is this fluidity that underpins the relationship between Basque nationalism and political violence. Political violence is here viewed as a cultural form in itself, representing a strategy within the wider struggle for cultural authority. The present study has, accordingly, argued that struggle and warfare emerged as ideological, symbolic, and strategic representations within the historical discourse of Basque nationalism and that this led, at least in part, within certain sectors of the Basque nationalist movement, to the growing endorsement for the potential use of political violence, an endorsement that assumed a reality with the formation of ETA in 1959.[4]

I would stress two further points about the emergence of a culture of political violence within Basque nationalism. First, the contest for the exercise of cultural authority was historically not only one within the Basque nationalist movement, but also between Basque and Spanish nationalism. Indeed, Spanish nationalism did not retreat from its own particular use of state force (whether by a constitutional monarchy, a republic, or a dictatorship) in the cultural struggle. Ultimately, this has been a spatial dynamic involving the contest for control of a particular site, in this case, cultural authority within the Basque Country. Second, the emergence of a culture of political violence within Basque nationalism took place within the context of a profound social and economic transformation of the Basque Country. Thus, in a temporal dynamic, profound social change influenced the idea of political violence, and contemporary Basque history has been marked by what might be termed the crisis of modernity.

Finally, and with specific reference to the emergence of ETA in 1959, the creation of a group theoretically willing to employ an armed struggle parodied (in the true meaning of the word–to be discussed in more detail later) the Basque nationalism projected by the PNV. The PNV was originally conceived by Arana as the political manifestation of a Romantic rearguard action against both modernity in general and the Spanish state in particular. However, the subsequent ideology of the party emphasized its commitment to Christian Democracy. Therefore, the PNV worked within the state (whenever possible) and dedicated itself to accommodation, rather than to confrontation. In many respects, ETA represented a rearguard action similar to that of Arana, although it took on (what can be termed with hindsight) a postmodern, rather than a Romantic vision. There is a common ground–hostility to modernity–between the two, and this common ground came to form the thematic relationship between nationalism and political violence.

In order to comprehend the importance of culture as a site of political struggle, one need only read Louis L. Snyder's and Ian Gibson's comments about the Basques referred to in the Introduction.[5] Even when speaking of terrorists (a subjective category in its own right), using terminology such as "hot-headed," "wild," and "irrational" serves only to objectify not only the said terrorists but, by implication, both Basque nationalists and Basques in general. Interestingly, if one were to look for hot-headed extremists in Spain at the turn of the twentieth century, one might be more tempted to go to Barcelona than Bilbao. Thus, the work of Snyder and Gibson represents an exercise in cultural authority that confuses contemporary discussion about the political violence affecting the Basque Country.

The present study has attempted to normalize a topic (Basque political violence) that is usually viewed of as external to an (undefined) norm. The very complexity of the historical discourse of Basque nationalism challenges the vague conception of terrorism as something external to supposed normal cultural or even political behavior.[6] On the contrary, violence (as conceived through representations of struggle and warfare) has been a normal feature of the historical discourse of Basque nationalism. Indeed, according to Antonio Elorza, there is an even longer precedent: War occupied such a prominent role in Basque history that it actually came to configure both a mentality and ideology (translated later into nationalism) for the Basque Country.[7]

Attempts to address the issue of Basque political violence from a moral standpoint are similarly problematic, for the emergence and development of the modern liberal state is itself intimately involved with political violence.[8] According to Edward W. Said,

> Legitimacy and normativeness–for example, in recent discussions of "terrorism" and "fundamentalism"–have either given or denied narratives to forms of crisis. If you conceive of one type of political movement in Africa or Asia [or in the Basque Country] as being "terrorist" you deny it narrative consequence, whereas if you grant it normative status (as in Nicaragua or Afghanistan) you impose on it the legitimacy of a complete narrative. Thus *our* people have been denied freedom, and therefore they organize, arm themselves, and fight and get freedom; *their* people, on the other hand, are gratuitous, evil terrorists. Therefore narratives are either politically and ideologically permissible, or not.[9]

Similarly, for Craig Calhoun,

> much of what we now think of as the peaceful patriotism of the long-established and prototypically modern Western nations is . . . the result of earlier bloodier histories. The process of consolidating states and nations was far from automatic. It was historically conflict-ridden in the states we now think of as stable democracies, just as it is conflict-ridden in emerging states. What now seem settled, almost natural national identities are the results of symbolic struggles and both cultural and very material violence.[10]

There is, then, an arbitrary discourse involved in the moral judgment of Basque political violence, the difference, say, between justifying the killing of innocent people as regrettable casualties of war or as the more euphemistic "collateral damage" (the unfortunate consequence of valid military operations) while condemning killings perpetrated by terrorists as uniformly and seemingly innately evil.

Of course, war and terrorism are different. Traditionally, war has involved some kind of combat between opposing forces, whereas terrorism implies the negation of such combat. Yet the trend of contemporary warfare, as demonstrated through the twentieth century, with its growing emphasis on aerial bombardment and the concomitant rise in civilian casualties with each conflict, is that the category of innocence for victims of politically motivated violence is just as hard to establish legally as, for example, the notion of terrorism itself. In fact, "the attempt to transfer the notion of 'innocent civilians' from the international law of war to the study of terrorism has foundered on the realization that innocence is another relative, unstable property."[11]

The issue is one of cultural space and the power to control that space. The growth, not only of the Spanish state, but of the modern nation-state in general and its metropolitan-centered discourse, has marginalized certain cultural groups. The response of these groups to modernism's marginalization has sometimes invoked the idea of a life-or-death struggle. Yet this struggle is itself denied normal narrative status by the state (including its media and academic institutions) and therefore becomes a problem to be resolved. For those denied their narrative, however, it has been, throughout, a question of survival.

Typically, the issue of Spanish nationalism has been little covered by the historiography of contemporary Spain, although in recent years, several authors have begun to address the question. As is evident from the findings here, the Spanish state promoted a specific project of national integration from at least the era of the mid-nineteenth century onward. This policy of integration, at various moments, assumed its own violence (intensity or vehemence) in the sustained assault on all forms of culture that diverged from a unitary idea of what constituted Spain and Spanishness–what may be termed "cultural violence."[12] Cultural violence is often symbolic (the marginalization of a language, for example), but this does not detract from its power, because actual violence (physical force) need not occur for a motive, idea, or policy to be violent. In the words of Pierre Bourdieu,

> *intimidation*, a symbolic violence which is not aware of what it is (to the extent that it implies no *act of intimidation*) can only be exerted on a person predisposed . . . to feel it, whereas others will ignore it . . . the cause of the timidity lies in the relation between the situation or the intimidating person (who may deny any intimidating intention) and the person intimidated, or rather, between the social conditions of production of each of them.[13]

In both the 1890s and the 1950s (and indeed, at various times in between), such social conditions existed in the Basque Country. Similarly, during both periods, the state (with the compliance of many Basques themselves) vigorously promoted an official Spanish nationalist ideology that denied Basque identity. In part, Basque nationalism emerged as a response to this, and the resulting struggle assumed ontological proportions involving questions of survival and existence. Indeed, for Juan Sisinio Pérez Garzón, "it is precisely Spanish nationalism, rather than the other [Basque] variety, which in its most extreme form justified forty years of dictatorship and which, paradoxically, was the breeding ground from which ETA would emerge and find its own justification."[14]

It is important to note that the Spanish state-building project manifested itself in a variety of forms, from the nineteenth-century liberal-education values of the Institución Libre de Enseñanza to the Second Republic's Misiones Pedagógicas and Franco's "new state." All three regimes actively promoted a division within Spanish society whereby straying too far from an ascribed norm implied an inferior status. Thus, it is disingenuous to ascribe to Basque nationalism alone the creation of a we/they dichotomy, as Patxo Unzueta maintains.[15] The very emergence of a modern national project in Spain was, at root, based on such categorizations.

This is a crucial point to bear in mind when considering the continuing role of ETA in Spain after the death of Franco in 1975 and the implementation of a new constitutional monarchy. According to Goldie Shabad and Francisco José Llera Ramo, "the culture of [Basque] violence and its social underpinnings persisted well after their raison d'être had disappeared," and "it is fortuitous that separatist violence did not occur in other ethnically distinct regions of Spain, such as Catalonia and Galicia. Had it spread to other areas and not been confined primarily to the Basque Country, Spanish democracy might have been stillborn."[16] Such discourse involves an obvious narrative ploy to invoke a moral right and wrong. It ascribes to the Spanish constitutional monarchy a normative status that is denied the "separatist violence" of the Basque "ethnically distinct *region*."

Indeed, most contemporary observers question the validity of ETA's role in a democratic state.[17] Asking why the political violence continued after 1975, once its raison d'être (Franco) had disappeared, Pérez-Agote answers: "because of a prophecy, a false prophecy, that by determining the behavior of the actors becomes a true prophecy for the very actors who had formulated it," the prophecy being "*that nothing has changed with democracy*; and the actors continue to act as if nothing has changed."[18] Yet however misguided it may seem for many observers, there was a raison d'être for ETA's continued existence after 1975.[19]

As I hope to have demonstrated, ETA did not simply appear as a response to the Franco dictatorship, although this was a key factor. In fact, there were a number of other reasons why ETA emerged, including the historic trajectory of Basque nationalism itself, the historical role that Spanish states (both liberal and republican democracies, as well as the dictatorships) played in fomenting an exclusive Spanish nationalism, and broader external factors, including anticolonial armed struggles serving as frames of reference and even intellectual or philosophical trends. Thus, "the dichotomy of Spain versus the Basque country was not merely cultural but political, not merely organizational but conceptual,"[20] and this at least partly explains the continued existence of and support for ETA. In short, reducing critical observation of ETA to the status of violent terrorist organization as opposed to the normative status of peaceful democracies not only ignores the organization's deeper intellectual and ideological roots, but also leads one into the trap of defining the world and its actors into the easy categories of "democrats" and "terrorists," a reading that still seems to occupy a place in the contemporary postnational discourse on culture.[21]

Joxe Azurmendi addresses the same question, arguing that positing democracy as something external to or other than violence denies the violent birth of European democracy itself in the French Revolution.[22] This is confirmed by David Held's definition of the modern nation-state, a definition that, borrowing from Max Weber, partly rests on the state's control or monopoly of violence as the only legitimate violence,[23] and numerous examples exist of Western liberal democracies embracing this concept, both using and encouraging organized political violence, often against noncombatants.[24] Ultimately, such considerations seem to be more about what Joseba Zulaika and William A. Douglass term "the politics of labeling," where "minimally stable categorical constructs" (such as dividing the world into democrats and terrorists) actually do not serve as way to understand terrorism or the use of political violence, but rather establish a political hierarchy: "The label 'terrorist,' rather than referring to a type of person situated in a particular society's political space and cultural domains, exudes generic or universal overtones. To the extent that it acquires social and cultural specificity, it does so... within an implicit hierarchy of world cultures in which the definer of terrorism occupies the apex and Arabs, Basques, Irish, or Sri Lankans are subordinated."[25]

At the same time, one should not consider ETA in monolithic terms, whether from a supportive or critical perspective. Like other political actors, ETA possesses a history of its own that has seen the organization go through several transformations since its formation in 1959. For example, after significant ideological and tactical changes in the mid-1960s (transforming ETA into a revolutionary socialist organization whose prime focus was now to be an armed struggle), several original founders left the organization between 1967 and 1968.[26] Indeed, the *violent* history of ETA–that moment when it began to use the specific tactic of political violence that had theoretically existed as a possibility since its inception–really began in 1968.[27] Important changes did take place within the group, and according to Zulaika, for example, ETA's increasing "political obsolescence" after Franco's death in 1975 has rested more on its own inability to conceive of the Spanish state in anything other than hegemonic terms, while this hegemony has been increasingly tested by a number of developments both internal and external to the state itself, especially those moments that have drawn the country into an international context, such as membership in NATO and the European Union. While I remain skeptical that the modern nation-state is really disappearing (witness the lukewarm welcome the proposed European Constitution received in 2005),[28] I would concur that in post–Franco Spain, "terrorism, far from posing a real 'external' threat, in most cases is well within the internal parameters of the power it opposes and ends up being co-opted by it to advance its otherwise most unsavory plans."[29] Indeed, the sometimes "unsavory" nature of post–Franco Spain is, itself, another contributing factor to the continued existence of ETA after 1975.[30]

The dialectic of Spanish/Basque nationalism, I have argued, is an overlooked relationship. And yet it remains a historically salient point that both ideologies have struggled with each other for cultural hegemony within the Basque Country. This struggle has not only been between the Spanish state and the Basque Country, but between Basques themselves. Further, when such a struggle assumes ontological proportions relating to the language a people use and their everyday way of life, it cannot fail to involve the most powerful emotions that people are capable of feeling. In such a situation, faced with a struggle for survival, a rearguard defense of one's culture that may or may not involve the use of violence becomes the norm. Elorza argues that there has been a historical ideological construction in the Basque Country, from the nineteenth century onward, whereby Basque virtue is seen as defending order through war.[31] One might extend this idea to say that ETA emerged as the product of a long-term ideological construction posited in opposition to the nationalism of the Spanish state and as the short-term response to the attempted extermination of the Basque culture by Franco.

This ideological construction was sustained by a symbolic recourse to suffering and agony and played out against the temporal setting of a social crisis arising from the imposition of modernization.[32] The agony of Basque nationalism and the symbolic recourse to suffering within its ideology drew momentum from defeat and persecution, whether imagined or real. Arana saw Loyola as the first martyr to the cause of Basque nationalism, and Arana himself was subsequently seen as the twentieth-century fallen hero of the cause. In the aftermath of the Civil War, Gernika became the new martyr of Basque nationalism. And yet Ekin attempted to break this cycle of ingrained suffering, principally through a recourse to the existential search for harmony between individual and group identity.[33]

Arana's ideology was framed as not only a response to the nationalism of the Spanish state, but also as a response to the modernizing project itself, for modernity was an ideology that denied both tradition and history,[34] and he sought to fight its consequences. According to his conceptual framework, encompassing, for example, the precise definitions of right and wrong taken from Loyola, an idea of struggle and warfare came to symbolize an attack on ambiguity. Warfare, however mythically portrayed, came to serve as an ideal affirmation of certainty in an uncertain world. At the same time, this ideology of struggle also called into question the morality of the modern, rational world and provided a new moral order based on the virtue of battle.[35] In this sense, it almost came to encompass a symbolic ideology of creation.[36]

The temporal context of modernity, its rise and fall, serves to frame the development of Basque nationalism itself from Arana to ETA. Yet it is also simplistic to view ETA as merely the rebirth of primitive Aranism,[37] for the very discourse of Ekin/ETA revealed that it was firmly rooted in the crisis-ridden modern world. If anything, the founding members of ETA were seeking to break free of the constraints of modernity while at the same time preserving the traditional cultural elements that they viewed as paramount to rooting their identity.[38] The close links between the existentialist movement sweeping Europe in the 1940s and 1950s and the emergence of Ekin as a cultural defense mechanism represent an essentialist search to resolve the problem of individual and group identity. At this point, the whole question of political violence in Basque nationalism assumed another dimension, one more reflective of nationalism and its inherent complexity.

Indeed, as I have suggested, ETA emerged as a parody of Basque nationalism in general and the PNV in particular. Parody is a subject's "imitative reference" to an object, entailing an implied critique of that object.[39] It is different from satire, for example, in being *next to* or *involved in* ("para" can mean both "against" and "beside") the object of its criticism. "Parody, then," argues Linda Hutcheon, "in its ironic 'trans-contextualization' and inversion, is repetition with a difference."[40] That critical and ironic difference, combined with an inevitable involvement in the very of its critique, gives parody a quality of self-reflection that is remarkably close to that experienced by the founders of Ekin in the 1950s.

There is a sense, moreover, that Ekin/ETA emerged as a parody of Basque nationalist discourse itself. The PNV, which had been formed in reaction to the rampant modernization overcoming the Basque Country, gradually became a part of that modernity.

For example, through the adoption of Christian Democracy in the post–World War II era, it transformed itself into an elitist and remote party, moving away from its original formation as a cross-class nationalist community, and its main exiled leadership became increasingly blind to a changing society in the Basque Country in the aftermath of the Civil War. However, Ekin/ETA was still involved in the nationalist community.[41] Ekin thus represented an attempt to go beyond modernity into a more pluralistic and ironic discourse that, through parody, recalled Arana's emphasis on the power of renewal.[42] Ekin utilized both traditional Basque nationalist ideas and contemporaneous global political and philosophical trends in the creation of its discourse, marking an attempt to renew Basque nationalism through a combination of old and new values. It was parodic in that it still represented Basque nationalism, although it was a discourse radically altered in certain of its forms–both a critique and an affirmation of the Basque nationalist project.

As Kepa Aulestia contends, violence has been an ever-present factor in the development of Basque nationalism.[43] However, he fails to note that violence has been germane to both the Spanish state-building process and modernization in general. Therefore, in the we/they dichotomy, a nationalist strategy used to justify particular forms of violence, it is not only radical Basque nationalism that has perpetuated the spiral, but the Spanish state itself. Furthermore, the relationship between Basque nationalism and political violence should not be marginalized as something morally deviant from an ill-defined norm. In a critique of a report on Basque political violence, it is argued that the report's authors' "fundamental assumption about Basque violence is that it *is* terrorism and therefore belongs to a particularly heinous category of behavior. Once established, it is the paradigm itself that defines the Basque problem. ETA *is* IRA *is* Baader-Meinhof *is* Brigata Rossa *is*. . . ."[44] The present study has sought to understand how and why violence specifically entered Basque nationalist mythology and ideology. Historically, there is a close relationship between the two, but this does not necessarily imply that Basque nationalism is naturally violent. If anything, an ironic underlying theme of the present study has been to imply the reverse: that the violence that did enter Basque nationalist discourse has been very precisely justified and defined according to certain moral codes. In contrast, violence elsewhere throughout the history of the modern Spanish state was either a random expression of social discontent (in fin-de-siècle Barcelona, for example) or reflective of the state-building project itself, and, in the guise of the Franco state at least, it was violence without any recourse to such moral concerns.[45]

This is reflective of a more general argument calling for historical investigation to overcome cultural marginalization and in favor of a stereotype-free discourse that seeks to place traditionally objectified subjects at the center of their own world. In this way, future studies of Basque nationalism and political violence will incorporate the idea that there is a precise historical and cultural dimension to the relationship between the two.

Notes

Notes, Introduction

1. Raymond Williams, "Culture is Ordinary," in *Resources of Hope: Culture, Democracy, Socialism*, ed. Robin Gable, with an introduction by Robin Blackburn (London: Verso, 1989), 3–18.

2. Richard English, *Armed Struggle: The History of the IRA* (London: Pan Books, 2003), 338. English says that he is "not really persuaded by the IRA's argument that their violence was necessary or beneficial," but neither is he satisfied "with a description of the IRA which casually or myopically condemns them" (384).

3. Joseba Zulaika, "Anthropologists, Artists, Terrorists: The Basque Holiday from History," *Journal of Spanish Cultural Studies* 4, no. 2 (2003): 139.

4. "The creation of modern states–and the wars and other struggles between them–both transform the way ethnicity figure's in people's lives and helps determine which pre-existing cultures or ethnic groups will flourish as nations and which will fail to define politically significant identities. Such states not only shaped national identity domestically, they organized the world of interstate relations in which nationalist aspirations flourished among stateless peoples." Craig Calhoun, *Nationalism* (Buckingham: Open University Press, 1997), 66.

5. The literature on nationalism is, as readers will appreciate, vast. Among others, the work of Elie Kedourie, *Nationalism* (London: Hutchinson, 1960); Ernest Gellner, *Nations and Nationalism* (Ithaca, NY: Cornell University Press, 1983); and Eric J. Hobsbawm, *Nations and Nationalism since 1780: Programme, Myth, Reality* (Cambridge: Cambridge University Press, 1990) established the modern credentials of nationalism as an instrumental, constructed phenomenon or process in which human agency was taken to be central to developing the idea of the nation. In contrast, Anthony D. Smith's work emphasized that successful nationalist movements did not emerge in a historical or cultural vacuum and that in prenational formations he labeled *ethnie* there might be some foundation to later modern nationalist claims. See, for example, *The Ethnic Origins of Nations* (Oxford: Blackwell, 1986) and *National Identity* (London: Penguin, 1991; rpt. Reno: University of Nevada Press, 1993). Benedict Anderson's *Imagined Communities: Reflections on the Origin and Spread of Nationalism*, rev. ed. (London: Verso, 1991), while grounding its analysis in the aforementioned instrumentalist or modern view of nationalism, also recognizes that successful nationalist mobilization requires generating a shared, albeit illusory or imagined, experience and that this was greatly aided by cultural means such as the power of discourse (and especially the written word) through a national language. In *Ethnonationalism: The Quest for Understanding* (Princeton, NJ: Princeton University Press, 1994), Walker Connor argues that the dominant literature on nationalism has tended to misinterpret the emotional pull of national feeling and questions the extent to which one can apply a purely rational analysis to the subject. Here, I acknowledge all the above in influencing the work that follows.

6. Louis L. Snyder, "Plurinational Spain: Basque and Catalan Separatism," in *Global Mini-Nationalisms: Autonomy or Independence* (Westport, CT: Greenwood Press, 1982), 101–2.

7. Ibid., 104–5.

8. English, *Armed Struggle*, 376.

9. Snyder bases his linguistic evaluation of Basque on the opinion of Paul Dickson, a "magazine writer based in Washington, D.C.," who wrote a travel article about the Basque Country in the late 1960s. See Paul Dickson, "The Separate Land," *Saturday Review* (September 7, 1968), 50–51.

10. Bill Bryson, *Mother Tongue: The English Language* (London: Hamish Hamilton, 1990; rpt., Harmondsworth, England: Penguin, 1991), 108 (page citations are to the reprint edition).

11. Ian Gibson, *Fire in the Blood: The New Spain* (London: Faber and Faber, 1992), xiv. I cite the same example in the introduction to my own *Modern Basque History: Eighteenth Century to the Present* (Reno: Center for Basque Studies, University of Nevada, Reno, 2003).

12. Ibid., 131.

13. Ibid., 133.

14. Ibid., 133, 135, 140.

15. From the Latin *negotium*, *discursus*, and *referendus* and the Greek *politikos*, respectively.

16. According to the linguist R. L. Trask, "the number of native Basque words (by which term I mean those lexical items which were certainly or probably in the language before the arrival of the Romans in the Basque Country) are now probably outnumbered in ordinary speech by words of Latin or Romance origin, though not by a large margin. Two thousand years of intense contact with Latin and Romance have had a profound effect on the Basque lexicon, though not so profound as to have obliterated its distinctively non-Romance (and non-Indo-European) character." See *The History of Basque* (London: Routledge, 1997), 249.

17. "There can be few parts of the world about which so many wild and inaccurate statements have been made and so much irresponsible and unauthoritative literature has been written, as that region of South-west France and North-west Spain which is inhabited by the Basques." Although written in 1930, incidentally by another foreign observer, these words resonate with significance in relation to Ian Gibson's portrayal of the Basque Country. See Rodney Gallop, *A Book of the Basques* (London: Macmillan, 1930; rpt., Reno: University of Nevada Press, 1970), xi (page citations are to the reprint edition).

18. Originally founded in West Germany in 1965 by a group of German, Italian, and Spanish Fascists, the Spanish Circle of Friends of Europe (Círculo Español de Amigos de Europa, CEDADE) established its headquarters in Barcelona in 1966. In 1973, a branch was opened in Madrid, and between them, the two cities account for just under half of the organization's twenty-five hundred members in Spain. From its center in Barcelona, CEDADE espouses an ideology of European unity based on racial grounds and promotes a virulent form of anti-Semitism. It publishes Nazi literature and music cassettes and is actively involved in professionally directed propaganda campaigns in both Spain and the rest of Europe. It might even be the case that CEDADE is the coordinating and documentation center for Europe's rising neo-Nazi movements. See Sheelagh Ellwood, "The Extreme Right in Spain: A Dying Species," in *The Far Right in Western and Eastern Europe*, eds. Luciano Cheles, Ronnie Ferguson, and Michalina Vaughan (London: Longman, 1995), 97–98 and 103–4.

19. "In 1936, in preparation for the Summer Olympic Games [in Berlin] ... Gypsies were being cleared from [the] streets [by the Nazis] as an eyesore, because visitors had to be 'spared the sight of the Gypsy disgrace', just as they were at the 1992 Summer Olympic Games in Barcelona. Just before the Berlin games, 600 Gypsies were forcibly detained in a cemetery and next to a sewage dump at Marzahn ... in Spain fifty-six years later, they were placed in the Campo de la Bota outside of the city." Ian Hancock, "Responses to the Porrajmos: The Romani Holocaust," in *Is the Holocaust Unique? Perspectives on Comparative Genocide*, ed. Alan S. Rosenbaum (Boulder, CO: Westview Press, 1996), 53.

20. I am reminded here of the notion of "moral panic," developed by Stuart Hall and his colleagues: "When the official reaction to a person, groups of persons or series of events is *out of all proportion* to the actual threat offered, when 'experts', in the form of police chiefs, the judiciary, politicians and editors, *perceive* the threat in all but identical terms, and appear to talk 'with one voice' of rates, diagnoses, prognoses and solutions, when the media representations universally stress 'sudden and dramatic' increases (in numbers involved or events) and 'novelty' above and beyond that which a sober, realistic appraisal could sustain, then we believe it is appropriate to speak of the beginnings of a *moral panic*." Stuart Hall et al., *Policing the Crisis: Mugging, the State, and Law and Order* (New York: Holmes & Meier, 1978), quoted by Houston A. Baker, Jr., foreword, in Paul Gilroy, *"There Ain't No Black in the Union Jack": The Cultural Politics of Race and Nation* (Chicago: University of Chicago Press, 1991), 3. Such moral panic is fomented by magnifying the transgression of the perceived perpetrators, so, for example, in 1970s Britain, politicians, the press, and others linked levels of rising crime and British industrial decline to immigration, drugs, and so on. For an example of "moral panic" writing about the Basque Country, see Barry Came, "The Taverna Terrorists: Basque Militants Target a Stunning New Museum," *Macleans* 110, no. 43 (October 27, 1997), in which the author talks of "the Basques' propensity for violence" (29) and describes the world of radical nationalist bars, where young militants listen to "deafening music," some of it in Euskara, "the mysterious language of the Basques" (28).

21. Jean-Paul Sartre, in *Enbata*, no. 236, December 30, 1971, quoted in Jean-Paul Sartre, *The Writings of Jean-Paul Sartre*, vol. 1, *A Bibliographical Life*, compiled by Michel Contat and Michel Rybalka, trans. Richard M. McCleary (Evanston, IL: Northwestern University Press, 1974), 572.

22. See Dick Hebdige, *Subculture: The Meaning of Style* (London: Methuen, 1979), 2–3.

23. See Joseba Zulaika, *Basque Violence: Metaphor and Sacrament* (Reno: University of Nevada Press, 1988).

24. Luke Gibbons, *Transformations in Irish Culture* (Cork: Cork University Press, 1996), 17–18.

25. See Antonio Elorza, "Guerra y fueros en los orígenes del nacionalismo vasco," in *Gernika: 50 años después (1937–1987). Nacionalismo, República, Guerra Civil*, ed. Manuel Tuñón de Lara (San Sebastián: Servicio Editorial Universidad del País Vasco/Argitarapen Zerbitzua Euskal Herriko Unibertsitatea, 1987).

26. Bertrand Russell, "On the Relations of Universals and Particulars," in *The Problem of Universals*, ed. with an introduction by Charles Landesman (New York: Basic Books, 1971), 27.

27. See Carl Boggs, *Intellectuals and the Crisis of Modernity* (Albany, NY: State University of New York Press, 1993), 145–46.

28. With much caution, one might allude to a sense of the postmodern in the strand of contemporary Basque nationalism favoring direct action in its discourse. As Susan Parman argues, "post-modernism is like Romanticism–a reaction against the orderly promise of Reason–which itself will promote a new communal understanding of the underworld." *Dream and Culture: An Anthropological Study of the Western Intellectual Tradition* (New York: Praeger, 1991), 111.

29. Benjamin I. Schwartz, "Culture, Modernity, and Nationalism–Further Reflections," *Daedalus* 122, no. 3 (Summer 1993): 225.

30. For an appraisal of this dynamic in the late twentieth century and possible future trends, see Tom Nairn, "Breakwaters of 2000: From Ethnic to Civic Nationalism," *New Left Review*, no. 214 (November/December 1995): 91–103.

31. As Hebdige says in regard to his preferred semiotic approach: "the simple notion of reading as the revelation of a fixed number of concealed meanings is discarded in favour of the idea of *polysemy* whereby each text is seen to generate a potentially infinite range of meanings. Attention is consequently directed towards the point–or more precisely, that level–in any given text where the principle of meaning itself seems most in doubt. Such an approach lays less stress on the primacy of structure and system in language ('langue'), and more upon the *position* of the speaking subject in discourse ('parole'). It is concerned with the *process* of meaning-construction rather than with the final product." *Subculture*, 2–3.

32. Raymond Williams, *Marxism and Literature* (Oxford: Oxford University Press, 1977), 11.

33. Homi K. Bhabha, *The Location of Culture* (London: Routledge, 1994), 7.

34. "The *basic* identity of European culture remains sheltered from 'foreign' influence, for the terminology portrays non-European contributions as indulgences or deviations on the part of Europeans." Jan Nederveen Pieterse, "Unpacking the West: How European is Europe?" in *Racism, Modernity and Identity: On the Western Front*, eds. Ali Rattansi and Sallie Westwood (Cambridge: Polity Press, 1994), 142.

35. Ibid., 211.

36. Antonio Gramsci, *An Antonio Gramsci Reader: Selected Writings, 1916–1935*, ed. David Forgacs (New York: Schocken Books, 1988), 194.

37. See Stuart Hall, "Gramsci and Us," in *The Hard Road to Renewal: Thatcherism and the Crisis of the Left* (London: Verso, 1988), 161–68.

38. Tom Nairn, *The Break-Up of Britain: Crisis and Neo-Nationalism*, 2nd ed. (London: NLB, 1981), 132.

39. Calhoun, *Nationalism*, 103. As in Calhoun's work (see esp. ch. 4), most general overviews of nationalism now involve fairly detailed discussion of state nationalism. See, for example, David McCrone, *The Sociology of Nationalism: Tomorrow's Ancestors* (London: Routledge, 1998).

40. "Regional identity" is a problematic concept itself, of course. What exactly constitutes a "region"? What is the region "regional" to? Might Spain, for example, be considered and talked about as a region of Europe? It may well be that the term "region" has a validity that the term "nation" does not, although in any coherent argument, this must first be established. See, for example, the discussion of the German concept of *Heimatkunde* (literally, knowledge of home areas) by Anne Buttimer, "Edgar Kant and Balto-Skandia: *Heimatkunde* and Regional Identity," in *Geography and National Identity*, ed. David Hooson (Oxford: Blackwell, 1994), 161–83.

41. For an excellent introduction to the nationalist project of Franco, see section 13, "Cultural Nationalism," of *Spanish Cultural Studies: An Introduction*, ed. Helen Graham and Jo Labanyi (Oxford: Oxford University Press, 1995), 215–28.

42. In the index, one can find references to "Nationalism:" "decentralization and," "ideology of," "organizations," "theories of," as well as "Basque nationalism," "Bourgeois nationalism," "Catalan nationalism," "Peripheral nationalism," and "Republicanism." See Juan Díez Medrano, *Divided Nations: Class, Politics, and Nationalism in the Basque Country and Catalonia* (Ithaca: Cornell University Press, 1995), 235.

43. Christopher Schmidt-Nowara, "After 'Spain': A Dialogue with Josep M. Fradera on Spanish Colonial Historiography," in *After the Imperial Turn: Thinking With and Through the Nation*, ed. Antoinette Burton (Durham: Duke University Press, 2003), 166–67.

44. Stanley G. Payne, "Nacionalismo español, nacionalismo vasco," in *Aula de cultura del Correo Español–El Pueblo Vasco*, vol. 12, ed. José Manuel González, (Bilbao: El Correo Español-El Pueblo Vasco, 1994), p. 111. M. K. Flynn recollects that

"attempts at interpreting variants of Spanish nationalism within a comparative framework with at least some of the peripheral nationalisms was [sic] often met with, if not outright rejection, then extreme scepticism, if my research experience in the late 1980s and early 1990s is representative." See "Constructed Identities and Iberia," *Ethnic and Racial Studies* 24, no. 5 (September 2001): 707–8.

45. As is the case with the life and work of José Ortega y Gasset, analyzed by P. García Isasti, "Nazionalismo espainiarrari buruz zenbait ohar," in *II Euskal mundu-biltzarra/II Congreso mundial vasco*, sec. 2, *Euskal Herriaren historiari buruzko biltzarra/Congreso de historia de Euskal Herria*, vol. 2, *Aro moderno eta gaur egungoa/Edad moderna y contemporánea* (Vitoria-Gasteiz: Eusko Jaurlaritzaren Argitalpen-Zerbitzu Nagusia/Servicio Central de Publicaciones del Gobierno Vasco, 1988), 269–80; and Julian White's exploration of the efforts to promote Spanish 'national' music, in "The Musical Avant-garde: Modernity and Tradition," in *Spanish Cultural Studies: An Introduction*, ed. Graham and Labanyi, 79–81.

46. Spanish nationalism and identity formation in its various forms is discussed in Clare Mar-Molinero and Angel Smith, eds., *Nationalism and the Nation in the Iberian Peninsula: Competing and Conflicting Identities* (Oxford: Berg, 1996); Sebastian Balfour examines the connections between loss of empire and Spanish nationalism in *The End of the Spanish Empire, 1898–1923* (Oxford: Clarendon Press, 1997); Carolyn P. Boyd's thorough investigation, *Historia Patria: Politics, History and National Identity in Spain 1875–1975* (Princeton, NJ: Princeton University Press, 1997), documents the parallel development of Spanish historiography and nationalism; José Álvarez Junco's comprehensive *Mater dolorosa: La idea de España en el siglo XIX* (Madrid: Taurus, 2001) explores varieties of Spanish nationalism in the nineteenth century and is complemented by an English-language summary of the same ideas in his "The Formation of Spanish Identity and its Adaptation to the Age of Nations," *History and Memory* 14, nos. 1/2 (Fall 2002): 13–36; Juan Sisinio Pérez Garzón demonstrates how nationalism filtered through various ideological guises in modern Spain: "State Nationalism, Cultural Nationalism and Political Alternatives," *Journal of Spanish Cultural Studies* 4, no. 1 (2003): 47–64; like Balfour, Ángel G. Loureiro addresses the link between Spain's loss of empire and the emergence of Spanish nationalist thought in "Spanish Nationalism and the Loss of Empire," *Journal of Spanish Cultural Studies* 4, no. 1 (2003): 65–76; while Xosé-Manoel Núñez discusses the phenomenon in its most contemporary guise. See "What is Spanish Nationalism Today? From Legitimacy to Crisis to Unfulfilled Renovation (1975–2000)," *Ethnic and Racial Studies* 24, no. 5 (September 2001): 719–52.

47. Terry Eagleton, *Ideology: An Introduction* (London: Verso, 1991), 223.

48. George Rudé, "Ideology and Popular Protest," in *The Face of the Crowd: Studies in Revolution, Ideology and Popular Protest*, ed. and intro. Harvey J. Kaye (Atlantic Highlands, NJ: Humanities Press International, 1988), 197–98.

49. Ibid., 202.

50. Hall, "Gramsci and Us," 166.

51. The Carlist Wars of 1833–39 and 1873–76 were fought specifically over different claims to the Spanish throne, but had as a more general precept the struggle between the bourgeois liberalism of the modernizing Spanish state and the traditional system of regional and local rights. This traditional system, based on a series of charters known as the *fueros*, guaranteed a certain degree of decision-making authority to the Basque provinces. The ultimate failure of Carlism to retain the *fueros* had an undeniable effect on encouraging the emergence and course of Basque nationalism in the late nineteenth century.

52. Charles Townshend, *Terrorism: A Very Short Introduction* (Oxford: Oxford University Press, 2002), 15–16.

53. Ibid., 74. Townshend dedicates a chapter to the connection between nationalism and terror. There, he contends that nationalism has been a more powerful influence on the use of political violence than, for example, the broad revolutionary ideology of various left-wing groups, precisely because of its wider motivational qualities. See ibid., ch. 5.

Notes, Chapter One

1. José Ignacio Ruiz Olabuénaga, "Los vascos, ¿violentados o violentantes?" in *Violencia y política en Euskadi*, ed. Fernando Reinares (Bilbao: Desclée de Brouwer, 1984), 157.

2. Theodore Zeldin, *An Intimate History of Humanity* (London: Sinclair-Stevenson, 1994; rpt., London: Minerva, 1995), 14–15 (page citations are to the reprint edition). See also George Boas, "Warfare in the Cosmos," in *Violence and Aggression in the History of Ideas*, ed. Philip P. Wiener and John Fisher (New Brunswick, NJ: Rutgers University Press, 1974), 7; and James Chowning Davies, "Aggression, Violence, Revolution, and War," in *Handbook of Political Psychology*, ed. Jeanne N. Knutson (San Francisco: Jossey-Bass Publishers, 1973), 245–46.

3. See José Álvarez Junco, "The Formation of Spanish Identity and Its Adaptation to the Age of Nations," *History and Memory* 14, nos. 1/2 (Fall 2002): 19–20.

4. César Molinas and Leandro Prados de la Escosura argue that Spain's social and economic modernization was perfectly normal within the context of Mediterranean society. See "Was Spain Different? Spanish Historical Backwardness Revisited," *Explorations in Economic History* 26, no. 4 (October 1989): 385–402. The more traditionally held view, that Spain

(and particularly Castile) did not effectively solve the problem of mobilizing its resources, integrating the population, and providing sufficiently cheap and flexible transportation in the socioeconomic transformation that took place between the eighteenth and nineteenth centuries, is discussed by David R. Ringrose. See his *Transportation and Economic Stagnation in Spain, 1750–1850* (Durham, NC: Duke University Press, 1970).

5. This is anachronistically termed the "Reconquest." According to James T. Monroe, this noun was not officially recorded by the Real Academia de la Lengua Española until 1843, does not appear in any known medieval text, and was first used in the late eighteenth century–that is, during the first throes of a nascent Spanish nationalism–by Leandro Fernández de Moratín and Gaspar Melchor de Jovellanos to denote retroactively the period between the battle of Covadonga (722) and the fall of Granada (1492). See James T. Monroe, "Improvised Invective in Hispano-Arabic Poetry and Ibn Quzmān's 'Zajal 87' (When Blond Meets Blonde)," in *Voicing the Moment: Improvised Oral Poetry and Basque Tradition*, ed. Samuel G. Armistead and Joseba Zulaika (Reno: Center for Basque Studies, University of Nevada, Reno, 2005), 156 n. 16.

6. "It is difficult to exaggerate the importance of this religious allegiance, which almost superseded and replaced the political link (the fact of being subjects of the same king)." Álvarez Junco, "The Formation of Spanish Identity," 16.

7. For a clear and succinct account of the difficulty in accepting the idea of Spain as a unified polity before the modern period, see Josep R. Llobera, "A Comment on Hasting's *The Construction of Nationhood*," *Nations and Nationalism* 9, no. 1 (2003): 16.

8. Álvarez Junco, "The Formation of Spanish Identity," 14–15.

9. Eduardo Manzano Moreno and Juan Sisinio Pérez Garzón, "A Difficult Nation? History and Nationalism in Contemporary Spain," *History and Memory* 14, nos. 1–2 (Fall 2002): 259–60.

10. Pedro Gonzalez Blasco, "Modern Nationalism in Old Nations as a Consequence of Earlier State-Building: The Case of Basque Spain," in *Ethnicity and Nation-Building: Comparative, International, and Historical Perspectives*, ed. Wendell Bell and Walter E. Freeman (Beverly Hills: Sage Publications, 1974), 342; Stanley G. Payne, *Basque Nationalism* (Reno: University of Nevada Press, 1975), 1. The debate over different historical interpretations of the birth of Spain is nicely summarized by Simon Barton. See "The Roots of the National Question in Spain," in *The National Question in Europe in Historical Context*, ed. Mikulá? Teich and Roy Porter (Cambridge: Cambridge University Press, 1993), 107.

11. Enric Ucelay Da Cal, "The Nationalisms of the Periphery: Culture and Politics in the Construction of National Identity," in *Spanish Cultural Studies: An Introduction*, ed. Helen Graham and Jo Labanyi (Oxford: Oxford University Press, 1995), 33–34.

12. Ken Medhurst, "Basques and Basque Nationalism," in *National Separatism*, ed. Colin H. Williams (Vancouver: University of British Columbia Press, 1982), 236. For an appreciation of how these different sectors were intricately linked to one another, see Juan Javier Pescador, *The New World inside a Basque Village: The Oiartzun Valley and Its Atlantic Emigrants, 1550–1800* (Reno: University of Nevada Press, 2004).

13. Paul Gilroy, *The Black Atlantic: Modernity and Double Consciousness* (London: Verso, 1993).

14. "The kingdom of Navarre possessed, and was allowed to retain, its own customs, coinage, and institutions, including a Cortes [parliament] and a *Diputación* [provincial council]," imparting it a "semi-autonomous government" within the new political regime. J. H. Elliot, *Imperial Spain 1469-1716* (1963; Harmondsworth: Penguin, 1983), 141.

15. The *fueros* changed from agreements based on oral tradition to a written code between the eleventh and thirteenth centuries and reflected what would be a constant theme of subsequent Spanish history: the struggle between centralism and separatism. See Robert P. Clark, *The Basques: The Franco Years and Beyond* (Reno: University of Nevada Press, 1979), 18–21.

16. In their seminal work, *Amerikanuak: Basques in the New World* (Reno: University of Nevada Press, 1975), 63, William A. Douglass and Jon Bilbao offer a clear overview of this system, contending that "Basque loyalties to Castilla [Castile] were contingent upon the monarch's respect for local tradition and autonomy.... These *fueros* were not privileges or concessions conferred at the pleasure of the king; rather, they were based upon centuries-old Basque legal traditions." For an appreciation of these codified laws in the case of Bizkaia, see Gregorio Monreal Zia, *The Old Law of Bizkaia (1452): Introductory Study and Critical Edition*, trans. William A. Douglass and Linda White, preface William A. Douglass (Reno: Center for Basque Studies, University of Nevada, Reno, 2005).

17. Before the industrial revolution, migration within Spain was primarily directed eastward, toward the Levante and Catalonia. This left the Basque provinces (particularly rural areas of Bizkaia and Gipuzkoa) free from outside influence. As a consequence, a set of sui generis ethnographic values were reinforced in the rural Basque world. See Santiago Genovés, *La violencia en el País Vasco y en sus relaciones con España (No todo es política)* (Barcelona: Editorial Fontanella/Hogar del Libro, 1986), 56.

18. Ucelay Da Cal, "The Nationalisms of the Periphery," 33.

19. For example, in accordance with regional Basque autonomy, the economic border of the Spanish state was situated on the Ebro River, the southern limit of Basque territory. This meant that imported goods paid no duty on entering the

Basque provinces and that peasants could therefore buy at relatively low prices. In 1717, the king declared that all customs stations should be transferred from the Ebro to the Basque coast, which provoked a widespread protest and peasant uprising. The duty stations were quickly returned to the Ebro to avoid further social disruption. See Clark, *The Basques: The Franco Years and Beyond*, 22–23.

20. Javier Corcuera Atienza, *Orígenes, ideología y organización del nacionalismo vasco (1876-1904)* (Madrid: Siglo XXI, 1979), 34. The second edition of this work has been revised and translated into English. See Javier Corcuera Atienza, *The Origins, Ideology, and Organization of Basque Nationalism, 1876–1903*, trans. Albert Bork and Cameron J. Watson (Reno: Center for Basque Studies, University of Nevada, Reno, 2007).

21. Juan Sisinio Pérez Garzón, "State Nationalism, Cultural Nationalism and Political Alternatives," *Journal of Spanish Cultural Studies* 4, no. 1 (2003): 49.

22. Antonio Elorza, "Guerra y fueros en los orígenes del nacionalismo vasco," in *Gernika: 50 años después (1937–1987). Nacionalismo, República, Guerra Civil*, ed. Manuel Tuñón de Lara (San Sebastián: Servicio Editorial Universidad del País Vasco/Argitarapen Zerbitzua Euskal Herriko Unibertsitatea, 1987), 15–17.

23. Ucelay Da Cal, "The Nationalisms of the Periphery," 34.

24. Joseba Gabilondo, "Historical Memory, Neoliberal Spain, and the Latin American Postcolonial Ghost: On the Politics of Recognition, Apology, and Reparation in Contemporary Spanish Historiography," *Arizona Journal of Hispanic Cultural Studies* 7 (2003): 259.

25. The word *guerrilla* first emerged in 1812 to denote the small-scale insurrectionary units fighting the French. For a discussion of the nature of guerrilla warfare and the symbolic importance of the guerrilla in Navarre and beyond, see Francisco Miranda Rubio, "El guerrillero navarro y su transcendencia," *Príncipe de Viana*, no. 165 (January–April 1982): 439–64.

26. On Fernando's return to Spain in 1814, however, the *fueros* were reinstated.

27. According to José María Portillo, "the idea of local and territorial autonomy through the implementation of 'ayuntamientos' and 'diputaciones provinciales' was introduced in the Spanish constitution of 1812 following the suggestions of a Mexican deputy (Miguel Ramos Arizpe) inspired by the Basque foral institutions–Juntas generales and diputaciones." Unpublished manuscript, quoted in Gabilondo, "Historical Memory, Neoliberal Spain, and the Latin American Postcolonial Ghost," 264 n. 8.

28. Pérez Garzón, "State Nationalism, Cultural Nationalism and Political Alternatives," 50.

29. Ibid., 51.

30. Manzano Moreno and Pérez Garzón, "A Difficult Nation?" 260.

31. Xosé Estévez highlights the complex and multifaceted nature of the nineteenth-century Carlist conflicts. They were most obviously struggles between defenders of the *ancien régime* and proponents of new liberal values, while also clearly representing a dynastic dispute. However, they were also social and economic in nature, with a wealthy, educated elite confronting its poorer, illiterate compatriots, a division reflected also in the urban versus rural dimension of the conflicts. Finally, and perhaps most contentiously, one might even contend that there was a "national" element to these conflicts–that, to some extent, at least, many Carlist sympathizers (in the Basque provinces) were fighting to preserve a Basque traditional way of life against the potential creation of a modern Spanish state. See Xosé Estévez, *Historia de Euskal Herria*, vol. 2, *Del hierro al roble* (Tafalla: Txalaparta, 1996), 257–70.

32. Corcuera Atienza, *Orígenes, ideología y organización del nacionalismo vasco*, 38.

33. Renato Barahona, *Vizcaya on the Eve of Carlism: Politics and Society, 1800–1833* (Reno: University of Nevada Press, 1989), 98.

34. Payne, *Basque Nationalism*, 43.

35. Ibid., 44.

36. George Borrow, *The Bible in Spain: Or, the Journeys, Adventures, and Imprisonments of an Englishman in An Attempt to Circulate the Scriptures in The Peninsula* (1843; rpt., London: J. M. Dent; New York: E. P. Dutton, 1906), 341–42 (page citations are to the reprint edition).

37. See Edward W. Said, *Culture and Imperialism* (London: Chatto & Windus, 1993; rpt., London: Vintage, 1994), 118–19 (page citations are to the reprint edition).

38. Vincent Garmendia, *El carlismo* (Paris: Masson et Cie, 1975), 29.

39. Gerald Brenan, *The Spanish Labyrinth: An Account of the Social and Political Background of the Civil War* (Cambridge: At the University Press; New York: The Macmillan Company, 1943), 208; Raymond Carr, *Spain 1808–1975* (Oxford: Oxford University Press, 1980), 187.

40. Martin Blinkhorn, *Carlism and Crisis in Spain, 1931-1939* (Cambridge: Cambridge University Press, 1975), 28.

41. Mikel Urquijo Goitia, "Carlismo y guerra en el origen del nacionalismo vasco," *Muga*, no. 93 (September 1995), 40.

42. These changes, as Eduardo Jorge Glas notes, left the Basque provinces more exposed to the centralization policies of the Spanish government. See *Bilbao's Modern Business Elite* (Reno: University of Nevada Press, 1997), 27.

43. In 1846, there were 514 Guardia Civil posts with 7,135 men, rising to 2,179 posts with 19,105 men in 1898. Adrian Shubert, *A Social History of Modern Spain* (London: Unwin Hyman, 1990), 181.

44. Pérez Garzón, "State Nationalism, Cultural Nationalism and Political Alternatives," 55.

45. Known as the Ley Moyano, it was seen as a compromise between the competition of church and state and was, as such, born with inherent weaknesses, although it did actually survive until well into the twentieth century. See Carolyn P. Boyd, *Historia Patria: Politics, History, and National Identity in Spain, 1875–1975* (Princeton, NJ: Princeton University Press, 1997), 3–7.

46. Marianne Heiberg, *The Making of the Basque Nation* (Cambridge: Cambridge University Press, 1989), 47. Cf. Said's description of Britain's imperialist educational system in India, where "students were taught not only English literature but also the inherent superiority of the English race." *Culture and Imperialism*, 121.

47. "In 1868 the so-called 'Glorious Revolution', definitively introducing democratic principles into mainstream constitutional practice, fixed the institutional sense of Spanish nationalism and its associated imagery." Ucelay Da Cal, "The Nationalisms of the Periphery," 35.

48. "In 1868, with the fall of Isabel II's throne, there emerged in Spain, as in 1975 with the death of Franco, a transition toward a democratic regime which would be contested by not inconsiderable numbers in the Basque Country. In both cases, radical opponents of the [new] system refused to accept a democratic system as a framework for their own political platform. In both cases, [their] radical and messianic nature drove the battle to a harsh extreme. In these two experiences the civil confrontation had some severe consequences for the Basque Country [because] the radicals attempted to deny their extreme nature to those followers who defended their proposals by peaceful means." Urquijo Goitia, "Carlismo y guerra," 47.

49. Payne, *Basque Nationalism*, 54.

50. Manuel Tuñón de Lara, Julio Valdeón Baruque, and Antonio Domínguez Ortiz, *Historia de España* (Barcelona: Editorial Labor, 1991), 460–61, 475.

51. Vicente Palacio Atard, *La España del siglo XIX, 1808–1898 (Introducción a la España contemporánea)*, 2nd ed. (Madrid: Calpe, 1981), 517.

52. In 1854 Cánovas published a book entitled *Historia de la decadencia de España* in which he specifically spoke about the decline in fortunes of the Spanish race. José Luis Orella Unzue, *Nueva invención de la España plurinacional* (Gasteiz: Arabera, 2000), 95–96.

53. "The governor ... was not merely a provincial administrator but a party hack working for party ends in a régime of official candidates proposed by the government in power for the time being." Carr, *Spain 1808–1975*, 370–71.

54. For an excellent description of the system, see Brenan, *The Spanish Labyrinth*, pt. 1, ch. 1, esp., 5–9; see also Palacio Atard, *La España del siglo XIX*, 523–32.

55. Jaime Vicens Vives, *Approaches to the History of Spain*, trans. and ed. Joan Connelly Ullman (Berkeley: University of California Press, 1967), 136.

56. "In the Basque provinces and Navarre... independent small farmers and a well-organized village society maintained traditional rules of governance. Here Cánovas countered by appointing the most respected patriarchs he could find to work with the Restoration. He also encouraged the industrialists of Bilbao, the major Basque city, to take charge of provincial life in a way they had not previously done." Robert W. Kern, *Liberals, Reformers and Caciques in Restoration Spain 1875–1909* (Albuquerque: University of New Mexico Press, 1974), 29.

57. Antonio Cánovas del Castillo, prologue to *Los Vascongadas* [The Basque provinces], by Miguel Rodríguez Ferrer (Madrid: J. Noguera, 1873), in Juan Madariaga Orbea, *Anthology of Apologists and Detractors of the Basque Language*, trans. Frederick H. Fornoff, María Cristina Saavedra, Amaia Gabantxo, and Cameron J. Watson (Reno: Center for Basque Studies, University of Nevada, Reno, 2006), 617–18.

58. Ibid., 618.

59. Shubert, *A Social History of Modern Spain*, 183.

60. Martin Guilbeau, *L'Euskal-Herria ou le Pays Basque: Historique et linguistique* (Paris: Association Française pour l'avancement des sciences, 1892), 6.

61. Cánovas del Castillo, prologue to *Los Vascongadas*, in Madariaga Orbea, *Anthology of Apologists and Detractors of the Basque Language*, 618.

62. Shubert, *A Social History of Modern Spain*, 173.

63. Shlomo Ben-Ami, "Basque Nationalism between Archaism and Modernity," *Journal of Contemporary History* 26, nos. 3–4 (September 1991): 494.

64. Joseph Harrison, "Heavy Industry, the State, and Economic Development in the Basque Region, 1876–1936," *The Economic History Review*, 2nd ser., 36, no. 4 (November 1983): 537.

65. Payne, *Basque Nationalism*, 61.

66. See Glas, *Bilbao's Modern Business Elite*, xiii.

67. Corcuera Atienza, *Orígenes, ideología y organización del nacionalismo vasco*, 65.

68. In 1868, a group of industrial workers in Bilbao had formed one of the earliest chapters in Western Europe of the First International. Cyrus Ernesto Zirakzadeh, *A Rebellious People: Basques, Protests, and Politics* (Reno: University of Nevada Press, 1991), 55.

69. The adjustment of Basque society to reflect the changes brought about by modernization is described by Antonio Elorza, *Ideologías del nacionalismo vasco, 1876–1937* (San Sebastián: L. Haranburu, 1978), 110.

70. The violence that swept Barcelona in the 1890s "gave it sad fame in the annals of world subversion," Vicens Vives observes. *Approaches to the History of Spain*, 140.

71. Palacio Atard, *La España del siglo XIX*, 595.

72. See Carr, *Spain 1808–1975*, 441–46.

73. In the Catalan case, Daniele Conversi describes language as a "core value" in the emergence of a nationalist movement, that is, the most apt element needed to epitomize the essence of a cultural group. See "Language or Race?: The Choice of Core Values in the Development of Catalan and Basque Nationalisms," *Ethnic and Racial Studies* 13, no. 1 (January 1990): 51, 53–55; see also the same author's "The Influence of Culture on Political Choices: Language Maintenance and Its Implications for the Catalan and Basque National Movements," *History of European Ideas* 16, nos. 1–3 (1993): 189–200.

74. Palacio Atard, *La España del siglo XIX*, 572.

75. Ibid., 574; Payne, *Basque Nationalism*, 70.

76. The late 1880s also witnessed the first stirrings of political action in favor of Galician regionalism, culminating in the formation of the Liga Gallega (Galician League) in 1891. Palacio Atard, *La España del siglo XIX*, 575.

77. See Christopher Schmidt-Nowara, "After 'Spain': A Dialogue with Josep M. Pradera on Spanish Colonial Historiography," in *After the Imperial Turn: Thinking With and Through the Nation*, ed. Antoinette Burton (Durham: Duke University Press, 2003), 157, 161.

78. Walter Nugent, *Crossings: The Great Transatlantic Migration, 1870–1914* (Bloomington: Indiana University Press, 1992), 101.

79. "Spanish civilians in Cuba preyed upon the island, and political office there was reserved for those seeking party service at home." Charles E. Chapman, *A History of Spain* (New York: The Macmillan Company, 1922), 506.

80. Elizabeth Wormeley Latimer, *Spain in the Nineteenth Century*, 5th ed. (Chicago: A. C. McClurg & Co., 1907), 412.

81. José Martí, "Our America," January 30, 1891, in *Hispanoamérica en lucha por su independencia* (México: Cuadernos Americanos), 115–17, trans. and quoted in Samuel L. Baily, ed., *Nationalism in Latin America* (New York: Alfred A. Knopf, 1971), 69.

82. See Benedict Anderson, *Imagined Communities: Reflections on the Origin and Spread of Nationalism*, rev. ed. (London: Verso, 1991), 26–28.

83. Palacio Atard, *La España del siglo XIX*, 561–62.

84. Pérez Garzón, "State Nationalism, Cultural Nationalism and Political Alternatives," 47.

85. Joseba Gabilondo, "State Melancholia: Spanish Nationalism, Specularity, and Performance. Notes on Antonio Muñoz Molina," in *From Stateless Nations to Postnational Spain*, eds. Silvia Bermúdez, Antonio Cortijo Ocaña and Timothy McGovern (Boulder, CO: Society of Spanish and Spanish-American Studies, 2002), 237–38.

86. Manzano Moreno and Pérez Garzón, "A Difficult Nation?" 266–67.

87. "Pompously christened the 'War of Africa', [it] gave rise to the greatest outpouring of patriotic rhetoric seen since the anti-Napoleonic war." Álvarez Junco, "The Formation of Spanish Identity," 28.

88. Eric Hobsbawm talks of the "anarchic and formidable world of Berber fighting clans" in Morocco. See *The Age of Empire 1875–1914* (London: Weidenfeld & Nicholson; New York: Pantheon, 1987; rpt., New York: Vintage Books, 1989), 279 (page citations are to the reprint edition).

89. Carr, *Spain 1808–1975*, 260.

90. Indeed, it is probably fair to say that Spanish nationalism was most evident in the region, due to the successful involvement of the Catalan volunteer force under General Prim. See Carr, *Spain 1808–1975*, 261; Payne, *Basque Nationalism*, 51; Payne, "Nacionalismo español, nacionalismo vasco," in *Aula de Cultura de El Correo Español–El Pueblo Vasco*, ed. José Manuel González, vol. 12, 109–27 (Bilbao: El Correo Español–El Pueblo Vasco, 1994), 117.

91. Álvarez Junco, "The Formation of Spanish Identity," 29.

92. Hobsbawm, *The Age of Empire 1875–1914*, 280–81.

93. Pérez Garzón, "State Nationalism, Cultural Nationalism and Political Alternatives," 60.

94. "[Spanish] Liberalism's stress on education and culture was integrally linked to emergent ideologies of nationalism, through which the ascendant bourgeoisie sought to integrate the rest of the population within the national territory into its own project." Helen Graham and Jo Labanyi, "Culture and Modernity: The Case of Spain," in *Spanish Cultural Studies: An Introduction*, ed. Graham and Labanyi, 9.

95. Manzano Moreno and Pérez Garzón, "A Difficult Nation?" 263.

96. Boyd, *Historia Patria*, 35–36.

97. Vicens Vives, *Approaches to the History of Spain*, 138; see also Carr, *Spain 1808–1975*, 469–72; Graham and Labanyi, "Culture and Modernity," 2; Boyd, *Historia Patria*, 30–36; and Inman Fox, *La invención de España. Nacionalismo liberal e identidad nacional* (Madrid: Cátedra, 1998), 27–34.

98. Manzano Moreno and Pérez Garzón, "A Difficult Nation?" 262–63; Pérez Garzón has also termed this the creation of a new "liturgy," "a Spanish/Castilian-centered ideology–or 'españolismo' as a mark of identity that could override class identities–was inculcated at all levels of society through the educational system, weak though it was in the nineteenth century." See "State Nationalism, Cultural Nationalism and Political Alternatives," 59.

99. Mª Victoria López-Cordón Cortezo, "La mentalidad conservadora durante la Restauración," in *La España de la Restauración: Política, economía, legislación y cultura*, ed. José Luis García, I Coloquio de Segovia sobre Historia de España dirigido por Manuel Tuñón de Lara ([Segovia]: n.p., n.d.), 85–86.

100. See Boyd, *Historia Patria*, 108–11.

101. Payne, "Nacionalismo español, nacionalismo vasco," 117; Boyd, *Historia Patria*, 68–69.

102. This is a debate with a number of contemporary ramifications. Indeed, some observers have questioned the manipulation of Spanish history in the Spanish autonomous communities such as the Basque Country and Catalonia. This in itself, of course, could be viewed as a form of Spanish nationalism. See Miguel A. Delgado, "Los historiadores consideran grave la manipulación de la historia de España que se enseña en algunas autonomías," *ABC* (Madrid), April 7, 1996, 74–76; and Manzano Moreno and Pérez Garzón, who highlight the political, as opposed to pedagogical, nature of this educational debate and conclude that Spanish nationalism is very much on the offensive. "A Difficult Nation?" 274–76.

103. See Richard J. Evans, "Introduction: Redesigning the Past. History in Political Transitions," *Journal of Contemporary History* 38, no. 1 (2003): 5–12.

104. Julian White, "The Musical Avant-garde: Modernity and Tradition," in *Spanish Cultural Studies: An Introduction*, ed. Graham and Labanyi, 79.

105. Manzano Moreno and Pérez Garzón, "A Difficult Nation?" 269.

106. Ángel G. Loureiro, "Spanish Nationalism and the Ghost of Empire," *Journal of Spanish Cultural Studies* 4, no. 1 (2003): 70.

107. Ibid., 71. Loureiro goes on to discuss the importance of race in not just the conservative thought represented by Menéndez y Pelayo, but also in liberal Spanish circles. He cites the liberal Rafael Altamira, who argued that Spain needed to defend the spirit of its race from the corrupting influences of both France and the United States (71).

108. Pérez Garzón, "State Nationalism, Cultural Nationalism and Political Alternatives," 60–61.

109. Manzano Moreno and Pérez Garzón, "A Difficult Nation?" 261.

110. Jon Juaristi, "El gueto vacío," in Juan Aranzadi, Jon Juaristi, and Patxo Unzueta, *Auto de terminación (Raza, nación y violencia en el País Vasco)* (Madrid: El País/Aguilar, 1994), 123; See also the opinion of Andrés de Blas that the Restoration, and more specifically the leadership of Cánovas, "established a level . . . of civil rights and freedoms comparable to the most advanced levels of European society." "Un recuerdo tranquilo," *El País* (Madrid), August 24, 1997, quoted in José Ignacio Lacasta-Zabalza, *España uniforme. El pluralismo enteco y desmemoriado de la sociedad española y de su conciencia nacional e intelectual* (Pamplona: Pamiela, 1998), 121.

111. See, for example, the classic work by Eugen Weber, *Peasants into Frenchmen: The Modernisation of Rural France, 1870–1914* (London: Chatto & Windus, 1977). Here, Weber contends that it took over a century of vigorous, modern

state-building, plus the effects of World War I, to fully cement the notion of modern France–developments that had few parallels in nineteenth-century Spain. For Weber, in particular, World War I represented an "immense step forward" (477) in French national integration, and the definitive moment from which time on France might be considered a modern, integrated state.

112. Manzano Moreno and Pérez Garzón, "A Difficult Nation?" 266. There is a growing field of studies that questions the innate realities of European states and point more to their nineteenth-century constructed quality. Apart from the already cited groundbreaking work by Weber, *Peasants into Frenchmen*, in the French case, some recent books have also challenged Anglocentric visions of British history. Among these works, see Linda Colley, *Britons: Forging the Nation 1707–1837* (New Haven: Yale University Press, 1992) and Laurence Brockliss and David Eastwood, eds. *A Union of Multiple Identities: The British Isles c.1750–c.1850* (Manchester: Manchester University Press, 1997). The work of Weber and Colley (among others) tends to emphasize the notion of (an often long and complex) process in constructing modern states, as well as the crucial factor of external warfare against European foes in cementing a concept of the nation.

113. Manzano Moreno and Pérez Garzón, "A Difficult Nation?" 271. This stands in stark contrast to the less conflictive creation of British national identity in the nineteenth century, which successfully managed to embrace Scotland and Wales, similarly important economic regions of the state, without engendering the same degree of center-periphery tensions. For Colley, the way in which British national identity was constructed actually allowed a sense of Britishness "to emerge alongside of, and not necessarily in competition with older, more organic attachments to England, Wales or Scotland, or to county or village." *Britons*, 18.

114. Manzano Moreno and Pérez Garzón, "A Difficult Nation?" 277–78.

115. Álvarez Junco, "The Formation of Spanish Identity," 24.

116. Paul Gilroy emphasizes "the ability of law and the ideology of legality to express and represent the nation state and national unity" so that unified national cultures are "articulated around the theme of legality and constitution." Thus, any transgression of the existent legal/constitutional framework becomes an attack on the nation-state itself. See "*There Ain't No Black in the Union Jack": The Cultural Politics of Race and Nation* (Chicago: University of Chicago Press, 1991), 74, 76.

Notes, Chapter Two

1. Santiago de Arana y Ansotegui never fully recovered from the emotional blow that defeat in 1876 had signaled for the Carlist cause. After the war, he suffered from depression "that at one point bordered on psychosis" and died in 1883. Stanley G. Payne, *Basque Nationalism* (Reno: University of Nevada Press, 1975), 65.

2. Jean-Claude Larronde, *El nacionalismo vasco: Su origen y su ideología en la obra de Sabino Arana-Goiri*, trans. Lola Valverde (San Sebastián: Editorial Txertoa, 1977), 64–65. See also Santiago de Pablo and Ludger Mees, *El péndulo patriótico: Historia del Partido Nacionalista Vasco, 1895–2005* (Barcelona: Crítica, 2005), 1–3.

3. Javier Corcuera, "Ese gran desconocido," interview by Eugenio Ibarzábal, *Muga*, no. 5 (April 1980), 10.

4. Daniele Conversi, *The Basques, the Catalans and Spain: Alternative Routes to Nationalist Mobilisation* (Reno: University of Nevada Press, 1997), 55.

5. Sabino Arana, quoted in Martín Ugalde, Eugenio Goienetxe, Federico Zabala, María Mina, and Ramón Sota, *Mesa redonda en torno a Sabino de Arana y Goiri* (Bilbao: Editorial Vizcaína, 1977), 13.

6. Larronde, *El nacionalismo vasco*, 66–67.

7. Ibid., 67.

8. Raymond Williams's comments on the Romantic reaction to the profound upheavals of the nineteenth century encapsulate the mood behind the development of Arana's ideas: "The emphasis on a general common humanity was evidently necessary in a period in which a new kind of society was coming to think of man as merely a specialized instrument of production. The emphasis on love and relationship was necessary not only within the immediate suffering but against the aggressive individualism and the primarily economic relationships which the new society embodied." *Culture and Society* (London: Chatto & Windus, 1958; rpt. with a postscript, Harmondsworth, England: Penguin Books, 1963), 59 (page citations are to the reprint edition).

9. William A. Douglass, "Sabino's Sin: Racism and the Founding of Basque Nationalism," in *Ethnonationalism in the Contemporary World: Walker Connor and the Study of Nationalism*, ed. Daniele Conversi (London: Routledge, 2002), 110 n. 20. Stanley G. Payne concludes that although one cannot speak of any direct influence on the young Arana from the burgeoning Catalan nationalist movement, "it may be reasonably inferred that the latter served as an indirect stimulus." *Basque Nationalism*, 68. Daniele Conversi echoes Payne's comments: "Although Catalanism had little influence on him, he was directly exposed to it. In particular, the renaissance of the Catalan language must have impressed him deeply, since he hoped to launch a similar revival for Euskara." *The Basques, the Catalans and Spain*, 57. Javier Corcuera, however, prefers to play down any specific Catalan influence as "minimal," although he does view the general rise of late nineteenth-century European

nationalist movements (in Ireland, for example) as establishing a general context for the young Arana's ideas. "Ese gran desconocido," 10.

10. Vicente Palacio Atard, *La España del siglo XIX, 1808–1898 (Introducción a la España contemporánea)*, 2nd ed. (Madrid: Calpe, 1981), 608. Even without counting the left bank of the city (the principal zone of industrial development), the figures are equally spectacular, with a population rising from 17,000 in 1857 to 85,000 in 1900. See Manuel Tuñón de Lara, Julio Valdeón Baruque, and Antonio Domínguez Ortiz, *Historia de España*) Barcelona: Editorial Labor, 1991), 464.

11. Bilbao later developed a tripartite political division after 1895 between liberals, socialists, and Basque nationalists that bequeathed the city a pluralist political heritage. See Juan Pablo Fusi, "El espíritu liberal, socialista y nacionalista de Bilbao," in *El País Vasco: Pluralismo y nacionalidad* (Madrid: Alianza Editorial, 1984), 147–60.

12. Joseph Harrison, "Heavy Industry, the State, and Economic Development in the Basque Region, 1876–1936," *The Economic History Review*, 2nd ser. 36, no. 4 (November 1983): 537. See also Eduardo Jorge Glas, *Bilbao's Modern Business Elite* (Reno: University of Nevada Press, 1997), ch. 4, "The Formation of Bilbao's Modern Business Elite," 108–32, for an appreciation of how this select group of families came to control industry and commerce in the city.

13. Gabriel Plata Parga, "Del liberalismo oligárquico al conservadurismo autoritario en Vizcaya (1875–1936)," in *II Euskal mundu-biltzarra/II Congreso Mundial Vasco*, sec.2, *Euskal Herriaren historiari buruzko biltzarra/Congreso de historia de Euskal Herria*, vol.5, *Aro moderno eta gaur egungoa/Edad moderna y contemporánea* (Vitoria-Gasteiz: Eusko Jaurlaritzaren Argitalpen-Zerbitzu Nagusia/Servicio Central de Publicaciones del Gobierno Vasco, 1988), 337.

14. For a comparative perspective on the relationship between migration and nationality, and the options of "fight" or "flight," see Raymond Pearson, *National Minorities in Eastern Europe, 1848–1945* (London: Macmillan, 1983), ch. 4, esp. 84–118.

15. Walter Nugent, *Crossings: The Great Transatlantic Migrations, 1870–1914* (Bloomington: Indiana University Press, 1992), 101. Nugent's map (102) indicates that, in broad terms, the core area of highest emigration was to be found in Galicia, in the northwest of the peninsula. Thereafter, emigration levels decrease in intensity the more one moves south and east, recording the highest Basque levels (in Spain) in Bizkaia and in Navarre.

16. Gloria P. Totoricagüena, *Identity, Culture, and Politics in the Basque Diaspora* (Reno: University of Nevada Press, 2004), 55. See ch. 3 of the same work, "The Formation of the Basque Diaspora," 55–80, for a fuller explanation of these factors. Palacio Atard confirms the importance of the mandatory military service imposed after 1876 in encouraging emigration. See *La España del siglo XIX*, 607. According to Daniel Alexander Gómez-Ibáñez, Spanish Basque migration to the Americas gained particular momentum after the Second Carlist War, during which time French Basques were also emigrating to avoid their military service. See *The Western Pyrenees: Differential Evolution of the French and Spanish Borderland* (Oxford: Clarendon Press, 1975), 107, 108. Furthermore, Adrian Shubert maintains that "in the two areas where languages other than Spanish were strongest, Catalonia and the Basque Provinces, the rate of avoidance of military service through cash redemptions and quota payments were highest; in the third, Galicians had the highest rate of avoidance." *A Social History of Modern Spain* (London: Unwin Hyman, 1990), 183–84.

17. William A. Douglass and Jon Bilbao. *Amerikanuak: Basques in the New World* (Reno: University of Nevada Press, 1975), 137. Exact figures of Basque-only migrants are impossible to calculate, although 200,000 is also the number used by José María Pérez de Arenaza Múgica and Javier Lasagabaster Olazábal, eds. *América y los Vascos. Presencia Vasca en América* (Gasteiz: Departamento de Cultura, Gobierno Vasco, 1991), quoted in Totoricagüena, *Identity, Culture, and Politics in the Basque Diaspora*, 63.

18. In 1877, Basque immigrants in Argentina established the Laurac Bat association to help new immigrants to the country and maintain links with their homeland. This association also, it should be noted, organized protests against the Spanish government for the abolition of the *fueros* in 1876. See Totoricagüena, *Identity, Culture, and Politics in the Basque Diaspora*, 68.

19. For an interesting account of different patterns of migration within this general trend and how such patterns affected Barakaldo, one of the towns on Greater Bilbao's left bank, see Mercedes Arbaiza Vilallonga, "Labor Migration during the First Phase of Basque Industrialization: The Labor Market and Family Motivations," *The History of the Family* 3, no. 2 (1998): 199–219.

20. Joseba Zulaika, *Caza, símbolo y eros*, trans. Lurdes Azurmendi (Madrid: Nerea, 1992), 83–84.

21. This was not, however, a rural outlook based on a defense of peasant interests, but rather the use of rural society as an ideal, basically as a contrast to the ills of modernization. Arana's rural emphasis looked to a precapitalist word of utopian harmony. Gurutz Jáuregui Bereciartu, *Ideología y estrategia política de ETA: Análisis de su evolución entre 1959 y 1968*, 2nd ed. (Madrid: Siglo XXI, 1985), 41.

22. Juan Aranzadi, *Milenarismo vasco (Edad de Oro, etnia y nativismo)* (Madrid: Taurus Ediciones, 1981), 441.

23. Joseba Zulaika, *Basque Violence: Metaphor and Sacrament* (Reno: University of Nevada Press, 1988), 107–10, 130; Aranzadi, *Milenarismo vasco*, 298–99. See also the assessment of William A. Douglass, for whom "the *baserria* is fixed in space

and durable as an identifiable unit through time." *Death in Murelaga: Funerary Ritual in a Spanish Basque Village* (Seattle: University of Washington Press, 1969), 18.

24. See de Pablo and Mees, *El péndulo patriótico*, 10–11.

25. Francisco Letamendia Belzunce [Ortzi, pseud.], *Introducción histórica: ETA en el franquismo*, vol. 1 of *Historia del nacionalismo vasco y de ETA* (San Sebastián: R & B Ediciones, 1994), 137.

26. Douglass, "Sabino's Sin," 105.

27. Conversi, *The Basques, the Catalans and Spain*, 63.

28. Juan Díez Medrano, *Divided Nations: Class, Politics, and Nationalism in the Basque Country and Catalonia* (Ithaca, NY: Cornell University Press, 1995), 78.

29. An interesting parallel is to be found in the case of Ireland, where ancient mythology served as a useful tool in the forging of a twentieth-century revolutionary ideology. According to Martin Williams, three themes were regularly associated with mythological references in all strands of Irish literature after 1878: fighting, redemption, and heroism, so that "even if some of the authors themselves intended the talk of war to be taken metaphorically rather than literally, it is easy to see how this idealization of fighting was potentially . . . congenial to insurrectionary nationalism; armed rebellion might seem much more attractive if portrayed as a heroic conflict." See "Ancient Mythology and Revolutionary Ideology in Ireland, 1878–1916," *The Historical Journal* 26, no. 2 (June 1983): 315, 317.

30. Such individuals "were thus launching a revolution as much cultural, even epistemological, as it was political. They were attempting to transform the symbolic framework through which people experienced social reality, and thus, to the extent that life is what we make of it all, that reality itself." Clifford Geertz, *The Interpretation of Cultures: Selected Essays* (New York: Basic Books, 1973), 239.

31. Friedrich Nietzsche, "*Thus Spoke Zarathustra*: A Book For All and None," in *Ecce Homo*, in *Basic Writings of Nietzsche*, trans. and ed. with commentaries Walter Kaufmann (New York: The Modern Library, 1968), 764–65.

32. "In Arana's view, a new ethnonationalist political movement was required to fill the void caused by the prostration and incapacity of Carlism to serve as an effective counterweight to Spain's unilateral abolition of Basque political autonomy and a 'Spanish invasion' which threatened to minoritize and marginate Basques in their own homeland, while raising a very real spectre of ethnic and class conflict." Douglass, "Sabino's Sin," 104.

33. The following argument is adapted from Elliot Oring's insightful discussion of the relationship between folklore and identity: "The Arts, Artifacts, and Artifices of Identity," *Journal of American Folklore* 107, no. 424 (Spring 1994), 211–33. I take "art" to mean a human creative process or activity requiring imaginative skill; an "artifact" to mean a man-made object of any material, verbal, or behavioral form that exists outside the life for which it was originally intended; and an "artifice" to mean a deliberately manufactured object that implies a process of cunning, skill, or even deception. These definitions are based on those offered by Oring. See "Arts, Artifacts, and Artifices," 213.

34. Douglass, "Sabino's Sin," 104.

35. Oring, "Arts, Artifacts, and Artifices," 224. Cultures and social groups are conceptualized in an ongoing process of construction and negotiation in Richard Handler, "Is 'Identity' a Useful Cross-Cultural Concept?" in *Commemorations: The Politics of National Identity*, ed. John R. Gillis (Princeton: Princeton University Press, 1994), 27.

36. De Pablo and Mees, *El péndulo patriótico*, 8.

37. Payne, *Basque Nationalism*, 69.

38. Javier Corcuera Atienza, *Orígenes, ideología y organización del nacionalismo vasco (1876–1904)* (Madrid: Siglo XXI, 1979), 201; Aranzadi, *Milenarismo vasco*, 336.

39. In the opinion of one historiographical study, *Bizkaya por su independencia* should not be considered a work of academic history, but rather a simple political manifesto. Andrés Mañaricúa, *Historiografía de Vizcaya (desde Lope García de Salazar a Labayru)*, 2nd ed. (Bilbao: La Gran Enciclopedia Vasca, 1973), 387–88, quoted in Corcuera Atienza, *Orígenes, ideología y organización del nacionalismo vasco*, 201 n. 73.

40. See Eric Hobsbawm's discussion of the importance of historical invention as a means of legitimizing nationalist political action and cementing group cohesion, "Introduction: Inventing Traditions," in *The Invention of Tradition*, ed. Eric Hobsbawm and Terence Ranger (Cambridge: Cambridge University Press, 1983), 7, 12.

41. Sabino Arana, *Bizkaya por su independencia* (1892; rpt., Bilbao: E.Verdes, 1932), 15 (page citations are to the reprint edition). All translations of this text are my own.

42. See both Conversi, *The Basques, the Catalans and Spain*, 59–61 and Douglass, "Sabino's Sin," for an appreciation of the racialist dimension of Arana's work and the context within which this was framed.

43. See Zulaika, *Basque Violence: Metaphor and Sacrament*, 238.

44. Walker Connor, "Beyond Reason: The Nature of the Ethnonational Bond," *Ethnic and Racial Studies* 16, no. 3 (July 1993): 382.

45. Patxo Unzueta, "El alma de Sabino Arana," in Juan Aranzadi, Jon Juaristi, and Patxo Unzueta, *Auto de terminación (Raza, nación y violencia en el País Vasco)* (Madrid: El País/Aguilar, 1994), 157–8. See also Aranzadi's analysis of the Arrigorriaga myth in *Milenarismo vasco*, 337–41, and Douglass on the separatist aspect of Arana's program and how this was configured in relation to the Basques' domination by Spain in "Sabino's Sin," 104–5.

46. Douglass, "Sabino's Sin," 104.

47. Payne, for example, is perhaps guilty of dismissively judging the book too literally when he concludes that it "consisted of a fanciful interpretation of four dimly understood battles in medieval Vizcayan history, which Arana converted into the guideposts of 'Vizcayan independence,' something which, of course, had never existed in any organized sense at any point in Vizcayan history." *Basque Nationalism*, 69.

48. Matthew Arnold (1822–88) was an early and influential critic of modernization. In *Culture and Anarchy* (1869), Arnold defines culture in a narrow sense as representing the best of all human capabilities. Terry Eagleton, *The Idea of Culture* (Oxford: Blackwell, 2000), 40–41. Eagleton goes on, however, to underscore the problems associated with culture as a direct substitute for religion: its elitism (if defined in a narrow way) and contested nature (if more broadly defined).

49. Aranzadi, *Milenarismo vasco*, 338. The figure of "Mother-Earth" is interesting, given the symbolism associated both with traditional society and religious belief. "Mary shines in compassion and splendor," observes Zulaika of the image production in a Basque sanctuary. "She is the port of salvation, the protective refuge, the always accessible solution. Resurrection and grace reside primarily in her." *Basque Violence: Metaphor and Sacrament*, 273.

50. Antonio Elorza, "Cultura e ideología en el País Vasco contemporáneo," in *II Euskal mundu-biltzarra/II Congreso mundial vasco*, sec. 2, *Euskal Herriaren historiari buruzko biltzarra/Congreso de historia de Euskal Herria*, vol. 5, *Aro moderno eta gaur egungoa/Edad moderna y contemporánea* (Vitoria-Gasteiz: Eusko Jaurlaritzaren Argitalpen-Zerbitzu Nagusia/Servicio Central de Publicacciones del Gobierno Vasco, 1988), 202. See also Aranzadi, *Milenarismo vasco*, 299–306.

51. Anthony D. Smith, *National Identity* (London: Penguin, 1991, rpt., Reno: University of Nevada Press, 1993), 78 (page citations are to the reprint edition).

52. Said, *Culture and Imperialism*, 61.

53. Zulaika, *Basque Violence: Metaphor and Sacrament*, 125.

54. John R. Gillis, "Introduction: Memory and Identity, The History of a Relationship," in *Commemorations: The Politics of National Identity*, ed. Gillis, 3, 5.

55. See Benedict Anderson's claim that imagining is a process of creating. Furthermore, "communities are to be distinguished, not by their falsity/genuineness, but by the style in which they are imagined." *Imagined Communities: Reflections on the Origin and Spread of Nationalism*, rev. ed. (London: Verso, 1991), 6.

56. Simon Schama, *Landscape and Memory* (London: Harper Collins, 1995; rpt., London: Fontana, 1996), 3–19 (page citations are to the reprint edition).

57. See Caroline Humphrey's investigation of Mongol culture, in which mountains are seen as "wholes" or "bodies" in an ego-centered system that views people and the land they inhabit as intimately linked. "Chiefly and Shamanist Landscapes in Mongolia," in *The Anthropology of Landscape: Perspectives on Place and Space*, ed. Eric Hirsch and Michael O'Hanlon (Oxford: Clarendon Press, 1995), 144.

58. Arana y Goiri, *Bizkaya por su independencia*, 22, 26.

59. "The very term *euskaldun* evokes an even more distant time.... It constitutes, in turn, a complete sentence of the language-town-territory relationship." Teresa del Valle, *Korrika: Basque Ritual for Ethnic Identity*, trans. Linda White (Reno: University of Nevada Press, 1994), 105.

60. Arana y Goiri, *Bizkaya por su independencia*, 23.

61. Ibid., 73.

62. Hobsbawm, *The Age of Empire 1875–1914* (London: Weidenfeld & Nicholson; New York: Pantheon, 1987; rpt., New York: Vintage Books, 1989), 148 (page citations are to the reprint edition).

63. Geertz, *The Interpretation of Cultures*, 144.

64. A people's "need to live in a world to which [they] can attribute some significance, whose essential import [they] feel [they] can grasp, often diverges from [their] concurrent need to maintain a functioning social organism." Ibid., 169.

65. Oring, "Arts, Artifacts, and Artifices," 212.

66. Arana y Goiri, *Bizkaya por su independencia*, 77–78.

67. "The deeply rooted and widespread belief that blood is the life of all organisms, human and animal, has given its sacrificial outpouring a peculiar efficacy as an expiation for wrong-doing as well as making it a cathartic agent in removing uncleanness and ritual defilements. When a tabu has been broken, a pollution incurred, or a god offended, wittingly or unwittingly, a life is required by way of propitiation in order that the evil and its consequences may be eliminated and divine favour and beneficence restored." E. O. James, *Sacrifice and Sacrament* (New York: Barnes & Noble, 1962), 104.

68. René Girard, *The Scapegoat*, trans. Yvonne Freccero (Baltimore: The Johns Hopkins University Press, 1986), 42. This would also justify Arana's essentialist view of the world with a precise beginning (the Creation) and end (Final Judgment) See 44 n. 13. See also Zulaika's discussion of the mythical void of *aske* and its relationship to the liberating principle of *askatasuna*, or freedom, in *Basque Violence: Metaphor and Sacrament*, 282.

69. Michel Foucault, *The History of Sexuality, Volume 1: An Introduction*, trans. Robert Hurley (New York: Vintage, 1990), 147. Ibn Khaldûn, a fourteenth-century Arab scholar assessed the importance of blood as follows: "(Respect for) blood ties is something natural among men, with the rarest exceptions. It leads to affection for one's relations and blood relatives, (the feeling that) no harm ought to befall them nor any destruction come upon them. One feels shame when one's relatives are attacked, and one wishes to intervene between them and whatever peril or destruction threatens them." Ibn Khaldûn, *The Muqaddimah: An Introduction to History*, trans. Franz Rosenthal, ed. and abr. N. J. Dawood, 2nd ed., Bollingen Series (Princeton: Princeton University Press, 1969), 98.

70. "The recognition that [blood] is the life principle in man and beast alike goes back . . . to the beginning of the Upper Palaeolithic, and ever since it has been regarded as the seat of vitality *par excellence* . . . it has been a potent agent in consolidating tribal relationships and effecting communication between the human and the sacred orders." James, *Sacrifice and Sacrament*, 60–61.

71. Arana y Goiri, *Bizkaya por su independencia*, 39, 41, 101. On the myth of the sacred Tree of Gernika, see Aranzadi, *Milenarismo vasco*, 341–46.

72. See George L. Mosse, who contends that the violence of World War I achieved a sacramental quality, because thousands of young men were prepared to die for their respective causes. This ideology, argues Mosse, a notion of masculine Romanticism through real or imaginary heroic deeds, subsequently led to the growth of nationalism in 1930s Europe. See *Fallen Soldiers: Reshaping the Memory of the World Wars* (New York: Oxford University Press, 1990).

73. David G. Gilmore, *Manhood in the Making: Cultural Concepts of Masculinity* (New Haven, CT.: Yale University Press, 1990), 166.

74. Robert Ardrey, *The Territorial Imperative: A Personal Inquiry into the Animal Origins of Property and Nations* (1967; rpt., London: Fontana, 1969), 362 (page citations are to the reprint edition). See also the argument that "to say war is inhuman is notoriously inappropriate. Almost the reverse: it is an exclusively human phenomenon . . . what *jus in bello* [a just war] attempts is to 'animalize' war." Francisco Murillo Ferrol, "Factores políticos de la violencia," *Revista Internacional de la Sociología*, 3d ser., no. 2 (May–August 1992), 69.

75. Zulaika, *Caza, símbolo y eros*, 90.

76. "Animals are used as signs that in an axis of nature/culture or reality/representation would stand closer to the nature and reality pole than to the metaphorical representation one." Zulaika, *Basque Violence: Metaphor and Sacrament*, 260.

77. Zulaika, *Basque Violence: Metaphor and Sacrament*, 188.

78. Ardrey, *The Territorial Imperative*, 280–81.

79. Zulaika, *Caza, símbolo y eros*, 79.

80. Arana y Goiri, *Bizkaya por su independencia*, 27, 32, 59, 68.

81. Robert Darnton, *The Great Cat Massacre and Other Episodes in French Cultural History* (New York: Basic Books, 1984; rpt., New York: Vintage Books, 1985), 193 (page citations are to the reprint edition); cf. Zulaika, *Basque Violence: Metaphor and Sacrament*, 242, 260; Girard, *The Scapegoat*, 48.

82. Ardrey, *The Territorial Imperative*, 366.

83. José María Satrústegui, *Antropología y lengua: (Tradición popular, memoria colectiva)* (Iruñea: José María Satrústegui, 1989), 89.

84. Zulaika, *Basque Violence: Metaphor and Sacrament*, 167.

85. "Performance, I would offer, constitutes . . . a point of departure, the nexus of tradition, practice and emergence." Richard Bauman, *Verbal Art as Performance* (Prospect Heights, IL: Waveland Press, 1977), 48.

86. For the complex relationships between myth, symbol, and memory, see Geertz, *The Interpretation of Culture*, 252; and Anthony D. Smith, *The Ethnic Origins of Nations.* (Oxford: Blackwell, 1986), 32.

87. Arana y Goiri, *Bizkaya por su independencia*, 28, 63.

88. Ibid., 46.

89. Simon Barton refers to the "imperfect sense of nationality" in the country, concluding: "The spectre that Spain might disintegrate never quite disappeared." "The Roots of the National Question in Spain," in *The National Question in Europe in Historical Context*, ed. Mikulá? Teich and Roy Porter (Cambridge: Cambridge University Press, 1993), 111, 121. See also ch. 1 of the present work.

90. Arana y Goiri, *Bizkaya por su independencia*, 41.

91. Ibid., 126.

92 Clark, *The Basques: The Franco Years and Beyond*, 47–48.

93. Hobsbawm, *The Age of Empire 1875–1914*, 57, 60. Said defines the terms thus: "'imperialism' means the practice, the theory, and the attitudes of a dominating metropolitan centre ruling a distant territory; 'colonialism', which is almost always a consequence of imperialism, is the implanting of settlements on distant territory." *Culture and Imperialism*, 8. For Tzvetan Todorov, this attitude is expressed as a feeling that, "one has the right to impose on others what one considers as the good, without concern as to whether or not this also good from the other's point of view. This postulate therefore implies a projection of the subject speaking about the universe, an identification of *my* values with *the* values." *The Conquest of America: The Question of the Other*, trans. Richard Howard (New York: Harper Colophon, 1985; rpt., New York: HarperPerennial, 1992), 154 (page citations are to the reprint edition).

94. "The Spanish Elections," *The Times* (London), March 6, 1893, 5, col. 6 and March 7, 1893, 5, col. 2.

95. "The Situation in Cuba," *The Times* (London), May 3, 1893, 5, col. 1.

96. Gerald Brenan, *The Spanish Labyrinth: An Account of the Social and Political Background of the Civil War* (Cambridge: At the University Press, 1943), 31.

97. Maura saw in the historical institutions of regional government a system that functioned successfully, as opposed to the crisis-torn unitary liberal system. See Raymond Carr, *Spain 1808–1975*, 2nd ed. (Oxford: Clarendon Press, 1982), 375.

98. The paradoxical nature of Maura's position in the Liberal Party is highlighted by his latent Carlist sympathies. Carlists and liberals had been *the* enemies par excellence throughout the nineteenth century. This animosity continued, in modified form, into the 1890s to the extent that, during the March 1893 election, a Carlist was murdered by a group of Liberal sympathizers in Nava del Rey (Valladolid). "The Spanish Elections," *The Times* (London), March 7, 1893, 5, col. 2.

99. Mercedes Cabrera, "El conservadurismo maurista en la Restauración: Los límites de la 'revolución desde arriba,'" in *La España de la Restauración: Política, economía, legislación y cultura*, ed. José Luis García Delgado, I Coloquio de Segovia sobre Historia Contemporánea de España dirigido por Manuel Tuñón de Lara ([Segovia]: n.p., n.d.), 59.

100. José María Jover Zamora, "La época de la Restauración panorama político-social, 1875–1902," in *Historia de España*, vol. 8, *Revolución burguesa oligarquía y constitucionalismo (1834–1923)*, ed. Manuel Tuñón de Lara (Barcelona: Editorial Labor, 1981), 370.

101. "Spain and Cuba," *The Times* (London), November 28, 1894, 5, col. 3.

102. Ibid.

103. Carr, *Spain 1808–1975*, 381. As noted, the parallels between the Cuban and Irish home rule initiatives of the 1880s are very illuminating.

104. Miguel Artola, "No había modo de evitar a Sabino Arana," interview by Eugenio Ibarzábal, *Muga*, no. 24 (1982), 41.

105. The meeting is analyzed in detail by Corcuera Atienza, *Orígenes, ideología y organización del nacionalismo vasco*, 205–13; see also Pedro de Basaldúa, *El libertador vasco: Sabino de Arana y Goiri* (Buenos Aires: Editorial Vasca Ekin, 1953), 65–70.

106. Sabino Arana to Engracio de Aranzadi y Etxeberría, November 20, 1897, in *Historia del nacionalismo vasco en sus documentos*, ed. Javier Corcuera and Yolanda Oribe (Bilbao: Eguzki Argitaldaria, 1991), vol. 1, 163 (hereafter cited as *Documentos*).

107. Sabino Arana, "El discurso de Larrazábal," June 3, 1893, in *Documentos*, vol. 1, 166.

108. See Zulaika, *Basque Violence: Metaphor and Sacrament*, 188.

109. This division is explored by Zirakzadeh in his examination of contemporary nonurban protest in the Basque Country. See Cyrus Ernesto Zirakzadeh, *A Rebellious People: Basques, Protests, and Politics* (Reno: University of Nevada Press, 1991), ch. 2, 33–52.

110. Arana y Goiri, "El discurso de Larrazábal," 166, 168.

111. Carmelo de Echegaray, "Héroes Ocultos," *Euskal-Erria* 28, no. 451 (January 20, 1893), 59.

112. Zulaika, *Basque Violence: Metaphor and Sacrament*, 111.

113. Javier Corcuera Atienza is recognized as the first historian of Basque nationalism to elucidate the different stages in the formation of Arana's nationalist ideology. He dates the incorporation of a policy more responsive to the reality of modernization to 1898, with a final phase dating from 1902. See *Orígenes, ideología y organización del nacionalismo vasco*, ch. 6, esp. 448–50, 465–72, and 512–75. An evaluation of Corcuera's work can be found in Granja Sainz, "El nacionalismo vasco: De la literatura histórica a la historiografía," *Historia contemporánea*, no. 7 (1992): 230–31; Letamendia Belzunce [Ortzi, pseud.], however, argues that the period of maximum intensity regarding nationalist activity coincided with the life span of the newsletter *Bizkaitarra* (1893–95). See *ETA en el franquismo*, 144.

114. Arana y Goiri, "El discurso de Larrazábal," 166.

115. "In many ways the wretched person's presence is enough to contaminate everything around him, infecting men and beasts with the plague, ruining crops, poisoning food, causing game to disappear, and sowing discord around him. Everything shrivels under his feet and the grass does not grow again. He produces disasters as easily as a fig tree produces figs. He need only be himself." Girard, *The Scapegoat*, 36.

116. The more one can convince one's followers of the brutal repression of a greater power, the easier it becomes to promote one's own form of violence, framed as a defensive mechanism against unjust attack. See Ignacio Sotelo, "Las raíces sociales de la violencia," *Revista Internacional de Sociología*, 3d ser., no. 2 (May–August 1992): 61.

117. Arana y Goiri, "El discurso de Larrazábal," 168.

118. Ibid., 169.

119. Negation is an important aspect of traditional Basque culture, ironically affirming precision and correctness. See Zulaika, *Basque Violence: Metaphor and Sacrament*, pt. 5, ch. 13, esp. 295–312. Elorza observes that "the political interpretation of the Basque Country [*Euskal Herria*] takes place through its negation–given that the national language cannot serve as the basis of a nationality in which it is a minority–and its substitution by a projective case, that future nation, but charged with archaic elements, that is *Euskadi* [the Basque Country]." "Cultura e ideología," 198.

120. Arana y Goiri, "El discurso de Larrazábal," 169.

121. George Boas, "Warfare in the Cosmos," in *Violence and Aggression in the History of Ideas*, ed. Philip P. Wiener and John Fisher (New Brunswick, NJ: Rutgers University Press, 1974), 9–10.

122. Mark Juergensmeyer, "Editor's Introduction: Is Symbolic Violence Related to Real Violence," *Terrorism and Political Violence* 3, no. 3 (Autumn 1991): 3.

123. This vision, posited as being predominantly negative rather than idealistic, is discussed by José Luis de la Granja Sainz. See *El nacionalismo vasco: Un siglo de historia* (Madrid: Editorial Tecnos, 1995), 65–71.

124. Arana y Goiri, "El discurso de Larrazábal," 167.

125. Jean-Claude Larronde, "Sabino de Arana-Goiri, el fundador," *Muga*, no. 93 (September 1995), 10. See the same author's "Sabino Arana," in *Los nacionalistas: Historia del nacionalismo vasco, 1876-1960*, ed. Santiago de Pablo, Besaide Series (Vitoria-Gasteiz: Fundación Sancho el Sabio, 1995), 58.

126. Arana y Goiri to Aranzadi y Etxeberría, November 20, 1897, in *Documentos*, vol. 1, 163.

127. Ibid.

128. Basaldúa, *El libertador vasco*, 71.

129. Sabino Arana, "1601'ko Bizkaya/Bizkaya en 1601," *Bizkaitarra*, no. 1, June 8, 1893, 1, col. 2.

130. Engracio de Aranzadi y Etxeberría [Kizkitza, pseud.], *Ereintza: Siembra de nacionalismo vasco, 1894–1912* (Zarauz: Editorial Vasca, 1935), 15.

131. It should be remembered that this was still very much a minority political movement. During its two-year life span, its total subscription (outside Bilbao) was just over three hundred people. It was, however, sent free to priests, teachers, and students, and monthly publication figures indicate around fifteen hundred copies. See Corcuera Atienza, *Orígenes, ideología y organización del nacionalismo vasco*, 213–14.

132. "Spain," *The Times* (London), June 22, 1893, 5, col. 3.

133. "Bomb Discovery at Seville," *The Times* (London), June 27, 1893, 5, col. 4.

134. "Spain," *The Times* (London), July 17, 1893, 5, col. 4.

135. "The Political Condition of Cuba," *The Times* (London), July 18, 1893, 5, col. 4.

136. Sabino Arana, "Recuerdo," *Bizkaitarra*, no. 14, August 31, 1894, 1, col. 1.

137. Sabino Arana, "A mi juicio," *Bizkaitarra*, no. 2, August 19, 1893, in *Documentos*, vol. 1, 174–75.

138. "Spain," *The Times* (London), August 25, 1893, 3, col. 4.

139. "Spain," *The Times* (London), August 29, 1893, 3, col. 5.

140. Ibid.

141. Corcuera Atienza, *Orígenes, ideología y organización del nacionalismo vasco*, 217.

142. Aranzadi y Etxeberría [Kizkitza, pseud.], *Ereintza: Siembra de nacionalismo vasco*, 12.

143. The Civil Guard developed "an essentially suspicious, if not openly hostile, attitude towards the bulk of the population. This is evident in the widespread hatred of the Guardia Civil among ordinary Spaniards. In large part this was a product of the ideology of the force, which was one of unambiguous social conservatism." Shubert, *A Social History of Modern Spain*, 181–82.

144. Furthermore, members of the Civil Guard were forbidden from serving in their native districts, which served only to alienate them from the communities which they served. See Carr, *Spain 1808–1975*, 233–34.

145. This point is made by Palacio Atard, who observes that there was a consistent failure on the part of Restoration Spain to integrate the emergent working class, preferring instead the politics of confrontation and repression. The same policy would be pursued in later years with the nationalists. See *La España del siglo XIX*, 587.

146. Payne views Restoration Spain as "reasonably tolerant but not democratic," *Basque Nationalism*, 77, whereas Enric Ucelay Da Cal criticizes what he sees as a "defensive and vicious" regime. "The Nationalisms of the Periphery: Culture and Politics in the Construction of National Identity," in *Spanish Cultural Studies: An Introduction*, ed. Helen Graham and Jo Labanyi, (Oxford: Oxford University Press, 1995), 35.

147. "Spain," *The Times* (London), August 29, 1893, 3, col. 5; Corcuera Atienza notes that during the Bilbao demonstrations, "The Marseillaise" was sung in conjunction with "Gernikako Arbola," as were the shouts of "Down with the bourgeoisie!" and "Long live the *fueros*!" *Orígenes, ideología y organización del nacionalismo vasco*, 218.

148. In an interview about these events, the Republican leader Manuel Ruiz Zorilla expressed surprise: "The whole of Spain was in a state of extreme agitation, and the gravest events would not surprise the public. San Sebastian was perhaps the one town in Spain from which the Republicans had the least to hope, as the Royal family spent a part of the summer there, and it had every reason to be staunchly Royalist." "Spain," *The Times* (London), August 29, 1893, 3, col. 5.

149. "Spain," *The Times* (London), August 31, 1893, 3, col. 5.

150. Aranzadi y Etxeberría [Kizkitza, pseud.], *Ereintza. Siembra de nacionalismo vasco*, 13.

151. "Riots in Spain," *The Times* (London), September 16, 1893, 5, col. 4.

152. Shubert, *A Social History of Modern Spain*, 193, 194.

153. It was named after its principal instigator, Simón Bernardo Zamacola. See Renato Barahona, *Vizcaya on the Eve of Carlism: Politics and Society, 1800–1833* (Reno: University of Nevada Press, 1989), 22, and Payne, *Basque Nationalism*, 36. Juan Aranzadi situates the Zamacolada within a historical social divide in the Basque provinces according to foral allegiance. See "La religión abertzale," in Aranzadi, Juaristi, and Unzueta, *Auto de terminación*, 85–86.

154. "Spain," *The Times* (London), September 29, 1893, 3, col. 4.

155. Ignacio Olabarri Gortazar, *Relaciones laborales en Vizcaya (1890–1936)* (Durango: Leopoldo Zugaza, 1978), 397–99.

156. See Juan Pablo Fusi, "El pluralismo vasco (notas para una definición del País Vasco contemporáneo)," in *El País Vasco: Pluralismo y nacionalidad*, 243–55.

157. See de Pablo and Mees, *El péndulo patriótico*, 6.

158. The anxiety caused by the violence had prompted the government to "adopt the most rigorous measures to crush Anarchism." "Spain," *The Times* (London), November 13, 1893, 5, col. 2.

159. "Spain and Morocco," *The Times* (London), November 13, 1893, 5, col. 2.

160. "Spain," *The Times* (London), November 25, 1893, 5, col. 3.

161. Sabino Arana, "El león español," *Bizkaitarra*, no. 4, December 17, 1893, 2, col. 3.

162. There are notable exceptions. William A. Douglass points out that Arana "empathized with the colonized peoples of the world, and would most certainly have sympathized with the views of Frantz Fanon," author of the seminal anticolonial text *The Wretched of the Earth* (1963). Furthermore, "in questioning the South African situation of his day, Arana denounced the aggression of the English against the Boers, as well as that of the Boers against the Kaffirs." See Douglass, "Sabino's Sin," 105. See also Jáuregui Bereciartu, *Ideología y estrategia política de ETA*, 25–30; Letamendia Belzunce [Ortzi, pseud.], *ETA en el franquismo*, 145.

163. Sabino Arana Goiri, *La patria de los vascos. Antología de escritos políticos*, compiled by Antonio Elorza (San Sebastián: R & B Ediciones, 1995), 258, quoted in Douglass, "Sabino's Sin," 106.

164. See Zulaika, *Basque Violence: Metaphor and Sacrament*, 282–83.

165. Conversi, *The Basques, the Catalans and Spain*, 60, 61. See, in general, Conversi's discussion off Arana's racialist ideas (59–61) and Douglass, "Sabino's Sin," for an appreciation of the extent to which race permeated late nineteenth-century social and political thought.

166. Díez Medrano, *Divided Nations*, 79. In recent years, the question of Arana's racism and its legacy for Basque nationalism as a whole have been vigorously promoted by a group of anti-Basque nationalist Spanish intellectuals (many of them Basque), leading to best-selling publications on the topic in Spain by practically all the leading figures associated with this group. See, for example, Antonio Elorza, *Tras la huella de Sabino Arana: Los orígenes totalitarios del nacionalismo vasco* (Madrid: Temas de Hoy, 2005) and Iñaki Ezquerra, *Sabino Arana, o, la sentimentalidad totalitaria* (Barcelona: Belaqva, 2003).

167. Joseba Zulaika, "Tropics of Terror: From Guernica's 'Natives' to Global 'Terrorists'," *Social Identities* 4, no. 1 (1998): 94, 95. Douglass also describes late nineteenth-century European racialist discourse. See "Sabino's Sin," 96–98.

168. Joseba Zulaika, "Anthropologists, Artists, Terrorists: The Basque Holiday from History," *Journal of Spanish Cultural Studies* 4, no. 2 (2003): 142. See also Joseba Zulaika, *Del Cromañon al Carnaval: Los vascos como museo antropológico* (Donostia: Erein, 1996) for a fuller explanation of this anthropological fascination with Basques. See also de Pablo and Mees, *El péndulo patriótico*, 12.

169. Douglass, "Sabino's Sin," 96. This is a view echoed by de Pablo and Mees, *El péndulo patriótico*, 12.

170. Granja Sainz, *El nacionalismo vasco*, 23–25.

171. One possible exception was the eighteenth-century Jesuit priest Manuel de Larramendi. According to both Julio Caro Baroja in *Los vascos* (Madrid: Ediciones Minotauro, 1958), 89, and Davydd Greenwood, in "Continuity in Change: Spanish Basque Ethnicity as a Historical Process," in *Ethnic Conflict in the Western World*, ed. Milton J. Esman (Ithaca, NY: Cornell University Press), 97–98 (both quoted in Douglass, "Sabino's Sin," 100), Larramendi employed abusive language toward Castilians, viewed Basque and Spanish identities as incompatible, and was a precursor of modern racists. However, Douglass disagrees with these conclusions, contending that Larramendi's diatribes against both Castilians and fellow Basques were more in keeping with those writers who defended Basque privileges based on cultural difference within the political context of the Spanish kingdom. "Sabino's Sin," 100–101.

172. Aranzadi, "La religión abertzale," 93.

173. The scientific study undertaken for the Association Française pour l'avancement des sciences by Martin Guilbeau. See *L'Eskal-Herria ou le Pays Basque*, esp. 2–5, 6, 8.

174. Glas, *Bilbao's Modern Business Elite*, 93. While this proportion is low compared with Spanish averages, where two-thirds of the active population were occupied in the primary sector, it still demonstrates a significant rural presence in Bizkaia. Moreover, it is likely that this percentage would have been even higher in the other Basque provinces.

175. A reference to military service. José Mª Basarrialde, "¡Viva Euskaria!" *Euskal-Erria* 28, no. 465 (June 10, 1893), 511.

176. Together with other cultural forms, both "national" and "international." See Serge Salaün, "The *Cuplé*: Modernity and Mass Culture," in *Spanish Cultural Studies*, ed. Graham and Labanyi, 93.

177. The history of *bertsolaritza* is described by Gorka Aulestia. See "El 'Bertsolarismo': Literatura Oral Improvisada del País Vasco," (Ph.D. diss., University of Nevada, Reno, 1987) and *Improvisational Poetry From the Basque Country*, foreword by William A. Douglass, trans. Lisa Corcostegui and Linda White (Reno: University of Nevada Press, 1995). See also Joxerra Garzia, Jon Sarasua, and Andoni Egaña, *The Art of Bertsolaritza: Improvised Basque Verse Singing* (Donostia: Bertsozale Elkartea; Andoain: Bertsolari Liburuak, 2001) and Samuel G. Armistead and Joseba Zulaika, eds., *Voicing the Moment: Improvised Oral Poetry and Basque Tradition* (Reno: Center for Basque Studies, University of Nevada, 2005).

178. Shlomo Ben-Ami, "Basque Nationalism between Archaism and Modernity," *Journal of Contemporary History* 26, nos. 3–4 (September 1991): 497. See Gorka Aulestia, *The Basque Poetic Tradition*, trans. Linda White (Reno: University of Nevada Press, 2000) for examples of Basque literature that may not be so archaic or savage.

179. Although a cursory glance at the numbers of books read at Donostia–San Sebastián's Municipal Public Library between the last quarter of 1892 and the third quarter of 1893 (the initial period of nationalist activity) has some interesting conclusions. While books consulted from the Basque section constituted between 20 and 30 percent of the total works checked out during the first three quarters, the combined total of Spanish history and literature books consulted never rose above 20 percent in the same period. During the third quarter of 1893 (including the vacation month of August), works consulted from the Basque section dropped to just under 13 percent of the total, whereas those of Spanish history and literature totaled just under 17 percent. It would seem, then, that the "reading classes" of Donostia–San Sebastián were not as averse to Basque culture as may have been portrayed. The figures are calculated from the information given in *Euskal-Erria* 28, no. 450 (January 10, 1893)–29, no. 477 (October 10, 1893).

180. Said, *Culture and Imperialism*, xxii–xxiii.

181. Ibid., xxix.

182. See the comments of Terry Eagleton on the case of Britain and Ireland, which, as we have been noting, bears some parallel to that between Spain and at least some sectors of Basque society. According to Eagleton, Matthew Arnold's *Culture and Anarchy* "might well have been rewritten as *Britain and Ireland.* The liberal humanist notion of Culture was constituted, among other things, to marginalize such peoples as the Irish." "Nationalism: Irony and Commitment," in Terry Eagleton, Frederic Jameson, and Edward W. Said, *Nationalism, Colonialism, and Literature* (Minneapolis: University of Minnesota Press, 1990), 33. See also similar conclusions with regard to Victorian Britain and the Highland Scots by Malcolm Chapman, *The Gaelic Vision in Scottish Culture* (London: Croom Helm; Montreal: McGill-Queens University Press, 1978).

183. Jon Juaristi, "El gueto vacío," in Aranzadi, Juaristi, and Unzueta, *Auto de terminación*, 128–29.

184. Todorov highlights the blurred distinctions between the reality of a religious civilization of sacrifice and a secular civilization of massacre. See *The Conquest of America*, 144–45.

185. Joseba Gabilondo, "State Melancholia: Spanish Nationalism, Specularity and Performance. Notes on Antonio Muñoz Molina," in *From Stateless Nations to Postnational Spain*, ed. Silvia Bermúdez, Antonio Cortijo Ocaña, and Timothy McGovern (Boulder, CO: Society of Spanish and Spanish-American Studies, 2002), 238–39.

186. Fredrik Barth, "Introduction," in *Ethnic Groups and Boundaries: The Social Organization of Culture Difference*, ed. Fredrik Barth, (Boston: Little, Brown and Co., 1969), 10.

187. Hayden White, "The Question of Narrative in Contemporary Historical Theory," *History and Theory* 23, no. 1 (1984), 31.

188. See Said's description of the power relations implied by imperialism in which the colonized always appear as anonymous collectives: "people on whom the economy and polity sustained by empire depend, but whose reality has not historically or culturally required attention." *Culture and Imperialism*, 75. Arana was, of course, equally guilty of disregarding those sectors of Basque society that did not fit his vision of an ideal and harmonious Bizkaia.

189. "Political expressions of militarism continued to emphasize the nation-building role of an imperial state in response to the threat of Catalan and Basque nationalist movements. These questioned the validity of both the liberal state as it came out of the nineteenth century and the heritage of the imperial past. Hereafter, Spanish and peripheral nationalisms have continued to feed off each other emotionally." Ucelay Da Cal, "The Nationalisms of the Periphery," 36.

Notes, Chapter Three

1. "Spain," *The Times* (London), January 4, 1894, 5, col. 3.

2. Including the attempted assassination of the governor of Barcelona. "A Spanish Governor Shot by an Anarchist," *The Times* (London), January 26, 1894, 3, cols. 3–4.

3. See Sabino Arana, "Los invasores," *Bizkaitarra*, no. 6, February 28, 1894, 3, col. 3, in which he discusses the murder of a Bizkaian by a *Maketo.* See also Javier Corcuera Atienza's discussion of Arana's ferocious hatred of Spain during this period, citing the article "Hipocresía y egoísmo," in *Bizkaitarra*, no. 5, January 29, 1894. *Orígenes, ideología y organización del nacionalismo vasco (1876–1904)* (Madrid: Siglo XXI, 1979), 349.

4. On the cabinet reshuffle and references to continuing the policy as before, see "The Spanish Cabinet," *The Times* (London), March 13, 1894, 5, col. 1 and "Spain," *The Times* (London), March 14, 1894, 5, col. 4.

5. "Spain," *The Times* (London), March 26, 1894, 3, col. 6.

6. Referring to the native population of the Philippines *The Times* of London observed that they were, "so bitterly hostile to the Spaniards that a change must come over the archipalago [sic] before their services can be utilized for its development. The problem of pacifying the Philippines has been rendered more difficult by the delay of centuries in taking the solution seriously in hand." "Spain and the Philippines," April 3, 1894, 5, col. 5.

7. In particular the nationalist movements of Ireland and Poland, two reference points consistently invoked by Arana for their similarities with the Basque case. See Sabino Arana [Iturribarri, pseud.], "Nuestros Males," *Bizkaitarra*, no. 7, March 31, 1894, 2, col. 3. The Irish and Poles remained the principal stateless nationalist movements of the era, although the emergence of Basque nationalism coincided also with the launch of Zionism by Theodor Herzl and the Young Wales movement under David Lloyd George. These movements also paralleled the slow demise of the Austro-Hungarian monarchy, which endured a decade of nationalist agitation within its reconstituted borders. It would, then, be fair to say that Europe in the 1890s experienced a wave of stateless nationalism alongside the statist nationalism of countries such as Britain, France, and, indeed, Spain. See Eric Hobsbawm, *The Age of Empire 1875–1914* (London: Weidenfeld & Nicholson; New York: Pantheon, 1987; rpt., New York: Vintage Books, 1989), 145, 156 (page citations are to the reprint edition).

8. Corcuera Atienza views this as a Bizkaian ideology that implied Basque nationalism, in that it suggested an independent federation of Basque states. From the spring of 1894 onward there would be a constant dialectic between Bizkaian and Basque visions of Arana's nationalism. *Orígenes, ideología y organización del nacionalismo vasco*, 225.

9. See Corcuera Atienza, *Orígenes, ideología y organización del nacionalismo vasco*, 221–241; Jean-Claude Larronde, *El nacionalismo vasco: Su origen y su ideología en la obra de Sabino Arana-Goiri*, trans. Lola Valverde (San Sebastián: Editorial Txertoa, 1977), 184–85; and Koldo San Sebastián, *Historia del Partido Nacionalista Vasco* (San Sebastián: Editorial Txertoa, 1984), 26–27.

10. On the history of the flag, see José María Bereciartúa, *Ikurriña. Historia y simbolismo* (Estella: Editorial Verbo Divino, 1977).

11. Sabino Arana, "Ikuŕin Bizkataŕa," *Egutegi Bizkataŕa* (1898), in *Documentos*, vol. 1, 226.

12. Eric Hobsbawm, "Mass-Producing Traditions: Europe, 1870–1914," in *The Invention of Tradition*, ed. Eric Hobsbawm and Terence Ranger (Cambridge: Cambridge University Press, 1983), 273, 280, 284.

13. Joanna Legaire, "Los símbolos y el Derecho," *El Mundo del País Vasco*, July 14, 1994, supplement, "Documentos. Cien años de ikurriña," 10, col. 1.

14. Mary LeCron Foster, "Symbolism: The Foundation of Culture," in *Companion Encyclopedia of Anthropology*, ed. Tom Ingold (London: Routledge, 1994), 366. See the description by Clifford Geertz of symbols such as flags as cultural acts or social events linking human experience. *The Interpretation of Cultures: Selected Essays* (New York: Basic Books, 1973), 91.

15 Gold, for instance, is perhaps one of the most commonly accepted symbols. As Marx observed, no chemist has been able to discover the physical value of gold. Its worth, throughout the history of the human experience, has been symbolic. Marshall Sahlins, "Goodbye to *Tristes Tropes*: Ethnography in the Context of Modern World History," *The Journal of Modern History* 65, no. 1 (March 1993), 12.

16. If one views the flag as an image on a material surface, then "the image documents [the] complex interplay between recollection and handiwork." Walter Melion and Susanne Küchler, "Introduction: Memory, Cognition, and Image Production," in *Images of Memory: On Remembering and Representation*, ed. Walter Melion and Susanne Küchler (Washington: Smithsonian Institution Press, 1991), 7.

17. Aristotle first viewed green as a medium between light and dark colors. Similarly, the Scholastic writer William of Auvergne believed green to be a mediator between black and white. By the late Middle Ages, green had come to represent a harmonious balance to red. See John Gage, *Color and Culture: Practice and Meaning from Antiquity to Abstraction* (Boston: Little, Brown and Co., 1993), 61, 82, 232.

18. There were, in total, ninety-four members of the Euskeldun Batzokija, fifty-six of whom had attended the inaugural celebrations in July 1894. Corcuera Atienza, *Orígenes, ideología y organización del nacionalismo vasco*, 235.

19. Ibid., 335–36 n. 66; Letamendia Belzunce, Francisco [Ortzi, pseud.], *Historia del nacionalismo vasco y de ETA*, vol. 1, *Introducción a la historia del País Vasco: ETA en el franquismo* (San Sebastián: R & B Ediciones, 1994), 146.

20. Sabino Arana, "El 25 de Octubre de 1839," *Bizkaitarra*, no. 16, October 31, 1894, 1, col. 1.

21. Ibid., 1, col. 3.

22. Sabino Arana, "La Cruz de San Andrés," *Bizkaitarra*, no. 17, November 30, 1894, 1, col. 1.

23. Sabino Arana, "Iñigo de Loyola," *Bizkaitarra*, no. 13, July 31, 1894, 2, col. 1.

24. Commenting on Loyola's seminal sixteenth-century text, *The Spiritual Exercises*, Roland Barthes remarks that "whoever reads [it] ... sees at first glance that the material is subjected to an incessant, painstaking, and almost obsessive separation; or more exactly, the *Exercises* is this separation itself, to which nothing is pre-existent: everything is immediately divided, subdivided, classified, numbered off in annotations, meditations, Weeks, points, exercises, mysteries, etc. A simple operation which myth attributes to the Creator of the world, separating day, night, man, woman, elements, and species, forms the continuing basis of Ignatian discourse: *articulation*." *Sade/Fourier/Loyola*, trans. Richard Miller (Baltimore: Johns Hopkins University Press, 1997), 52.

25. Joseba Zulaika, *Basque Violence: Metaphor and Sacrament* (Reno: University of Nevada Press, 1988), 334–38.

26. "The Conservative journals are the loudest in denouncing what they regard as the danger arising from the indifference manifested by the Government in allowing the Carlists to make such a bold display of their power in the provinces. This section of the Press attributes to the Carlist movement the extraordinary military and other precautions now being adopted near the residence of the Royal Family and the special measures taken for the protection of the Premier." "The Carlists," *The Times* (London), August 16, 1894, 3, col. 4.

27. "Riots in Spain," *The Times* (London), September 14, 1894, 3, col. 5.

28. Helen Graham and Jo Labanyi, "Culture and Modernity: The Case of Spain," in *Spanish Cultural Studies: An Introduction*, ed. Helen Graham and Jo Labanyi (Oxford: Oxford University Press, 1995), 5.

29. "Few nationalisms in the modern world can be said to have been permeated and shaped by a single person, but Basque nationalism is an exception, since it owes most of its symbols and values to one man." Daniele Conversi, *The Basques, the Catalans and Spain: Alternative Routes to Nationalist Mobilisation.* (Reno: University of Nevada Press, 1997), 53.

30. "The implicit power and responsibility of historical accounts in such a system assigns considerable value to the affective qualities of the text, and by extension, grants it some . . . degree of fictive licence." Marian Rothstein, "When Fiction is Fact: Perceptions in Sixteenth-Century France," *Studies in Philology* 83, no. 3 (Summer 1986): 375.

31. "The Crisis in Spain," *The Times* (London), November 2, 1894, 5, col. 5.

32. "Spain and Cuba," *The Times* (London), November 28, 1894, 5, col. 3.

33. "Spain and Cuba," *The Times* (London), December 6, 1894, 5, col. 6.

34. *Casticismo* has been defined as Spanish "cultural nationalism." The word *castizo* means "typically Spanish" and from the late nineteenth century on has been particularly associated with Castile. See *Spanish Cultural Studies: An Introduction*, ed. Graham and Labanyi, 420.

35. According to Jon Juaristi, these essays (the second part was published in June 1895) precipitated the literary and philosophical movement known as the "generation of '98," a movement of sweeping intellectual criticism that highlighted the roots of the perennial crisis in Spanish society. "El gueto vacío," in Juan Aranzadi, Jon Juaristi, and Patxo Unzueta, *Auto de terminación (Raza, nación y violencia en el País Vasco)* (Madrid: El País/Aguilar, 1994), first published in *Letra Internacional* (Spring 1987), 123. Two years later, Unamuno published his first novel: an indictment of the violence witnessed in the Bilbao of his youth during the Second Carlist war and a lament for the recourse to warfare in Cuba. In the book, he wrote that "only in the refuge of true and profound peace is war understood and justified. . . . Not outside war, but within it, in its very heart, peace must be sought: peace in war itself." Miguel de Unamuno, *Peace in War: A Novel*, trans. Allen Lacey and Martin Nozick with Anthony Kerrigan, Bollingen Series, 85.1 (1897; rpt., Princeton: Princeton University Press, 1983), 383 (page citations are to the reprint edition).

36. "The Spanish Cabinet Crisis," *The Times* (London), March 18, 1895, 5, col. 1. In Barcelona, a military court took matters into its own hands by ordering the arrest of two newspaper editors. "The Spanish Ministerial Crisis," *The Times* (London), March 20, 1895, 5, col. 2.

37. "The Spanish Cabinet Crisis," *The Times* (London), March 22, 1895, 5, col. 2.

38. "Spanish Affairs," *The Times* (London), March 28, 1895, 5, col. 3.

39. Ibid.

40. "Spain and Cuba," *The Times* (London), March 29, 1895, 5, col. 3.

41. "Spain and Cuba," *The Times* (London), April 2, 1895, 5, col. 3.

42. For a detailed account of the provisions of this law, see Corcuera Atienza, *Orígenes, ideología y organización del nacionalismo vasco*, 237.

43. Sabino Arana, "Ellos y nosotros," *Bizkaitarra*, no. 25, April 24, 1895, 1, col. 3.

44. Herodotus, *The Histories*, trans. Aubrey de Sélincourt, rev. with an introduction and notes by A. R. Burn, rev. ed. (Harmondsworth, England: Penguin Books, 1972), 583.

45. Hedva Ben-Israel, "Nationalism in Historical Perspective," *Journal of International Affairs* 45, no. 2 (Winter 1992): 368.

46. See Zulaika, *Basque Violence: Metaphor and Sacrament*, pt. 5.

47. Ibid., 230.

48. As a contemporary assessment of *ekintza* puts it: "Action can represent a cultural way of resolving a concern through the visible experiential of movement. It provides a sensation of already being part of the solution to the problem. When this action occurs in a group, it has a power that can prolong the enthusiasm of the moment and carry over to the specific actions within ordinary life." Teresa del Valle, *Korrika: Basque Ritual for Ethnic Identity*, trans. Linda White (Reno: University of Nevada Press, 1994), 43–44.

49. Sabino Arana, *Bizkaitarra*, no. 26, May 12, 1895, 1, col. 1.

50. Sabino Arana, "¿Qué somos?" *Bizkaitarra*, no. 28, June 16, 1895, 1, col. 2.

51. Such distinctions are seminal in the reactive force of violence. See, for example, Bruce Kapferer, *Legends of People, Myths of State: Violence, Intolerance, and Political Culture in Sri Lanka and Australia* (Washington: Smithsonian Institution Press, 1988), ch. 2, 29–48.

52. Ander Gurruchaga, *El código nacionalista vasco durante el franquismo* (Barcelona: Anthropos, 1985), 46–52.

53. Arana y Goiri, "¿Qué somos?," 1, cols. 2–5. These elements are discussed in detail by Corcuera Atienza, *Orígenes, ideología y organización del nacionalismo vasco*, ch. 5; Stanley G. Payne, *Basque Nationalism* (Reno: University of Nevada Press, 1975), 72–77; Gurruchaga, *El código nacionalista vasco durante el franquismo*, 109–21; and Conversi, *The Basques, the Catalans and Spain*, 53–68.

54. Arana y Goiri, "¿Qué somos?," 2, col. 2.

55. On its formation and composition, see Corcuera Atienza, *Orígenes, ideología y organización del nacionalismo vasco*, 413–19, and Letamendia Belzunce [Ortzi, pseud.], *ETA en el franquismo*, 149.

56. Principally the articles in question were dedicated to the *gudariak*, or Basque soldiers who fought in the Second Carlist war. See Pedro Antonio de Ormaetxea [pseud. Maitetsea], "Gudarijak," *Bizkaitarra*, no. 29, June 30, 1895, 1, cols. 2–4 and no. 30, July 7, 1895, 1, cols. 1–2. See also two hymns devoted to Loyola, the words of which are printed in *Bizkaitarra*, no. 31, July 28, 1895, 1, cols. 1–2.

57. "Today saw before trial the case against Sabino de Arana for the crime of rebellion." *El Nervión* (Bilbao), November 18, 1895, in *Documentos*, vol. 1, 628.

58. See Angel Jausoro [pseud. Neu], "Abolición y Reconquista," and Engracio de Aranzadi y Etxeberría [pseud. Baso-Jaun], "¡Vengan escobas!" *Bizkaitarra*, suppl. 4, July 21, 1895, 1–2; even according to the standards set by Arana, the articles were virulent in their prose. Indeed, their more direct, less metaphorical content must have been responsible for the official condemnation. For example, Jausoro referred to the post–1876 settlement as a "blood tribute" and the Restoration period as "that armed peace" (1, col. 2). Aranzadi's racial diatribe against Spanish immigrants called for their symbolic sweeping away: "We have to declare a war without mercy on that sick element that has entered our cities, of which it is master, that has penetrated our towns, of which it is tyrannical oppressor.... But, for such a fight... we should provide ourselves with no more than a broom; it would be disregarding the quality of our enemy, building him up, praising him, to allow anything else in his presence" (2, col. 2).

59. Payne, *Basque Nationalism*, 77; Larronde, "Sabino Arana," 65; San Sebastián, *Historia del Partido Nacionalista Vasco*, 27.

60. Daniel de Irujo, "Discurso del abogado Sr. Irujo ante el Tribunal," in *Documentos*, vol. 1, 631. The speech was later published under the title *Inocencia de un patriota* (The innocence of a patriot) in Buenos Aires in 1913, becoming a nationalist classic. Payne, *Basque Nationalism*, 85 n. 34.

61. The offending phrase was originally written by Engracio de Aranzadi y Etxeberría in "La invasión maketa en Gipuzkoa," *Bizkaitarra*, no. 32, September 5, 1895, in *Documentos*, vol. 1, 666, and is repeated in his *Ereintza: Siembra de nacionalismo vasco, 1894–1912* (Zarauz: Editorial Vasca, 1935), 17–18. *The Times* (London) described Maceo as, "a daring mulatto adventurer, brave, unscrupulous, and cruel, who gained his living before the outbreak of the insurrection as chief of a band of brigands." "The Cuban Question From the Spanish Point of View," September 19, 1895, 8, col. 2.

62. Aranzadi y Etxeberría [Kizkitza, pseud.], *Ereintza: Siembra de nacionalismo vasco*, 18; Letamendia Belzunce [Ortzi, pseud.], *ETA en el franquismo*, 149.

63. Sabino Arana to Paulina Arana y Goiri [his sister], [ca. September 14, 1895], in *Documentos*, vol. 1, 464–66. Cf. the fate of the anarchists tried for one of their most infamous acts: the Liceo Opera House bombing in Barcelona in 1893 that killed twenty-one people. The accused were tried first by a civil magistrate and then handed over to the military authorities. "The Anarchists," *The Times* (London), January 4, 1894, 5, col. 2.

64. Corcuera Atienza, *Orígenes, ideología y organización del nacionalismo vasco*, 238; Larronde, "Sabino Arana," 65; San Sebastián, *Historia del Partido Nacionalista Vasco*, 27.

65. Aranzadi y Etxeberría [Kizkitza, pseud.], *Ereintza: Siembra de nacionalismo vasco*, 18.

66. "The Cuban Revolt," *The Times* (London), September 16, 1895, 3, cols. 1–2.

67. "The Cuban Question From the Spanish Point of View," *The Times* (London), September 19, 1895, 8, col. 1.

68. Aranzadi y Etxeberría [Kizkitza, pseud.], *Ereintza: Siembra de nacionalismo vasco*, 19. See also Payne, *Basque Nationalism*, 43–45. For the relationship between Carlism and Basque nationalism, see Mikel Urquijo Goitia, "Carlismo y guerra en el origen del nacionalismo vasco," *Muga*, no. 93 (September 1995), 40–47.

69. Luis de Arana y Goiri to Angel de Zabala, Bilbao, January 20, 1896, in *Documentos*, vol. 2, 149.

70. Weyler is described by Raymond Carr as "the military incarnation of the policy of resistance to the end." *Spain 1808–1975*, 2nd ed. (Oxford: Clarendon Press, 1982), 385. *The Times* of London referred to one of Weyler's subsequent campaigns in Cuba as "marked by the destruction of property and the despair of the peaceful inhabitants." "Spain and Cuba," March 8, 1897, 8, col. 2.

71. "Bomb Outrage in Madrid," *The Times* (London), February 21, 1896, 5, col. 4.

72. Sabino Arana to Angel de Zabala, Bilbao, March 3, 1896, in *Documentos*, vol. 2, 150.

73. This point is made by San Sebastián, *Historia del Partido Nacionalista Vasco*, 30.

74. The matter was taken up by Arana's brother Luis, who wrote that he would do everything he could, "because they attack him every day until he has to leave." Luis de Arana y Goiri to Angel de Zabala, Bilbao, March 10, 1896, in *Documentos*, vol. 2, 151.

75. Sabino Arana to Angel de Zabala, Bilbao, June 22, 1896, in *Documentos*, vol. 2, 158.

76. The bombing resulted in a death toll of around fifteen and fifty injuries. "The Barcelona Bomb Outrage," *The Times* (London), September 9, 1896, 3, col. 2.

77. "Taxation Riots in Spain," *The Times* (London), August 6, 1896, 3, col. 3.

78. "Spain and Her Colonies," *The Times* (London), September 1, 1896, 3, col. 2.

79. Juan Valera, "Las dos rebeliones" (1896), in *Obras completas*, vol. 3 (Madrid: Agular, 1947), 1032, quoted in Ángel G. Loureiro, "Spanish Nationalism and the Ghost of Empire," *Journal of Spanish Cultural Studies* 4, no. 1 (2003): 71.

80. Luis de Arana y Goiri to Angel de Zabala, Bilbao, September 21, 1896, in *Documentos*, vol. 2, 160.

81. Manuel Tuñón de Lara, Julio Valdeón Baruque, and Antonio Domínguez Ortiz, *Historia de España* (Barcelona: Editorial Labor, 1991), 480.

82. On this manipulation and the distribution of municipal politics in Bilbao, see Corcuera Atienza, *Orígenes, ideología y organización del nacionalismo vasco*, 307–14.

83. Letamendia Belzunce [Ortzi, pseud.], *ETA en el franquismo*, 144.

84. Corcuera Atienza, *Orígenes, ideología y organización del nacionalismo vasco*, 335. See also Payne, *Basque Nationalism*, 77, and San Sebastián, *Historia del Partido Nacionalista Vasco*, 30.

85. Sabino Arana, "El Partido Carlista y los fueros Vasco-Nabarros," *Hoja Suelta* (Bilbao), February 20, 1897, 1, col. 1.

86. Ibid., cols. 2–3.

87. These ideas would confirm the conclusion drawn by Larronde that, although Arana never explicitly stated it, he owed an ideological debt of allegiance to German thinkers such as Herder and Fichte. See Larronde, *El nacionalismo vasco*, 19–22.

88. However, this point is contested by one unsigned article that argues that Basque nationalists did not look to either Cuba or the Philippines for inspiration. See "Relaciones entre los nacionalistas cubano y filipino y el nacionalismo vasco en el marco de la crisis de 1898," *Muga*, no. 55 (June 1986), 27–28.

89. "Spain and Cuba," *The Times* (London), March 8, 1897, 8, col. 2.

90. "Four of the prisoners fell dead immediately, but Alsina remained on his knees not even wounded. At the second volley he fell, but was not killed outright, and it was not till a third volley had been fired that he was pronounced to be dead." "The Barcelona Anarchists," *The Times* (London), May 5, 1897, 8, col. 2.

91. "The Duke of Tetuan and Señor Comas appointed seconds, who, after deliberating for more than an hour, decided that there was no ground for a duel." "Spain," *The Times* (London), May 24, 1897, 8, col. 1.

92. It was less anti-Spanish in theory, at least. Arana told Aranzadi that the anti-Spanish rhetoric of *Bizkaitarra* had been due to a lack of historical consciousness on the part of its readership. "Today," he continued, "and above all in Bizkaia, there is no need to speak against Spain . . . today I would write a newspaper in which nothing, [or] the very minimum would be directed against Spain." Sabino Arana to Engracio de Aranzadi y Etxeberría, Bilbao, November 13, 1897, in *Documentos*, vol. 2, 349.

93. Sabino Arana, "Los civilizadores de América," *Baseritara*, no. 1, May 2, 1897, 3, col. 4, and 4, col. 1.

94. The methods of Spanish torture were also detailed by the correspondent, William Tallace of the Howard Association. They included "burning the flesh with hot irons, tearing out finger-nails with pincers, bodily mutilations, compression of the skull by metal instruments, and other modes of treatment, both indecent and savage." "Spain and the Torture," *The Times* (London), June 7, 1897, 10, col. 6.

95. "Spain and the Torture," *The Times* (London), August 3, 1897, 6, col. 3.

96. Michel Foucault, *The History of Sexuality, Volume 1: An Introduction*, trans. Robert Hurley (New York: Vintage Books, 1990), 58–59.

97. Hobsbawm, *The Age of Empire 1875–1914*, 24.

98. Sabino Arana, "Martires de la Patria," *Baseritara*, no. 4, May 23, 1897, 1, col. 1.

99. Sabino Arana, "La Ley del 76," *Baseritara*, no. 13, July 25, 1897, 2, col. 1.

100. In 1891 Rizal wrote that "the spectre of subversion has been used so often to frighten us that, from being a mere nursery tale, it has acquired a real and positive existence. . . . If the sight of it should lead our Country and its Government to reflexion, we shall be happy." "To the Filipino People and Their Government," in *The Subversive (El Filibusterismo)*, trans. León Mª Guerrero (1891; rpt., Bloomington: Indiana University Press, 1962), vii (page citations are to the reprint edition).

101. The full text is reproduced in Sabino Arana, "Una poesía de Rizal," *Baseritara*, no. 15, August 8, 1897, 4, cols. 2–3. See Rizal's "Último adiós (Last goodbye), written as he awaited his execution by the Spanish authorities. See also Benedict Anderson, *Imagined Communities: Reflections on the Origin and Spread of Nationalism*, rev. ed (London: Verso, 1991), 142–43.

102. "The Assassination of the Spanish Premier," *The Times* (London), August 10, 1897, 3, col. 1.

103. Sabino Arana to Angel de Zabala, Bilbao, August 8, 1897, in *Documentos*, vol. 2, 443.

104. "Spain," *The Times* (London), August 17, 1897, 3, col. 1.

105. The verse attacked Cánovas as a "crook" or "villain" who had "destroyed" Basque homes and taken away the *fueros*. His death, according to Txirrita, was by God's grace. The full text and an appreciation of his life and work appear in Gorka Aulestia, "El 'Bertsolarismo': Literatura Oral Improvisada del País Vasco." Ph.D. diss., University of Nevada, Reno, 1987, 141–44. and in idem, Gorka Aulestia, *Improvisational Poetry from the Basque Country*, trans. Lisa Corcostegui and Linda White (Reno: University of Nevada Press, 1995), 88–95.

106. "The Late Señor Canovas," *The Times* (London), August 12, 1897, 3, col. 6, and "Execution of Angiolillo," *The Times* (London), August 21, 1897, 5, col. 2.

107. "Spanish Politics," *The Times* (London), August 28, 1897, 3, col. 6.

108. Joseba Zulaika, "Terror, Totem, and Taboo: Reporting on a Report," *Terrorism and Political Violence* 3, no. 1 (Spring 1991): 44.

109. The decree was published in full by *The Times* (London). "Spain and Her Colonies," November 29, 1897, 8, cols. 2–3.

110. Luis de Arana y Goiri to Angel de Zabala, Bilbao, November 14, 1897, in *Documentos*, vol. 2, 535.

111. "Spain and Her Colonies," *The Times* (London), December 18, 1897, 7, col. 4.

112. "Spain and Her Colonies," *The Times* (London), December 20, 1897, 5, col. 6.

113. Corcuera Atienza, *Orígenes, ideología y organización del nacionalismo vasco*, 446–47; cf. "Spain and Cuba," *The Times* (London), February 8, 1898, 2, col. 6.

114. There was, for instance, a widespread social protest during the March elections. The disturbances were few, but relatively strong, especially in the mining areas around Bilbao. "The Spanish Elections," *The Times* (London), March 29, 1898, 5, col. 2. That summer, the mining protest spread to Catalonia, where seventeen thousand men were out of work. "The authorities," reported *The Times* (London), "are using every possible means to avert a conflict and improve the situation." June 23, 1898, 5, col. 2.

115. "The Scene in the Cortes on Wednesday," *The Times* (London), April 22, 1898, 4, col. 1.

116. According to Larronde, this act constituted the first act of terrorism between Basque and Spanish nationalists in the modern age. "Sabino de Arana-Goiri, el fundador," 13.

117. The disturbances were located chiefly in Andalusia, Extremadura, Murcia, Castile, and the coal-mining areas of Asturias. Madrid, Barcelona, and Bilbao, perhaps fearful of a mass uprising, were spared trouble due to municipal implementation of preventative measures such as the distribution of free food to the needy. Adrian Shubert, *A Social History of Modern Spain* (London: Unwin Hyman, 1990), 194.

118. Sabino Arana to Angel de Zabala, [Bilbao], [ca. June 13, 1898], in *Documentos*, vol. 2, 552.

119. Joseba Gabilondo, "Postnationalism, Fundamentalism, and the Global Real: Historicizing Terror/ism and the New North American/Global Ideology," *Journal of Spanish Cultural Studies* 3, no.1 (2002): 69.

120. Ángel G. Loureiro would appear to agree, arguing that, "in spite of repeated characterization of the outcome of the Spanish American war as a 'national disaster' . . . such expression points to nothing more than the reiteration of the topical view regarding Spain's decline that had been bandied about well before 1898." "Spanish Nationalism and the Ghost of Empire," 67.

121. José Álvarez Junco, "The Formation of Spanish Identity and its Adaptation to the Age of Nations." *History and Memory* 14, nos. 1–2 (Fall 2002): 32.

122. Gabilondo, "Postnationalism, Fundamentalism, and the Global Real," 69.

123. Luis de Arana y Goiri to Angel de Zabala, Bilbao, June 30, 1898, in *Documentos*, vol. 2, 553.

124. Luis de Arana y Goiri to Angel de Zabala, Bilbao, July 9, 1898, in *Documentos*, vol. 2, 554.

125. Corcuera Atienza, *Orígenes, ideología y organización del nacionalismo vasco*, 445–48; José Luis de la Granja Sainz, *El nacionalismo vasco: Un siglo de historia* (Madrid: Editorial Tecnos, 1995), 34, 35–36; Martín de Ugalde, *Nueva síntesis de la historia del País Vasco*, vol. 2 (Donostia: Elkar, 1983), 669.

126. Javier Corcuera, "La difícil definición del 'problema vasco,'" in *Violencia y política en Euskadi*, ed. Fernando Reinares (Bilbao: Desclée de Brouwer, 1984), 40.

127. Mikel Azurmendi, "Etnicidad y violencia en el suelo vasco," *Claves de Razón Práctica*, no. 43 (June 1994): 35.

128. See Joxe A. Otaegi, "Biolentzia, biolentziak," *Jakin*, no. 9 (January–March 1979): 108.

129. Payne, *Basque Nationalism*, 79–81.

130. Douglass, "Sabino's Sin," 104.

131. Conversi, *The Basques, the Catalans and Spain*, 77.

132. Martin Jay, *Fin-de-Siècle Socialism and Other Essays* (New York: Routledge, 1988), 1.

133. H. Stuart Hughes, *Consciousness and Society: The Reorientation of European Social Thought 1890–1930* (New York: Alfred A. Knopf, 1958), 113–15.

134. Walter Laqueur, "Fin-de-Siècle: Once More With Feeling," *Journal of Contemporary History* 31 (1996): 10, 13.

Notes, Chapter Four

1. Eric Hobsbawm, *The Age of Extremes: The Short History of the Twentieth Century 1914–1991* (London: Michael Joseph, 1994; rpt., London: Abacus, 1995), 6 (page citations are to the reprint edition).

2. Daniele Conversi, *The Basques, the Catalans and Spain: Alternative Routes to Nationalist Mobilisation* (Reno: University of Nevada Press, 1997), 77.

3. "President [Woodrow] Wilson put his faith in national self-determination as a force for freedom and peaceful felicity. If the most fundamental cause of war in 1914 had really been a frustration of the ambitions cherished by small nations, rather than a thwarting of the greed harboured by larger ones, then his creed might have had more sense." Michael Biddiss, "Nationalism and the Moulding of Modern Europe," *History* 79, no. 257 (October 1994): 421–22.

4. As to the legitimacy of the principle, it has been argued that "self-determination–again , an actual legal arrangement that provides a group independence or more legal authority within a state–is rooted in moral autonomy, which not only grounds democracy and, derivatively, self-determination, but is also the map with which we negotiate the minefield of qualifications which threaten to explode on us." Daniel Philpott, "In Defense of Self-Determination," *Ethics* 105, no. 2 (January 1995): 353.

5. Jesús Mª de Leizaola Sánchez, in Marga Otaegui and Xosé Estévez, "Protagonistas de la historia vasca (1923–1950): Partido Nacionalista Vasco," *Cuadernos de Sección Historia-Geografía*, no. 7 (1984): 24.

6. Hobsbawm, *The Age of Extremes*, 65.

7. Gloria Totoricagüena, *Identity, Culture, and Politics in the Basque Diaspora* (Reno: University of Nevada Press, 2004), 69. According to data gathered by Totoricagüena, there were approximately a quarter of a million Basque immigrants in Argentina in 1908.

8. Eduardo Jorge Glas, *Bilbao's Modern Business Elite* (Reno: University of Nevada Press, 1997), 213.

9. "The Cuban Revolution gave Spain a net inflow of about 110,000 transatlantic migrants in 1897–1899, contrasting with a net outflow of 153,000 in 1895–1896." Walter Nugent, *Crossings: The Great Transatlantic Migrations, 1870–1914* (Bloomington: Indiana University Press, 1992), 104.

10. "With few exceptions, except for the Catalans, the really rich men in Spain after 1900 were Basques." Raymond Carr, *Spain 1808–1975*, 2nd ed. (Oxford: Clarendon Press, 1982), 406.

11. Ibid., 464.

12. Vicente Palacio Atard, *La España del siglo XIX, 1808–1898 (Introducción a la España contemporánea)*, 2nd ed. (Madrid: Calpe, 1981), 609–10.

13. José Alvarez Junco, "Rural and Urban Popular Cultures," in *Spanish Cultural Studies: An Introduction*, ed. Helen Graham and Jo Labanyi (Oxford: Oxford University Press, 1995), 82.

14. Sebastian Balfour, "The Loss of Empire, Regenerationism, and the Forging of a Myth of National Identity," in *Spanish Cultural Studies: An Introduction*, ed. Graham and Labanyi, 25–26, 30.

15. "[Iron ore] mining increased the capital of a local group of entrepreneurs, which reduced the need for institutional support that seems to characterize other late industrializers." Glas, *Bilbao's Modern Business Elite*, 210.

16. See Joseph Harrison, "Heavy Industry, the State, and Economic Development in the Basque Region, 1876–1936," *The Economic History Review*, 2nd ser., 36, no. 4 (November 1983): 539–41.

17. Alvaro Chapa, *La vida cultural de la villa de Bilbao 1917–1936* (Bilbao: Ayuntamiento de Bilbao/Bilboko Udala, 1989), 29–30.

18. Juan Pablo Fusi, *El País Vasco: Pluralismo y nacionalidad* (Madrid: Alianza Editorial, 1984), 14.

19. John K. Walton and Jenny Smith, "The First Spanish Seaside Resorts," *History Today* 44, no. 8 (August 1994): 23–25.

20. John K. Walton and Jenny Smith, "The Rhetoric of Community and the Business of Pleasure: The San Sebastián Waiters' Strike of 1920," *International Review of Social History* 39 (1994): 6, 24.

21. Walton and Smith, "The First Spanish Seaside Resorts," 26.

22. Fusi, *El País Vasco: Pluralismo y nacionalidad*, 14.

23. John K. Walton, "Planning and Seaside Tourism: San Sebastián, 1863–1936," *Planning Perspectives* 17 (2002): 12, 14. For an excellent comparative analysis of social change in Bilbao and Donostia–San Sebastián during the period (as well for the similarities and differences therein) and between Liverpool and Blackpool in England, see John K. Walton, Martin Blinkhorn, Colin Pooley, David Tidswell, and Michael J. Winstanley, "Crime, Migration and Social Change in North-West England and the Basque Country, c.1870–1930," *British Journal of Criminology* 39, no. 1, special issue (1999): 90–112.

24. Letamendia Belzunce [Ortzi, pseud.], *Historia del nacionalismo vasco y de ETA*, vol. 1. *Introducción a la historia del País Vasco: ETA en el franquismo* (San Sebastián: R & B Ediciones, 1994), 155–56.

25. Marianne Heiberg, *The Making of the Basque Nation*, (Cambridge: Cambridge University Press, 1989), 171, 177, 179.

26. Fusi, *El País Vasco. Pluralismo y nacionalidad*, 15.

27. Rosario Galdos Urrutia, *Estructura y dinámica de la población alavesa (1900–1981)* (Vitoria-Gasteiz: Diputación Foral de Álava, Departamento de Cultura/Arabako Foru Aldundia, Cultura Saila, 1990), 99.

28. Pilar Erdozáin Azpilicueta, *Propiedad, familia y trabajo en la Navarra contemporánea* (Pamplona: Gobierno de Navarra, Departamento de Educación y Cultura, 1999), 79–83, 101–8.

29. Stanley G. Payne, *Basque Nationalism* (Reno: University of Nevada Press, 1975), 78. See also Conversi, *The Basques, the Catalans and Spain*, 25–36.

30. Engracio de Aranzadi, *Patriotismo: Conferencia leída por su autor en el "Centro Vasco" de Bilbao, el día 22 de Mayo de 1904* (Bilbao: José de Astuy, 1904), 21.

31. José Luis de la Granja Sainz, *El nacionalismo vasco: Un siglo de historia* (Madrid: Editorial Tecnos, 1995), 37.

32. Indeed, the party was forced into a position of semiclandestinity in 1904, when its main leaders (including Zabala) were imprisoned after the publication of an article that was considered to be against the interests of the state. Ludger Mees, "La Restauración y la dictadura de Primo de Rivera," in *Los nacionalistas: Historia del nacionalismo vasco, 1876–1960*, ed. Santiago de Pablo, Beasaide Series (Vitoria-Gasteiz: Fundación Sancho el Sabio, 1995), 81.

33. However, it was in 1906, too, that a major doctrinal work of Basque nationalism was published: *Ami vasco*, by the Navarrese friar Father Goicoechea Oroquieta, who wrote under the pseudonym Evangelista de Ibero. It reaffirmed much of Arana's original doctrine while at the same time eschewing violence as a political tactic. Payne, *Basque Nationalism*, 88. Mees views the work as an ideological continuation of Sabino Arana's radical vision, but with a provision that allowed for gradual modernization within the party. "La Restauración," 92. In the opinion of Granja Sainz, the work constituted the nationalist catechism. *El nacionalismo vasco, movimiento obrero y cuestión social (1903–1923)* (Bilbao: Fundación Sabino Arana, 1992), 37.

34. Of the electoral system itself, Gerald Brenan remarks that "one notices as time goes on the ever-increasing amount of force that was needed to produce the desired results. More and more frequently police and bands of roughs had to be called in to keep away hostile voters, whilst landlords were obliged to make it clear to their hitherto docile tenants or labourers that failure to vote for the right man would bring eviction and dismissal." *The Spanish Labyrinth: An Account of the Social and Political Background of the Civil War* (Cambridge: At the University Press, 1943), 18–19.

35. Ibid., 30–31. See Jon Juaristi's argument in *El linaje de Aitor: La invención de la tradición vasca* (Madrid: Taurus, 1987), ch. 1, which seems limited if one takes the view that a fully constructed state would not enact a law like that of 1906.

36. *Enciclopedia General Ilustrada del País Vasco*, s.v. "Mendigoizale."

37. Brenan, *The Spanish Labyrinth*, 34.

38. Frances Lannon, "The Social Praxis and Cultural Politics of Spanish Catholicism," in *Spanish Cultural Studies: An Introduction*, ed. Graham and Labanyi, 42–43.

39. Brenan, *The Spanish Labyrinth*, 34.

40. Robert Darnton, "Workers Revolt: The Great Cat Massacre of the Rue Saint-Séverin," in *The Great Cat Massacre and Other Episodes in French Cultural History* (New York: Basic Books, 1984; rpt., New York: Vintage Books, 1985), 75–104 (page citations are to the reprint edition).

41. Brenan, *The Spanish Labyrinth*, 34–35; Carr, *Spain 1808–1975*, 483–85.

42. E. P. Thompson, "Folklore, Anthropology, and Social History," *The Indian Historical Review* 3, no. 2 (January 1977): 254.

43. David Held, "The Development of the Modern State," in *Modernity: An Introduction to Modern Societies*, ed. Stuart Hall, David Held, Don Hubert, and Kenneth Thompson (Oxford: Blackwell, 1996), 71.

44. Enric Ucelay Da Cal, "The Nationalisms of the Periphery: Culture and Politics in the Construction of National Identity," in *Spanish Cultural Studies: An Introduction*, ed. Graham and Labanyi, 38.

45. Mees, "La Restauración," 88.

46. Sira García Casado and Jesús Mª Abad Ruiz, "Evolución ideológica del Partido Nacionalista Vasco, 1913–1918," *Cuadernos de Alzate*, no. 4 (1986): 82. See also Chapa, *La vida cultural*, 23–24.

47. "I understand the Basque nationalist community to be a social collectivity cross-cutting class distinctions and aware of a nationalist consciousness which exhibits itself through ideological elements, cultural mores and social practices, and which politically has the PNV as its central, but not its sole, axis." José Luis Granja, "The Basque Nationalist Community During the Second Spanish Republic (1931–1936)," in *Basque Politics: A Case Study in Ethnic Nationalism*, ed. William A. Douglass, Basque Studies Program Occasional Papers Series, no. 2 (Reno: Associated Faculty Press and Basque Studies Program, 1985), 157–58.

48. "To be an ethnic party, the party does not have to command an exclusive hold on the allegiance of group members. It is how the *party's* support is distributed, and not how the *ethnic group's* support is distributed, that is decisive." Donald L. Horowitz, *Ethnic Groups in Conflict* (Berkeley University of California Press, 1985), 293.

49. Alain Darré, "Le Parti nationaliste basque: Un mouvement périphérique et totalisant," *Revue Française de Science Politique* 40, no. 2 (April 1990): 252.

50. Letamendia Belzunce [Ortzi, pseud.], *ETA en el franquismo*, 157.

51. Mees, *El nacionalismo vasco*, 345.

52. José Mª de Ojarbide, "Destellos de historia vasca: Artifices famosos," *Euzkadi*, no. 121, June 3, 1913, 1, col. 2.

53. Antonio Elorza argues that Basque nationalists inherited a mythical ideology from Carlism, whereby Basques defended peace and order through war, and that Basque nationalism, as encapsulated by Arana, existed as a desperate agony, with the noble Basques constantly struggling against more powerful enemies. See "Guerra y fueros en los orígenes del nacionalismo vasco," in *Gernika: 50 años después (1937–1987). Nacionalismo, República, Guerra Civil*, ed. Manuel Tuñón de Lara (San Sebastián: Servicio Editorial Universidad del País Vasco/Argitalpen Zerbitzua Euskal Herriko Unibertsitatea, 1987), 19, 21.

54. L. de Otxaita, "Impresiones. Los mendigoi-zales," *Euzkadi*, no. 153, July 5, 1913, 1, col. 2.

55. Mees, "La Restauración," 90.

56. Payne, *Basque Nationalism*, 93–94.

57. Ibid., 92.

58. Ludger Mees, "Luis de Arana Goiri y la crisis de la Communión Nacionalista en 1915–16," *Muga*, no. 69 (June 1989), 42.

59. Payne, *Basque Nationalism*, 95.

60. Blas de Gárate, interview by Carlos Blasco Olaetxea, "José y Blas de Gárate," in Fondo de Carlos Blasco Olaetxea, Irargi: Centro de Patrimonio Documental de Euskadi (Bergara, Gipuzkoa), box no. 4, 2 (hereafter cited as Blasco Olaetxea MSS).

61. Lezo de Urreztieta, "Un aberriano," interview by Eugenio Ibarzábal, *Muga*, no. 4 (March 1980), 8.

62. Javier Real Cuesta, "El P.N.V. en 1917: De la intransigencia al oportunismo político," *Letras de Deusto* 6, no. 12 (July–December 1976), 117.

63. Délégation Basque, *Le nationalisme basque et le Gouvernement espagnol* (Lausanne: Imprimerie Vaudoise, 1916), 5–8.

64. See Harrison, "Heavy Industry," 544–45.

65. [Francesc Cambó], *Conferencia pronunciada por D. Francisco Cambó en el Teatro de los Campos Elíseos de Bilbao, el día 28 de enero de 1917* (Bilbao: Jesús Alvarez, 1917), 10, 13.

66. Cambó remarked in the speech that it was not necessarily rich people who should be defended, but wealth itself. *Conferencia*, 18.

67. Real Cuesta, "El P.N.V. en 1917," 120–21; Payne, *Basque Nationalism*, 95–96.

68. Ucelay Da Cal, "The Nationalisms of the Periphery," 38.

69. Carr, *Spain 1808–1975*, 500–501.

70. Brenan, *The Spanish Labyrinth*, 60.

71. Payne, *Basque Nationalism*, 96; Mees, "La Restauración," 100.

72. Brenan, *The Spanish Labyrinth*, 64–65. The debate over whether the *juntas* could ever have joined the Assembly is interesting. According to Ucelay Da Cal, "the colonial wars of the 1890s tended to polarize what had previously been a juridical debate about administrative organization pursued by politicians in parliament, transforming it into a controversial issue central to the rise of mass participation in Spanish politics. The subject of devolution was thus turned into a potentially violent conflict between the officer corps, viscerally unitarist after being defeated by Cuban separatists, and the new, alternative, non-Spanish nationalists in industrialized Catalonia and the Basque Country, who loved to bait centralist opinion with allusions to Cuba." "The Nationalisms of the Periphery," 37–38.

73. Real Cuesta, "El P.N.V. en 1917," 128–29, 137.

74. Payne, *Basque Nationalism*, 96; Real Cuesta, "El P.N.V. en 1917," 132–33.

75. Mees, "La Restauración," 104.

76. Payne, *Basque Nationalism*, 97–98.

77. Joseba Mikel de Urquijo y Goitia, "La crisis de 1917. Las reivindicaciones autonómicas en el País Vasco," in *II Euskal mundu-biltzarra/II Congreso mundial vasco*, sec. 2, *Euskal Herriaren historiari buruzko biltzarra/Congreso de historia de Euskal Herria*, vol. 7, *Aro moderno eta gaur egungoa/Edad moderna y contemporánea* (Vitoria-Gasteiz: Eusko Jaurlaritzaren Argitalpen-Zerbitzu Nagusia/Servicio Central de Publicaciones del Gobierno Vasco, 1988), 276.

78. José Luis de la Granja Sainz, *Nacionalismo y II República en el País Vasco: Estatutos de autonomía, partidos y elecciones. Historia de Acción Nacionalista Vasca: 1930–1936* (Madrid: Centro de Investigaciones Sociológicas/Siglo XXI, 1986), 7; Granja Sainz, *El nacionalismo vasco*, 37.

79. José María Lorenzo Espinosa, *Gudari: Una pasión útil. Vida y obra de Eli Gallastegi (1892–1974)* (Tafalla: Txalaparta, 1992), 59.

80. Ludger Mees, "Luis Arana Goiri," 43.

81. See Eric J. Hobsbawm, *The Age of Revolution, 1789–1848* (London: Weidenfeld & Nicholson, 1962; rpt., London: Abacus, 1977), 164–65 (page citations are to the reprint edition).

82. Enrique Montero, "Reform Idealized: The Intellectual and Ideological Origins of the Second Republic," in *Spanish Cultural Studies: An Introduction*, ed. Graham and Labanyi, 126–27. There were, naturally, regional counterparts to this vision of nationalism, such as the classicist *noucentistas* of Catalonia and the Basque Studies Congresses of 1918–36 that, rejecting Arana's fear of modernization and science, attempted to quantify and measure Basque identity. On the latter, see Jacqueline Urla, "Being Basque, Speaking Basque: The Politics of Language and Identity in the Basque Country," Ph.D. diss., University of California, Berkeley, 1987.

83. Jesús de Sarría, *Ideología del nacionalismo vasco* (Bilbao: E. Verdes, 1918), 77–78, 79, 82.

84. Koldo San Sebastián, "Jesús de Sarría: Un nacionalista vasco 'heterodoxo,'" *Muga*, no. 7 (June 1980), 57.

85. Payne, *Basque Nationalism*, 99–100.

86. See Antonio Elorza, "Cultura e ideología en el País Vasco contemporáneo," in *II Euskal mundu-biltzarra/II Congreso Mundial*. Sec. 2, *Euskal Herriaren historiari buruzko biltzarra/Congreso de historia de Euskal Herria*, vol. 5, *Aro moderno eta gaur egungoa/Edad moderna y contemporánea* (Vitoria-Gasteiz: Eusko Jaurlaritzaren Argitalpen-Zerbitzu Nagusia/Servicio Central de Publicaciones del Gobierno Vasco, 1988), 204.

87. Tomás Otaegui, *Nacionalismo basko (su actual carácter)* (Buenos Aires: n.p., 1922), 82–83.

88. Robert W. Kern, *Red Years/Black Years: A Political History of Spanish Anarchism, 1911–1937* (Philadelphia: Institute for the Study of Human Issues, 1978), 56–57.

89. Harrison, "Heavy Industry," 542; Payne, *Basque Nationalism*, 98–100.

90. Jesús de Sarría, *Patria Vasca* (Bilbao: Editorial Vasca, 1920), 83.

91. Ibid., 85.

92. San Sebastián, "Jesús de Sarría," 58.

93. Walton and Smith, "The Rhetoric of Community," 3–4, 19.

94. "The riots which followed the *soka-muturra* bullock-running custom in the Old Town main square were a . . . warning, although they took place safely in the depths of January in 1902; and the pre-Lent Carnival was always a source of worry about the exportation of unruliness from the Old Town, with regular attempts to control it through a mixture of patronage and repression." Walton and Smith, "The Rhetoric of Community," 25.

95. Payne, *Basque Nationalism*, 99.

96. Paul Preston, *Franco: A Biography* (London: Harper Collins, 1993; rpt., London: Fontana, 1995), 29 (page citations are to the reprint edition).

97. See Carr, *Spain 1808–1975*, 516–23; Preston, *Franco: A Biography*, 25–34.

98. Mees, *Nacionalismo vasco, movimiento obrero*, 347.

99. Roland Barthes, "The Death of the Author," in *Image, Music, Text*, trans. Stephen Heath (New York: Hill and Wang, 1977), 143.

100. The "concept first" theory states that people acquire vague concepts (of things, ideas, or emotions) before the ability to articulate them specifically. For example, children will have an idea of what a house is before they can actually describe it in detail. See Maurice Bloch, "Language, Anthropology and Cognitive Science," *Man* 26, no. 2 (June 1991): 184–86.

Notes, Chapter Five

1. Thomas Carlyle, *On Heroes, Hero Worship, and the Heroic in History*, ed. for study by John Chester Adams (Boston, Chicago, and New York: Houghton Mifflin, 1907), 15.

2. See Theodore Zeldin, *An Intimate History of Humanity* (London: Sinclair-Stevenson, 1994; rpt., London: Minerva, 1995), 16 (page citations are to the reprint edition).

3. "San Ignacio. Prudencia y fortaleza," *Euzkadi*, no. 1267, July 31, 1916, 1, cols. 2–3.

4. "'National Prophets' express . . . ideas in their words and often in their lives and call for better realization of the ideas; these ideas thus become the normative form and goal of national life." Hans Kohn, *Prophets and Peoples: Studies in Nineteenth Century Nationalism* (New York: Octagon Books, 1975), 3.

5. "En el 14 aniversario del Maestro. Solemnidad de ayer," *Euzkadi*, no. 1785, November 27, 1917, 1, cols. 2–3.

6. Lezo de Urreztieta, "Un aberriano," interview by Eugenio Ibarzábal. *Muga*, no. 4 (March 1980): 8.

7. Zabalgunde-Batzordia, "Los patriotas de Euzkadi ante la tumba del Maestro," *Aberri*, no. 72, June 10, 1922, 2, cols. 2–4.

8. Gorka Aulestia, "El 'Bertsolarismo': Literatura Oral Improvisada del País Vasco," Ph.D. diss., University of Nevada, Reno, 1987, 6. "Bertsolaritza is a form of artistic expression that involves intense mental exercise and creative and rewarding work. It is performed in the gymnasium of the mind where one thinks as one sings, and improvises without pausing to correct errors. . . . Technically, bertsolaritza is a Basque genre of oral improvised poetry created by folk-poets for an audience." Gorka Aulestia, *Improvisational Poetry from the Basque Country*, trans. Lisa Corcostegui and Linda White (Reno: University of Nevada Press, 1995), 21.

9. Joseba Zulaika, *Basque Violence: Metaphor and Sacrament* (Reno: University of Nevada Press, 1988), 215–16, 225–26.

10. "In the Basque case, I would say 'doing' in the sense of 'being'. It is a 'doing' that can arise from improvisation." Teresa del Valle, *Korrika: Basque Ritual for Ethnic Identity*, trans. Linda White (Reno: University of Nevada Press, 1994), 43.

11. According to Zulaika, the *bertsolari* "has been the unchallenged troubadour, the singer of the desires of rebellious youth. As a poet, he is the hero's memory; as a singer, he is the community's political voice. No other men are able to appreciate the value of Euskera as profoundly and vitally as the bertsolariak." *Basque Violence: Metaphor and_Sacrament*, 231.

12. See Aulestia, "El 'Bertsolarismo,'" 148–54, and *Improvisational Poetry from the Basque Country*, 95–99.

13. Aulestia, *Improvisational Poetry from the Basque Country*, 96.

14. According to James W. Fernandez, "the rising nationalisms of the nineteenth century made much use of folklore to typify and thus create new national identities around new national boundaries, but there is no reason for folklorists to be the acquiescent agents of such nationalism." "Folklorists as Agents of Nationalism: Asturian Legends and the Problem of Identity," in *Fairy Tales and Society: Illusion, Allusion, and Paradigm*, ed. Ruth B. Bottigheimer (Philadelphia: University of Pennsylvania Press, 1986), 135. See my own observation that "throughout the course of Basque nationalism [folklore] has stressed the importance of memory as a primary call to origins" and "made frequent use of folkloric genres as a discursive element of its rhetoric." Cameron Watson, "Folklore and Basque Nationalism: Language, Myth, Reality," *Nations and Nationalism* 2, no. 1 (1996): 31.

15. Engracio de Aranzadi y Etxeberría [Kizkitza, pseud.], "Un gran vasco: Enbeita tař Kepa," *Euzkadi*, no. 2752, October 21, 1920, 1, col. 3. See a similar article about the same *bertsolari* by the radical nationalists, "Nuestro homenaje a Enbeita' tař Kepa," *Aberri*, no. 88, October 7, 1922, 3, cols. 2–3.

16. Zulaika, *Basque Violence: Metaphor and Sacrament*, 231.

17. Stanley G. Payne, *Basque Nationalism* (Reno: University of Nevada Press, 1975), 43–45.

18. Engracio de Aranzadi y Etxeberría [Kizkitza, pseud.], "Zumalakarregi," *Euzkadi*, no. 3112, October 29, 1922, 1, col. 3.

19. Mikel Urquijo Goitia, "Carlismo y guerra en el origen del nacionalismo vasco," *Muga*, no. 93 (September 1995), 46.

20. Santiago Genovés, *La violencia en el País Vasco y en sus relaciones con España (No todo es política)* (Barcelona: Editorial Fontanella/Hogar del Libro, 1986), 84. See also Zeldin's conclusion that, "war has remained prestigious so long as it has been valued as the most dangerous of all excitements.... Humans have continued to fight wars not merely because they cannot agree, but even more because so many of them have loved the exhilarating sensations it created." *An Intimate History of Humanity*, 214–15.

21. "Las proclamaciones de Pradera: En defensa de los héroes de Amayur," *Euzkadi*, no. 2818, January 18, 1921, 1, cols. 3–4.

22. "En memoria de los héroes de Amayur," *Hermes*, no. 85 (1922), 35.

23. Napartarra, "¡Amayur!" *Euzkadi*, no. 3029, July 21, 1922, 1, col. 3.

24. [Jesús María de Leizaola], "Los vascos y la independencia de América," *Euzkadi*, no. 2856, March 4, 1921, 1, col. 6.

25. The history of Basque migration to and settlement in the Americas is complex. The classic categorization, by William A. Douglass and Jon Bilbao, is that migrant Basques were mercenaries, missionaries, mariners, and merchants, as well as sheepmen. See *Amerikanuak: Basques in the New World* (Reno: University of Nevada Press, 1975), esp. chs. 2 and 3, 61–176. See also Gloria Totoricagüena, *Identity, Culture, and Politics in the Basque Diaspora* (Reno: University of Nevada Press, 2004), ch. 3, 55–80, where she outlines this complexity. For example, Basques went to the Americas as faithful collaborators in the Spanish imperial thrust, migrants to the newly independent republics of the nineteenth century, and economic and political refugees.

26. Dořkaitz, "El militarismo en la Diputación," *Aberri*, no. 57, February 24, 1922, 2, col. 1.

27. Kis., "¡Resurreción!" *Aberri*, no. 96, November 30, 1922, 1, col. 4.

28. Gudalgai, "Crónicas de la guerra. En el frente inglés. Aviadores y zapadores. La lección de heroísmo," *Euzkadi*, no. 1208, June 1, 1916, 5, col. 3.

29. [Gudalgai], "¿Paz ó guerra?," *Euzkadi*, no. 1792, December 4, 1917, 1, col. 4.

30. "Euzkaldun gudari azkarrak," *Euzkadi*, no. 1066, January 9, 1916, 1, col. 1.

31. The Irish name for the IRA, Óglaigh na hÉireann, had actually been used by the Volunteers since 1913, but their title was not officially changed until 1922. Richard English, *Armed Struggle: The History of the IRA* (London: Pan Books, 2003), 394 n. 39.

32. Martin Williams, "Ancient Mythology and Revolutionary Ideology in Ireland, 1878–1916," *The Historical Journal* 26, no. 2 (June 1983): 325.

33. English, *Armed Struggle*, 5–6.

34. Ibid., 7, 14.

35. Letamendia Belzunce [Ortzi, pseud.], *ETA en el franquismo*, 159.

36. Engracio de Aranzadi y Etxeberría [Kizkitza, pseud.], "Ante la revolución irlandesa. Enseñanzas católicas sobre la revolución," *Euzkadi*, no. 1203, May 27, 1916, 1, col. 4.

37. Ibid., 2, col. 1.

38. Engracio de Aranzadi y Etxeberría [Kizkitza, pseud.], "Ante la revolución irlandesa. El imperio de lo retumbante," *Euzkadi*, no. 1204, May 28, 1916, 1, col. 4.

39. "El estado libre de Irlanda," *Aberri*, no. 46, December 17, 1921, 1, col. 3.

40. Elías de Gallastegui [Gudari, pseud.], *Por la libertad vasca*, vol. 1, *En plena lucha* (Bilbao: E. Verdes, 1933), 131. Trifón Echeberria, a young Basque militant of the 1930s, argued that the youth wing of the nationalists, through its Bilbao section, began to feel a particular affinity with the Irish cause from the time of the Easter Rising onward. See Eugenio Ibarzábal, ed., *50 años de nacionalismo vasco 1928–1978(A través de sus protagonistas)* (San Sebastián: Ediciones Vascas, 1978), 121.

41. "I think there is evidence," notes Martin Williams in regard to the Irish case, "to indicate that the ideals of heroic mythology played a significant part in shaping 1916 and its aftermath. They may not have directly influenced many to take up arms, but their tone and their language gave an epic quality to the whole national struggle." "Ancient Mythology," 323.

42. Luis de Eleizalde [Axe, pseud.], "El Ulster vasco," *Euzkadi*, no. 1669, July 22, 1917, 2, col. 1.

43. See, for example, Ramón de Belaustegigoitia, "Nacionalistas y sinn-feiners," *Euzkadi*, no. 1675, July 28, 1917.

44. Luis de Eleizalde [Axe, pseud.], "'Sinn-fein', Nacionalismo y Ulster," *Euzkadi*, no. 2776, November 14, 1920, 1, col. 2.

45. Ibid., 1, col. 4.

46. Letamendia Belzunce [Ortzi, pseud.] overlooks this change in policy by only making reference to the 'anglophile' policy of the CNV. See *ETA en el franquismo*, 159.

47. "Muere asesinado Michael Collins: Irlanda pierde en él a uno de sus más preclaros hijos," *Euzkadi*, no. 3057, August 24, 1922, 1, col. 5.

48. "El estado libre de Irlanda," *Aberri*, no. 46, December 17, 1921, 1, col. 4.

49. Uritarte, "El problema irlandés," *Aberri*, no. 60, March 18, 1922, 2, col. 3.

50. Elías de Gallastegui [Gudari, pseud.], "Pascua revolucionaria: ¡Y un día nos fusilarán!" *Aberri*, no. 112, March 31, 1922, 1, cols. 3–4.

51. Eugenio Ibarzábal, "Sabino Arana y su herencia," *Muga*, no. 4 (March 1980), 2–3.

52. Urreztieta, "Un aberriano," 26.

53. Alberto de Olabarria, "África, para los africanos: ¿Se prepara en África un movimiento antieuropeo?" *Euzkadi*, no. 2850, June 25, 1921, 1, cols. 4–5.

54. "Ante Melilla," *Euzkadi*, no. 2888, August 10, 1921, 1, col. 3.

55. "Bajo el sol africano," *Euzkadi*, no. 2889, August 11, 1921, 1, col. 3.

56. Engracio de Aranzadi y Etxeberría [Kizkitza, pseud.], "España, Marruecos, Euskadi," *Euzkadi*, no. 3099, October 13, 1922, 1, col. 3.

57. Ibid.

58. Ibargarondo tar Kepa, "El viaje de la muerte," *Aberri*, no. 35, September 30, 1921, 3, col. 3.

59. "¡Soldado vasco que vuelves…!" *Aberri*, no. 88, October 7, 1922, 1, col. 4.

60. Daniele Conversi, "Domino Effect or Internal Developments? The Influences of International Events and Political Ideologies on Catalan and Basque Nationalism," *West European Politics* 16, no. 3 (July 1993): 245–70.

61. Ibid., 249, 252.

62. Luke Gibbons, *Transformations in Irish Culture* (Cork: Cork University Press, 1996), 3.

63. Cf. English's description of radical Irish nationalist thought in the period 1916–21; a discourse believing that, "Ireland should properly be seen as an independent culture and polity, fully separate from a Britain that had oppressed and obscured it for centuries. Authentic Irishness would be restored by a process of de-anglicization." *Armed Struggle*, 25.

64. "Medidas extremas: A los nacionalistas," *Euzkadi*, no. 1504, April 7, 1917, 1, col. 2.

65. "Ante la revolución española: Indignación hipócrita," *Euzkadi*, no. 2510, January 11, 1920, 1, cols. 2–3.

66. S., "El estado moderno y la revolución," *Euzkadi*, no. 2521, January 22, 1920, 1, col. 4.

67. Luis de Eleizalde [Axe, pseud.] "Acción nacionalista: Eusko-Gastedi-Batza'rentzat," *Euzkadi*, no. 2560, March 23, 1920, 1, col. 3.

68. Luis de Eleizalde [Axe, pseud.], "Democracia y servicio militar," *Euzkadi*, no. 2572, April 3, 1920, 1, col. 3.

69. Founded in Bilbao in 1901 as a newspaper dedicated to restoring foral rights and defending Catholic interests in the liberal state, *La Gaceta del Norte* played a mediating role between *Euzkadi* and the conservative monarchist daily, *El Pueblo Vasco*. Alvaro Chapa, *La vida cultural de la villa de Bilbao 1917–1936* (Bilbao: Ayuntamiento de Bilbao/Bilboko Udala, 1989), 20–21.

70. *Euzkadi* then went on to discuss the events of August 1893 and a similar disturbance during the past year in which 130 individuals were taken from the Basque center in Donostia–San Sebastián, stoned and some of them injured, then transported them to the town's prison in the old quarter. "La razón de la Guardia Civil," *Euzkadi*, no. 2630, May 30, 1920, 1, col. 3.

71. "Monstruoso," *Euzkadi*, no. 2737, October 5, 1920, 2, col. 3.

72. "¡Sangre vasca! El suceso de ayer en Erandio: El sargento de la Guardia Civil, padre de dos huelgistas, mata a un obrero vasco," *Euzkadi*, no. 2742, October 10, 1920, 1, col. 6.

73. "Después de la muerte de Txarterina: El paro de ayer," *Euzkadi*, no. 2744, October 12, 1920, 1, col. 5. A personal account of the "alarming" period between 1920 and 1923, including the death of Txarterina, by one of ELA/STV's founders, Manuel Robles-Aranguiz, appears in *50 años de nacionalismo vasco 1928–1978*, ed. Ibarzábal, 59.

74. Urreztieta, "Un aberriano," 8.

75. Jesús de Sarría, *Patria vasca* (Bilbao: Editorial Vasca, 1920), 129–31.

76. Quoted in Payne, *Basque Nationalism*, 101.

77. Robert Darnton asserts that "pigeon-holing is . . . an exercise in power. . . . All social action flows through boundaries determined by classification schemes . . . Setting up boundaries and policing them is therefore a serious business." *The Great Cat Massacre and Other Episodes in French Cultural History* (New York: Basic Books, 1984; rpt, New York: Vintage Books, 1985), 192–93 (page citations are to the reprint edition).

78. Terry Eagleton, "Nationalism: Irony and Commitment," in Terry Eagleton, Frederic Jameson, and Edward W. Said, *Nationalism, Colonialism, and Literature* (Minneapolis: University of Minnesota Press, 1990), 25–26.

Notes, Chapter Six

1. Enrique Montero, "Reform Idealized: The Intellectual and Ideological Origins of the Second Republic," in *Spanish Cultural Studies: An Introduction*, ed. Helen Graham and Jo Labanyi (Oxford: Oxford University Press, 1995), 124–32.

2. Raymond Carr, *Spain 1808–1975*, 2nd ed. (Oxford: Clarendon Press, 1982), 603.

3. Gerald Brenan, *The Spanish Labyrinth: An Account of the Social and Political Background of the Civil War* (Cambridge: At the University Press; New York: The Macmillan Company, 1943), 229–32.

4. In particular, the works of George L. Steer, *The Tree of Gernika: A Field Study of Modern War* (London: Hodder and Stoughton, 1938) and Claude G. Bowers, *My Mission to Spain: Watching the Rehearsal for World War II* (New York: Simon and Schuster, 1954).

5. Carr, *Spain 1808–1975*, 531; Brenan, *The Spanish Labyrinth*, 238–39.

6. Carr, *Spain 1808–1975*, 605–15.

7. Juan J. Linz, "Church and State in Spain from the Civil War to the Return of Democracy," *Daedalus* 20, no. 3 (Summer 1991): 160–61.

8. Frances Lannon, "The Political Debate within Catholicism," in *Spanish Cultural Studies: An Introduction*, ed. Graham and Labanyi, 140–41.

9. Sanjurjo was the most popular general in Spain, thanks to his exploits in Morocco, which had earned him the nickname "'Lion of the Rif.' The coup, which took place in August 1932, was more of a protest against what the plotters saw as the radical nature of the government than against the state itself. Although it failed, it emphasized the fragile nature of the new regime. See Carr, *Spain 1808–1975*, 618–19.

10. Juan Pablo Fusi, "The Basque Question 1931–7," in *Revolution and War in Spain 1931–1939*, ed. Paul Preston (London: Methuen, 1984), 191.

11. Christopher Cobb, "The Republican State and Mass Educational-Cultural Initiatives, 1931–1936," in *Spanish Cultural Studies: An Introduction*, ed. Graham and Labanyi, 135–36.

12. Both her parents had suffered similar fates. Her father, a merchant-marine captain, had struggled to pass the official exams in Spanish, while her mother could remember being made to wear "the ring" on her finger for speaking Basque at school, a punishment that allowed the bearer to remove the ring only when a pupil denounced another for speaking Basque. See the recollections of Asunción Caro in Ronald Fraser, *Blood of Spain: An Oral History of the Spanish Civil War* (London: Allen Lane, 1979; rpt. with a new intro., London: Pimlico, 1986), 537 (page citations are to the reprint edition).

13. Cobb, "The Republican State and Mass Educational-Cultural Initiatives, 1931–1936," in *Spanish Cultural Studies: An Introduction*, ed. Graham and Labanyi, 136–37.

14. "The division, traditional in Euskadi, between industrial urban centers in the hands of the left, and rural or semirural areas under Carlist or nationalist power came about in April 1931 [the date of the proclamation of a provisional Republican government] and characterized Basque political life during the Republic." José Luis de la Granja, "Cinco años de República en Euskadi," *Historia Contemporánea*, no. 1 (1988): 97.

15. Stanley G. Payne, *Basque Nationalism* (Reno: University of Nevada Press, 1975), 103.

16. Joseph Harrison, "Heavy Industry, the State, and Economic Development in the Basque Region, 1876–1936," *The Economic History Review*, 2nd ser., 36, no. 4 (November 1983): 548–49.

17. Cyrus Ernesto Zirakzadeh, *A Rebellious People: Basques, Protests, and Politics* (Reno: University of Nevada Press, 1991), 54–59.

18. Brenan, *The Spanish Labyrinth*, 222.

19. Antonio Miguel Bernal, "Cambio económico y modernización social, 1880–1936," *Historia Contemporánea*, no. 4 (1990): 177.

20. Marianne Heiberg, "Inside the Moral Community: Politics in a Basque Village," in *Basque Politics: A Case Study in Ethnic Nationalism*, ed. William A. Douglass, Basque Studies Program Occasional Papers Series, no. 2 (Reno: Associated Faculty Press and Basque Studies Program, 1985), 294–95. "The medium and smaller towns in [Bizkaia and Gipuzkoa] were

more genuinely urbanized than those elsewhere... even small towns had been strongly affected by industrialization and changes in business and social organization. They had a high literacy rate, lived within the structure of modern communications, and were fully aware of the non-Basque immigration into the industrial areas and the pressures for secularization and rapid change radiating from those zones." Payne, *Basque Nationalism*, 105.

21. This actually foreshadowed the more famous efforts of Republican propaganda during the formative years of the new regime. See Cipriano Ramos, "El nacionalismo vasco durante la dictadura de Primo de Rivera," *Letras de Deusto*, no. 31 (January–April 1985): 137–67, and Cameron J. Watson, "Basque Nationalism during the Dictatorship of Primo de Rivera, 1923–1930," M.A. thesis, University of Nevada, Reno, 1992.

22. J. L. de la Granja Sainz, "El Aranismo, ideología dominante del Partido Nacionalista Vasco en los años treinta: Acta de la Asamblea de Bergara," in *II Euskal mundu biltzarra/II Congreso mundial vasco*, sec. 2, *Euskal Herriaren historiari buruzko biltzarra/Congreso de historia de Euskal Herria*, vol. 5, *Aro moderno eta gaur egungoa/Edad moderna y contemporánea* (Vitoria-Gasteiz: Eusko Jaurlaritzaren Argitalpen-Zerbitzu Nagusia/Servicio Central de Publicaciones del Gobierno Vasco, 1988), 419.

23. A succinct biography of Aguirre is given by Robert P. Clark in his introduction to *Escape via Berlin: Eluding Franco in Hitler's Europe*, by José Antonio de Aguirre (1945; rpt. with an intro. and annotations by Robert P. Clark, Reno and Las Vegas: University of Nevada Press, 1991), 1–15 (page citations are to the reprint edition).

24. Antonio Elorza, "Cultura e ideología en el País Vasco contemporáneo." in *II Euskal mundu-biltzarra/II Congreso Mundial*, sec. 2, *Euskal Herriaren historiari buruzko biltzarra/Congreso de historia de Euskal Herria*, vol. 5, *Aro moderno eta gaur egungoa/Edad moderna y contemporánea* (Vitoria-Gasteiz: Eusko Jaurlaritzaren Argitalpen-Zerbitzu Nagusia/Servicio Central de Publicaciones del Gobierno Vasco, 1988), 206.

25. José Luis de la Granja, "El nacionalismo vasco entre la autonomía y la independencia," in *Los nacionalismos en la España de la II República*, ed. Justo G. Beramendi and Ramón Maiz (Madrid: Siglo XXI, 1991), 106.

26. José Luis de la Granja Sainz, "The Basque Nationalist Community During the Second Spanish Republic (1931–1936)," in *Basque Politics: A Case Study in Ethnic Nationalism*, ed. Douglass, 160. For a full discussion of the ANV, see Granja Sainz, *Nacionalismo y II República en el País Vasco. Estatutos de autonomía, partidos y elecciones. Historia de Acción Nacionalista Vasca: 1930–1936* (Madrid: Centro de Investigaciones Sociológicas/Siglo XXI, 1986), and Eduardo Renobales, *ANV, el otro nacionalismo: Historia de Acción Nacionalista Vasca–Eusko Abertzale Ekintza* (Tafalla: Txalaparta, 2005).

27. This was the opinion of the PNV's José de Gárate. See "José y Blas de Gárate," Blasco Olaetxea MSS, 4.

28. J. J. Diaz Freire, "La proclamación de la II República como restauración de la dignidad popular," in *II Euskal mundu biltzarra/II Congreso mundial vasco*, sec. 2, *Euskal Herriaren historiari buruzko biltzarra/Congreso de historia de Euskal Herria*, vol. 5, *Aro moderno eta gaur egungoa/Edad moderna y contemporánea* (Vitoria-Gasteiz: Eusko Jaurlaritzaren Argitalpen-Zerbitzu Nagusia/Servicio Central de Publicaciones del Gobierno Vasco, 1988), 250.

29. "Ambrosio Igual," in Blasco Olaetxea MSS, box no. 5, file 5, 46, 1.

30. The events are detailed by one of the members of what became the Jagi Jagi Party, Trifón Echeberria, in *50 años de nacionalismo vasco 1928–1978 (A través de sus protagonistas)*, ed. Eugenio Ibarzábal (San Sebastián: Ediciones Vascas, 1978), 117–18.

31. Lezo de Urreztieta, "Un aberriano," interview by Eugenio Ibarzábal. *Muga*, no. 4 (March 1980), 18.

32. Trifón Etarte, quoted in Fraser, *Blood of Spain*, 536.

33. Txiřika, "Un paso al frente," *Jagi Jagi*, no. 20, February 4, 1933, 1, col. 3.

34. PNV member José de Gárate observed at the time that, in his opinion, Gallastegui's quest for independence was always going to be unattainable in the prevalent conditions. Furthermore, in the 1930s, Gallastegui could not count on such able followers as he had had in the years preceding the coup of Primo de Rivera. "José y Blas de Gárate," Blasco Olaetxea MSS, 5–6.

35. Urreztieta, "Un aberriano," 18.

36. The results are published and discussed in detail in Payne, *Basque Nationalism*, 122.

37. Juan Pablo Fusi, "The Basque Question 1931–7," 185. See the same author's assessment in "Política y nacionalidad," in *II Euskal mundu-biltzarra/II Congreso mundial vasco*, sec. 2, *Euskal Herriaren historiari buruzko biltzarra/Congreso de historia de Euskal Herria*, vol. 7, *Aro moderno eta gaur egungoa/Edad moderna y contemporánea* (Vitoria-Gasteiz: Eusko Jaurlaritzaren Argitalpen-Zerbitzu Nagusia/Servicio Central de Publicaciones del Gobierno Vasco, 1988), 15.

38. Granja makes this point in "El nacionalismo vasco entre la autonomía y la independencia," 108. The same author argues that an ideological change within the PNV began during the period from 1934 to 1936 and that by the 1950s, the party could be regarded as Christian Democrat and therefore similar to other such parties across Europe at that time. See Granja, "The Basque Nationalist Community," 161–62.

39. Shlomo Ben-Ami, "Basque Nationalism Between Archaism and Modernity," *Journal of Contemporary History* 26, nos. 3–4 (September 1991): 497.

40. For example, religion had been a unifying factor between Basque nationalists and their Carlist cousins in Navarre. One such Carlist, a Navarrese peasant named Antonio Izu, recalled with horror his later experiences in the Civil War when venturing out of his home province: "There wasn't merely a difference between the Basque and Navarrese clergy and the clergy in the rest of Spain; the gulf was so wide it went beyond being a difference. The communists in Navarre were more religious than the priests in Castile." See Fraser, *Blood of Spain*, 125.

41. Alfonso Pérez-Agote, "The Role of Religion in the Definition of a Symbolic Conflict: Religion and the Basque Problem," *Social Compass* 33, no. 4 (1986): 419.

42. Granja, "El nacionalismo vasco entre la autonomía y la independencia," 101–2.

43. These methods included a blend of old and new, as Basque nationalism made ready use of both the influential *bertsolariak* and radio broadcasts. See "Teodoro Hernandorena," Blasco Olaetxea MSS, box no. 5, file 5 (43), 20.

44. Urreztieta, "Un aberriano," 15.

45. "Teodoro Hernandorena," Blasco de Olaetxea MSS, 10.

46. "Juan Beistegui: Su historia y la del Batallón Loyola," in Fondo Luis Ruiz de Aguirre, Irargi: Centro de Patrimonio Documental de Euskadi (Bergara, Gipuzkoa), 12–13 (hereafter cited as Ruiz de Aguirre MSS).

47. Quoted in Fraser, *Blood of Spain*, 539.

48. Ibid; Urreztieta recalled that immigration was *the* dominant social change in Bizkaia during the era and that the mutual incomprehension between groups led to an inevitable intolerance. "Un aberriano," 22.

49. As recalled by the president of ANV in Barakaldo (Bizkaia), Luis Ruiz de Aguirre Urkijo, in Marga Otaegui and Xosé Estévez, "Protagonistas de la historia vasca (1923–1950): Acción Nacionalista Vasca," *Cuadernos de Sección Historia-Geografía*, no. 7 (1984): 74–75.

50. These works include reprints of *Ami vasco* (1931) and Aranzadi's *La nación vasca* (1931), together with new studies, such as *Formulario* (1932) by Luis de Arana, *Nacionalismo y confesionalidad* (1931) by Federico Belausteguigoitia, *Sólo JEL basta* (1933) by Ceferino Jemein, and the later publication of Manuel Eguileor, *Nacionalismo vasco* (1936). Granja, "El nacionalismo vasco entre la autonomía y la independencia," 108–9.

51. "Juan Beistegui: Su historia y la del Batallón Loyola," Ruiz de Aguirre MSS, 21–24.

52. Urreztieta, "Un aberriano," 25.

53. Miguel de Ergabia, *Jaungoikua eta Lege Zaŕa: La Eŕibera por JEL* (Bilbao: n.p., 1933), 69.

54. Manuel Eguileor [Ikasle, pseud.], *Responsabilidad: Conferencia leída en Juventud Vasca de Bilbao, en el XXX aniversario de su fundación* (n.p.: n.p., 1934), 8.

55. "Juan Beistegui: Su historia y la del Batallón Loyola," Ruiz de Aguirre MSS, 13.

56. Granja, "Cinco años de República en Euskadi," 102.

57. José María Jimeno Jurío, in *50 años de nacionalismo vasco 1928–1978*, ed. Ibarzábal, 134–37.

58. Granja, "El nacionalismo vasco entre la autonomía y la independencia," 114.

59. Quoted in Fraser, *Blood of Spain*, 536.

60. Eŕotari, "Aparece el tricornio siniestro," *Jagi Jagi*, no.20, February 4, 1933, 7, cols. 1–4.

61. Elías de Gallastegui [Gudari, pseud.], "Programas y conductas," *Jagi Jagi*, no. 20, February 4, 1933, 3, col. 1.

62. Martin Blinkhorn argues that the PNV failed to make any political headway in Navarre during this time. See "'The Basque Ulster': Navarre and the Basque Autonomy Question under the Spanish Second Republic," *Historical Journal* 17, no. 3 (September 1974): 595–613. However, Josu Chueca talks of a "spectacular growth" for the PNV in Navarre at an organizational and membership level (with the founding of numerous Basque centers, for example), although, because of the electoral system, the party could not break a two-party stranglehold in the province between the Republican-Socialist alliance and a right-wing bloc composed of various groups. See "El nacionalismo vasco en Navarra," in *Los nacionalistas: Historia del nacionalismo vasco, 1876–1960*, Beasaide Series (Vitoria-Gasteiz: Fundación Sancho el Sabio, 1995), 293–301. See also José María Jimeno Jurío's argument in *Navarra jamás dijo no al Estatuto Vasco* (Tafalla: Txalaparta, 1997), 59–60, that during the early years of the Republic, there was widespread support in Navarre for a common Basque-Navarrese statute of autonomy. For example, in August 1931, a majority of Navarrese city halls voted in favor of a Basque-Navarrese statute, as opposed to a purely Navarrese one.

63. Granja, "El nacionalismo vasco entre la autonomía y la independencia," 114.

64. Manuel Irujo, in *50 años de nacionalismo vasco*, ed. Ibarzábal, 15–16.

65. The failure of Basque nationalism to capture sufficient support in Navarre was accurately summarized by Mario Ozcodi, a Navarrese Carlist at the time: "We didn't feel sufficiently identified with the Basque country to exchange dependence on Madrid for dependence on Bilbao and San Sebastián." Quoted in Fraser, *Blood of Spain*, 541.

66. Both Chueca, in "El nacionalismo vasco en Navarra," 293–301 and Jimeno Jurío, in *Navarra jamás dijo no al Estatuto Vasco*, allude to the potential irregularities of the 1932 vote by Navarrese city halls on the question of the adherence of Navarre to the Basque autonomy statute. See also Josu Chueca, *El nacionalismo vasco en Navarra (1931–1936)* (Bilbao: Universidad del País Vasco, Servicio Editorial, 1999).

67 Granja, "El nacionalismo vasco entre la autonomía y la independencia," 117; Granja also refers to "an impressive growth in [the PNV's] militantism" during the 1930s. "The Basque Nationalist Community," 161.

68. Granja, "The Basque Nationalist Community," 160.

69. Carr, *Spain 1808–1975*, 628–29.

70. Ibid., 635.

71. Fusi, "Política y nacionalidad," 16.

72. Stanley G. Payne, "Nacionalismo español, nacionalismo vasco," in *Aula de Cultura de El Correo Español–El Pueblo Vasco*, ed. José Manuel González, vol. 12 (Bilbao: El Correo Español-El Pueblo Vasco, 1994), 120–21.

73. Ibid., 121. See also the discussion of Ortega y Gasset's Spanish nationalism by P. García Isasti, "Nazionalismo espainiarrari buruz zenbait ohar," in *II Euskal mundu-biltzarra/II Congreso mundial vasco*, sec. 2, *Euskal Herriaren historiari buruzko biltzarra/Congreso de historia de Euskal Herria*, vol. 5, *Aro moderno eta gaur egungoa/Edad moderna y contemporánea* (Vitoria-Gasteiz: Eusko Jaurlaritzaren Argitalpen-Zerbitzu Nagusia/Servicio Central de Publicaciones del Gobierno Vasco, 1988), 272–78.

74. Fusi, "Política y nacionalidad," 16.

75. Carr, *Spain 1808–1975*, 637–39.

76. "Prieto [the Basque Socialist leader] appeared on the same platform as José Aguirre [the PNV leader], singing 'The Tree of Guernika,' and the fierce local quarrels of the U.G.T. and the Basque Catholic Unions ceased to trouble the meeting halls and streets of Bilbao. Thus began the strange alliance between the anti-clerical left and the Catholic Basques which was to be consummated in the common defence of the Republic in the Civil War. The Basque Nationalists found an even more surprising ally in the Communists who presented nationalism as part of the social revolution and published a paper in Basque." Carr, *Spain 1808–1975*, 630. According to Manuel de Irujo, it was Prieto who initiated the dialogue between the two parties. See Manuel Irujo in *50 años de nacionalismo vasco 1928–1978*, ed. Ibarzábal, 25.

77. Granja, "El Aranismo," 424.

78. Teodoro Hernandorena, Blasco Olaetxea MSS, 26.

79. Blas de Gárate, "José y Blas de Gárate," Blasco Olaetxea MSS, 7–9.

80. Granja, "Cinco años de República en Euskadi," 106. According to Robert W. Kern, the summer of 1934 had seen a confluence of nationalist and revolutionary aspirations to the extent that "the Basque National Action Association demanded a boycott of the national parliament as a result of setbacks suffered by a proposal of Basque autonomy in Madrid. Since the CNT and the UGT had thousands of members in the industrial centers of Barcelona and Bilbao, it was inevitable that regionalist politics soon dominated everything else." *Red Years/Black Years: A Political History of Spanish Anarchism, 1911–1937* (Philadelphia: Institute for the Study of Human Issues, 1978), 128.

81. Manuel Robles-Aranguiz, in *50 años de nacionalismo vasco 1928–1978*, ed. Ibarzábal, 62.

82. Quoted in Fraser, *Blood of Spain*, 540.

83. Urreztieta, "Un aberriano," 19.

84. "Our decisions–through action or omission–can influence the development [and] direction of the others' lives." Manuel Eguileor [Ikasle, pseud.], *Responsabilidad*, 4.

85. Fusi, "The Basque Question 1931–7," 197.

86. "Juan Beistegui: Su historia y la del Batallón Loyola," Ruiz de Aguirre MSS, 14–19.

87. Fusi, "The Basque Question 1931–7," 198–99.

88. Taking Navarre into account, the PNV share fell to 28 percent. See Payne, *Basque Nationalism*, 147–48.

89. Carr, *Spain 1808–1975*, 645.

90. Martin Blinkhorn, "Carlism and the Crisis of the 1930s," *Journal of Contemporary History* 7, nos. 3–4 (July–October 1972), 85.

91. Jimeno Jurío, in *50 años de nacionalismo vasco 1928–1978*, ed. Ibarzábal, 138–39.

92. Elías Etxeberria, a member of the central council of the party (the Euzkadi Buru Batzar) recalled that the CNT were the best-armed political group in 1934 and that the PNV had only twenty or thirty pistols at its disposal. Blasco Olaetxea MSS, box no. 4, file 4 (30), 4–5.

93. "Juan Beistegui: Su historia y la del Batallón Loyola," Ruiz de Aguirre MSS, 27–34.

94. Payne, *Basque Nationalism*, 161–62.

95. See, for example, the recollection of Gipuzkoan PNV member Mariano Estornés, who maintains that at the outbreak of the uprising in Donostia–San Sebastián, the party had absolutely no arms at its disposal. Idoia Estornés, "El PNV y el 18 de julio," *El Mundo del País Vasco* (Bilbao), October 12, 1995, 5, col. 1.

96. "Nacionalismo Bretón: Buena Lección," *Jagi Jagi*, no. 100, May 9, 1936, 4, col. 1.

97. See "Teodoro Hernandorena," Blasco Olaetxea MSS, 10–11.

98. See Santiago de Pablo, and Ludger Mees, *El péndulo patriótico: Historia del Partido Nacionalista Vasco, 1895–2005* (Barcelona: Crítica, 2005), 204.

99. See Granja, "El nacionalismo vasco entre la autonomía y la independencia," 111–13.

100. Manuel Eguileor Orueta [Bizkargi, pseud.], *Nacionalismo Vasco* (Abando: n.p., 1936), 66–67.

101. Ibid., 67–69.

102. Urreztieta, "Un aberriano," 26.

103. Quoted in Fraser, *Blood of Spain*, 56.

104. Ibid., 57.

105. Payne, *Basque Nationalism*, 163.

106. Ibid., 164.

Notes, Chapter Seven

1. Joseba Zulaika, *Basque Violence: Metaphor and Sacrament* (Reno: University of Nevada Press, 1988), 16.

2. Iwona Irwin-Zarecka, *Frames of Remembrance: The Dynamics of Collective Memory* (New Brunswick: Transaction Publishers, 1994), 52.

3. Robert Darnton notes that "when we cannot get a proverb, or a joke, or a ritual, or a poem, we know that we are on to something. By picking at a document where it is most opaque, we may be able to unravel an alien system of meaning. The thread might even lead into a strange and wonderful world view." *The Great Cat Massacre and Other Episodes in French Cultural History* (New York: Basic Books, 1984; rpt., New York: Vintage Books, 1985), 5 (page citations are to the reprint edition).

4. See Natalie Zemon Davis, "Anthropology and History in the 1980s," *Journal of Interdisciplinary History* 12, no. 2 (Autumn 1981): 268.

5. Hugh Thomas, *The Spanish Civil War*, 3rd ed. (Harmondsworth, England: Penguin, 1977), 239; Stanley G. Payne, *Basque Nationalism* (Reno: University of Nevada Press, 1975), 164.

6. Quoted in Ronald Fraser, *Blood of Spain: An Oral History of the Spanish Civil War* (London: Allen Lane, 1979; rpt., with a new intro., London: Pimlico, 1986), 123 (page citations are to the reprint edition).

7. "Like Franco, [Mola was] deeply affected by the loss of empire in 1898. He was born the son of a soldier in Cuba, Spain's richest colony ... on his return to Spain after the loss of the island in the Spanish-American war, he found 'a country emptied of itself' and a 'degenerated people, and ambience of abdication'." Michael Richards, *A Time of Silence: Civil War and the Culture of Repression in Franco's Spain, 1936–1945* (Cambridge, MA: Cambridge University Press, 1998), 48.

8. Negotiations between Mola and the Carlists continued through the eve of the uprising itself. In Pamplona–Iruñea, there was a popular expectancy that something was afoot, reinforced no doubt by the heady atmosphere created by the annual running of the bulls in the festival of San Fermín. As Thomas observes, many of the young men taking part in the festival would, within a week, be enrolled in the Carlist forces of Navarre. See *The Spanish Civil War*, 201–5.

9. Quoted in Fraser, *Blood of Spain*, 121.

10. Thomas speculates on the decision, which, he argues, seemed strange at the time in a province regarded as the bastion of support for the insurgents: "There is no easy explanation. The spirit of the Right was enraged and fearful, and many people's blood was up. The new military authorities in nationalist Spain also found it almost as hard to control 'spontaneous' actions as the government did." *The Spanish Civil War*, 260.

11. Payne, *Basque Nationalism*, 164.

12. Josu Chueca, "El nacionalismo vasco en Navarra," in *Los nacionalistas: Historia del nacionalismo vasco 1876–1960*, ed. Santiago de Pablo, Beasaide Series (Vitoria-Gasteiz: Fundación Sancho el Sabio, 1995), 301.

13. Julián Aguirre y Basterra and Francisco Aguirre y Basterra, in *50 años de nacionalismo vasco 1928–1978 (A través de sus protagonistas)*, ed. Eugenio Ibarzábal (San Sebastián: Ediciones Vascas, 1978), 94–95.

14. Santiago de Pablo, "El nacionalismo vasco en Álava," in *Los nacionalistas*, 330.

15. Though evidently some Civil Guards and Assault Guards remained loyal to the Republic, according to the testimony of Julián and Francisco Aguirre. See Julián Aguirre y Basterra and Francisco Aguirre y Basterra, in *50 años de nacionalismo vasco 1928–1978*, ed. Ibarzábal, 95.

16. Javier Ugarte, "Represión como instrumento de acción política del 'nuevo estado' (Álava, 1936–1939)," in *II Euskal mundu-biltzarra/II Congreso mundial vasco*, sec. 2, *Euskal Herriaren historiari buruzko biltzarra/Congreso de historia de Euskal Herria*, vol. 7, *Aro moderno eta gaur egungoa/Edad moderna y contemporánea* (Vitoria-Gasteiz: Eusko Jaurlaritzaren Argitalpen-Zerbitzu Nagusia/Servicio Central de Publicaciones del Gobierno Vasco, 1988), 253–54.

17. Javier Ugarte and Antonio Rivera, "La guerra civil en el País Vasco: La sublevación en Álava," *Historia Contemporánea*, no. 1 (1988): 191.

18. The leadership of the PNV was left unharmed to the extent that Julián Aguirre could actually leave the capital to meet with two Bizkaian PNV leaders, Juan Ajuriaguerra and Jesús Solaun, to discuss party strategy. See Julián Aguirre y Basterra and Francisco Aguirre y Basterra, in *50 años de nacionalismo vasco 1928–1978*, ed. Ibarzábal, 95.

19. Ugarte, "Represión," 260; de Pablo, "El nacionalismo vasco en Álava," 329–33.

20. Payne, *Basque Nationalism*, 165; Thomas, *The Spanish Civil War*, 237.

21. Quoted in Fraser, *Blood of Spain*, 191.

22. According to Pedro Basabilotra, later secretary to the head of the PNV militia, "The right [in the fall of 1936] was even worse than the left. Assassinations committed by so-called religious believers, by people with so-called education, were even more unpardonable than those committed by the under-privileged and the poor." Quoted in Fraser, *Blood of Spain*, 191.

23. Payne, *Basque Nationalism*, 165.

24. As recalled by a member of Euzko Gaztedi (the PNV youth section), José Manuel Irardi, interview by Carlos Blasco Olaetxea, in *Diálogos de guerra: Euskadi 1936* (San Sebastián: Gráficas Izarra, 1983), 15, 23.

25. Ibid., 25.

26. A full account of the battle is given by Thomas, *The Spanish Civil War*, 377–80. See also Payne, *Basque Nationalism*, 167–68.

27. Andrés Plazaola, interview by Blasco Olaetxea, *Diálogos de guerra: Euskadi 1936*, 27.

28. José Manuel Irardi, interview by Blasco Olaetxea, *Diálogos de guerra: Euskadi 1936*, 29.

29. This actually allowed, given the exigencies of war, for the creation of what virtually amounted to a separate Basque state. "The collapse of the Republican state in the Basque provinces permitted the creation not of a revolutionary authority, but of a new state, specifically Basque, a bourgeois state for the defense of property and the Church that, while organizing the country's defense against the military adversaries of Basque freedom, led the victorious struggle against the internal revolutionary movement." Pierre Broué and Emile Témime, *The Revolution and the Civil War in Spain*, trans. Tony White (Cambridge, MA: MIT Press, 1970), 139.

30. Lezo de Urreztieta, "Un aberriano," interview by Eugenio Ibarzábal. *Muga*, no. 4 (March 1980), 24.

31. Trifón Echeberria, in *50 años de nacionalismo vasco 1928–1978*, ed. Ibarzábal, 129. See also the view of another Jagi Jagi member, Trifón Etarte: "we had always believed that the statute was a trap–a trap very similar to that in which Ireland had fallen after the First World War." Quoted in Fraser, *Blood of Spain*, 193.

32. Ibid.

33. Payne, *Basque Nationalism*, 179.

34. Juan Manuel Epalza, quoted in Fraser, *Blood of Spain*, 192.

35. Gonzalo Nardiz, in *50 años de nacionalismo vasco 1928–1978*, ed. Ibarzábal, 160–61; Payne, *Basque Nationalism*, 183.

36. A full list of the battalions (including those associated with the left) is given in Payne, *Basque Nationalism*, 261–64.

37. Robert P. Clark, *The Basques: The Franco Years and Beyond*, (Reno: University of Nevada Press, 1979), 76.

38. Clark continues: "For the Basques, the Spanish Civil War was one of those rare psychological moments in history when an entire culture passes through an experience of the deepest significance, and is never quite the same again." *The Basques: The Franco Years and Beyond*, 76.

39. Luis Ruiz de Aguirre, interview by Blasco Olaetxea, in *Diálogos de guerra: Euskadi 1936*, 35.

40. Gonzalo Nardiz, in *50 años de nacionalismo vasco 1928–1978*, ed. Ibarzábal, 169.

41. Payne, *Basque Nationalism*, 191–92. There was also, however, among the insurgent forces, a new corps, the Black Arrows, numbering eight thousand Spaniards and led by Italian officers. Thomas, *The Spanish Civil War*, 614.

42. The Ambassador in Spain (Bowers), then in France, to the Secretary of State, St. Jean de Luz, April 12, 1937, 852.00/5238, no. 1272, *Foreign Relations of the United States: Diplomatic Papers, 1937*, vol. 1, *General* (Washington, D.C.: United States Government Printing Office, 1954), 281 (hereafter cited as FRUS).

43. Fraser, *Blood of Spain*, 395; Clark, *The Basques: The Franco Years and Beyond*, 70; Thomas, *The Spanish Civil War*, 616.

44. Payne, *Basque Nationalism*, 192–93.

45. The Ambassador in Spain (Bowers), then in France, to the Secretary of State, St. Jean de Luz, April 12, 1937, 852.00/5238, no. 1272, FRUS (1937), vol. 1, 281–82. See also Bowers's later account in the autobiography, Claude G. Bowers, *My Mission to Spain: Watching the Rehearsal for World War II* (New York: Simon and Schuster, 1954), 343; Clark, *The Basques*, 70; Thomas, *The Spanish Civil War*, 616. A volunteer army chaplain, Father José Maria Basabilotra, went to the town as soon of his unit's troops had returned on leave. He described the planes of the Condor Legion (which he saw on their second raid on the town) as "grey, rather beautiful and sinister," thinking at the time that the rebels had "done this to demoralize us at the front." Quoted in Fraser, *Blood of Spain*, 396.

46. The force had rapidly gained a reputation for its brutality in the southern campaign, an inheritance of Franco's tactics during the Moroccan war of the early 1920s. See Thomas, *The Spanish Civil War*, 371–75.

47. A lucid description of the battle is given by *The Times* of London's correspondent in the Basque Country during the war. See George L. Steer, *The Tree of Gernika: A Field Study of Modern War* (London: Hodder and Stoughton, 1938), 210–27. For an excellent biography of Steer, see Nicholas Rankin, *Telegram from Guernica: The Extraordinary Life of George Steer, War Correspondent* (London: Faber and Faber, 2003).

48. Marianne Heiberg's study of the village offers a harrowing account of the attack: "the Moors [the Army of Africa] descended on the farms lying at the base of the mountain [Intxorta]. They entered one farmhouse and killed a PNV supporter. In a neighbouring farm, the Moors entered with hand grenades and killed the *baserritar* [peasant] and some *gudaris* they found hiding. In another *baserri* on the fringe of the village nucleus, the Moors attempted to rape a 14-year-old girl. The father tried to defend his young daughter and was shot; he died instantly. The daughter ran to her father and put her arms around him in a futile attempt to protect him. The Moors fired again, shattering both the farmer's head and the girl's hand. The girl's mother was found hiding in the stables. She was first raped then shot through the back and shoulders. On most farms the Moors stole what they could and destroyed much of what they could not steal." Marianne Heiberg, "Inside the Moral Community: Politics in a Basque Village," in *Basque Politics: A Case Study in Ethnic Nationalism*, ed. William A. Douglass, Basque Studies Program Occasional Papers Series, no. 2 (Reno: Associated Faculty Press and Basque Studies Program, 1985), 299.

49. Steer, *The Tree of Gernika*, 226.

50 "Simón," interview by Joseba Zulaika, in *Basque Violence: Metaphor and Sacrament*, 24.

51. The following description of the offensive is taken from Clark, *The Basques: The Franco Years and Beyond*, 69–72; Payne, *Basque Nationalism*, 192–96; and Thomas, *The Spanish Civil War*, 623–31.

52. Clark, *The Basques: The Franco Years and Beyond*, 70. Thomas discusses the problems associated with assessing the destruction. See *The Spanish Civil War*, 625.

53. Father Dionisio Ajanguiz, quoted in Fraser, *Blood of Spain*, 399.

54. "Guernica," *The Times* (London), April 28, 1937, 17, col. 3.

55. Steer, *The Tree of Gernika*, 239, 241.

56. The Ambassador in Spain (Bowers), then in France, to the Secretary of State, St. Jean de Luz, April 30, 1937, 852.00/5276, no. 253, FRUS (1937), vol. 1, 290.

57. Bowers, *My Mission to Spain*, 344.

58. Fusi, "Política y nacionalidad," 18.

59. See Preston, *Franco: A Biography*, 245–46.

60. Payne, *Basque Nationalism*, 183.

61. "All the time aeroplanes have flown over Bilbao, occasionally dropping bombs in the centre of the city. . . . In all these raids the Junkers and Heinkel bombers circle at leisure over the population for the moral effect produced." *The Times* (London), April 30, 1937, 16, col. 1.

62. Gonzalo Nardiz, in *50 años de nacionalismo vasco 1928–1978*, ed. Ibarzábal, 169.

63. Jesús Solaun, in *50 años de nacionalismo vasco 1928–1978*, ed. Ibarzábal, 255.

64. It was also decided to escort rebel prisoners to the front in order to protect them from left-wing reprisals before the city ultimately fell. Clark, *The Basques: The Franco Years and Beyond*, 72; Payne, *Basque Nationalism*, 212; Thomas, *The Spanish Civil War*, 693.

65. Clark, *The Basques: The Franco Years and Beyond*, 72; Thomas, *The Spanish Civil War*, 693.

66. See Payne, *Basque Nationalism*, 212.

67. Quoted in Fraser, *Blood of Spain*, 413.

68. On the significance of Lauaxeta as a martyr of Basque nationalism, see Joseba Zulaika, *ETAren hautsa* (Irun: Alberdania, 2006), 25–28. Here (26), Zulaika recalls visiting an exhibition about the poet in Bilbao in January 2006 where he read the following lines in the visitors' book: "With great emotion I recall the last meeting with Lauaxeta in the lobby before going to the Court Martial that we were being tried by in the Gasteiz cavalry barracks, where we had been transferred, together with my father and four brothers, in the same vehicle, on May 15, 1937. He informed us that, resignedly, he expected the death penalty but that we would be alright. My father and brother spoke every day with him, because they helped the priest that celebrated a daily mass and he attended in truly pious fashion. He was a good Christian and a good *abertzale* [patriot]. From the heart. Ignacio Elejalde."

69. Thomas, *The Spanish Civil War*, 718–19; Clark, *The Basques: The Franco Years and Beyond*, 73–74.

70. Thomas, *The Spanish Civil War*, 720.

71. Luis Sansinenea, in *50 años de nacionalismo vasco 1928–1978*, ed. Ibarzábal, 201–2.

72. Ibid., 202; Fraser, *Blood of Spain*, 412.

73. The Ambassador in Spain (Bowers), then in France, to the Secretary of State, St. Jean de Luz, December 13, 1937, 852.00/7112, no. 1384, FRUS (1937), vol. 1, 465–66.

74. Bowers, *My Mission to Spain*, 350.

75. See Ignacio Olabarri and Fernando Meer, "Aproximación a la Guerra Civil en el País Vasco (1936–1939) como un conflicto de ideas," *Cuadernos de Sección Historia-Geografía*, no. 17 (1990): 144–45.

76. "Social memory identifies a group, giving it a sense of its past and defining its aspirations for the future." James Fentress and Chris Wickham, *Social Memory* (Oxford: Blackwell, 1992), 25.

77. Zulaika, *Basque Violence: Metaphor and Sacrament*, 34.

78. Regarding the importance of local observation, Malcolm Chapman notes: "Locally-produced and locally-received ideas about (say) nations, are not a kind of quirky distortion of reality that exists in its properly realised and objective form elsewhere. 'France' does not exist somewhere, in any tangible or objective form, other than in the ideas Frenchmen have of it. Some of these ideas feel more concrete than others (ideas, say, about where the frontier runs), but they are none the less conceptual for all that. . . . France, because of its size, does not have a conceptual status any different from the smaller units of social life with which the social anthropologist might feel happier." "Fieldwork, Language and Locality in Europe, from the North," in *Europe Observed*, ed. João de Pina-Cabral and John Campbell (London: Macmillan, 1992), 48–49.

79. James Clifford, *The Predicament of Culture: Twentieth-Century Ethnography, Literature, Art* (Cambridge, MA: Harvard University Press, 1988), 340.

80. Clifford Geertz, *The Interpretation of Cultures: Selected Essays* (New York: Basic Books, 1973), 20.

81. Lasting barely two weeks, the offensive claimed the lives of eight hundred *gudariak*, as well as four thousand wounded. Clark, *The Basques: The Franco Years and Beyond*, 65.

82. Luis Ruiz de Aguirre, in Marga Otaegui and Xosé Estévez, "Protagonistas de la historia vasca (1923–1950): Partido Nacionalista Vasco." *Cuadernos de Sección Historia-Geografía*, no. 7 (1984): 69–70.

83. Luis Ruiz de Aguirre, interview by Blasco Olaetxea, in *Diálogos de guerra: Euskadi 1936*, 42–43.

84. Ibid., 44.

85. Ibid.

86. Ibid. 45–46.

87. Zulaika, *Basque Violence: Metaphor and Sacrament*, 32–34.

88. See Helen Graham and Jo Labanyi's cautionary advice: "As someone once pointed out on hearing the Spanish civil war referred to as a text: 'my father died in that text.'" "Culture and Modernity: The Case of Spain," in *Spanish Cultural Studies: An Introduction*, ed. Helen Graham and Jo Labanyi (Oxford: Oxford University Press, 1995), 5.

89. Zulaika, *Basque Violence: Metaphor and Sacrament*, 32.

90. Ibid., 33.

91. Joseba Elosegi, *Quiero morir por algo* (Barcelona: Plaza & Janes, 1977), 22.

92. Ibid., 32.

93. Ibid., 49.

94. Joseba Elosegi, interview by Blasco Olaetxea, *Diálogos de guerra: Euskadi 1936*, 77.

95. Ibid., 83.

96. Elosegi, *Quiero morir por algo*, 133.

97. Ibid.

98. Ibid., 135–36.

99. Elosegi, interview by Blasco Olaetxea, *Diálogos de guerra: Euskadi 1936*, 84.

100. Elosegi, *Quiero morir por algo*, 141–42.

101. Steer, *The Tree of Gernika*, 243.

102. The despair, it should be noted, was commonly felt among all Basques. A seventeen-year-old Communist miner from Bizkaia, Saturnino Calvo, was also fighting the insurgent forces. He recalled that "the effect of Guernica on the soldiers of my JSU [Juventudes Socialistas Unificadas–Unified Socialist Youth] battalion was much worse than if they had been in combat and suffered casualties. . . . To know that women and children were being killed in the rearguard–we saw the ambulances on the road below our positions–demoralized them." Quoted in Fraser, *Blood of Spain*, 401.

103. Zulaika, *Basque Violence: Metaphor and Sacrament*, 33.

104. Clifford, *The Predicament of Culture*, 341.

105. Zulaika, *Basque Violence: Metaphor and Sacrament*, 35.

106. Irwin-Zarecka, *Frames of Remembrance*, 101–02.

107. Cf. Fentress and Wickham, *Social Memory*, 80, 85.

Notes, Chapter Eight

1. Max Gallo, *Spain Under Franco: A History*, trans. Jean Stewart (New York: E. P. Dutton, 1974), 73.

2. See Michael Richards's thorough examination of what he defines as Franco's "reconstruction of the nation by looking at how violence, religion, gender, language, psychiatry, economics and the state came together in the idea of *self-sufficiency*." *A Time of Silence: Civil War and the Culture of Repression in Franco's Spain, 1936–1945* (Cambridge: Cambridge University Press, 1998), 1.

3. Ander Gurruchaga, *El código nacionalista vasco durante el franquismo* (Barcelona: Anthropos, 1985), 161; Michael Richards, "'Terror and Progress': Industrialization, Modernity, and the Making of Francoism," in *Spanish Cultural Studies: An Introduction*, ed. Helen Graham and Jo Labanyi (Oxford: Oxford University Press, 1995), 173.

4. Richards, "'Terror and Progress,'" 178–79 and *A Time of Silence*, 11, 30; Paul Preston, "The Urban and Rural *Guerrilla* of the 1940s," in *Spanish Cultural Studies: An Introduction*, ed. Graham and Labanyi, 230. Gurruchaga discusses some of the various estimations of those executed after 1939. See *El código nacionalista vasco durante el franquismo*, 282n.

5. Rafael Abella, *La vida cotidiana en España bajo el régimen de Franco* (Barcelona: Editorial Argos Vergara, 1985), 27.

6. "The Franco dictatorship (1939–1975) consecrated the hegemony of a Catholic and traditionalist version of Spanish nationalism (*National-Catholicism*), which centred its nationalist discourse around the essentialist affirmation of Catholic Spain basically identified with Castile." Xosé-Manoel Núñez, "What is Spanish Nationalism Today?: From Legitimacy to Crisis to Unfulfilled Renovation (1975–2000)," *Ethnic and Racial Studies* 24, no. 5 (September 2001): 720.

7. Formed in 1933, the Falange Española (Spanish Fascist Party) had been led by the charismatic José Antonio Primo de Rivera, son of former dictator Miguel Primo de Rivera. It was a minority party before the outbreak of hostilities in 1936, but quickly grew to rival the fanaticism of the Carlists. However, José Antonio's execution by the pro-Republic forces in November 1936 deprived the party of its figurehead, and Franco was able gradually to incorporate the great majority of Falange members into his own authoritarian movement. See Stanley G. Payne, *Falange: A History of Spanish Fascism* (Stanford, CA: Stanford University Press, 1961) and Sheelagh M. Ellwood, *Spanish Fascism in the Franco Era: Falange Española de las JONS 1936–76* (New York: St. Martin's Press, 1987).

8. Javier Tusell, *La España de Franco: El poder, la oposición y la política exterior durante el franquismo* (Madrid: Historia 16, 1989), 53–55.

9. In the Gipuzkoan village of Elgeta, after Franco's triumph, local Carlists (who had been the rural power brokers prior to World War I, but who had subsequently lost their status through increased economic independence for the peas-

antry) became the power elite once more. The local head of FET y de las JONS became the Movimiento's overseer. His reports to the civil governor would form the basis of who was elected to the municipal council and the right to obtain a passport, driver's license, permission to open a store, access to social benefits, and much more. Marianne Heiberg, *The Making of the Basque Nation* (Cambridge: Cambridge University Press, 1989), 197–99.

10. Stanley G. Payne, *The Franco Regime 1936–1975* (Madison: University of Wisconsin Press, 1987), 413.

11. Raymond Carr, *Modern Spain 1875–1980* (Oxford: Oxford University Press, 1980), 165.

12. This was the case with the disappearance from the political scene of Gil Robles and the CEDA during the early stages of the Civil War, the gradual fall from grace of the Falangists, and the isolation of the Spanish monarchists. See Sergio Vilar, "Sobre el franquismo y contra Franco," in Ricardo de la Cierva and Sergio Vilar, *Pro y contra Franco: Franquismo y antifranquismo* (Barcelona: Editorial Planeta, 1985), 34–36.

13. Meaning "leader," this was the title officially adopted by Franco in a Spanish equivalent to *duce* or *führer*.

14. Tusell, *La España del Franco*, 87–97.

15. [Annex] Suggested United States Position on Spain at April Session of the United Nations General Assembly, Washington, March 1, 1949, in a Memorandum by the Director of the Office of European Affairs (Hickerson) to the Assistant Secretary of State (Rusk), Washington, March 4, 1949, 501.BC Spain/3-449, Department of State, *Foreign Relations of the United States: Diplomatic Papers, 1949*, vol. 4, *Western Europe* (Washington, D.C.: United States Government Printing Office, 1954), 281 (hereafter cited as FRUS), 731.

16. Payne, *The Franco Regime 1936–1975*, 417–19.

17. "American Bases in Spain: An Alternative to N.A.T.O.?" *The Manchester Guardian Weekly* (London), May 8, 1958, 3, col. 1.

18. "Spain Submits to Economic Surgery," *The Manchester Guardian Weekly* (London), July 23, 1959, 7, col. 2.

19. "Spanish Donkey for General Eisenhower," *The Times* (London), April 7, 1956, 6, col. 6.

20. There is debate over an exact definition of the Francoist state. According to Raymond Carr and Juan Pablo Fusi Aizpurua, it would be difficult to classify the country as totalitarian, for it did not ever fully seek mass mobilization. Rather, it should be classified as a "stabilized authoritarian regime" that sought only the "passive acceptance" of its people. *Spain: Dictatorship to Democracy*, 2nd ed. (London: George Allen & Unwin, 1981), 47. However, Paul Preston contends that such a definition depends too much on "an exclusivist definition of fascism in Spain" (namely, limited to the Falange) and that Franco's Spain, a corporative state bereft of free trade unions, a left-wing press, and political parties, might rightly be considered totalitarian and even fascist. See "Spain," in *Fascism in Europe*, 2nd ed., ed. S. J. Woolf (London: Methuen, 1981), 330–31, 351.

21. The Chargé in Spain (Culbertson) to the Secretary of State, Madrid, June 20, 1950, 752.00/6-2050, in *FRUS* (1950), vol. 3, *Western Europe*, 1565.

22. Richards observes that "physical and economic repression in the wake of the Spanish civil war were used as a way of disciplining the lower orders of society and confirming their defeat… the concept of autarky offered a potential way of achieving the essential aims of this brutal vision of modernity: repression, the concentration of economic power and industrialization." "'Terror and Progress'," 176.

23. Carr, *Modern Spain 1875–1980*, 156; Carr and Fusi Aizpurua, *Spain: Dictatorship to Democracy*, 52.

24. Adrian Shubert, *A Social History of Modern Spain* (London: Unwin Hyman, 1990), 251.

25. Heiberg, *The Making of the Basque Nation*, 200.

26. There was a traditional pattern of emigration in Basque rural society because the domestic group organization did not allow excess membership. This, however, was compounded by a growing rural exodus throughout the twentieth century. See William A. Douglass, *Echalar and Murelaga: Opportunity and Rural Exodus in Two Spanish Basque Villages* (New York: St. Martin's Press, 1975), 120, 136–49.

27. Eduardo Sevilla Guzmán, "The Peasantry and the Franco Régime," in *Spain in Crisis: The Evolution and Decline of the Franco Régime*, ed. Paul Preston (New York: Barnes & Noble, 1976), 104.

28. Tusell, *La España de Franco*, 86.

29. For example, in 1950, the Madrid City Council stated that 40 percent of the milk consumed in the city was more water than milk. This was the result of a daily demand for four hundred thousand liters of milk, while only two hundred thousand liters entered the capital every day. Abella, *La vida cotidiana en España*, 89.

30. "The period 1936–45 witnessed a brutal repression simultaneous with a rapid reclamation of power by social elites. These elites both supported violence and had a vision of the future, albeit one which re-cycled a great deal of the past. The regime ultimately oversaw profound economic change and development, but was established through violence and suffering." Richards, *A Time of Silence*, 10.

31. The Chargé in Spain (Culbertson) to the Secretary of State, Madrid, June 20, 1950, 752.00/6-2050, *FRUS* (1950), vol. 3, *Western Europe*, 1564–65.

32. "'Progress' in the wake of the Spanish civil war entailed a terroristic reversion to primitivism." Richards, "'Terror and Progress,'" 181.

33. "Franco sought to carry centralization, which was one of the hallmarks of Spanish liberalism, to its logical extreme and make Spain a culturally homogenous nation, something which no Spanish government had ever achieved or, for that matter, even attempted." Shubert, *A Social History of Modern Spain*, 246.

34. Herbert R. Southworth, *El mito de la Cruzada de Franco* (Barcelona: Plaza & Janes, 1986), 315, 317; Gurruchaga, *El código nacionalista vasco durante el franquismo*, 143. Franco's rebellion of 1936 was referred to in a "Joint Letter of the Spanish Bishops to the Bishops of the Whole World" (June 1937) as an "armed plebiscite." Shubert, *A Social History of Modern Spain*, 233.

35. Alicia Alted, "Education and Political Control," in *Spanish Cultural Studies: An Introduction*, ed. Graham and Labanyi, 197; Gurruchaga, *El código nacionalista vasco durante el franquismo*, 158–59. The American chargé d'affaires in Madrid, Paul T. Culbertson, reserved a particular loathing for the official religious hierarchy in Spain, referring to a "backward, bigoted church, whose concepts look to the building of church treasures of gold and jewels and not the social uplift and well-being of the people." The Chargé in Spain (Culbertson) to the Secretary of State, Madrid, June 20, 1950, 752.00/6-2050, *FRUS* (1950), vol. 3, *Western Europe*, 1564.

36 Thomas J. Hamilton, *Appeasement's Child: The Franco Regime in Spain* (New York: Alfred A. Knopf, 1943), 210.

37. Shubert, *A Social History of Modern Spain*, 235. See also Alfonso Pérez-Agote's assertion that, "the State ... made the Church the basic institution of development and control in the ideological field in Spain." "The Role of Religion in the Definition of a Symbolic Conflict: Religion and the Basque Problem." *Social Compass* 33, no. 4 (1986): 423.

38. Alted, "Education and Political Control," 196.

39. Richards, *A Time of Silence*, 7.

40. Gurruchaga, *El código nacionalista vasco durante el franquismo*, 156–61.

41. Pérez-Agote, "The Role of Religion in the Definition of a Symbolic Conflict," 422.

42. Alted, "Education and Political Control," 197. Francoist culture, in the opinion of Carr, was "compounded of Tridentine Catholicism and the remnants of a Falangist imperialism, which ... found its ideal in the Spain of Philip II." *Modern Spain 1875–1980*, 163.

43. "Individuo 18," interview by Alfonso Pérez-Agote, in *La reproducción del nacionalismo vasco*: *El caso vasco* (Madrid: Centro de Investigaciones Sociológicas/Siglo XXI, 1984), 187. An updated version of this work has been translated into English. See Alfonso Pérez-Agote, *The Social Roots of Basque Nationalism*, trans. Cameron Watson and William A. Douglass, foreword by William A. Douglass (Reno: University of Nevada Press, 2006). See also the story of "Martín" as recounted to Joseba Zulaika about his teacher: "He was a staunch Francoist and would castigate harshly anyone speaking Basque, either in the school or in the street. He had *chivatos* [informers] to tell him who had been speaking in Basque and then would hit them in school." *Basque Violence: Metaphor and Sacrament* (Reno: University of Nevada Press, 1988), 37.

44. Jo Labanyi, "Censorship and the Fear of Mass Culture," in *Spanish Cultural Studies: An Introduction*, ed. Graham and Labanyi, 208.

45. Joseba Elosegi, *Quiero morir por algo* (Barcelona: Plaza & Janes, 1977), 238. See also the account of postwar prohibitions on the use of Euskara in the Basque-speaking village of Elgeta (Gipuzkoa) in Heiberg, *The Making of the Basque Nation*, 199–200.

46. Carr, *Modern Spain 1875–1980*, 164.

47. These films did encompass some regional cultures (particularly Andalusia's), but not that of the Basque Country. See Peter Evans, "Cifesa: Cinema and Authoritarian Aesthetics," in *Spanish Cultural Studies: An Introduction*, ed. Graham and Labanyi, 215–22.

48. The book, *Raza* (Race), was made into a film by the nephew of the former dictator Primo de Rivera. It depicts, in a less than subtle self-portrait of Franco himself, the life of José Churruca (interestingly a Basque last name), the son of a military family who becomes a hero during the Civil War. Virginia Higginbotham, *Spanish Film Under Franco* (Austin: University of Texas Press, 1988), 19.

49. Julian White, "Music and the Limits of Cultural Nationalism," in *Spanish Cultural Studies: An Introduction*, ed. Graham and Labanyi, 225–26.

50. Emma Dent Coad, "Constructing the Nation: Francoist Architecture," in *Spanish Cultural Studies: An Introduction*, ed. Graham and Labanyi, 223–25.

51. The figure is calculated from an estimate of sixteen thousand deaths of those loyal to the Republic and just over eight thousand insurgents. See Angel García-Sanz Marcotegui, "La población vasco-navarra entre 1930 y 1960: Los efectos de guerra y los cambios demográficos," *Boletín del Instituto Gerónimo de Ustariz*, no. 4 (1990): 98, 102.

52. This was a tactic employed throughout Spain as the Falangists sought to root out any remaining dissent and physically destroy it. See Gallo, *Spain Under Franco: A History*, 65. See also Richards, *A Time of Silence*, 42.

53. See Robert P. Clark, *The Basques: The Franco Years and Beyond* (Reno: University of Nevada Press, 1979), 80–82.

54. Ibid., 83.

55. Elosegi, *Quiero morir por algo*, 215, 217. See also the description of conditions in the Dueso jail as cited by Clark, *The Basques: The Franco Years and Beyond*, 83–84.

56. "Martin," interview by Zulaika in *Basque Violence: Metaphor and Sacrament*, 24.

57. Ibid., 84.

58. Hamilton, *Appeasement's Child*, 23.

59. Ibid., 24, 31.

60. Ibid., 32.

61. "Suffering... is not a raw datum, a natural phenomenon we can identify and measure, but a social status that we extend or withhold. We extend or withhold it largely on whether the sufferer falls within our moral community." David B. Morris, "About Suffering: Voice, Genre, and Moral Community," *Daedalus* 125, no.1 (Winter 1996): 40.

62. See José Mari Garmendia, *Historia de ETA*, vol. 1 (San Sebastián: L. Haranburu, 1979), 12.

63. "To support the PNV... was, according to Francoist authorities, to be a 'separatist' and separatism had become, in practice, a capital crime." Richards, *A Time of Silence*, 42.

64. Alfonso Pérez-Agote, *La reproducción del nacionalismo*, 79. See also Gurruchaga, *El código nacionalista vasco durante el franquismo*, 284–85.

65. "*Mark* is... our generic term for perceived or inferred conditions of deviation from a prototype or norm that *might* initiate the stigmatizing process.... The marked person may or may not be *stigmatized*. To mark a person implies that the deviant condition has been noticed and recognized as a problem in the interaction of the relationship. To stigmatize a person generally carries a further implication that the mark has been linked by an attributional process to dispositions that discredit the bearer, i.e., that 'spoil' his identity." Edward E. Jones, Amerigo Farina, Albert A. Hastorf, Hazel Markus, Dale T. Miller, and Robert A. Scott, with a special contribution by Rita S. de French, *Social Stigma: The Psychology of Marked Relationships* (New York: W. H. Freeman, 1984), 8.

66. See Juan Aranzadi, *Milenarismo vasco* (Edad de Oro, etnia y nativismo) (Madrid: Taurus Ediciones, 1981), Jon Juaristi, *El linaje de Aitor: La invención de la tradición vasca* (Madrid: Taurus, 1987), Juan Aranzadi, Jon Juaristi, and Patxo Unzueta, *Auto de terminación (Raza, nación y violencia en el País Vasco)* (Madrid: El País/Aguilar, 1994), and "Introduction: Inventing Traditions," in *The Invention of Tradition*, ed. Eric Hobsbawm and Terence Ranger (Cambridge: Cambridge University Press, 1983).

67. Carr and Fusi Aizpurua, *Spain: Dictatorship to Democracy*, 159.

68. "The Spanish state itself further contributed to the perception of 'us' versus 'them' by distinguishing the Basque territory from the rest of Spain through the imposition of 12 'states of exception' [a virtual proclamation of martial law, between 1956 and Franco's death in 1975] which, by specifically discriminating against the Basque provinces, delegitimated the social reality of a unified Spanish nation and, in turn, legitimated the social construct of a distinct Basque nation." Francisco Llera, José M. Mata, and Cynthia Irvin, "ETA: From Secret Army to Social Movement–The Post-Franco Schism of the Basque Nationalist Movement," *Terrorism and Political Violence* 5, no. 3 (Autumn 1993): 107; See also Robert P. Clark, *The Basque Insurgents: ETA, 1952–1980* (Madison: University of Wisconsin Press, 1984), 241.

69. In Joseba Zulaika's study of the Gipuzkoan village of Itziar, he observes that "*gosia* (hunger) is vivid in the villagers' memory of the postwar situation" and that misery, hatred, division, fear, and guilt permeated their everyday lives. "For the villagers, who were startled by this runaway situation, *gerra ondorena* (the postwar) was a time of economic and psychological atonement for the preceding chaos and a period of slow return to normal cultural models of behavior." *Basque Violence: Metaphor and Sacrament*, 34–35.

70. Gurruchaga, *El código nacionalista vasco durante el franquismo*, 172.

71. According to one study of the Navarrese village of Etxalar (Echalar), *gau lana* (night work) became a major source of income for the villagers in the post–Civil War era: "Everything," explains Douglass, "from buttons to truck transmissions passed through Echalar on the backs of runners." Furthermore, "throughout the period of active contraband there was scarcely a household in Echalar which did not benefit.... Most adolescent and adult males could count upon employment several nights a week. Women and children also earned salaries serving as lookouts and carrying messages.... Vil-

lagers report that during its most active years the contraband traffic eclipsed agriculture as the most important economic activity in the village." *Echalar and Murelaga*, 118–19.

72. "Spain fears a war in the near future because she is to-day at the end of her resources. In certain regions there is famine." Galeazzo Ciano, *Ciano's Diary 1939–1943*, ed. with an introduction by Malcolm Muggeridge, foreword by Sumner Welles (London: William Heinemann, 1947), 100.

73. "Silence stands in opposition to every voice, weak or strong, ordinary or unique, prosaic or poetic. The basic opposition between voice and silence matters here because suffering, like pain, with which it so often intermingles, exists in part beyond language." David B. Morris, "About Suffering: Voice, Genre, and Moral Community," 27.

74. Abella maintains that public spaces such as parks, the street, and any public premises were the targets of extreme vigilance on the part of the state. See *La vida cotidiana en España*, 41.

75. The Basque family is discussed by William A. Douglass in *Death in Murelaga: Funerary Ritual in a Spanish Basque Village* (Seattle: University of Washington Press, 1969), 83–105.

76. Marianne Heiberg, "Urban Politics and Rural Culture: Basque Nationalism," in *The Politics of Territorial Identity: Studies in European Regionalism*, ed. Stein Rokkan and Derek W. Urwin (London: Sage Publications, 1982), 372–73.

77. See Richards's comments about the "defeated" throughout Spain: "memories of pain, or of shame were internalised and are not easy to recapture, articulate or interpret. The Spanish Civil War and its devastating aftermath represented an overwhelming sense of loss in many ways. Defeat represented more than military failure: it also meant a loss of the past, of identity and ideals, and of visions of the future." *A Time of Silence*, 28.

78. Pérez-Agote, *La reproducción del nacionalismo vasco*, 88–90.

79. Ibid., 97.

80. Gurruchaga, *El código nacionalista vasco durante el franquismo*, 325–26.

81. "The potential rebel must believe that by rebelling he will improve his lot. This implies that there must be somebody, or some recognisable group, to blame for his misfortune: something to rebel against." Brian Crozier, *The Rebels: A Study of Post–War Insurrections* (Boston: Beacon Press, 1960), 9.

82. Clark, *The Basques: The Franco Years and Beyond*, 81.

83. Pérez-Agote, *La reproducción del nacionalismo vasco*, 99.

84. Zulaika, *Basque Violence: Metaphor and Sacrament*, 39–41. According to a founding member of Ekin (and later ETA), José Manuel Agirre, his presidency of a local JOC chapter was an experience that helped shape his later activism. José Manu Agirre, interview by Xabier Amuriza in *Euskadi eta Askatasuna, Euskal Herria y Libertad*, vol. 1, *1952-1965, De Ekin a ETA*, ed. Luis Nuñez (Tafalla: Txalaparta, 1993), 204.

85. Jesús Azcona, "To Be Basque and to Live in Basque Country: The Inequalities of Difference," in *Democracy and Ethnography: Constructing Identities in Multicultural Liberal States*, ed. Carol J. Greenhouse with Roshanak Kheshti (Albany: State University of New York Press, 1998), 168.

86. See Pérez-Agote, *La reproducción del nacionalismo vasco*, 103–5.

87. Gurruchaga, *El código nacionalista vasco durante el franquismo*, 364.

88. Heiberg, *The Making of the Basque Nation*, 154–59.

89. Ibid., 201.

90. As Gloria Totoricagüena notes, however, support from the diaspora communities was also complicated by numerous factors. For example, pro-Franco media elements labeled Basques as Communists and anti-Catholic, and in general, the Catholic Church throughout the Americas supported the Franco regime. Similarly, right-wing politics in Latin America also made criticism of Franco difficult. See *Identity, Culture and Politics in the Basque Diaspora* (Reno: University of Nevada Press, 2004.), 70–74.

91. The network functioned primarily for passing information about Spain by Basque agents between the French, British, and Americans and for transporting information across the Franco-Spanish border, particularly about German movements in France. The period is described in detail by one of the agents. See Joseba Elosegui, in *50 años de nacionalismo vasco 1928–1978*, ed. Ibarzábal, 328.

92. Clark, *The Basques: The Franco Years and Beyond*, 91.

93. Emilio López Adán [Beltza, pseud.], *El nacionalismo vasco en el exilio 1937–1960* (San Sebastián: Editorial Txertoa, 1977), 14.

94. Pedro Ordoki, in *50 años de nacionalismo vasco 1928–1978*, ed. Ibarzábal, 299–301.

95. Ordoki, in *50 años de nacionalismo vasco 1928–1978*, ed., Ibarzábal, 301–03; Clark, *The Basques: The Franco Years and Beyond*, 92; López Adán [Beltza, pseud.], *El nacionalismo vasco en el exilio*, 18–19; Francisco Letamendia Belzunce [Ortzi, pseud.], *ETA en el franquismo* (San Sebastián: R & B Ediciones, 1994), 209.

96. López Adán [Beltza, pseud.], *El nacionalismo vasco en el exilio*, 19.

97. "The PNV of the 1940s was fundamentally an organization with a paramilitary structure. Composed of what came to be called the Basque Resistance . . . the PNV, in addition to its political sections, possessed an armed wing named *Euzko Naia*, formed out of the old leaders and officials of the Basque Army, and alongside it, in clandestine activity . . . [the Secret] Services." Eugenio Ibarzábal, "Así nació ETA. A los 20 años de su aparición," *Muga*, no. 1 (June 1979), 79. Euzko Naia had actually been formed in 1941 under the leadership of Lino de Lazkano. Koldo San Sebastián, "El PNV durante el primer franquismo," in *Los nacionalistas: Historia del nacionalismo vasco, 1876–1960*, ed. Santiago de Pablo (Vitoria-Gasteiz: Fundación Sancho el Sabio, 1995), 172.

98. Ibarzábal, "Así nació ETA," 89.

99. López Adán [Beltza, pseud.], *El nacionalismo vasco en el exilio*, 32. During his American exile in World War II, the Basque president, Aguirre, had established a close friendship with exiled European Christian Democrats such as Jacques Maritain, Luigi Sturzzo, Frans Van Cawalaert, and Paul Van Zeelan. In 1946, the PNV sent an official representation to the Congress of Christian Democracy in Rome, and the following year, after a meeting of European Christian Democrats in the PNV's Paris headquarters, an organization was formed to coordinate the various European parties. San Sebastián, "El PNV durante el primer franquismo," 176.

100. López Adán [Beltza, pseud.], *El nacionalismo vasco en el exilio*, 23.

101. Clark, *The Basques: The Franco Years and Beyond*, 103; López Adán [Beltza, pseud.], *El nacionalismo vasco en el exilio*, 35; Letamendia Belzunce [Ortzi, pseud.], *ETA en el franquismo*, 210. See also the personal testimony of Joseba Elosegi, who took part in planting of an *ikurriña* on the Buen Pastor cathedral in Donostia–San Sebastián on the tenth anniversary of Franco's uprising, *Quiero morir por algo*, 279, and Elosegui, in *50 años de nacionalismo vasco 1928–1978*, ed. Ibarzábal, 333–34.

102. López Adán mentions two cases: that of José Aguirre, who was murdered after shouting "Gora Euzkadi" ("Long live the Basque Country") during the fiestas of Bilbao in 1946, and Txomin Letamendi, a member of the resistance, who was detained in August 1946 and subsequently executed. *El nacionalismo vasco en el exilio*, 34.

103. Letamendia Belzunce [Ortzi, pseud.], *ETA en el franquismo*, 211.

104. Ordoki, in *50 años de nacionalismo vasco 1928–1978*, ed. Ibarzábal, 303–4.

105. "Bakunin," quoted in Eduardo Pons Prades, *Guerrillas españolas 1936–1960* (Barcelona: Editorial Planeta, 1977), 428.

106. Ordoki, in *50 años de nacionalismo vasco 1928–1978*, ed. Ibarzábal, 305; Elosegui, in *50 años de nacionalismo vasco 1928–1978*, ed. Ibarzábal, 334.

107. Joseba Elosegi, *Quiero morir por algo*, 269.

108. Abella overlooks this fact, stating that the 1951 Barcelona strike marked the first challenge to public order in the Francoist state. *La vida cotidiana en España*, 123.

109. "Strikes in Bilbao: Government Official's Statement," *The Times* (London), May 10, 1947, 3, col. 4.

110. Clark, *The Basques: The Franco Years and Beyond*, 104; Letamendia Belzunce [Ortzi, pseud.], *ETA en el franquismo*, 211.

111. "Strikes in Spain: Wide Movement in Industrial North," *The Times* (London), April 24, 1951, 4, col. 6.

112. "Spanish Strike Ending: Demand for Release of Prisoners," *The Times* (London), April 26, 1951, 3, col. 6.

113. "Renewal of Unrest," *The Times* (London), April 27, 1951, 6, col. 4.

114. "General Strike in Pamplona," *The Times* (London), May 9, 1951, 5, col. 4.

115. "Arrested Men to Be Released," *The Times* (London), May 12, 1951, 5, col. 2.

116. See Clark, *The Basques: The Franco Years and Beyond*, 105–06.

117. Ibid., 106.

118. In the opinion of the Spanish police, "the recent strikes in Catalonia and the three Basque provinces were organized and directed from the French side of the Pyrenean frontier . . . [and] reference is made to the 'complicity of separatists and foreign freemasons' on the one hand and to the infiltration of separatist elements among the local Basque Catholic workers on the other." "Causes of Spanish Unrest: Agitators Arrested," *The Times* (London), May 16, 1951, 3, col. 5.

119. "Falangists claim it is they and not the shilly-shallying authorities of the régime who will break the strikes." "Foreign Agencies Blamed for Disturbances," *The Times* (London), May 22, 1951, 3, col. 3.

120. See "Restlessness in Spain," *The Times* (London), May 29, 1951, 5, col. 4, and "Spain's Domestic Troubles: Gen. Franco's Scapegoats," *The Times* (London), June 11, 1951, 3, col. 3.

121. Richards, *A Time of Silence*, 170.

122. Memorandum of Conversation by Mr. John Y. Millar of the Office of Western European Affairs, Washington, March 27, 1950, 752.00/3-2750, *FRUS* (1950), vol. 3, *Western Europe*, 1557.

123. López Adán [Beltza, pseud.], *El nacionalismo vasco en el exilio*, 72.

124. Ibid., 58–62, 77–84.

125. Clark, *The Basques: The Franco Years and Beyond*, 245–46.

126. See Juan Ajuriaguerra, in *50 años de nacionalismo vasco 1928–1978*, ed. Ibarzábal, 337–39; San Sebastián, "El PNV durante el primer franquismo," 177.

Notes, Chapter Nine

1. Søren Kierkegaard, "The First Love: A Comedy in One Act by Scribe," trans. J. L. Heiberg, in *Either/Or: Part I*, ed. with an introduction and notes by Howard V. Hong and Edna H. Hong (1843; rpt., Princeton: Princeton University Press, 1987), 237–38.

2. The better works to treat this early period are Eugenio Ibarzábal, "Así nació ETA"; Jon Nicolás, "El grupo 'Ekin' y los primeros pasos," "Integración en Euzko gaztedi, 1956–57," and "Nacimiento de ETA (1958)," in ETA, *Documentos Y*, vol. 1 (Donostia: Editorial Lur, 1979), 25–32 (hereafter cited as *Documentos Y*); Gurutz Jáuregui Bereciartu, *Ideología y estrategia política de ETA: Análisis de su evolución entre 1959 y 1968*, 2nd ed. (Madrid: Siglo XXI, 1985), pt. 1, esp. 48–83; and Robert P. Clark, *The Basque Insurgents: ETA, 1952–1980* (Madison: University of Wisconsin Press, 1984), pt. 1, esp. 20–27. Other works that record the events leading to the formation of ETA include José Mari Garmendia, *Historia de ETA*, 2 vols. (San Sebastián: L. Haranburu, 1979), vol. 1, 11–18; Mercè Ibarz, *Breu Història d'ETA* (Barcelona: Ediciones la Magrana, 1981), 31–46; and Peter Waldmann, *Militanter Nationalismus im Baskenland* (Frankfurt am Main: Vervuert Verlag, 1990), 61–97, 101–104.

3. According to a founding member of ETA, Iulen de Madariaga, "One cannot understand ETA without the six or seven introductory years, under the name Ekin ... The historic decision, the authentic embryo of the military wing, of not confining ourselves to purely political and cultural activity, [dates] also from that era." Quoted in Antoni Batista, *Madariaga: De las armas a la palabra* (Barcelona: RBA Libros, 2007), 78.

4. This group actually bore a striking similarity to the future Ekin. Formed in 1943 as a reaction against the perceived inactivity of the PNV, it had an international character (its center was in the Dutch town of Leiden) and remained reasonably independent through the 1940s. However, it gradually moved closer to the PNV (through contact with the resistance movement) and in the early 1950s, it was officially incorporated into the party structure. Koldo San Sebastián, "El PNV durante el primer franquismo," in *Los nacionalistas: Historia del nacionalismo vasco, 1876–1960*, ed. Santiago de Pablo (Vitoria-Gasteiz: Fundación Sancho el Sabio, 1995), 172; Clark, *The Basque Insurgents: ETA, 1952–1980*, 24–25.

5. Iulen de Madariaga, interview by Juan P. Bator, *Punto y Hora de Euskal Herria*, no. 49 (August 18–24, 1977), 22. For a full biography of Madariaga, see Batista, *Madariaga: De las armas a la palabra*.

6. José Luis Alvarez Enparantza [Txillardegi, pseud.], *Euskal Herria helburu* (Tafalla: Txalaparta, 1994), 180–82.

7. "The ease with which we were arrested and the consequences of that roundup–the almost total destruction of the organization–called to our attention what it meant to act clandestinely, and it made it clear to us that serious and continuous work required that we improve our security standards, and that idea would have important consequences in the future." José Luis Alvarez Enparanza [Txillardegi, pseud.], in *50 años de ncionalismo vasco 1928–1978 (A través de sus protagonistas)*, ed. Eugenio Ibarzábal (San Sebastián: Ediciones Vascas, 1978, 362; the translation is that of Clark in *The Basque Insurgents: ETA, 1952–1980*, 25. See also Jáuregui Bereciartu, *Ideología y estrategia política de ETA*, 76–77.

8. Ibarz, *Breu Història d'ETA 1959–1979*, 44.

9. "M.P.s' Protest Returned: Action by Spanish Ambassador," *The Times* (London), March 17, 1954, 8, col. 2. "Emilio Jose Agote said that when he was arrested in May, 1951, the police laid him across a table with his head hanging over one end and his feet over the other. Then they beat his stomach with rubber truncheons. This treatment went on for three consecutive days before they asked him to make his statement." "17 Basques on Trial: Alleged Organization of 1951 Strike," *The Times* (London), March 26, 1954, 5, col. 3.

10. "Sentences in Basque Trial: Three Men Acquitted," *The Times* (London), March 31, 1954, 8, col. 4.

11. As mentioned previously, there were ideological differences between the PNV's exiled leadership and Ajuriaguerra. These tensions were further compounded when Telesforo Monzón resigned from the Basque government in 1953, leading a faction of the party that advocated noncooperation with other (Spanish) exiled pro-Republic groups and that represented, to some extent, a reaction against a policy of moderation within the party. There was even an emerging division between two party stalwarts over whether Navarre should remain in the official PNV project for Basque self-determination. Manuel de Irujo believed that it should, whereas Jesús María de Leizaola favored its removal. See Garmendia, *Historia de ETA*, vol. 1, 17–18; and Clark, *The Basques: The Franco Years and Beyond*, 112; Luigi Bruni, *ETA: Historia política de una lucha armada* (Bilbo: Txalaparta, 1987), 29–30.

12. Ibarzábal, "Así nació ETA," 78.

13. Interview with José Luis Alvarez Enparantza [Txillardegi, pseud.], *Garaia*, no.1 (September 1976), quoted in *Documentos Y*, vol. 1, 9.

14. Iulen de Madariaga was actually a student in the university's Faculty of Law. Madariaga, interview by Bator, *Punto y Hora de Euskal Herria*, 22.

15. They also collected books from wherever they could, such as those formerly held by the PNV's *batzokiak*, or cultural centers. They found the *batzokiak* of Algorta, Asua, and Sestao (all in different suburbs of greater Bilbao) particularly rich sources for their endeavors. Nicolás, "El grupo 'Ekin,'" in *Documentos Y*, vol. 1, 25.

16. Alvarez Enparantza [Txillardegi, pseud.], *Euskal Herria helburu*, 137–40; Txillardegi, in *50 años de nacionalismo vasco 1928-1978*, ed. Ibarzábal, 362–63; "The ideas that were discussed, in the beginning with a friend, entailed a strong shock for [their] personal conscience in many aspects, in the insecurity with which they defended themselves, [and] their own doubts were motives for great vacillations that held up the formation of [even] a minimal collective conscience of struggle." Nicolás, "El grupo 'Ekin'," *Documentos Y*, vol. 1, 25.

17. Alvarez Enparantza [Txillardegi, pseud.], *Euskal Herria helburu*, 139; Ibarzábal, "Así nació ETA," 78; José Manu Agirre, interview by Xabier Amuriza, *Euskadi eta Askatasuna*, vol. 1, 204.

18. Madariaga, interview by Bator, *Punto y Hora de Euskal Herria*, 22.

19. The title of the group may have been influenced by a publishing company of the same name in Buenos Aires. Jáuregui Bereciartu, *Ideología y estrategia política de ETA*, 76; José Manu Agirre, interview by Xabier Amuriza, *Euskadi eta Askatasuna*, vol. 1, 204–5.

20. Alvarez Enparantza [Txillardegi, pseud.], *Euskal Herria helburu*, 137.

21. Julen [Iulen de] Madariaga, "Lutte revolutionnaire en Euskadi: Etat de guerre larvée," in *Documentos Y*, vol. 9, 387, 389.

22. Alvarez Enparantza [Txillardegi, pseud.], *Euskal Herria helburu*, 137.

23. In Luigi Bruni's opinion, Ekin's "ideological plans differed little from those of classical [Basque] nationalism; their readings were those works of Sabino Arana, Eleizalde, and Aranzadi. It joined in them a strong conscience of national oppression and a great interest in the Basque language that some of them did not even know." *ETA: Historia política de una lucha armada*, 29.

24. Eguileor was the former *aberriano* and author of *Nacionalismo vasco* (1936), a book maintaining that a potential recourse to force would be perfectly congruent with the early idealism of Arana (See ch. 6); Robles-Aranguiz was one of the founders of the Basque nationalist union (ELA-STV) and a provincial representative during the Second Republic; Sota was one of the historic *aberrianos*.

25. Txillardegi, in *50 años de nacionalismo vasco 1928–1978*, ed. Ibarzábal, 363; Alvarez Enparantza [Txillardegi, pseud.], *Euskal Herria helburu*, 183.

26. Alvarez Enparantza [Txillardegi, pseud.], *Euskal Herria helburu*, 204–05; See also Madariaga's recollection that "we had a great reverence and an enormous sympathy toward the [Basque Nationalist] party for the simple reason that in the brief history of the resurrection of the Basque national conscience, the PNV, with its defects and ups and downs, was the real force that had done most for Euskadi." Interview by Bator, *Punto y Hora de Euskal Herria*, 22.

27. As Murray Edelman observes, the use of metaphor and myth in political discourse is as much a means of reinforcement for the user as it is meant to influence an audience: "Leaders ... often have an interest in encouraging acceptance of the myths and in accepting themselves; motivation is not irrelevant to perception." *Politics as Symbolic Action: Mass Arousal and Quiescence*, Institute for Research on Poverty Monograph Series (Chicago: Markham Publishing Company, 1971), 63.

28. Madariaga, "Lutte revolutionnaire en Euskadi," in *Documentos Y*, vol. 9, 389.

29. "Nationalism itself suffered a generational crisis. The new generation born in the bosom of nationalism faced conditions in which even though they had to consider themselves heirs of the Civil War's outcome, they distanced themselves ostensibly in relation to the immediate postwar. To that extent, they did not feel as if they had lost the war, nor did they accept the situation as a punishment for a defeat of which they were not the victims. Therefore, neither did they feel chained to quiet and passive means that meant that the resistance did not in fact exist. The PNV's politics of waiting was losing, before the eyes of that new generation, the prestige that a democratic legitimacy, so remote in time, could offer." Kepa Aulestia, *Días de viento sur: La violencia en Euskadi* (Barcelona: Editorial Antárdida/Empúries, 1993), 19.

30. The Ekin notebooks are reproduced in full in the multivolume work of documents concerning ETA. Their titles are: *Fueros y leyes* (*Fueros* and laws), *La Federación Europea* (The European Federation), *Normas generales* (General rules), *Un bosquejo de la historia vasca hasta 1512* (A search for Basque history through 1512), *Moral de resistencia nacionl* (The ethics of national resistance), *Fueros-Instituciones* (*Fueros*-institutions), and *Euskera y patriotismo vasco* (Basque and Basque patriotism). See *Documentos Y*, vol. 1, 77–109, and for the White Book, 149–298.

31. Ekin, "Moral de resistencia nacional," in *Documentos Y*, vol. 1, 94–95.

32. See Ekin, "Euskera y patriotismo vasco," in *Documentos Y*, vol. 1, 103–09.

33. Clark, *The Basque Insurgents: ETA, 1952–1980*, 25–26. See also Ibarz, *Breu Historia d'ETA 1959-1979*, 44.

34. Alvarez Enparantza [Txillardegi, pseud.], *Euskal Herria helburu*, 207.

35. Ibarzábal, "Así nació ETA," 78.

36. Letter by Txillardegi, José Manuel Agirre, José María Benito del Valle, and Iulen de Madariaga, Bilbao, December 8, 1979, *Muga*, no. 3 (February 1980), 14.

37. Ekin, "Fueros-Leyes," in ETA, *Documentos Y*, 78, 80.

38. Manuel de Irujo, "La República Vasca," *Euzko Deya*, no. 223 (January 1959), 13.

39. Clark, *The Basque Insurgents: ETA, 1952–1980*, 26.

40. Ekin, *La Federación Europea*, in *Documentos Y*, vol. 1, 85.

41. Ibarzábal argues that there was little difference between the PNV and Ekin in terms of their respective political programs. "Así nació ETA," 85. However, this is challenged by one of Ekin's founders. According to Txillardegi, a PNV representative, Eli Etxeberria, told Ekin that "the slogan JEL [Jaungoikua eta lege zarra–God and the Old Laws] is untouchable. If you start anything with such things, we will close all doors to you." See Txillardegi, "Así nació ETA," *Punto y Hora de Euskal Herria*, no. 130 (21–28 June 1979), 16. See also the opinion of other Ekin members, José María Benito del Valle and José Manu Aguirre, "El nacimiento de ETA," *Punto y Hora de Euskal Herria*, no. 150 (8–15 November 1979), 17.

42. José Mari Benito del Valle and José Manu Agirre, "ETA: Historia e historias," *Punto y Hora de Euskal Herria*, no. 134 (19–26 July 1979), 44.

43. Ibid., 177. See also Txillardegi, in *50 años de nacionalismo vasco 1928–1978*, ed. Ibarzábal, 364–65.

44. José Antonio Etxebarrieta, "Breve resumen de la historia de ETA," unpublished article (1968), in *Documentos Y*, vol. 1, 18; Ibarzábal, "Así nació ETA," 78; Clark, *The Basque Insurgents: ETA, 1952–1980*, 26.

45. Txillardegi, in *50 años de nacionalismo vasco 1928–1978*, ed. Ibarzábal, 363.

46. Space precludes a discussion here of the question regarding the involvement of the PNV's secret service in the Ekin-PNV dialogue of the 1950s. Suffice to say that it remains one of the most contentious points of historical debate, one without any apparent solution. Ibarzábal makes a detailed and seemingly convincing case that the rise of Ekin/ETA would have been impossible without the aid of at least some members of the PNV secret service: "Ekin created the spider's web," concludes Ibarzábal, "but it would not have been possible without the collaboration of Murua [a member of the PNV's secret services], to the extent that one might dare say that without the help given by the *Servicios*, [only with] difficulty would Ekin have been able to develop an authentic organization." See "Así nació ETA," 83–85. For their part, four of the original Ekin members refute this claim, arguing that the development of Ekin was, from the outset, exclusively autonomous. See the letter by Txillardegi, Agirre, Benito del Valle, and Madariaga, Bilbao, December 8, 1979, 13–14.

47. Ibarzábal, "Así nació ETA," 82–83.

48. Although certain less welcoming members of EG referred to the 'I' as standing for *Ikasle* (Student). Nicolás, "Integración en Euzko Gaztedi, 1956–57," in *Documentos Y*, vol. 1, 29n.

49. Clark, *The Basque Insurgents: ETA, 1952–1980*, 24. There were from the outset, however, differences between the two groups. EGI enjoyed a greater membership owing to its more open recruitment policy. It was also more folkloric, as well as being tolerated, although closely supervised, by the police. On the other hand, Ekin was considered by EGI as a group of boorish, aloof, and snobbish intellectuals, closed and secretive in their organization. Nicolás, "El grupo 'Ekin'," in *Documentos Y*, vol. 1, 27. Joseba Zulaika, citing evidence from one of the original Ekin members (Txillardegi), points out that in many ways, it was the spirit of critical inquiry and self-reflection, more than "pure" activism, that originally differentiated Ekin from the EG. *ETAren hautsa* (Irun: Alberdania, 2006), 117.

50. Ibarzábal, "Así nació ETA," 84; Clark, *The Basque Insurgents: ETA, 1952–1980*, 26; Jáuregui Bereciartu, *Ideología y estrategia política de ETA*, 77.

51. Alvarez Enparanza [Txillardegi, pseud.] in *50 años de nacionalismo vasco 1928–1978*, ed. Ibarzábal, 365.

52. Ibarzábal, "Así nació ETA," 84.

53. Alvarez Enparantza [Txillardegi, pseud.], *Euskal Herria helburu*, 187.

54. "The rector of [Madrid] university ... recently informed General Franco of the 'increasing deviation' among pupils from the 'ideals inspired by the national rising of July 18, 1936.'" "Student Unrest in Madrid: More Anti-Falange Incidents," *The Times* (London), February 9, 1956, 7, col. 1 The anti-Franco movement of the mid-1950s was, to some extent, predicted by the young Spanish writer Juan Goytisolo, whose first novel, *Juegos de mano* (translated into English as *The Young Assassins*) captured a youthful desire to protest through concrete action. In the novel, the personal failure of a young activist to

kill a politician reflects, for Goytisolo, the failure of a generation. See Max Gallo, *Spain Under Franco: A History*, trans. Jean Stewart (New York: E. P. Dutton & Co., 1974), 217.

55. "Kingdom without a King: Spanish Régime's Future in the Melting-Pot," *The Times* (London), February 13, 1956, 9, col. 6.

56. "Unrest in Pamplona: Governor's Warning Defied," *The Times* (London), April 12, 1956, 8, col. 5; "Spanish Reply to Strikes: Drastic Measures by Government," *The Times* (London), April 16, 1956, 8, col. 4.

57. "40,000 Now Out at Bilbao: Spread of Basque Labour Troubles: Factories Closed," *The Times* (London), April 27, 1956, 10, col. 5; "Bilbao Shipyard Lock-Out: Shop Stewards' Arrest," *The Times* (London), April 28, 1956, 5, col. 5.

58. "Unrest in Spain," *The Times* (London), May 1, 1956, 11, col. 2.

59. Francisco Javier de Landáburu, *La causa del pueblo vasco (Razones de una actitud: Posibilidades de actuación)* (1956; rpt., 3rd ed. Bilbao: Editorial Geu Argitaldaria, 1977), 29–37 (page citations are to the reprint edition).

60. Ibid., 46.

61. Ibid., 53, 59.

62. Ibid., 63–64.

63. Particularly by Jáuregui Bereciartu, who makes the important point that Landáburu stressed the importance of Euskara, as well as the role of the young nationalists, in his overall vision of the nationalist cause. See *Ideología y estrategia política de ETA*, 22, 75–76.

64. "Las reuniones del P.N.V.," *Alderdi*, no. 115, October 1956, 4.

65. "En el XX aniversario del Gobierno de Euzkadi," *Alderdi*, no. 115 (October 1956), 6.

66. John Sullivan, *ETA and Basque Nationalism: The Fight for Euskadi, 1890–1986* (London: Routledge, 1988), 30; Ibarzábal, "Así nació ETA," 85.

67. "Despite not forming part of ETA, his [Krutwig's] work played an important role for many years, influencing many of its militants." Bruni, *ETA: Historia política de una lucha armada*, 30.

68. Although his words would prove, within the space of a few years, prophetic. Alvarez Enparantza [Txillardegi, pseud.], *Euskal Herria helburu*, 191–92.

69. "Conclusiones adoptadas a propuesta de la Sección Política," in López Adán [Beltza, pseud.], *El nacionalismo vasco en el exilio 1937–1960* (San Sebastián: Txertoa, 1977), 138.

70. EGI's members, as Marianne Heiberg points out, "tended to come from the smaller new industrial towns, were often Basque-speakers, had a vocational, rather than academic, training, and were anti-intellectual with little patience for theorizing of any kind. It was these people, in particular, who had been recruited to nationalism by priests. During the 1950s while *Ekin* organized study groups, EG members covered the walls and streets of the Basque country with political slogans and broadsheets. EG represented the militant base of ETA, a base over which the leadership would never manage to gain effective political control." *The Making of the Basque Nation* (Cambridge: Cambridge University Press, 1989), 106.

71. Sullivan, *ETA and Basque Nationalism*, 30.

72. Zulaika, *Basque Violence: Metaphor and Sacrament*, 43.

73. Juan Ajuriaguerra, in *50 años de nacionalismo vasco 1928–1978*, ed. Ibarzábal, 340.

74. Clark, *The Basque Insurgents: ETA, 1952–1980*, 26; José María Portell, *Los hombres de ETA* (Barcelona: Dopesa, 1974), 12–13.

75. Ibarzábal, "Así nació ETA," 85; Clark, *The Basque Insurgents: ETA, 1952–1980*, 26–27; Letamendia Belzunce [Ortzi, pseud.], *Historia del nacionalismo vasco y de ETA*, vol. 1., *Introducción a la historia del País Vasco: ETA en el franquismo* (San Sebastián: R & B Ediciones, 1994), 253.

76. Alvarez Enparanza [Txillardegi, pseud.], in *50 años de nacionalismo vasco 1928–1978*, ed. Ibarzábal, 366.

77. Madariaga, interview by Bator, *Punto y Hora de Euskal Herria*, 22. Referring to the same quote, Ekin members Benito del Valle and Agirre saw it as symbolic of the PNV's obsessive monopolistic intentions. See "ETA: Historia e historias," *Punto y Hora de Euskal Herria*, 45.

78. Iulen de Madariaga, quoted in Batista, *Madariaga: De las armas a la palabra*, 79.

79. Ibarzábal, "Así nació ETA," 86.

80. Alvarez Enparanza [Txillardegi, pseud.], in *50 años de nacionalismo vasco 1928–1978*, ed. Ibarzábal, 366.

81. Ajuriaguerra, in *50 años de nacionalismo vasco 1928–1978*, ed. Ibarzábal, 340; Ibarzábal, "Así nació ETA," 86.

82. Alvarez Enparanza [Txillardegi, pseud.], in *50 años de nacionalismo vasco 1928–1978*, ed. Ibarzábal, 366–67.

83. Ajuriaguerra, in *50 años de nacionalismo vasco 1928–1978*, ed. Ibarzábal, 345.

84. Clark, *The Basque Insurgents: ETA, 1952–1980*, 27.

85. Nicolás, "Integración en Euzko Gaztedi, 1956–57," in *Documentos Y*, vol. 1, 30; Madariaga, interview by Bator, *Punto y Hora de Euskal Herria*, 22.

86. Ibarzábal, "Así nació ETA," 88–89. That said, some members of EGI who had been closely identified with Ekin chose to remain within the party structure. Such was the case with José Murua. See Txillardegi, in *50 años de nacionalismo vasco 1928–1978*, ed. Ibarzábal, 367.

87. Jáuregui Bereciartu, *Ideología y estrategia política de ETA*, 81–82.

88. Alvarez Enparanza [Txillardegi, pseud.], in *50 años de nacionalismo vasco 1928–1978*, ed. Ibarzábal, 370; Alvarez Enparantza [Txillardegi, pseud.], *Euskal Herria helburu*, 195; Ibarzábal, "Así nació ETA," 89. According to Txillardegi, the name ETA signified two ideals: "'Euzkadi': a free Basque Country [Euskal Herria], in the manner of a state, within the states of the world. 'Askatasuna' [Freedom]: the free man within Euzkadi." "De Santoña a Burgos," (1972), in *Documentos Y*, vol. 1, 22.

89. Madariaga claims that ETA was not founded on any specific day. Rather, it came into being as part of a process that had already begun in 1958. He remarks that July 31, 1959 was merely the date that Txillardegi notified the Basque government in exile of ETA's existence. See Batista, *Madariaga: De las armas a la palabra*, 82–83.

90. A reference to the Greek Cypriot organization that had employed direct action throughout the 1950s. See Alvarez Enparantza [Txillardegi, pseud.], *Euskal Herria helburu*, 195, and Batista, *Madariaga: De las armas a la palabra*, 82.

91. Alvarez Enparanza [Txillardegi, pseud.], in *50 años de nacionalismo vasco 1928-1978*, ed. Ibarzábal, 369–70.

92. Madariaga, interview by Bator *Punto y Hora de Euskal Herria*, 22.

93. Ibid., 25.

94. Sullivan, *ETA and Basque Nationalism*, 30.

95. Jáuregui Bereciartu, *Ideología y estrategia política de ETA*, 82–83.

Notes, Chapter Ten

1. "One should not forget that new currents in European thought, from atheism to existentialism, from Marxism to Maoism, [and] from anti-colonialism to nihilism, dominated ETA's ideological formation. When 'freedom' was mentioned, one mostly thought about political freedom, but in the work of Sartre and other existentialists . . . that word carried with it a special philosophical meaning that could be understood only in tandem with modernity. A group like ETA could not have come about until the second half of the twentieth century." Joseba Zulaika, *ETAren hautsa* (Irun: Alberdania, 2006), 53.

2. José Luis Alvarez Enparantza [Txillardegi, pseud.], *Euskal herria helburu* (Tafalla: Txalaparta, 1994), 140.

3. Ibid.

4. Jean-Paul Sartre, "A More Precise Characterization of Existentialism," in *Action* (December 1944), quoted in *The Writings of Jean-Paul Sartre*, vol. 2, *Selected Prose*, ed. Michel Contat and Michel Rybalka, trans. Richard McCleary (Evanston: Northwestern University Press, 1974), 157.

5. Martin Heidegger, "Letter on Humanism" (1946), in *Basic Writings from Being and Time (1927) to The Task of Thinking (1964)*, ed. with a general intro. and intros. to each sec., David Farrell Krell (New York: Harper & Row, 1977), 193.

6. Alvarez Enparantza [Txillardegi, pseud.], *Euskal Herria helburu*, 141.

7. Sartre, "A More Precise Characterization of Existentialism," in *The Writings of Jean-Paul Sartre*, vol. 2, 157.

8. "Thinking is not merely *l'engagement dans l'action* for and by beings, in the sense of the actuality of the present situation. Thinking is *l'engagement* by and for the truth of Being." Heidegger, "Letter on Humanism," 193, 194.

9. Gabriel Marcel, *Being and Having: An Existentialist Diary* (1949; rpt., Gloucester, MA: Peter Smith, 1976), 173 (page citations are to the reprint edition).

10. Sartre, "A More Precise Characterization of Existentialism," 158.

11. Ibid., 159.

12. Søren Kierkegaard, "The Tragic in Ancient Drama Reflected in the Tragic in Modern Drama: A Venture in Fragmentary Endeavor," in *Either/Or: Part I*, ed. and trans. Howard V. Hong and Edna H. Hong (Princeton, NJ: Princeton University Press, 1987), 150.

13. Ibid., 150.

14. Sartre, "A More Precise Characterization of Existentialism," 158.

15. "ETA was no more than the continuation of EKIN.... EKIN... was born and developed autonomously." Benito del Valle, José Mari, and José Manu Agirre, "El nacimiento de ETA," *Punto y Hora de Euskal Herria*, no. 150 (8–15 November 1979): 17; Ekin "was our spontaneous creation." Iulen de Madariaga, interview by Juan P. Bator, *Punto y Hora de Euskal Herria*, no. 49 (18–24 August 1977): 22.

16. Marcel, *Being and Having: An Existentialist Diary*, 159.

17. Ibid., 172.

18. Sartre, "A More Precise Characterization of Existentialism," 160.

19. Marc Légasse, *Paroles d'un anarchiste basque* (Bayonne: Darracq, 1948), 14.

20. "Few figures in the modern Basque nationalist movement are more enigmatic than Marc Légasse." James E. Jacob, *Hills of Conflict: Basque Nationalism in France* (Reno: University of Nevada Press, 1994), 122. Légasse has also been described as "a scathing and explosive Basque who adores parody, although one will never find bitterness in his words." *Enciclopedia General Ilustrada del País Vasco*, s.v. "Légasse Celaya, Marc." See Amaia Ereñaga, *Marc Légasse: Un rebelde burlón* (Tafalla: Txalaparta, 1997) for a biography.

21. Jacob, *Hills of Conflict*, 70, 103; *Enciclopedia General Ilustrada del País Vasco*, s.v. "Légasse Celaya, Marc."

22. According to Emilio López Adán [Beltza, pseud.], the letter is significant for its interpretation of the PNV as relegating the idea of Basque unity (the unity of Spanish and French Basques) in order to placate the French state's reception of Basque nationalist exiles as a legal constituent part of the exiled Spanish pro-Republic community. *El nacionalismo vasco en el exilio 1937–1960* (San Sebastián: Txertoa, 1977), 46.

23. The letter is reproduced in detail by Jacob, *Hills of Conflict*, 125–57, and in full by López Adán [Beltza, pseud.], *El nacionalismo vasco en el exilio 1937–1960*, 112–17.

24. Marc Légasse to José Antonio de Aguirre Lecube, Ciboure, March 25, 1946, quoted in Jacob, *Hills of Conflict*, 126.

25. Légasse, *Paroles d'un anarchiste basque*, 7.

26. Ibid., 10, 11.

27. Marc Légasse, *Le "Séparatisme Basque" est-il un existentialisme?* ([Biarritz]: Cahiers Internationaux d'Etudes Humanistes, 1951), 7.

28. Marc Légasse, "De la contrebande considérée comme une obligation de conscience." *Gure Herria*, no. 2 (March–April 1952), 104.

29. Légasse, *Le "Séparatisme Basque" est-il un existentialisme?* 5.

30. Légasse stands out as one of the few critics of Basque history and culture within the nationalist movement itself. Consider, for example, the following scathing attack on the vision of Basque history that noted the Basques' "noble" involvement in Spanish imperialism: "Hyperchauvinist Basques! Calm down. It is not necessary to shout from the roof tops that the Basques discovered America and gave the world Loyola. The discovery of America produced: syphilis and the atomic bomb. And Ignatius of Loyola: the Jesuits. There is truly nothing to boast about." *Paroles d'un anarchiste basque*, 12.

31. Légasse, *Le "Séparatisme Basque" est-il un existentialisme?* 6 n1, 8.

32. Ibid., 6.

33. Légasse, "De la contrabande," 107, 110.

34. Légasse, *Paroles d'un anarchiste basque*, 16.

35. Ibid., 34.

36. Ibarz, *Breu Història d'ETA 1959–1979* (Barcelona: Ediciones la Magrana, 1981), 43.

37. "Oteiza... participated actively with ETA in the 1960s–although he later became one of its harshest critics–and until the 1980s he acted as the main ideological guru for its political-military branch. Ideological and operational leaders of ETA, such as Txabi Etxebarrieta, Patxo Unzueta, or Pertur, were personal friends of Oteiza and were singularly influenced by him." Zulaika, "Anthropologists, Artists, Terrorists: The Basque Holiday from History," *Journal of Spanish Cultural Studies* 4, no. 2 (2003): 146.

38. See in particular, *Quousque tandem... ! Ensayo de interpretación estética del alma vasca* (Zarautz: Auñamendi, 1963) and *Ejercicios espirituales en un túnel: En busca y encuentro de nuestra identidad pérdida*, 2nd ed. (Donostia: Hordago, 1984). A selection of Oteiza's works are translated into English in Jorge Oteiza, *Oteiza's Selected Writings*, ed. Joseba Zulaika, trans. Frederick Fornoff (Reno: Center for Basque Studies, University of Nevada, Reno, 2003). In this volume, see also Joseba Zulaika's "Introduction: Oteiza's Return from the Future" (9–81).

39. *Diccionario Enciclopédico del País Vasco*, s.v. "Oteiza Embil, Jorge de."

40. Jesús Azcona, *Etnia y nacionalismo vasco: Una aproximación desde la antropología* (Barcelona: Anthropos, 1984), 176.

41. Zulaika, "Introduction: Oteiza's Return from the Future," in Oteiza, *Oteiza's Selected Writings*, 49–51.

42. Miguel Pelay Orozco, *Oteiza. Su vida, su obra, su pensamiento, su palabra* (Bilbao: Editorial La Gran Enciclopedia Vasca, 1978), 471–72.

43. An account of the problems is given by the Basque artist Nestor Basterrechea, in *50 años de nacionalismo vasco 1928–1978*, ed. Ibarzábal, 349–57.

44. Ibid., 355–56.

45. *Diccionario Enciclopédico del País Vasco*, s.v. "Oteiza Embil, Jorge de."

46. Azcona, *Etnia y nacionalismo vasco*, 193–95.

47. Ibid., 192, 203.

48. Ibid., 203, 223.

49. Zulaika, *Basque Violence: Metaphor and Sacrament*, 282–83.

50. Zulaika, "Anthropologists, Artists, Terrorists," 143.

51. Jorge Oteiza, interview in Pelay Orozco, *Oteiza*, 400.

52. Jorge Oteiza, quoted in Pelay Orozco, *Oteiza*, 516.

53. Oteiza, *Ejercicios espirituales en un túnel*, 298, quoted in Zulaika, "Introduction: Oteiza's Return from the Future," 57.

54. Basterrechea, in *50 años de nacionalismo vasco 1928–1978*, ed. Ibarzábal, 357.

55. Walter J. Ong, *Orality and Literacy: The Technologizing of the Word* (London: Methuen, 1982), 178.

56. These questions have been adapted from Robert Darnton, *The Kiss of Lamourette: Reflections in Cultural History* (New York: W. W. Norton, 1990), 131–34.

57. Ibid., 187; Wolfgang Iser argues that "the study of a literary work should concern not only the actual text but also, and in equal measure, the actions involved in responding to that text." "Interaction Between Text and Reader," in *The Reader in the Text: Essays on Audience and Interpretation*, ed. Susan R. Suleiman and Inge Crosman (Princeton, NJ: Princeton University Press, 1980), 106.

58. Paul B. Armstrong, *Conflicting Readings: Variety and Validity in Interpretation* (Chapel Hill: The University of North Carolina Press, 1990), 13.

59. José Mari Benito del Valle and José Manu Agirre, "ETA: Historia e historias," *Punto y Hora de Euskal Herria*, no. 134 (19–26 July 1979): 45; Agirre recalls that Ireland and Israel stood out as examples of the successful use of an armed struggle. José Manu Agirre, interview by Xabier Amuriza, *Euskadi eta Askatasuna*, vol. 1, 205.

60. According to a biography of Madariaga, Menachem Begin's *The Revolt* was a "referential text" for the founders of ETA. Antoni Batista, *Madariaga: De las armas a la palabra* (Barcelona: RBA Libros, 2007), 83–84.

61. Menachem Begin, *The Revolt*, rev. ed. (1951; rpt., New York: Nash Publishing, 1977), 40–41 (page citations are to the reprint edition).

62. "Life in the underground enforces seclusion and seclusion makes deep thinking possible." Ibid., 148.

63. Alvarez Enparantza [Txillardegi, pseud.], *Euskal Herria helburu*, 138, 183; Madariaga, interview by Bator, *Punto y Hora de Euskal Herria*, 22; José Manu Agirre, interview by Xabier Amuriza, *Euskadi eta Askatasuna*, vol. 1, 204.

64. Hermilio Oloriz, *La cuestión foral: Reseña de los principales acontecimientos ocurridos desde Mayo de 1893, á julio de 1894* (Pamplona: Imprenta Provincial, 1894), 22.

65. Ibid., 25.

66. Arturo Campión, "La personalidad euskara en la historia y la literatura. Conferencia leída en el Centro Basko de Bilbao el día 27 de Abril de 1901," in *Discursos políticos y literarios* (Pamplona: Erice y García, 1907), 126.

67. Padre Bernadino de Estella, *Historia vasca* (Bilbao: Emeterio Verdes Achirica, 1931), 386.

68. Engracio de Aranzadi y Etxeberría [Kizkitza, pseud.], *La nación vasca* (Bilbao: Verdes, 1931), 28, 29.

69. Ibid., 131–32.

70. In a stimulating essay on ETA, Zulaika contends that this cultural milieu of the 1950s bequeathed the founders of Ekin, together most obviously with existentialism, varied ideological and intellectual influences to which they were extremely open: Arana's original conception of Basque nationalism, Marxism, and even Christian social activism. However, Ekin, and later ETA, while drawing from these ideological sources, also implied a break with them in a post-Arana, post-Marxist, and post-Christian way. This, Zulaika argues, was the truly revolutionary turn of the organization. See Zulaika, *ETAren hautsa*, 29–34.

71. Alfonso Pérez-Agote, "The Role of Religion in the Definition of a Symbolic Conflict," *Social Compass* 33, no. 4 (1986): 424.

72. See Zulaika, *ETAren hautsa*, 116–18.

73. Beate Krais discusses a similar repression in regard to women in society. See "Gender and Symbolic Violence: Female Oppression in the Light of Pierre Bourdieu's Theory of Social Practice," in *Bourdieu: Critical Perspectives*, ed. Craig Calhoun, Edward LiPuma, and Moishe Postone (Chicago: The University of Chicago Press, 1993), 156–58.

74. Ibid., 172.

75. Jesús Azcona, "To Be Basque and to Live in Basque Country: The Inequalities of Difference," in *Democracy and Ethnography: Constructing Identities in Multicultural Liberal States*, ed. Carol J. Greenhouse with Roshanak Kheshti (Albany, NY: State University of New York Press, 1998), 167.

76. Zulaika neatly summarizes what the formation of ETA originally implied, before it took part in any violent action: a different way of conceiving Basque identity, based on language more than race, a critical revision of Basque culture, and the formulation of a new political consciousness in which a theoretically independent Basque Country might fit into a new Europe–all the while reinforcing the sense of Basque identity through individual and group freedom. Zulaika, *ETAren hautsa*, 128.

77. Zulaika, "Tropics of Terror," 100.

78. This was not only a legacy of Arana, but also a common theme of Western thought in general, dating from Aristotle, for example, who saw suffering as an indispensable component of tragedy. Likewise, for Ekin, there was an implied dialectic between the common suffering of the Basque people and the tragedy of Basque society in the 1950s. On tragedy see David B. Morris, "About Suffering: Voice, Genre, and Moral Community," *Daedalus* 125, no. 1 (Winter 1996): 35.

Notes, Conclusion

1. See Ernest Gellner, *Nations and Nationalism* (Ithaca, NY: Cornell University Press, 1983), Eric J. Hobsbawm, *Nations and Nationalism since 1780: Programme, Myth, Reality* (Cambridge: Cambridge University Press, 1990), and Eric J. Hobsbawm and Terence Ranger, eds., *The Invention of Tradition* (Cambridge: Cambridge University Press, 1983).

2. I borrow the mirror metaphor from the stimulating work of Begoña Aretxaga. In her exploration of contemporary political violence in the Basque Country, Aretxaga argues that there is a spectral quality to the manner in which antagonists in the conflict have seen each other, leading ultimately to a kind of mirroring process whereby state and stateless political violence come to resemble one another. See "A Hall of Mirrors: On the Spectral Character of Basque political Violence," in *Basque Politics and Nationalism on the Eve of the Millennium*, Basque Studies Program Occasional Papers Series, no. 6, ed. William A. Douglass, Carmelo Urza, Linda White, and Joseba Zulaika (Reno: Basque Studies Program, University of Nevada, Reno, 1999), 115–26, and *States of Terror: Begoña Aretxaga's Essays* (Reno: Center for Basque Studies, University of Nevada, Reno, 2005).

3. Luke Gibbons, *Transformations in Irish Culture* (Cork: Cork University Press, 1996), 8.

4. Citing Martha Crenshaw, *Revolutionary Terrorism: The FLN in Algeria, 1954–1962* (Stanford: Hoover Institution Press, 1978), Charles Townshend notes that many terrorist groups build up what he terms "ideological or moral endorsement" through an "'inspiring quality' [that] is often neglected, especially by conservative writers who are concerned to deny any legitimacy to terrorist action in pursuit of agitational or revolutionary goals." See *Terrorism: A Very Short Introduction* (Oxford: Oxford University Press, 2002), 12.

5. Louis L. Snyder, "Plurinational Spain: Basque and Catalan Separatism," in *Global Mini-Nationalisms: Autonomy or Independence* (Westport, CT: Greenwood Press, 1982) and Ian Gibson, *Fire in the Blood: The New Spain* (London: Faber and Faber, 1992).

6. An interesting parallel to the abstract and universalizing tendencies of many works within terrorism studies can be found in the unique quality ascribed to the Holocaust. One work critiques this tendency, which also makes use of what it terms "unnecessarily vacuous abstractions." "Recourse to such abstract universalisms," it continues, "fails to account for real event-specifics like context, scope, and dimension; intention; methods; opportunity; blame; and responsibility." Alan S. Rosenbaum, "Introduction," in *Is the Holocaust Unique? Perspectives on Comparative Genocide*, ed. with an intro. by Alan S. Rosenbaum, forward by Israel W. Charny (Boulder, CO: Westview Press, 1996), 3.

7. Antonio Elorza, "Guerra y fueros en los orígenes del nacionalismo vasco," in *Gernika: 50 años después (1937–1987). Nacionalismo, República, Guerra Civil*, ed. Manuel Tuñón de Lara (San Sebastián: Servicio Editorial Universidad del País Vasco/Argitalpen Zerbitzua Euskal Herriko Unibertsitatea, 1987), 14.

8. In the pre-Columbian Americas, there were as many as two thousand distinct peoples whose cultural differences were greater than those of the different European peoples. Today, there is nothing left of most of them. Yet the West does

not confront the genocide of its past (through education or the media, for example) with anything like the same passion that it brings to identifying and condemning terrorists. See David E. Stannard, "Uniqueness as Denial: The Politics of Genocide Scholarship," in *Is the Holocaust Unique?* 163–208.

9. Edward W. Said, "Representing the Colonized: Anthropology's Interlocutors," *Critical Inquiry* 15, no. 2 (Winter 1989), 221–22.

10. Calhoun, *Nationalism* (Buckingham: Open University Press, 1997), 85.

11. Townshend, *Terrorism: A Very Short Introduction*, 7. See his general discussion of terrorism and war, 6–8.

12. "Cultural violence makes direct and structural violence look, even feel, right–or at least not wrong.... One way cultural violence works is by changing the moral color of an act from red/wrong to green/right or at least to yellow/acceptable.... Another way is by making reality opaque, so that we do not see the violent act or fact, or at least not as violent." Johan Galtung, "Cultural Violence," *Journal of Peace Research* 27, no. 3 (1990), 291–92.

13. Pierre Bourdieu, *Language and Symbolic Power*, ed. with an intro. by John B. Thompson, trans. Gino Raymond and Matthew Adamson (Cambridge, MA: Harvard University Press, 1991), 51.

14. Juan Sisinio Pérez Garzón, "State Nationalism, Cultural Nationalism and Political Alternatives," *Journal of Spanish Cultural Studies* 4, no. 1 (2003): 47.

15. Patxo Unzueta, *Los nietos de la ira. Nacionalismo y violencia en el País Vasco* (Madrid: El País/Aguilar, 1988), 62.

16. Goldie Shabad and Francisco José Llera Ramos, "Political Violence in a Democratic State: Basque Terrorism in Spain," in *Terrorism in Context*, ed. Martha Crenshaw (University Park: The Pennsylvania State University Press, 1995), 425, 468–69. The article itself, of course, draws a clear moral distinction between *Basque* terrorism (political violence) and Spain (a democratic state).

17. See, for example, the triumphalist nature of studies by Paul Preston, *The Triumph of Democracy in Spain* (London: Methuen, 1986) and David Gilmour, *The Transformation of Spain: From Franco to the Constitutional Monarchy* (London: Quartet Books, 1985), which argue against the validity of ETA in a liberal democratic state.

18. Alfonso Pérez-Agote, "Self-Fulfilling Prophecy and Unresolved Meaning: Basque Political Violence in the Twenty-First Century," in *Empire & Terror: Nationalism/Postnationalism in the New Millennium*, ed. Begoña Aretxaga, Dennis Dworkin, Joseba Gabilondo, and Joseba Zulaika (Reno: Center for Basque Studies, University of Nevada, Reno, 2005), 177. Pérez-Agote goes on to argue that after 1975, radical Basque nationalism became increasingly self-referential, relying on a kind of unresolved mourning for its original object (the dictatorship), so that violence actually progressively became "the end," rather than "the means," of the struggle.

19. Cf. Crenshaw's assessment that the use of political violence can be "a willful choice made by an organization for political and strategic reasons, rather than as the unintended outcome of psychological or social factors." See "The Logic of Terrorism: Terrorist Behavior as a Product of Strategic Choice," in *Origins of Terrorism: Psychologies, Ideologies, Theologies, States of Mind*, ed. Walter Reich, Woodrow Wilson Center Series (Cambridge: Cambridge University Press, 1990), 7–8.

20. Francisco Llera, José M. Mata, and Cynthia Irvin, "ETA: From Secret Army to Social Movement–The Post-Franco Schism of the Basque Nationalist Movement," *Terrorism and Political Violence* 5, no. 3 (Autumn 1993): 108.

21. Imanol Galfarsoro, *Kultura eta identitate erbesteratuak (Nomadologia subalternoak)* (Iruña: Pamiela, 2005), 46–48. See also Joan Ramon Resina, who takes a wry look at the national basis of postnational discourse in Spain. See "Post-national Spain? Post-Spanish Spain?," *Nations and Nationalism* 8, no. 3 (2002): 377–96.

22. Joxe Azurmendi, *Demokratak eta biolentoak* (Donostia: Elkar, 1997), 28. Ironically, the etymological origins of the word "terrorism" derive from that very moment–the birth of liberal democracy and the modern state in Europe during the French Revolution and Robespierre's reign of terror. See Joseba Zulaika and William A. Douglass, *Terror and Taboo: The Follies, Fables, and Faces of Terrorism* (New York: Routledge, 1996), 106.

23. David Held, "The Development of the Modern State," in *Modernity: An Introduction to Modern Societies*, ed. Stuart Hall, David Held, Don Hubert, and Kenneth Thompson (Oxford: Blackwell, 1996), 71. See also the observation that this legitimate *norm* (democracy, the nation-state, or whatever it may be) in effect forms a kind of status quo, and "violence in its defense is 'natural,'" yet "the resort to violence in the furtherance of alternative political agendas is 'unnatural.'" Zulaika and Douglass, *Terror and Taboo*, 112.

24. See, for example, Alexander George, ed. *Western State Terrorism* (New York: Routledge, 1991).

25. Zulaika and Douglass, *Terror and Taboo*, 94, 101.

26. "With the withdrawal of Txillardegi and the others from ETA, a significant phase of the movement came to a close. Those who remained behind were in command of a newly reorganized clandestine political force with a coherent ideology and a commitment to armed struggle." Robert P. Clark, *The Basque Insurgents: ETA, 1952–1980* (Madison: University of Wisconsin Press, 1984), 46–47.

27. Although the first fatality as a result of ETA activity was reputedly that of an unborn child, Begoña Urroz, in 1960. Her mother lost the baby after being too close to an explosive device set off by ETA. By extending the first fatality as a result of ETA activity to 1960, one also, by definition, extends the list of those victims of state repression to that same date. The best source to document all the casualties associated with political violence in contemporary Basque history is Sabino Ormazabal Elola, *Sufrimenduaren mapa (osatugabea)/Un mapa (inacabado) del sufrimiento* (Bilbo: Manu Robles-Arangiz Institutoa, 2003).

28. Resina observes that "the state may be weaker now in some respects, but it still wields formidable power. It can determine the evolution or involution of historical groups, since, in the march toward globalisation, admission to suprastate organisations is paved by the state. More than anything else, the entitling role, vested in the state by the etiquette of world power, explains the nationalistic scramble for a place in the global sun." "Post-national Spain? Post-Spanish Spain?" 394.

29. Joseba Zulaika, "Nourishment by the Negative: National Subalternity, Antagonism, and Radical Democracy," in *Empire and Terror: Nationalism/Postnationalism in the New Millennium*, ed. Begoña Aretxaga, Dennis Dworkin, Joseba Gabilondo, and Joseba Zulaika (Reno: Center for Basque Studies, University of Nevada, Reno, 2005), 130. See also Townshend's observation that "pure" terrorism, judged statistically, actually poses little substantial danger to the Western liberal state. That said, it is, of course, impossible to ignore it, precisely because of the deep-rooted public anxiety about the security of life and property. See *Terrorism: A Very Short Introduction*, 115–16.

30. It is beyond the scope of the present work to address the deficiencies of post-Franco, democratic Spain. Unfortunately, within the historiography of the period, few critical voices have emerged. A recent example of the somewhat overly generous trend in analyzing contemporary Spain is Daniele Conversi's "The Smooth Transition: Spain's 1978 Constitution and the Nationalities Question," *National Identities* 4, no. 3 (2002): 223–44. By contrast, one study that addresses some of the fault lines in post-1975 Spain and specifically the creation of government-sponsored, yet secret death squads in the 1980s is Paddy Woodworth, *Dirty War, Clean Hands: ETA, the GAL and Spanish Democracy* (Cork: Cork University Press, 2001). From another perspective, in *States and Regions in the European Union: Institutional Adaptation in Germany and Spain* (Cambridge: Cambridge University Press, 2002), Tanja A. Börzel highlights the inherently conflictive nature of the post-1975 autonomous political settlement, contrasting its many problems with the more effective administrative organization of a true federal state, Germany.

31. Elorza, "Guerra y Fueros," 19.

32. This recalls Martin Jay's examination of the relation between melancholy and apocalyptic thought at the close of the nineteenth century: "There can be little doubt that the symptoms of melancholy... approximate very closely those of apocalyptic thinking: deep and painful dejection, withdrawal of interest in everyday life, diminished capacity to love, paralysis of the will, and, most important of all, radical lowering of self-esteem accompanied by fantasies of punishment for assumed moral transgressions." *Force Fields: Between Intellectual History and Cultural Critique* (New York: Routledge, 1993), 92.

33. Although it is outside the scope of this study, one might speculate that the violent turn of ETA–that is, its definitive recourse to an armed struggle in 1968, when, after shooting dead a Civil Guard, Juan Pardines, ETA's leading ideologue, Txabi Etxebarrieta, was in turn gunned down by another Civil Guard patrol–both broke with the original basis on which Ekin was formed and returned once more to the martyr syndrome that had defined one current of Basque nationalist thought since Arana. See Zulaika, *ETAren hautsa*, 23.

34. "It should be recognized that modernism is not first of all a set of forms, a historical sequence of works and texts, but an ideology. Like any ideology certain core values, interests, and powers are veiled and rationalized." Robert Morris, "Words and Images in Modernism and Postmodernism," *Critical Inquiry* 15, no. 2 (Winter 1989), 341.

35. "The colonizing discourse of a triumphant modernist rationality and male order sniffs at... fragmentation. It is similarly impatient with the 'inconsistency' of subaltern narratives and statements. We are uncomfortable with truncated narratives and undisciplined fragments, and can scarcely make them our own. We seek, rather, to appropriate and unify them in fully connected, neatly fashioned historical accounts, without any jagged edges if possible." Gyanendra Pandey, "Voices From the Edge: The Struggle to Write Subaltern Histories," *Ethnos* 60, nos. 3–4 (1995), 239.

36. See the discussion of war and modernity by Modris Eksteins, *Rites of Spring: The Great War and the Birth of the Modern Age* (London: Bantam Press, 1989' rpt, London: Black Swan, 1990), 126–39, 286–90 (page citations are to the reprint edition).

37. Unzueta, *Los nietos de la ira*, 53.

38. However, the subsequent development of the group may confirm Zulaika's claim that "one might say that ETA has been the true symptom of the modern Basque Country." *ETAren hautsa*, 54.

39. Joseph A. Dane, *Parody: Critical Concepts Versus Literary Practices, Aristophenes to Sterne* (Norman: University of Oklahoma Press, 1988), 4.

40. Linda Hutcheon, *A Theory of Parody: The Teachings of Twentieth-Century Art Forms* (New York: Methuen, 1985), 32.

41. This point is made by José Mari Garmendia, although he does not explain the parodic discourse of ETA. See *Historia de ETA*. 2 vols. (San Sebastián: L. Haranburu, 1979), vol. 1, 117.

42. Ibid., 112–15.

43. Kepa Aulestia, *Días de viento sur: La violencia en Euskadi* (Barcelona: Editorial Antárdida/Empúries, 1993), 142–43.

44. Zulaika and Douglass, *Terror and Taboo*, 49–50.

45. Michael Richards's detailed study of the early years of Franco's Spain argues that state violence was methodical and organized, directed toward the elimination of opponents (the enemy). It was, in effect, programmed political violence (based on ideological assumptions) that was never questioned, only encouraged. *A Time of Silence: Civil War and the Culture of Repression in Franco's Spain, 1936–1945* (Cambridge: Cambridge University Press, 1998), 31–34.

Glossary

Aberrianos: Members of the PNV's youth wing during the early decades of the twentieth century who followed the original intransigent line of Arana through their newspaper, *Aberri.*

Acción Nacionalista Vasca (ANV): Basque Nationalist Action. A nondenominational and republican nationalist party formed in 1930. It rejected the traditionalism of the PNV.

Baserri(a): The traditional farmstead and primary focus of identity in rural Basque culture.

Baserritarra(k): Basque peasant(s).

Bertsolari(a): A Basque versifier.

Bertsolaritza: The Basque troubadorial tradition of extemporaneous versifying.

Caciques: Corrupt and powerful local political leaders in nineteenth-century Spain.

Caciquismo: The system of bossism.

Carlism: A traditionalist monarchist political movement dating from 1833 that rejected liberal secularism and all forms of modernization.

Castellano: The Spanish language (literally, Castilian).

Casticismo: A Spanish (or more specifically Castilian) cultural nationalism.

Communión Nacionalista Vasca (CNV): The Basque Nationalist Communion. The name by which the original PNV was known between 1916 and 1930.

Conciertos económicos: Fiscal pacts between the Spanish state and the individual Basque provinces established after the Second Carlist War.

Confederación Española de Derechas Autónomas (CEDA): Spanish Confederation of Right-Wing Groups. A Spanish Catholic authoritarian coalition party founded in 1933.

Confederación Nacional de Trabajo (CNT): National Work Confederation. The anarchist labor union formed out of the merger of several smaller groups in 1911.

Cortes: Spanish constituent legislature or congress.

Ekin: Student activist group formed during 1951–52. Some of its members later went on to form ETA.

Euskadi/Euzkadi: Literally "Basque Land." The name given the Basque Country by Sabino Arana.

Euskaldun: A Basque speaker.

Euskalerriacos: Members of the Sociedad Euskalerria.

Euskara/Euskera: The Basque language.

Eusko Gaztedi del Interior (EGI): The youth wing of the PNV, renamed in 1956 with the amalgamation of Ekin.

Eusko Ikasle Alkartasuna (EIA): The Society of Basque Students. Formed in Leiden (Holland) in 1943 as an independent group of exiled nationalists. It was later incorporated by the PNV in the early 1950s.

Eusko Langileen Alkartasuna (ELA): The Basque name for STV. See Solidaridad de Trabajadores Vascos.

Euzkadi ta Askatasuna (ETA): Basque Country and Freedom. The direct action group formed in 1959.

Euzko Gaztedi (EG): See Juventud Vasca.

Euzko Gudarostea: The Basque nationalist army which fought during the Spanish Civil War.

Falange Española: Spain's Fascist movement, founded in 1933. In 1937 it was merged, by Franco, with the Carlists to form Falange Española Tradicionalista de las JONS.

Fueros: A set of medieval charters whereby the Spanish political sovereign granted exemptions and protections to influential regional constituencies (such as the Basque provinces) in return for political support.

Foral: Of or pertaining to the fueros.

Guardia Civil: Civil Guard. A National paramilitary Spanish police force created in 1844.

Gudariak: Basque nationalist soldiers during the Spanish Civil War.

Jagi Jagi: Literally "Arise, Arise." A breakaway faction of the PNV in 1934 that sought outright independence for the Basque Country, as opposed to the party line of autonomy.

Juventud Vasca: Basque Youth. Known as Euzko Gaztedi in Basque. The youth wing of the PNV, created in 1904.

Laurak Bat: Literally "the four in one." A Basque foral protest group created in 1884 to defend the regional privileges of Navarre.

Mendigoizaleak/Mendigoizales: Mountaineers. A nationalist group of mountaineers affiliated with the PNV. The mountaineers were often the party's most enthusiastic activists.

Partido Nacionalista Vasco (PNV): Basque Nationalist Party. The hegemonic nationalist party created in 1895. It adopted a new name (see Communión Nacionalista Vasca) between 1916 and 1930, during which time the *aberrianos* (see above) took the title PNV in a party split. The two wings reunited in 1930, taking the original PNV title.

Partido Socialista Obrero de España (PSOE): The Spanish Socialist Party. Founded in 1879.

Requetés: Navarrese Carlist militia during the Spanish Civil War.

Sociedad Euskalerria: The Basque Country Society. A Bizkaian foral party, created in the mid-1880s, that attempted to blend both liberal and traditional sympathies.

Solidaridad de Trabajadores Vascos (STV): Originally known as Solidaridad de Obreros Vascos. The Basque nationalist labor union, created in 1911 and affiliated with the PNV.

Unión General de Trabajadores (UGT): General Workers' Union. The Spanish socialist labor union founded in 1888. It affiliated with the PSOE in 1918.

Bilbliography

PRIMARY MATERIAL

Archives and Private Papers

Archivo de los PP. Benedictinos. Lazkao, Gipuzkoa (Spain)

Basque Studies Program, later renamed the Center for Basque Studies. University of Nevada, Reno (U.S.A.)

Public Record Office. Kew (U.K.)

Irargi: Centro de Patrimonio Documental de Euskadi. Bergara, Gipuzkoa (Spain)

Fondo de Carlos Blasco Olaetxea

Fondo de Luis Ruiz de Aguirre

Universidad de Deusto. Deusto, Bizkaia (Spain)

Fondo de Fernando de Abrisqueta

Government Documents and Records

Department of State. *Foreign Relations of the United States.* Diplomatic Papers: Western Europe, 1937, 1949–50. Washington: United States Government Printing Office, 1954, 1975–1977.

Foreign Office. *Documents on British Foreign Policy 1919–1939.* Edited by W. N. Medlicott and Douglas Dakin. Assisted by Gillian Bennett. Second Series, vols.17–18. London: Her Majesty's Stationery Office, 1979.

Contemporary Accounts, Published Documents, and Memoirs

Aguirre, José Antonio de. *Escape via Berlin: Eluding Franco in Hitler's Europe.* 1945. Reprint with an introduction and annotations by Robert P. Clark, Reno and Las Vegas: University of Nevada Press, 1991.

Alvarez Enparantza, José Luis [Txillardegi, pseud.]. "Así nació ETA." *Punto y Hora de Euskal Herria,* no. 130 (June 21–28, 1979): 15–16.

——. *Euskal Herria helburu.* Tafalla: Txalaparta, 1994.

Alvarez Enparantza, José Luis [Txillardegi, pseud.], José Manuel Aguirre, José María Benito del Valle, and Julen Madariaga. Letter. *Muga*, no. 3 (February 1980), 13–14.

Arana y Goiri, Sabino de. *Bizkaya por su independencia.* 1892. Reprint, Bilbao: E. Verdes, 1932.

Aranzadi y Etxeberría, Engracio de [Kizkitza, pseud.]. *Patriotismo: Conferencia leída por su autor en el "Centro Vasco" de Bilbao, el día 22 de Mayo de 1904.* Bilbao: José de Astuy, 1904.

———. *La nación vasca.* Bilbao: Verdes, 1931.

———. *Ereintza: Siembra de nacionalismo vasco, 1894–1912.* Zarauz: Editorial Vasca, 1935.

Basaldúa, Pedro de. *El libertador vasco: Sabino de Arana y Goiri.* Buenos Aires: Editorial Vasca Ekin, 1953.

Begin, Menachem. *The Revolt.* 1951. Rev. ed. Reprint, New York: Nash Publishing, 1977.

Benito del Valle, José Mari, and José Manu Agirre. "ETA: Historia e historias." *Punto y Hora de Euskal Herria*, no. 134 (19–26 July 1979): 44–45.

———. "El nacimiento de ETA." *Punto y Hora de Euskal Herria*, no. 150 (8–15 November 1979): 17.

Borrow, George. *The Bible in Spain: Or, the Journeys, Adventures, and Imprisonments of an Englishman in an Attempt to Circulate the Scriptures in the Peninsula.* London: J. M. Dent; New York: E. P. Dutton, 1906.

Bowers, Claude G. *My Mission to Spain: Watching the Rehearsal for World War II.* New York: Simon and Schuster, 1954.

[Cambó, Francesc]. *Conferencia pronunciada por D. Francisco Cambó en el Teatro Campos Elíseos de Bilbao, el día 28 de enero de 1917.* Bilbao: Jesús Alvarez, 1917.

Campión, Arturo. "La personalidad euskara en la historia y la literatura: Conferencia leída en el Centro Basko de Bilbao el día 27 de Abril de 1901." In *Discursos políticos y literarios.* Pamplona: Erice y García, 1907.

Ciano, Galeazzo. *Ciano's Diary.* Edited with an introduction by Malcolm Muggeridge. Foreword by Sumner Welles. London: William Heinemann, 1947.

Corcuera, Javier and Yolanda Oribe, *Historia del nacionalismo vasco en sus documentos.* 3 vols. Bilbao: Eguzki Argitaldaria, 1991.

Délégation Basque, *Le nationalisme basque et le Gouvernement espagnol.* Lausanne: Imprimerie Vaudoise, 1916.

Eguileor, Manuel. *Responsibilidad: Conferencia leída en Juventud Vasca de Bilbao en el XX aniversario de su fundación.* N.p.: n.p., 1934.

———. [Bizkargi, pseud.]. *Nacionalismo vasco.* Abando: n.p., 1936.

Elosegi, Joseba. *Quiero morir por algo.* Barcelona: Plaza & Janes, 1977.

Ergabia, Miguel de. *Jaungoikua eta Lege Zaŕa: La Eŕibera por JEL.* Bilbao: n.p., 1933.

Estella, Padre Bernadino de. *Historia vasca.* Bilbao: Emeterio Verdes Achirica, 1931.

ETA. *Documentos Y.* 18 vols. Donostia: Editorial Lur, 1979–1981.

Gallastegui, Elías de [Gudari, pseud.]. *Por la libertad vasca.* Vol. 2, *En plena lucha.* Bilbao: E. Verdes, 1933.

Guilbeau, Martin. *L'Euskal-Herria ou le Pays Basque: Historique et linguistique.* Paris: Association Française pour l'avancement des sciences, 1892.

Hamilton, Thomas J. *Appeasement's Child: The Franco Regime in Spain.* New York: Alfred A. Knopf, 1943.

Heidegger, Martin. "Letter on Humanism." In *Basic Writings from Being and Time (1927) to the Task of Thinking (1964).* Edited with a general introduction and introductions to each section by David Farrell Krell, 193–242. New York: Harper & Row, 1977.

Kierkegaard, Søren. *Either/Or: Part I.* Edited with an introduction and notes by Howard V. Hong and Edna H. Hong. Reprint, Princeton, NJ: Princeton University Press, 1987.

Landáburu, Francisco Javier de. *La causa del pueblo vasco (Razones de una actitud. Posibilidades de actuación).* 1956. Reprint, 3rd ed. Bilbao: Editorial Geu Argitaldaria, 1977.

Latimer, Elizabeth Wormeley. *Spain in the Nineteenth Century.* 5th ed. Chicago: A. C. McClurg & Co., 1907.

Legasse, Marc. *Paroles d'un anarchiste basque.* Bayonne: Darracq, 1948.

———. *Le "Séparatisme Basque" est-il un existentialisme?* [Biarritz]: Cahiers Internationaux d'Etudes Humanistes, 1951.

———. "De la contrabande considérée comme une obligation de conscience." *Gure Herria,* no. 2 (March–April 1952): 104–13.

Madariaga Orbea, Juan. *Anthology of Apologists and Detractors of the Basque Language.* Translated by Frederick H. Fornoff, María Cristina Saavedra, Amaia Gabantxo, and Cameron J. Watson. Reno: Center for Basque Studies, University of Nevada, Reno, 2006.

Marcel, Gabriel. *Being and Having: An Existentialist Diary.* 1949. Reprint, Gloucester, MA: Peter Smith, 1976.

Oloriz, Hermilio. *La cuestión Foral: Reseña de los principales acontecimientos ocurridos desde Mayo de 1893, á julio de 1894.* Pamplona: Imprenta Provincial, 1894.

Otaegui, Tomás. *Nacionalismo basko (su actual carácter).* Buenos Aires: n.p., 1922.

Oteiza, Jorge. *Quousque tandem . . . ! Ensayo de interpretación estética del alma vasca.* Zarautz: Auñamendi, 1963.

———. *Ejercicios espirituales en un túnel: En busca y encuentro de nuestra identidad pérdida.* 2nd ed. Donostia: Hordago, 1984.

———. *Oteiza's Selected Writings.* Edited by Joseba Zulaika. Translated by Frederick Fornoff. Reno: Center for Basque Studies, University of Nevada, Reno, 2003.

Rizal, José. *The Subversive (El Filibusterismo).* Translated by León Mª Guerrero. 1891. Reprint, Bloomington: Indiana University Press, 1962.

Sarría, Jesús de. *Ideología del nacionalismo vasco.* Bilbao: E. Verdes, 1918.

———. *Patria vasca.* Bilbao: Editorial Vasca, 1920.

Sartre, Jean-Paul. *The Writings of Jean-Paul Sartre.* 2 vols. Compiled by Michel Contat and Michel Rybalka. Translated by Richard M. McCleary. Evanston, IL: Northwestern University Press, 1974.

Steer, George L. *The Tree of Gernika: A Field Study of Modern War.* London: Hodder and Stoughton, 1938.

Unamuno, Miguel de. *Peace in War: A Novel.* Translated by Allen Lacey and Martin Nozick with Anthony Kerrigan. Bollingen Series, 85.1. 1897. Reprint, Princeton, NJ: Princeton University Press, 1983.

Published Interviews

Agirre, José Manu. Interview by Xabier Amuriza. *Euskadi eta Askatasuna, Euskal Herria y Libertad,* vol. 1, 1952-1965, *De Ekin a ETA*, edited by Luis Nuñez, 203-8. Tafalla: Txalaparta, 1993.

Blasco Olaetxea, Carlos. *Diálogos de guerra: Euskadi 1936.* San Sebastián: Gráficas Izarra, 1983.

Fraser, Ronald. *Blood of Spain: An Oral History of the Spanish Civil War.* London: Allen Lane, 1979. Reprint with a new introduction, London: Pimlico, 1986.

Ibarzábal, Eugenio, ed. *50 años de nacionalismo vasco 1928–1978 (A través de sus protagonistas).* San Sebastián: Ediciones Vascas, 1978.

Madariaga, Iulen de. Interview by Juan P. Bator. *Punto y Hora de Euskal Herria,* no. 49 (18–24 August 1977): 21–25.

Otaegui, Marga, and Xosé Estévez, "Protagonistas de la historia vasca (1923–1950): Partido Nacionalista Vasco." *Cuadernos de Sección Historia-Geografía,* no. 7 (1984): 17–39.

———. "Protagonistas de la historia vasca (1923–1950): Acción Nacionalista Vasca." *Cuadernos de Sección Historia-Geografía,* no. 7 (1984): 67–90.

Pelay Orozco, Miguel. *Oteiza: Su vida, su obra, su pensamiento, su palabra.* Bilbao: Editorial La Gran Enciclopedia Vasca, 1978.

Urreztieta, Lezo de. "Un aberriano." Interview by Eugenio Ibarzábal. *Muga,* no. 4 (March 1980), 6–26.

Journals, Periodicals, and Newspapers

Aberri (Bilbao), 1921–22.

Alderdi (n.p.), 1956.

Baseritara (Bilbao), 1897.

Bizkaitarra (Bilbao), 1893, 1894–95.

Euskal-Erria (San Sebastián), 1893.

Euzkadi (Bilbao), 1913, 1916–17, 1920–22.

Euzko Deya (Mexico City), 1959.

Hermes (Bilbao), 1922.

Jagi Jagi (Bilbao), 1933, 1936.

The Manchester Guardian Weekly (London), 1958–59.

The Times (London), 1893–98, 1937, 1951, 1954, 1956.

SECONDARY MATERIAL

Books and Articles

Abella, Rafael. *La vida cotidiana en España bajo el régimen de Franco*. Barcelona: Editorial Argos Vergara, 1985.

Alted, Alicia. "Education and Political Control." In *Spanish Cultural Studies: An Introduction*, edited by Helen Graham and Jo Labanyi, 196–201. Oxford: Oxford University Press, 1995.

Álvarez Junco, José. "Rural and Urban Popular Cultures." In *Spanish Cultural Studies: An Introduction*, edited by Helen Graham and Jo Labanyi, 82–90. Oxford: Oxford University Press, 1995.

———. *Mater Dolorosa: La idea de España en el siglo XIX*. Madrid: Taurus, 2001.

———. "The Formation of Spanish Identity and Its Adaptation to the Age of Nations." *History and Memory* 14, nos. 1–2 (Fall 2002): 13–36.

Anderson, Benedict. *Imagined Communities: Reflections on the Origin and Spread of Nationalism*. Rev. ed. London: Verso, 1991.

Aranzadi, Juan. *Milenarismo vasco (Edad de Oro, etnia y nativismo)*. Madrid: Taurus Ediciones, 1981.

———. *El escudo de Arquíloco: Sobre mesías, mártires y terroristas*. 2 vols. Madrid: Machado Libros, 2001.

Aranzadi, Juan, Jon Juaristi, and Patxo Unzueta. *Auto de terminación (Raza, nación y violencia en el País Vasco)*. Madrid: El País/Aguilar, 1994.

Arbaiza Vilallonga, Mercedes. "Labor Migration during the First Phase of Basque Industrialization: The Labor Market and Family Motivations." *The History of the Family* 3, no. 2 (1998): 199–219.

Ardrey, Robert. *The Territorial Imperative: A Personal Inquiry into the Animal Origins of Property and Nations*. 1967. Reprint, London: Fontana, 1969.

Aretxaga, Begoña. "A Hall of Mirrors: On the Spectral Character of Basque Political Violence." In *Basque Politics and Nationalism on the Eve of the Millennium*, Basque Studies Program Occasional Papers Series, no. 6, edited by William A. Douglass, Carmelo Urza, Linda White, and Joseba Zulaika, 115–26. Reno: Basque Studies Program, University of Nevada, Reno, 1999.

———. *States of Terror: Begoña Aretxaga's Essays*. Reno: Center for Basque Studies, University of Nevada, Reno, 2005.

Armistead. Samuel G., and Joseba Zulaika, eds. *Voicing the Moment: Improvised Oral Poetry and Basque Tradition.* Reno: Center for Basque Studies, University of Nevada, Reno, 2005.

Armstrong, John A. *Nations Before Nationalism.* Chapel Hill: University of North Carolina Press, 1982.

Armstrong, Paul B. *Conflicting Readings: Variety and Validity in Interpretation.* Chapel Hill: University of North Carolina Press, 1980.

Artola, Miguel. "No había modo de evitar a Sabino Arana." Interview by Eugenio Ibarzábal. *Muga,* no. 24 (1982), 38–47.

Aulestia, Gorka. "El 'Bertsolarismo': Literatura Oral Improvisada del País Vasco." Ph.D. diss., University of Nevada, Reno, 1987.

———. *Improvisational Poetry from the Basque Country.* Foreword by William A. Douglass. Translated by Lisa Corcostegui and Linda White. Reno: University of Nevada Press, 1995.

———. *The Basque Poetic Tradition.* Foreword by Linda White. Translated by Linda White. Reno: University of Nevada Press, 2000.

Aulestia, Kepa. *Días de viento sur: La violencia en Euskadi.* Barcelona: Editorial Antárdida/Empúries, 1993.

Azcona, Jesús. *Etnia y nacionalismo vasco: Una aproximación desde la antropología.* Barcelona: Anthropos, 1984.

———. "To Be Basque and to Live in Basque Country: The Inequalities of Difference." In *Democracy and Ethnography: Constructing Identities in Multicultural Liberal States,* edited by Carol J. Greenhouse with Roshanak Kheshti, 163–77. Albany, NY: State University of New York Press, 1998.

Azurmendi, Joxe. *Demokratak eta biolentoak.* Donostia: Elkar, 1997.

Azurmendi, Mikel. "Etnicidad y violencia en el suelo vasco." *Claves de Razón Práctica,* no. 24 (June 1994): 35.

Baily, Samuel L., ed. *Nationalism in Latin America.* New York: Alfred A. Knopf, 1971.

Balfour, Sebastian. "The Loss of Empire, Regenerationism, and the Forging of a Myth of National Identity." In *Spanish Cultural Studies: An Introduction,* edited by Helen Graham and Jo Labanyi, 25–31. Oxford: Oxford University Press, 1995.

———. *The End of the Spanish Empire, 1898–1923.* Oxford: Clarendon Press, 1997.

Barahona, Renato. *Vizcaya on the Eve of Carlism: Politics and Society, 1800–1833.* Reno: University of Nevada Press, 1989.

Barth, Fredrik. "Introduction." In *Ethnic Groups and Boundaries: The Social Organization of Culture Difference,* edited by Frederik Barth, 9–38. Boston: Little, Brown and Co., 1969.

Barthes, Roland. "The Death of the Author." In *Image, Music, Text.* Translated by Stephen Heath, 142–48. New York: Hill and Wang, 1977.

———. *Sade/Fourier/Loyola.* Translated by Richard Miller. Baltimore: Johns Hopkins University Press, 1997.

Barton, Simon. "The Roots of the National Question in Spain." In *The National Question in Europe in Historical Context*, edited by Mikulá? Teich and Roy Porter, 106–27. Cambridge: Cambridge University Press, 1993.

Batista, Antoni. *Madariaga: De las armas a la palabra.* Barcelona: RBA Libros, 2007.

Bauman, Richard. *Verbal Art as Performance*. Prospect Heights, IL: Waveland Press, 1977.

Ben-Ami, Shlomo. "Basque Nationalism Between Archaism and Modernity." *Journal of Contemporary History* 26, nos. 3–4 (September 1991): 493–521.

Ben-Israel, Hedva. "Nationalism in Historical Perspective." *Journal of International Affairs* 45, no. 2 (Winter 1992): 367–97.

Bereciartúa, José María. *Ikurriña: Historia y simbolismo*. Estella: Editorial Verbo Divino, 1977.

Bernal, Antonio Miguel. "Cambio económico y modernización social, 1880–1936." *Historia Contemporánea* 4 (1990): 173–84.

Bhabha, Homi K. *The Location of Culture*. London: Routledge, 1977.

Biddiss, Michael. "Nationalism and the Moulding of Modern Europe." *History* 7, no. 257 (October 1994): 412–32.

Blaut, James M. *The National Question: Decolonizing the Theory of Nationalism*. London: ZED, 1987.

Blinkhorn, Martin. "Carlism and the Crisis of the 1930s." *Journal of Contemporary History* 7, nos. 3–4 (July–October 1972): 65–88.

———. "'The Basque Ulster'": Navarre and the Basque Autonomy Question under the Spanish Second Republic." *Historical Journal* 17, no. 3 (September 1974): 595–613.

———. *Carlism and Crisis in Spain, 1931–1939*. Cambridge: Cambridge University Press, 1975.

Bloch, Maurice. "Language, Anthropology and Cognitive Science." *Man* 26, no. 2 (June 1991): 183–98.

Boas, George. "Warfare in the Cosmos." In *Violence and Aggression in the History of Ideas*, edited by Philip P. Wiener and John Fisher, 3–14. New Brunswick, NJ: Rutgers University Press, 1974.

Bogdanor, Vernon. "Overcoming the Twentieth Century: Democracy and Nationalism in Central and Eastern Europe." *The Political Quarterly* 66, no. 1 (January–March 1995): 84–97.

Boggs, Carl. *Intellectuals and the Crisis of Modernity*. Albany: State University of New York Press, 1993.

Börzel, Tanja A. *States and Regions in the European Union: Institutional Adaptation in Germany and Spain*. Cambridge: Cambridge University Press, 2002.

Bourdieu, Pierre. *Language and Symbolic Power*. Edited with an introduction by John B. Thompson. Translated by Gino Raymond and Matthew Adamson. Cambridge, MA.: Harvard University Press, 1991.

Boyd, Carolyn P. *Historia Patria: Politics, History, and National Identity in Spain, 1875–1975.* Princeton, NJ: Princeton University Press, 1997.

Brass, Paul R. *Ethnicity and Nationalism: Theory and Comparison.* New Delhi: Sage, 1991.

Brenan, Gerald. *The Spanish Labyrinth: An Account of the Social and Political Background of the Civil War.* Cambridge: At the University Press; New York: The Macmillan Company, 1943.

Breuilly, John. *Nationalism and the State.* New York: St. Martin's Press, 1982.

Brockliss, Laurence and David Eastwood, eds. *A Union of Multiple Identities: The British Isles c.1750–c.1850.* Manchester: Manchester University Press, 1997.

Broué, Pierre, and Emile Témime, *The Revolution and the Civil War in Spain.* Translated by Tony White. Cambridge, MA: The MIT Press, 1970.

Bruni, Luigi. *ETA: Historia política de una lucha armada.* Bilbo: Txalaparta, 1987.

Bryson, Bill. *Mother Tongue: The English Language.* London: Hamish Hamilton, 1990. Reprint, Harmonsworth, England: Penguin, 1991.

Buttimer, Anne. "Edgar Kant and Balto-Skandia: *Heimatkunde* and Regional Identity." In *Geography and National Identity*, edited by David Hooson, 161–83. Oxford: Blackwell, 1994.

Cabrera, Mercedes. "El conservadurismo maurista en la Restauración: Los límites de la 'revolución desde arriba.'" In *La España de la Restauración: Política, economía, legislación*, edited by José Luis García Delgado, 55–69. I Coloquio de Segovia sobre Historia Contemporánea de España dirigido por Manuel Tuñón de Lara. [Segovia]: n.p., n.d.

Calhoun, Craig. *Nationalism.* Buckingham: Open University Press, 1997.

Came, Barry. "The Taverna Terrorists: Basque Militants Target a Stunning New Museum," *Macleans* 110, no. 43 (October 27, 1997): 28–29.

Carlyle, Thomas. *On Heroes, Hero Worship, and the Heroic in History*, edited for study by John Chester Adams. Boston: Houghton Mifflin, 1907.

Caro Baroja, Julio. *Los vascos.* Madrid: Ediciones Minotauro, 1958.

Carr, Raymond. *Modern Spain 1875–1980.* Oxford: Oxford University Press, 1980.

———. *Spain 1808–1975.* 2nd ed. Oxford: Clarendon Press, 1982.

Carr, Raymond, and Juan Pablo Fusi Aizpurua. *Spain: Dictatorship to Democracy.* 2nd ed. London: George Allen & Unwin, 1981.

Chapa, Alvaro. *La vida cultural de la villa de Bilbao 1917–1936.* Bilbao: Ayuntamiento de Bilbao/Bilboko Udala, 1989.

Chapman, Charles E. *A History of Spain.* New York: The Macmillan Company, 1922.

Chapman, Malcolm. *The Gaelic Vision in Scottish Culture.* London: Croom Helm; Montreal: McGill-Queens University Press, 1978.

———. "Fieldwork, Language and Locality in Europe, from the North." In *Europe Observed*, edited by João de Pina-Cabral and John Campbell, 39–55. London: Macmillan, 1992.

Chowning Davies, James. "Aggression, Violence, Revolution, and War." In *Handbook of Political Psychology*, edited by Jeanne N. Knutson, 234–60. San Francisco: Jossey-Bass Publishers, 1973.

Chueca, Josu. "El nacionalismo vasco en Navarra." In *Los nacionalistas: Historia del nacionalismo vasco 1876–1960*, edited by Santiago de Pablo, 283–307. Beasaide Series. Vitoria-Gasteiz: Fundación Sancho el Sabio, 1995.

———. *El nacionalismo vasco en Navarra (1931–1936)*. Bilbao: Universidad del País Vasco, Servicio Editorial, 1999.

Cierva, Ricardo de la, and Sergio Vilar. *Pro y contra Franco: Franquismo y antifranquismo*. Barcelona: Editorial Planeta, 1985.

Clark, Robert P. *The Basques: The Franco Years and Beyond*. Reno: University of Nevada Press, 1979.

———. "Language and Politics in Spain's Basque Provinces." *West European Politics* 4, no. 1 (1981): 85–103.

———. *The Basque Insurgents: ETA, 1952–1980*. Madison: University of Wisconsin Press, 1984.

———. *Negotiating with Euzkadi ta Askatasuna (ETA): Obstacles to Peace in the Basque Country*. Reno: University of Nevada Press, 1990.

Clifford, James. *The Predicament of Culture: Twentieth-Century Ethnography, Literature, Art*. Cambridge, MA: Harvard University Press, 1988.

Cobb, Christopher. "The Republican State and Mass Educational-Cultural Initiatives, 1931–1936." In *Spanish Cultural Studies: An Introduction*, edited by Helen Graham and Jo Labanyi, 133–38. Oxford: Oxford University Press, 1995.

Colley, Linda. *Britons: Forging the Nation 1707–1837*. New Haven, CT: Yale University Press, 1992.

Connor, Walker. "Beyond Reason: The Nature of the Ethnonational Bond." *Ethnic and Racial Studies* 16, no. 3 (July 1993): 373–89.

———. *Ethnonationalism: The Quest For Understanding*. Princeton, NJ: Princeton University Press, 1994.

Conversi, Daniele. "Language or Race?: The Choice of Core Values in the Development of Catalan and Basque Nationalisms." *Ethnic and Racial Studies* 13, no. 1 (January 1990): 50–70.

———. "Domino Effect or Internal Developments? The Influences of International Events and Political Ideologies on Catalan and Basque Nationalism." *West European Politics* 16, no. 3 (July 1993): 245–70.

———. "The Influence of Culture on Political Choices: Language Maintenance and Its Implications for the Catalan and Basque National Movements." *History of European Ideas* 16, nos. 1–3 (1993): 189–200.

———. *The Basques, the Catalans and Spain: Alternative Routes to Nationalist Mobilisation*. Reno: University of Nevada Press, 1997.

———. "The Smooth Transition: Spain's 1978 Constitution and the Nationalities Question." *National Identities* 4, no. 3 (2002): 223–44

Corcuera Atienza, Javier. *Orígenes, ideología y organización del nacionalismo vasco (1876–1904).* Madrid: Siglo XXI, 1979.

———. "Ese gran desconocido." Interview by Eugenio Ibarzábal. *Muga*, no. 5 (April 1980), 8–29.

———. "La difícil definición del 'problema vasco.'" In *Violencia y política en Euskadi*, edited by Fernando Reinares, 37–53. Bilbao: Desclée de Brouwer, 1984.

———. *The Origins, Ideology, and Organization of Basque Nationalism, 1876–1903.* Translated by Albert Bork and Cameron J. Watson. Reno: Center for Basque Studies, University of Nevada, Reno, 2007.

Crenshaw, Martha. *Revolutionary Terrorism: The FLN in Algeria, 1954–1962.* Stanford: Hoover Institution Press, 1978.

———. "The Logic of Terrorism: Terrorist Behavior as a Product of Strategic Choice." In *Origins of Terrorism: Psychologies, Ideologies, Theologies, States of Mind*, edited by Walter Reich, Woodrow Wilson Center Series, 7–24. Cambridge: Cambridge University Press, 1990.

Crozier, Brian. *The Rebels: A Study of Post–War Insurrections.* Boston: Beacon Press, 1960.

Dane, Joseph A. *Parody: Critical Concepts Versus Literary Practices, Aristophenes to Sterne.* Norman: University of Oklahoma Press, 1988.

Darnton, Robert. *The Great Cat Massacre and Other Episodes in French Cultural History.* New York: Basic Books, 1984. Reprint, New York: Vintage Books, 1985.

———. *The Kiss of Lamourette: Reflections in Cultural History.* New York: W. W. Norton, 1990.

Darré, Alain. "Le Parti nationaliste basque: Un mouvement périphérique et totalisant." *Revue Française de Science Politique* 40, no. 2 (April 1990): 250–70.

Davis, Natalie Z. "Anthropology and History in the 1980s." *Journal of Interdisciplinary History* 12, no. 2 (Autumn 1981): 267–75.

Delgado, Miguel A. "Los historiadores consideran grave la manipulación de la historia de España que se enseña en algunas autonomías." *ABC*, April 7, 1996, 74–76.

del Valle, Teresa. *Korrika: Basque Ritual for Ethnic Identity.* Translated by Linda White. Reno: University of Nevada Press, 1994.

Dent Coad, Emma. "Constructing the Nation: Francoist Architecture." In *Spanish Cultural Studies: An Introduction*, edited by Helen Graham and Jo Labanyi, 223–25. Oxford: Oxford University Press, 1995.

Deutsch, Karl W. *Nationalism and Social Communication: An Enquiry Into the Foundations of Nationality.* New York: The Technology Press of the Massachusetts Institute of Technology and John Wiley and Sons, 1953.

———. *Nationalism and Its Alternatives.* New York: Knopf, 1969.

Diaz Freire, J. J. "La proclamación de la II República como restauración de la dignidad popular." In *II Euskal mundu biltzarra/II Congreso mundial vasco.* Sec. 2, *Euskal Herriaren historiari buruzko biltzarra/Congreso de historia de Euskal Herria.* Vol. 5, *Aro moderno eta gaur egungoa/Edad modern ay contemporánea,* 245–54. Vitoria-Gasteiz: Euskal Jaurlaritzaren Argitalpen-Zerbitzu Nagusia/Servicio Central de Publicaciones del Gobierno Vasco, 1988.

Diccionario enciclopédico del País Vasco

Dickson, Paul. "The Separate Land." *Saturday Review,* September 7, 1968, 50–51.

Díez Medrano, Juan. *Divided Nations: Class, Politics, and Nationalism in the Basque Country and Catalonia.* Ithaca, NY: Cornell University Press, 1995.

Douglass, William A. *Death in Murelaga: Funerary Ritual in a Spanish Basque Village.* Seattle: University of Washington Press, 1969.

———. *Echalar and Murelaga: Opportunity and Rural Exodus in Two Spanish Basque Villages.* New York: St. Martin's Press, 1975.

———. "A Critique of Recent Trends in the Analysis of Ethnonationalism." *Ethnic and Racial Studies* 11, no. 2 (1988): 192–206.

———., ed. *Essays in Basque History and Social Anthropology.* Reno: Basque Studies Program, 1989.

———. "Sabino's Sin: Racism and the Founding of Basque Nationalism," in *Ethnonationalism in the Contemporary World: Walker Connor and the Study of Nationalism,* ed. Daniele Conversi, 95–112. London: Routledge, 2002

Douglass, William A., and Jon Bilbao, *Amerikanuak: Basques in the New World.* Reno: University of Nevada Press, 1975.

Eagleton, Terry. "Nationalism: Irony and Commitment." In Terry Eagleton, Frederic Jameson, and Edward W. Said. *Nationalism, Colonialism, and Literature,* 23–39. Minneapolis: University of Minnesota Press, 1990.

———. *Ideology: An Introduction.* London: Verso, 1991.

———. *The Idea of Culture.* Oxford: Blackwell, 2000.

Edelman, Murray. *Politics as Symbolic Action: Mass Arousal and Quiescence.* Institute for Research on Poverty Monograph Series. Chicago: Markham Publishing Company, 1971.

Eksteins, Modris. *Rites of Spring: The Great War and the Birth of the Modern Age.* London: Bantam Press, 1989. Reprint, London: Black Swan, 1990.

Elliot, J. H. *Imperial Spain 1469–1716.* 1963. Harmondsworth: Penguin, 1983.

Ellwood, Sheelagh M. *Spanish Fascism in the Franco Era: Falange Española de las JONS 1936–76.* New York: St. Martin's Press, 1987.

———. "The Extreme Right in Spain: A Dying Species." In *The Far Right in Western and Eastern Europe,* edited by Luciano Cheles, Ronnie Ferguson, and Michalina Vaughan, 91–107. London: Longman, 1995.

Elorza, Antonio. *Ideologías del nacionalismo vasco, 1876–1937.* San Sebastián: L. Haranburu, 1978.

———. "Guerra y fueros en los orígenes del nacionalismo vasco." In *Gernika: 50 años después (1937–1987). Nacionalismo, República, Guerra Civil*, edited by Manuel Tuñón de Lara, 11–23. San Sebastián: Servicio Editorial Universidad del País Vasco/Argitalpen Zerbitzua Euskal Herriko Unibertsitatea, 1987.

———. "Cultura e ideología en el País Vasco contemporáneo." In *II Euskal mundu-biltzarra/II Congreso Mundial*. Sec. 2, *Euskal Herriaren historiari buruzko biltzarra/Congreso de historia de Euskal Herria*. Vol. 5, *Aro moderno eta gaur egungoa/Edad moderna y contemporánea*, 195–210. Vitoria-Gasteiz: Eusko Jaurlaritzaren Argitalpen-Zerbitzu Nagusia/Servicio Central de Publicaciones del Gobierno Vasco, 1988.

———. *Tras la huella de Sabino Arana: Los orígenes totalitarios del nacionalismo vasco*. Madrid: Temas de Hoy, 2005.

Elorza, Antonio, José María Garmendia, Gurutz Jáuregui, and Florencio Domínguez Iribarren, eds. *La historia de ETA*. Madrid: Temas de Hoy, 2000.

Enciclopedia general ilustrada del País Vasco.

English, Richard. *Armed Struggle: The History of the IRA*. London: Pan Books, 2003.

Erdozáin Azpilicueta, Pilar. *Propiedad, familia y trabajo en la Navarra contemporánea*. Pamplona: Gobierno de Navarra, Departamento de Educación y Cultura, 1999.

Ereñaga, Amaia. *Marc Légasse: Un rebelde burlón*. Tafalla: Txalaparta, 1997.

Escudero, Manu. *Euskadi: Dos communidades*. San Sebastián: L. Haranburu, 1978.

Estévez, Xosé. *De la Triple Alianza al Pacto de San Sebastián (1923–1930)*. San Sebastián: Universidad de Deusto, 1991.

———. *Historia de Euskal Herria*. Vol. 2. *Del hierro al roble*. Tafalla: Txalaparta, 1996.

Estornés Zubizarreta, Idoia. *La construcción de una nacionalidad vasca: El autonomismo de Eusko-Ikaskuntza (1918–1931)*. San Sebastián: Eusko-Ikaskuntza, 1990.

———. "El PNV y el 18 de julio." *El Mundo del País Vasco*, October 12, 1995, 5.

Evans, Peter. "Cifesa: Cinema and Authoritarian Aesthetics." In *Spanish Cultural Studies: An Introduction*, edited by Helen Graham and Jo Labanyi, 215–22. Oxford: Oxford University Press, 1995.

Evans, Richard J. "Introduction: Redesigning the Past. History in Political Transitions." *Journal of Contemporary History* 38, no. 1 (2003): 5–12.

Ezquerra, Iñaki. *Sabino Arana, o, la sentimentalidad totalitaria*. Barcelona: Belaqva, 2003.

Fentress, James, and Chris Wickham. *Social Memory*. Oxford and Cambridge, MA: Blackwell, 1992.

Fernandez, James W. "Folklorists as Agents of Nationalism: Asturian Legends and the Problem of Identity." In *Fairy Tales and Society: Illusion, Allusion, and Paradigm*, edited by Ruth B. Bottigheimer, 133–46. Philadelphia: University of Pennsylvania Press, 1986.

Flynn, M. K. "Constructed Identities and Iberia." *Ethnic and Racial Studies* 24, no. 5 (September 2001): 703–18.

Foucault, Michel. *The History of Sexuality, Volume 1: An Introduction*. Translated by Robert Hurley. New York: Vintage Books, 1990.

Fox, Inman. *La invención de España: Nacionalismo liberal e identidad nacional.* Madrid: Cátedra, 1998.

Fusi, Juan Pablo. *Política obrera en el País Vasco (1880–1923).* Madrid: Ediciones Turner, 1975.

———. *El problema vasco en la II República.* Madrid: Ediciones Turner, 1979.

———. *El País Vasco: Pluralismo y nacionalidad.* Madrid: Alianza Editorial, 1984.

———. "The Basque Question 1931–7." In *Revolution and War in Spain 1931–1939*, edited by Paul Preston, 182–201. London: Methuen, 1984.

———. "Política y nacionalidad." In *II Euskal mundu-biltzarra/II Congreso mundial vasco.* Sec. 2, *EuskalHerriaren historiari buruzko biltzarra/Congreso de historia de Euskal Herria.* Vol. 7, *Aro moderno eta gaur egungoa/Edad moderna y contemporánea*, 3–24. Vitoria-Gasteiz: Eusko Jaurlaritzaren Argitalpen-Zerbitzu Nagusia/Servicio Central de Publicaciones del Gobierno Vasco, 1988.

Gabilondo, Joseba. "Postnationalism, Fundamentalism, and the Global Real: Historicizing Terror/ism and the New North American/Global ideology." *Journal of Spanish Cultural Studies* 3, no. 1 (2002): 57–86.

———. "State Melancholia: Spanish Nationalism, Specularity and Performance. Notes on Antonio Muñoz Molina." In *From Stateless Nations to Postnational Spain*, edited by Silvia Bermúdez, Antonio Cortijo Ocaña, and Timothy McGovern, 237–71. Boulder, CO: Society of Spanish and Spanish-American Studies, 2002.

———. "Historical Memory, Neoliberal Spain, and the Latin American Postcolonial Ghost: On the Politics of Recognition, Apology, and Reparation in Contemporary Spanish Historiography." *Arizona Journal of Hispanic Cultural Studies* 7 (2003): 247–66.

Gage, John. *Color and Culture: Practice and Meaning From Antiquity to Abstraction.* Boston: Little, Brown and Co., 1993.

Gal, Susan. "Bartók's Funeral: Representations of Europe in Hungarian Political Rhetoric." *American Ethnologist* 18, no. 3 (1991): 440–58.

Galdos Urrutia, Rosario. *Estructura y dinámica de la población alavesa (1900–1981).* Vitoria-Gasteiz: Diputación Foral de Álava, Departamento de Cultura/Arabako Foru Aldundia, Cultura Saila, 1990.

Galfarsoro, Imanol. *Kultura eta identitate erbesteratuak (Nomadologia subalternoak).* Iruña: Pamiela, 2005.

Gallo, Max. *Spain Under Franco: A History.* Translated by Jean Stewart. New York: E. P. Dutton & Co., 1974.

Gallop, Rodney. *A Book of the Basques.* London: Macmillan, 1930. Reprint, Reno: University of Nevada Press, 1970.

Galtung, Johan. "Cultural Violence." *Journal of Peace Research* 27, no. 3 (1990): 291–305.

García Casado, Sira, and Jesús Mª Abad Ruiz. "Evolución ideológica del Partido Nacionalista Vasco, 1913–1918." *Cuadernos de Alzate*, no. 4 (1986): 81–87.

García de Cortázar, Fernando and José Manuel Azcona. *El nacionalismo vasco.* Madrid: Historia 16, 1991.

García Isasti, P. "Nazionalismo espainiarrari buruz zenbait ohar." In *II Euskal mundubiltzarra/II Congreso mundial vasco.* Sec. 2, *Euskal Herriaren historiari buruzko biltzarra/Congreso de historia de Euskal Herria.* Vol. 5, *Aro moderno eta gaur egungoa/Edad moderna y contemporánea,* 269–80. Vitoria-Gasteiz: Eusko Jaurlaritzaren Argitalpen-Zerbitzu Nagusia/Servicio Central de Publicaciones del Gobierno Vasco, 1988.

García-Sanz Marcotegui, Angel. "La población vasco-navarra entre 1930 y 1960: Los efectos de la guerra y los cambios demográficos." *Boletín del Instituto Gerónimo de Ustariz,* no. 4 (1990): 96–110.

García Venero, Maximiano. *Historia del nacionalismo vasco 1793–1936.* Madrid: Editora Nacional, 1945.

———. *Historia del nacionalismo vasco.* Madrid: Editora Nacional, 1968.

Garmendia, José Mari. *Historia de ETA.* 2 vols. San Sebastián: L. Haranburu, 1979.

Garmendia, Vincent. *El carlismo.* Paris: Masson et Cie, 1975.

Garzia, Joxerra, Jon Sarasua, and Andoni Egaña. *The Art of Bertsolaritza: Improvised Basque Verse Singing.* Donostia: Bertsozale Elkartea; Andoain: Bertsolari Liburuak, 2001.

Geertz, Clifford. *The Interpretation of Cultures: Selected Essays.* New York: Basic Books, 1973.

Gellner, Ernest. *Nations and Nationalism.* Ithaca, NY: Cornell University Press, 1983.

Genovés, Santiago. *La violencia en el País Vasco y en sus relaciones con España (No todo es política).* Barcelona: Editorial Fontanella/Hogar del Libro, 1986.

George, Alexander, ed. *Western State Terrorism.* New York: Routledge, 1991.

Gibbons, Luke. *Transformations in Irish Culture.* Cork: Cork University Press, 1996.

Gibson, Ian. *Fire in the Blood: The New Spain.* London: Faber and Faber, 1992.

Gillis, John R. "Introduction. Memory and Identity: The History of a Relationship." In *Commemorations: The Politics of National Identity,* edited by John R. Gillis, 3–24. Princeton, NJ: Princeton University Press, 1994.

Gilmore, David G. *Manhood in the Making: Cultural Concepts of Masculinity.* New Haven, CT: Yale University Press, 1990.

Gilmour, David. *The Transformation of Spain: From Franco to the Constitutional Monarchy.* London: Quartet Books, 1985.

Gilroy, Paul. *"There Ain't No Black in the Union Jack": The Cultural Politics of Race and Nation.* Chicago: University of Chicago Press, 1991.

———. *The Black Atlantic: Modernity and Double Consciousness.* London: Verso, 1993.

Girard, René. *The Scapegoat.* Translated by Yvonne Freccero. Baltimore: The Johns Hopkins University Press, 1986.

Glas, Eduardo Jorge. *Bilbao's Modern Business Elite.* Reno: University of Nevada Press, 1997.

Gómez-Ibáñez, Daniel Alexander. *The Western Pyrenees: Differential Evolution of the French and Spanish Borderland.* Oxford: Clarendon Press, 1975.

Gonzalez Blasco, Pedro. "Modern Nationalism in Old Nations as a Consequence of Earlier State-Building: The Case of Basque Spain." In *Ethnicity and Nation-Building: Comparative, International, and Historical Perspectives*, edited by Wendell Bell and Walter E. Freeman, 341–73. Beverly Hills: Sage Publications, 1974.

Graham, Helen and Jo Labanyi. "Culture and Modernity: The Case of Spain." In *Spanish Cultural Studies: An Introduction*, edited by Helen Graham and Jo Labanyi, 1–19. Oxford: Oxford University Press, 1995.

Gramsci, Antonio. *An Antonio Gramsci Reader: Selected Writings, 1916–1935*, edited by David Forgacs. New York: Schocken Books, 1988.

Granja Sainz, José Luis de la. "The Basque Nationalist Community During the Second Spanish Republic (1931–1936)." In *Basque Politics: A Case Study in Ethnic Nationalism*, edited by William A. Douglass, 155–73. Basque Studies Program Occasional Papers Series, no. 2. Reno: Associated Faculty Press and Basque Studies Program, 1985.

———. *Nacionalismo y II República en el País Vasco: Estatutos de autonomía, partidos y elecciones. Historia de Acción Nacionalista Vasca: 1930–1936.* Madrid: Centro de Investigaciones Sociológicas/Siglo XXI, 1986.

———. "Cinco años de República en Euskadi." *Historia Contemporánea*, no. 1 (1988): 95–108.

———. "El Aranismo, ideología dominante del Partido Nacionalista Vasco en los años treinta: Acta de la Asamblea de Bergara." In *II Euskal mundu biltzarra/Congreso mundial vasco.* Sec. 2, *Euskal Herriaren historiari buruzko biltzarra/Congreso de historia de Euskal Herria.* Vol. 5, *Aro moderno eta gaur egungoa/Edad moderna y contemporánea*, 417–30. Vitoria-Gasteiz: Eusko Jaurlaritzaren Argitalpen-Zerbitzu Nagusia/Servicio Central de publicaciones del Gobierno Vasco, 1988.

———. *República y Guerra Civil en Euskadi: Del Pacto de San Sebastián al de Santoña.* Oñati: Instituto Vasco de Administración Pública, 1990.

———. "El nacionalismo vasco entre la autonomía y la independencia." In *Los nacionalismos en la España de la II República*, edited by Justo G. Beramendi and Ramón Maiz, 101–25. Madrid: Siglo XXI, 1991.

———. "La historiografía reciente sobre el nacionalismo vasco." *Cuadernos de Alzate*, no. 15 (October 1991): 80–88.

———. "El nacionalismo vasco: De la literatura histórica a la historiografía." *Historia contemporánea*, no. 7 (1992): 209–36.

———. *El nacionalismo vasco: Un siglo de historia.* Madrid: Editorial Tecnos, 1995.

Greenfeld, Liah. *Nationalism: Five Roads to Modernity.* Cambridge, MA : Harvard University Press, 1992.

Greenwood, Davydd. "Continuity in Change: Spanish Basque Ethnicity as a Historical Process." In *Ethnic Conflict in the Western World*, edited by Milton J. Esman, 81–102. Ithaca, NY: Cornell University Press.

Gurruchaga, Ander. *El código nacionalista vasco durante el franquismo.* Barcelona: Anthropos, 1985.

Hall, Stuart. *The Hard Road to Renewal: Thatcherism and the Crisis of the Left.* London: Verso, 1988.

______, et al., *Policing the Crisis: Mugging, the State, and Law and Order.* New York: Holmes & Meier, 1978.

Hancock, Ian. "Responses to the Porrajmos: The Romani Holocaust." In *Is the Holocaust Unique? Perspectives on Comparative Genocide*, edited by Alan S. Rosenbaum, 39–64. Boulder, CO: Westview Press, 1996.

Handler, Richard. "Is 'Identity' a Useful Cross-Cultural Concept?" In *Commemorations: The Politics of National Identity*, edited by John R. Gillis, 27–40. Princeton, NJ: Princeton University Press, 1994.

Harrison, Joseph. "Heavy Industry, the State, and Economic Development in the Basque Region, 1876–1936." *The Economic History Review*, 2nd ser., 36, no. 4 (November 1983): 535–51.

Hebdige, Dick. *Subculture: The Meaning of Style.* London: Methuen & Co., 1979.

Hechter, Michael. *Internal Colonialism: The Celtic Fringe in British National Development, 1536–1966.* Berkeley: University of California Press, 1975.

Heiberg, Marianne. "Urban Politics and Rural Culture: Basque Nationalism." In *The Politics of Territorial Identity: Studies in European Regionalism*, edited by Stein Rokkan and Derek W. Urwin, 355–87. London: Sage Publications, 1982.

———. "Inside the Moral Community: Politics in a Basque Village." In *Basque Politics: A Case Study in Ethnic Nationalism*, edited by William A. Douglass, 285–307. Basque Studies Program Occasional Papers Series, no. 2. Reno: Associated Faculty Press and Basque Studies Program, 1985.

———. *The Making of the Basque Nation.* Cambridge: Cambridge University Press, 1989.

Held, David. "The Development of the Modern State." In *Modernity: An Introduction to Modern Societies*, edited by Stuart Hall, David Held, Don Hubert, and Kenneth Thompson, 55–89. Oxford: Blackwell, 1996.

Herodotus. *The Histories.* Translated by Aubrey de Sélincourt. Revised with an introduction and notes by A. R. Burn. Rev. ed. Harmondsworth, England: Penguin Books, 1972.

Higginbotham, Virginia. *Spanish Film Under Franco.* Austin: University of Texas Press, 1988.

Hobsbawm, Eric J. *The Age of Revolution, 1789–1848.* London: Weidenfeld & Nicholson, 1962. Reprint, London: Abacus, 1977.

———. "Introduction: Inventing Traditions." In *The Invention of Tradition*, edited by Eric Hobsbawm and Terence Ranger, 1–14. Cambridge: Cambridge University Press, 1983.

———. "Mass-Producing Traditions: Europe, 1870–1914." In *The Invention of Tradition*, edited by Eric Hobsbawm and Terence Ranger, 263–307. Cambridge: Cambridge University Press, 1983.

———. *The Age of Empire 1875–1914.* London: Weidenfeld & Nicholson; New York: Pantheon, 1987. Reprint, New York: Vintage Books, 1989.

———. *Nations and Nationalism Since 1780: Programme, Myth, Reality*. Cambridge: Cambridge University Press, 1990.

———. *The Age of Extremes: The Short History of the Twentieth Century 1914–1991.* London: Michael Joseph, 1994. Reprint, London: Abacus, 1995.

Horowitz, Donald L. *Ethnic Groups in Conflict.* Berkeley: University of California Press, 1985.

Hroch, Miroslav. *Social Preconditions of National Revival in Europe: A Comparative Analysis of the Social Composition of Patriotic Groups Among the Smaller European Nations.* Cambridge: Cambridge University Press, 1985.

Hughes, H. Stuart. *Consciousness and Society: The Reorientation of European Social Thought 1890–1930.* New York: Alfred A. Knopf, 1958.

Humphrey, Caroline. "Chiefly and Shamanist Landscapes in Mongolia." In *The Anthropology of Landscape: Perspectives on Place and Space*, edited by Eric Hirsch and Michael O'Hanlon, 135–62. Oxford: Clarendon Press, 1995.

Hutcheon, Linda. *A Theory of Parody: The Teachings of Twentieth–Century Art Forms.* New York: Methuen, 1985.

Hutchinson, John. *The Dynamics of Cultural Nationalism: The Gaelic Revival and the Creation of the Irish Nation State.* London: Allen & Unwin, 1987.

Ibarz, Mercè. *Breu Història d'ETA*. Barcelona: Ediciones la Magrana, 1981.

Ibarzábal, Eugenio. "Así nació ETA: A los 20 años de su aparición." *Muga*, no. 1 (June 1979), 76–89.

———. "Sabino Arana y su herencia." *Muga*, no. 4 (1980), 2–5.

Ignatieff, Michael. *Blood and Belonging: Journeys into the New Nationalism.* New York: Farrar, Straus and Giroux, 1993.

Irwin-Zarecka, Iwona. *Frames of Remembrance: The Dynamics of Collective Memory.* New Brunswick, NJ: Transaction Publishers, 1994.

Iser, Wolfgang. "Interaction Between Text and Reader." In *The Reader in the Text: Essays on Audience and Interpretation*, edited by Susan R. Suleiman and Inge Crosman, 106–19. Princeton, NJ: Princeton University Press, 1980.

Jacob, James E. *Hills of Conflict: Basque Nationalism in France.* Reno: University of Nevada Press, 1994.

James, E. O. *Sacrifice and Sacrament.* New York: Barnes & Noble; London: Thames and Hudson, 1962.

Jáuregui Bereciartu, Gurutz. *Ideología y estrategia política de ETA: Análisis de su evolución entre 1959 y 1968.* 2nd ed. Madrid: Siglo XXI, 1985.

Jay, Martin. *Fin-de-Siècle Socialism and Other Essays*. New York: Routledge, 1988.

———. *Force Fields: Between Intellectual History and Cultural Critique*. New York: Routledge, 1993.

Jimeno Jurío, José María. *Navarra jamás dijo no al Estatuto Vasco*. Tafalla: Txalaparta, 1997.

Jones, Edward E., Amerigo Farina, Albert A. Hastorf, Hazel Markus, Dale T. Miller, and Robert A. Scott, with a special contribution by Rita S. de French. *Social Stigma: The Psychology of Marked Relationships*. New York: W. H. Freeman, 1984.

Jover Zamora, José María. "La época de la Restauración panorama político-social, 1875–1902." In *Historia de España*, vol. 8, *Revolución burguesa oligarquía y constitucionalismo (1834–1923)*, edited by Manuel Tuñón de Lara, 269–406. Barcelona: Editorial Labor, 1981.

Juaristi, Jon. *El linaje de Aitor: La invención de la tradición vasca*. Madrid: Taurus, 1987.

———. "El gueto vacío." In Juan Aranzadi, Jon Juaristi, and Patxo Unzueta. *Auto de terminación (Raza, nación y violencia en el País Vasco)*, 115–136. Madrid: El País/Aguilar, 1994. First published in *Letra Internacional* (Spring 1987).

Juergensmeyer, Mark. "Editor's Introduction: Is Symbolic Violence Related to Real Violence?" *Terrorism and Political Violence* 3, no. 3 (Autumn 1991): 1–8.

Kapferer, Bruce. *Legends of the People, Myths of the State: Violence, Intolerance, and Political Culture in Sri Lanka and Australia*. Washington, D.C.: Smithsonian Institution Press, 1988.

Kedourie, Elie. *Nationalism*. London: Hutchinson, 1960.

Kern, Robert W. *Liberals, Reformers and Caciques in Restoration Spain 1875–1909*. Albuquerque: University of New Mexico Press, 1974.

———. *Red Years/Black Years: A Political History of Spanish Anarchism, 1911–1937*. Philadelphia: Institute for the Study of Human Issues, 1978.

Khaldûn, Ibn. *The Muqaddimah: An Introduction to History*. Translated by Franz Rosenthal. Edited and abridged by N. J. Dawood. 2nd ed. Bollingen Series. Princeton, NJ: Princeton University Press, 1967.

Kohn, Hans. *The Idea of Nationalism: A Study in Its Origins and Background*. New York: Macmillan, 1944.

———. *Prophets and Peoples. Studies in Nineteenth-Century Nationalism*. New York: Octagon Books, 1975.

Kohr, Hans. "Disunion Now: A Plea For a Society Based Upon Small Autonomous Units." *The Commonweal* (September 26, 1941): 540–42.

Krais, Beate. "Gender and Symbolic Violence: Female Oppression in the Light of Pierre Bourdieu's Theory of Social Practice." In *Bourdieu: Critical Perspectives*, edited by Craig Calhoun, Edward LiPuma, and Moishe Postone, 156–77. Chicago: University of Chicago Press, 1993.

Kupchan, Charles A. "Introduction: Nationalism Resurgent." In *Nationalism and Nationalities in the New Europe*, edited by Charles A. Kupchan, 1–14. Ithaca, NY: Cornell University Press, 1995.

Labanyi, Jo. "Censorship or the Fear of Mass Culture." In *Spanish Cultural Studies: An Introduction*, edited by Helen Graham and Jo Labanyi, 207–14. Oxford: Oxford University Press, 1995.

Lacasta-Zabalza, José Ignacio. *España uniforme: El pluralismo enteco y desmemoriado de la sociedad española y de su conciencia nacional e intelectual.* Pamplona: Pamiela, 1998.

Lannon, Frances. "The Social Praxis and Cultural Politics of Spanish Catholicism." In *Spanish Cultural Studies: An Introduction*, edited by Helen Graham and Jo Labanyi, 40–45. Oxford: Oxford University Press, 1995.

———. "The Political Debate within Catholicism." In *Spanish Cultural Studies: An Introduction*, edited by Helen Graham and Jo Labanyi, 139–44. Oxford: Oxford University Press, 1995.

Laqueur, Walter. "Fin-de-Siècle: Once More With Feeling." *Journal of Contemporary History* 31 (1996): 5–47.

Larronde, Jean-Claude. *El nacionalismo vasco: Su origen y su ideología en la obra de Sabino Arana-Goiri.* Translated by Lola Valverde. San Sebastián: Editorial Txertoa, 1977.

———. "Sabino de Arana-Goiri, el fundador." *Muga*, no. 93 (September 1995), 6–25.

———. "Sabino Arana." In *Los nacionalistas: Historia del nacionalismo vasco, 1876–1960*, edited by Santiago de Pablo, 49–74. Besaide Series. Vitoria-Gasteiz: Fundación Sancho el Sabio, 1995.

LeCron Foster, Mary. "Symbolism: The Foundation of Culture." In *Companion Encyclopedia of Anthropology*, edited by Tom Ingold, 366–95. London: Routledge, 1994.

Legaire, Joanna. "Los símbolos y el Derecho." *El Mundo del País Vasco.* Supplement, "Documentos. Cien años de ikurriña." July 14, 1994, 10.

Letamendia, Pierre. *Nationalismes au Pays Basque.* Bordeaux: Presses Universitaires de Bordeaux, 1987.

Letamendia Belzunce, Francisco [Ortzi, pseud.]. *Historia de Euskadi. El nacionalismo vasco y ETA.* Paris: Ruedo Ibérico, 1975.

———. *Euskadi: Pueblo y nación.* 7 vols. San Sebastián: Kriselu-Sendoa, 1990.

———. *Historia del nacionalismo vasco y de ETA.* Vol. 1. *Introducción a la historia del País Vasco: ETA en el franquismo.* San Sebastián: R & B Ediciones, 1994.

Linz, Juan J. "Church and State in Spain from the Civil War to the Return of Democracy." *Daedalus* 20, no. 3 (Summer 1991): 159–78.

Llera, Francisco, José M. Mata, and Cynthia Irvin. "ETA: From Secret Army to Social Movement–The Post-Franco Schism of the Basque Nationalist Movement." *Terrorism and Political Violence* 5, no. 3 (Autumn 1993): 106–34.

Llobera, Josep R. "A Comment on Hasting's *The Construction of Nationhood.*" *Nations and Nationalism* 9, no. 1 (2003): 15–17.

López Adán, Emilio [Beltza, pseud.]. *El nacionalismo vasco 1876–1936.* San Sebastián: Txertoa, 1976.

———. *Nacionalismo vasco y clases sociales.* San Sebastián: Txertoa, 1976.

———. *El nacionalismo vasco en el exilio 1937–1960.* San Sebastián: Txertoa, 1977.

———. *Del carlismo al nacionalismo burgués.* San Sebastián: Txertoa, 1978.

López-Cordón Cortezo, Mª Victoria. "La mentalidad conservadora durante la Restauración." In *La España de la Restauración: Política, economia, legislación y cultura*, edited by José Luis García, 71–109. I Coloquio de Segovia sobre Historia de España dirigido por Manuel Tuñón de Lara. [Segovia]: n.p., n.d.

Lorenzo Espinosa, José María. *Gudari: Una pasión útil. Vida y obra de Eli Gallastegi.* Tafalla: Txalaparta, 1992.

Loughlin, John. "A New Deal for France's Regions and Linguistic Minorities." *West European Politics* 8, no. 3 (1985): 101–13.

Loureiro, Ángel G. "Spanish Nationalism and the Ghost of Empire." *Journal of Spanish Cultural Studies* 4, no. 1 (2003): 65–76.

Mainer, José Carlos. *Regionalismo, burguesía y cultura: Los casos de Revista de Aragón (1900–1905) y Hermes (1917–1922).* Barcelona: A. Redondo, 1974.

Mañaricúa, Andrés. *Historiografía de Vizcaya (desde Lope García de Salazar a Labayru).* 2nd ed. Bilbao: La Gran Enciclopedia Vasca, 1973.

Manzano Moreno, Eduardo, and Juan Sisinio Pérez Garzón, "A Difficult Nation? History and Nationalism in Contemporary Spain." *History and Memory* 14, nos. 1–2 (Fall 2002): 259–84.

Mar-Molinero, Clare, and Angel Smith, eds. *Nationalism and the Nation in the Iberian Peninsula: Competing and Conflicting Identities.* Oxford: Berg, 1996.

Martínez-Peñuela, A. *Antecedentes y primeros pasos del nacionalismo vasco en Navarra: 1878–1918.* Pamplona: Gobierno de Navarra, 1989.

McCrone, David. *The Sociology of Nationalism: Tomorrow's Ancestors.* London: Routledge, 1998.

Medhurst, Ken. "Basques and Basque Nationalism." In *National Separatism*, edited by Colin H. Williams, 235–61. Vancouver: University of British Columbia, 1982.

Mees, Ludger. "Luis de Arana Goiri y la crisis de la Communión Nacionalista en 1915–16." *Muga*, no. 69 (June 1989), 38–43.

———. *El nacionalismo vasco, movimiento obrero y cuestión social (1903–1923).* Bilbao: Fundación Sabino Arana, 1992.

———. "La Restauración y la dictadura de Primo de Rivera." In *Los nacionalistas: Historia del nacionalismo vasco, 1876–1960*, edited by Santiago de Pablo, 75–111. Beasaide Series. Vitoria-Gasteiz: Fundación Sancho el Sabio, 1995.

Melion, Walter, and Susanne Küchler. "Introduction: Memory, Cognition, and Image Production." In *Images of Memory: On Remembering and Representation*, edited by Walter Melion and Susanne Küchler, 1–46. Washington, D.C,: Smithsonian Institution Press, 1991.

Minogue, K.R. *Nationalism.* New York: Basic Books, 1967.

Miranda Rubio, Francisco. "El guerrillero navarro y su trascendencia." *Príncipe de Viana*, no. 165 (January–April 1982): 439–64.

Mitxelena, Koldo. "Sabino Arana según Jean-Claude Larronde." *Muga*, no. 1 (June 1979), 100–104.

Molinas, César, and Leandro Prados de la Escosura, "Was Spain Different? Spanish Historical Backwardness Revisited." *Explorations in Economic History* 26, no. 4 (October 1989): 385–402.

Monreal Zia, Gregorio. *The Old Law of Bizkaia (1452): Introductory Study and Critical Edition.* Translated by William A. Douglass and Linda White. Preface by William A. Douglass. Reno: Center for Basque Studies, University of Nevada, Reno, 2005.

Monroe, James T., "Improvised Invective in Hispano-Arabic Poetry and Ibn Quzmān's "Zajal 87" (When Blond Meets Blonde)," in *Voicing the Moment: Improvised Oral Poetry and Basque Tradition*, edited by Samuel G. Armistead and Joseba Zulaika, 135–59. Reno: Center for Basque Studies, University of Nevada, Reno, 2005.

Montero, Enrique. "Reform Idealized: The Intellectual and Ideological Origins of the Second Republic." In *Spanish Cultural Studies: An Introduction*, edited by Helen Graham and Jo Labanyi, 124–33. Oxford: Oxford University Press, 1995.

Morris, David B. "About Suffering: Voice, Genre, and Moral Community." *Daedalus* 125, no. 1 (Winter 1996): 25–45.

Morris, Robert. "Words and Images in Modernism and Postmodernism." *Critical Inquiry* 15, no. 2 (Winter 1989): 337–47.

Mosse, George L. *Fallen Soldiers: Reshaping the Memory of the World Wars.* New York: Oxford University Press, 1990.

Murillo Ferrol, Francisco. "Factores políticos de la violencia." *Revista Internacional de la Sociología*, 3rd ser., no. 2 (May-August): 67–77.

Nairn, Tom. *The Break-Up of Britain: Crisis and Neo-Nationalism.* 2nd ed. London: NLB, 1981.

———. "Breakwaters of 2000: From Ethnic to Civic Nationalism." *New Left Review*, no. 214 (November/December 1995): 91–103.

Nederveen Pieterse, Jan. "Unpacking the West: How European is Europe?" In *Racism, Modernity and Identity: On the Western Front*, edited by Ali Rattansi and Sallie Westwood, 129–49. Cambridge: Polity Press, 1994.

Nietzsche, Friedrich. *Basic Writings of Nietzsche.* Translated and edited with commentaries by Walter Kaufmann. New York: The Modern Library, 1968.

Nugent, Walter. *Crossings: The Great Transatlantic Migrations, 1870–1914.* Bloomington: Indiana University Press, 1992.

Núñez, Xosé-Manoel. "Historical Research on Regionalism and Peripheral Nationalism in Spain: A Reappraisal." *European Culture Research Centre Research Report.* Florence: European University Institute, 1992.

———. "What is Spanish Nationalism Today?: From Legitimacy to Crisis to Unfulfilled Renovation (1975–2000)." *Ethnic and Racial Studies* 24, no. 5 (September 2001): 719–52.

Olábarri Gortazar, Ignacio. *Relaciones laborales en Vizcaya (1890–1936)*. Durango: Leopoldo Zugaza, 1978.

Olábarri, Ignacio, and Fernando Meer. "Aproximación a la Guerra Civil en el País Vasco (1936–1939) como un conflicto de ideas." *Cuadernos de Sección Historia-Geografía*, no. 17 (1990): 141–72.

Ong, Walter J. *Orality and Literacy: The Technologizing of the Word*. London: Methuen, 1982.

Orella Unzue, José Luis. *Nueva invención de la España plurinacional.* Gasteiz: Arabera, 2000.

Oring, Elliot. "The Arts, Artifacts, and Artifices of Identity." *Journal of American Folklore* 107, no. 424 (Spring 1994): 211–33.

Ormazabal Elola, Sabino. *Sufrimenduaren mapa (osatugabea)/Un mapa (inacabado) del sufrimiento.* Bilbo: Manu Robles-Arangiz Institutoa, 2003.

Otaegi, Joxe A. "Biolentzia, biolentziak." *Jakin*, no. 9 (January–March 1979): 104–18.

Pablo, Santiago de. *El nacionalismo vasco en Alava (1907–1936)*. Bilbao: Ekin, 1988.

———., ed. *Los nacionalistas. Historia del nacionalismo vasco 1876–1960.* Beasaide Series. Vitoria-Gasteiz: Fundación Sancho el Sabio, 1995.

———. "El nacionalismo vasco en Álava." In *Los nacionalistas: Historia del nacionalismo vasco 1876–1960*, edited by Santiago de Pablo, 309–41. Beasaide Series. Vitoria-Gasteiz: Fundación Sancho el Sabio, 1995.

Pablo, Santiago de, and Ludger Mees. *El péndulo patriótico: Historia del Partido Nacionalista Vasco, 1895–2005.* Barcelona: Crítica, 2005.

Palacio Atard, Vicente. *La España del siglo XIX, 1808–1898 (Introducción a la España contemporánea)*. 2nd ed. Madrid: Calpe, 1981.

Pandey, Gyanendra. "Voices From the Edge: The Struggle to Write Subaltern Histories." *Ethnos* 60, nos. 3–4 (1995): 223–42.

Parman, Susan. *Dream and Culture: An Anthropological Study of the Western Intellectual Tradition.* New York: Praeger, 1991.

Payne, Stanley G. *Falange: A History of Spanish Fascism.* Stanford, CA: Stanford University Press, 1961.

———. *Basque Nationalism.* Reno: University of Nevada Press, 1975.

———. *The Franco Regime 1936–1975.* Madison: The University of Wisconsin Press, 1987.

———. "Nacionalismo español, nacionalismo vasco." In *Aula de Cultura de El Correo Español–El Pueblo Vasco*, edited by José Manuel González, vol. 12, 109–27. Bilbao: El Correo Español–El Pueblo Vasco, 1994.

Pearson, Raymond. *National Minorities in Eastern Europe, 1848–1945.* London: Macmillan, 1983.

Pérez-Agote, Alfonso. *La reproducción del nacionalismo: El caso vasco.* Madrid: Centro de Investigaciones Sociológicas/Siglo XXI, 1984.

———. "The Role of Religion in the Definition of a Symbolic Conflict: Religion and the Basque Problem." *Social Compass* 33, no. 4 (1986): 419–35.

———. "Self-Fulfilling Prophecy and Unresolved Mourning: Basque Political Violence in the Twenty-First Century." In *Empire and Terror: Nationalism/Postnationalism in the New Millennium*, edited by Begoña Aretxaga, Dennis Dworkin, Joseba Gabilondo, and Joseba Zulaika, 177–98. Reno: Center for Basque Studies, University of Nevada, Reno, 2005.

———. *The Social Roots of Basque Nationalism.* Translated by Cameron Watson and William A. Douglass. Foreword by William A. Douglass. Reno: University of Nevada Press, 2006.

Pérez Garzón, Juan Sisinio. "State Nationalism, Cultural Nationalism and Political Alternatives." *Journal of Spanish Cultural Studies* 4, no. 1 (2003): 47–64.

Pérez de Arenaza Múgica, José María, and Javier Lasagabaster Olazábal, eds. *América y los Vascos: Presencia vasca en América.* Gasteiz: Departamento de Cultura, Gobierno Vasco, 1991.

Pescador, Juan Javier. *The New World Inside a Basque Village: The Oiartzun Valley and Its Atlantic Emigrants, 1550–1800.* Reno: University of Nevada Press, 2004.

Philpott, Daniel. "In Defense of Self–Determination." *Ethics* 105, no. 2 (January 1995): 352–85.

Plata Parga, Gabriel. "Del liberalismo oligárquico al conservadurismo autoritario en Vizcaya (1875–1936)." In *II Euskal mundu-biltzarra/II Congreso mundial vasco.* Sec. 2, *Euskal Herriaren historiari buruzko biltzarra/Congreso de historia de Euskal Herria.* Vol. 5, *Aro moderno eta gaur egungoa/Edad moderna y contemporánea*, 335–43. Vitoria-Gasteiz: Eusko Jaurlaritzaren Argitalpen-Zerbitzu Nagusia/Servicio Central de Publicaciones del Gobierno Vasco, 1988.

Pons Prades, Eduardo. *Guerrillas españolas 1936–1960.* Barcelona: Editorial Planeta, 1977.

Portell, José María. *Los hombres de ETA.* Barcelona: Dopesa, 1974.

Preston, Paul. "Spain." In *Fascism in Europe*, edited by S. J. Woolf, 329–351. 2nd ed. London York: Methuen, 1981.

———. *The Triumph of Democracy in Spain.* London: Methuen, 1986.

———. *Franco: A Biography.* London: Harper Collins, 1993. Reprint, London: Fontana, 1995.

———. "The Urban and Rural *Guerrilla* of the 1940s." In *Spanish Cultural Studies: An Introduction*, edited by Helen Graham and Jo Labanyi, 229–37. Oxford: Oxford University Press, 1995.

Ramos, Cipriano. "El nacionalismo vasco durante la dictadura de Primo de Rivera." *Letras de Deusto*, no. 31 (January–April 1985): 137–67.

Rankin, Nicholas. *Telegram from Guernica: The Extraordinary Life of George Steer, War Correspondent.* London: Faber and Faber, 2003.

Real Cuesta, Javier. "El P.N.V. en 1917: De la intransigencia al oportunismo político." *Letras de Deusto* 6, no. 12 (July–December 1976): 113–40.

"Relaciones entre los nacionalistas cubano y filipino y el nacionalismo vasco en el marco de la crisis de 1898." *Muga*, no. 55 (June 1986), 27–28.

Renobales, Eduardo. *ANV, el otro nacionalismo: Historia de Acción Nacionalista Vasca–Eusko Abertzale Ekintza*. Tafalla: Txalaparta, 2005.

Resina, Joan Ramon. "Post-national Spain? Post-Spanish Spain?" *Nations and Nationalism* 8, no. 3 (2002): 377–96.

Richards, Michael. "'Terror and Progress': Industrialization, Modernity, and the Making of Francoism." In *Spanish Cultural Studies: An Introduction*, edited by Helen Graham and Jo Labanyi, 173–82. Oxford: Oxford University Press, 1995.

———. *A Time of Silence: Civil War and the Culture of Repression in Franco's Spain, 1936–1945*. Cambridge: Cambridge University Press, 1998.

Ringrose, David R. *Transportation and Economic Stagnation in Spain, 1750–1850*. Durham, NC: Duke University Press, 1970.

Rokkan, Stein, and Derek W. Urwin. *Economy, Territory, Identity: Politics of West European Peripheries*. London: Sage, 1983.

Rosenbaum, Alan S. "Introduction." In *Is the Holocaust Unique? Perspectives on Comparative Genocide*, edited with an introduction by Alan S. Rosenbaum. Foreword by Israel W. Charney, 1–9. Boulder, CO: Westview Press, 1996.

Rothstein, Marian. "When Fiction is Fact: Perceptions in Sixteenth-Century France." *Studies in Philology* 83, no. 3 (Summer 1986): 359–75.

Rudé, George. "Ideology and Popular Protest." In *The Face in the Crowd: Studies in Revolution, Ideology and Popular Protest*, edited and introduced by Harvey J. Kaye, 197–204. Atlantic Highlands, NJ: Humanities Press International, 1988.

Ruiz Olabuénaga, José Ignacio. "Los vascos, ¿violentados o violentantes?" In *Violencia y política en Euskadi*, edited by Fernando Reinares, 149–68. Bilbao: Desclée de Brouwer, 1984.

Russell, Bertrand. "On the Relations of Universals and Particulars." In *The Problem of Universals*, edited with an introduction by Charles Landesman, 21–35. New York: Basic Books, 1977. First published in the *Proceedings of the Aristotelian Society*, 12 (1911–12).

Sahlins, Marshall. "Goodbye to *Tristes Tropes*: Ethnography in the Context of Modern World History." *The Journal of Modern History* 65, no. 1 (March 1993): 1–25.

Said, Edward W. "Representing the Colonized: Anthropology's Interlocutors." *Critical Inquiry* 15, no. 2 (Winter 1989): 205–225.

———. *Culture and Imperialism*. London: Chatto & Windus, 1993. Reprint, London: Vintage, 1994.

Salaün, Serge. "The *Cuplé*: Modernity and Mass Culture." In *Spanish Cultural Studies: An Introduction*, edited by Helen Graham and Jo Labanyi, 90–94. Oxford: Oxford University Press, 1995.

San Sebastián, Koldo. "Jesús de Sarría: Un nacionalista vasco 'heterodoxo'." *Muga*, no. 7 (June 1980), 48–58.

———. *Historia del Partido Nacionalista Vasco*. San Sebastián: Editorial Txertoa, 1984.
———. "El PNV durante el primer franquismo." In *Los nacionalistas: Historia del nacionalismo vasco, 1876–1960*, edited by Santiago de Pablo, 145–77. Beasaide Series. Vitoria-Gasteiz: Fundación Sancho el Sabio, 1995.

Satrústegui, José María. *Antropología y lengua (Tradición popular, memoria colectiva)*. Iruñea: José María Satrústegui, 1989.

Schama, Simon. *Landscape and Memory*. London: Harper Collins, 1995. Reprint, London: Fontana, 1996.

Schmidt-Nowara, Christopher. "After 'Spain': A Dialogue with Josep M. Pradera on Spanish Colonial Historiography." In *After the Imperial Turn: Thinking With and Through the Nation*, edited by Antoinette Burton, 157–69. Durham, NC: Duke University Press, 2003.

Schwartz, Benjamin I. "Culture, Modernity, and Nationalism–Further Reflections." *Daedalus* 122, no. 3 (Summer 1993): 207–226.

Seton-Watson, Hugh. *Nations and States: An Enquiry Into the Origins of Nations and the Politics of Nationalism*. Boulder, CO.: Westview Press, 1977.

Sevilla Guzmán, Eduardo. "The Peasantry and the Franco Régime." In *Spain in Crisis: The Evolution and Decline of the Franco Régime*, edited by Paul Preston, 101–24. New York: Barnes & Noble, 1976.

Shabad, Goldie, and Francisco José Llera Ramo. "Political Violence in a Democratic State: Basque Terrorism in Spain." In *Terrorism in Context*, edited by Martha Crenshaw, 410–69. University Park: Pennsylvania State University Press, 1995.

Shafer, Boyd C. *Nationalism: Myth and Reality*. New York: Harcourt Brace, 1955.
———. *Faces of Nationalism: New Realities and Old Myths*. New York: Harcourt Brace Jovanovich, 1972.

Shubert, Adrian. *A Social History of Modern Spain*. London: Unwin Hyman, 1990.

Smith, Anthony D. *Nationalism in the Twentieth Century*. New York: New York University Press, 1979.
———. *The Ethnic Origins of Nations*. Oxford: Blackwell, 1986.
———. *National Identity*. London: Penguin, 1991. Reprint, Reno: University of Nevada Press, 1993.

Snyder, Louis L. "Plurinational Spain: Basque and Catalan Separatism." In *Global Mini-Nationalisms: Autonomy or Independence*, 101–15. Westport, CT: Greenwood Press, 1982.

Solozábal, Juan José. *El primer nacionalismo vasco. Industrialismo y conciencia nacionl*. Madrid: Túcar, 1975.

Sotelo, Ignacio. "Las raíces sociales de la violencia." *Revista Internacional de Sociología*, 3rd ser., no. 2 (May–August 1992): 53–66.

Southworth, Herbert R. *El mito de la Cruzada de Franco*. Barcelona: Plaza & Janes, 1986.

Stannard, David E. "Uniqueness as Denial: The Politics of Genocide Scholarship." In *Is the Holocaust Unique? Perspectives on Comparative Genocide*, edited with an introduction by Alan S. Rosenbaum. Foreword by Israel W. Charney, 163–208. Boulder, CO: Westview Press, 1996.

Sullivan, John. *ETA and Basque Nationalism: The Fight for Euskadi, 1890–1986.* London: Routledge, 1988.

Thomas, Hugh. *The Spanish Civil War.* 3rd ed. Harmondsworth, England: Penguin, 1977.

Thompson, E. P. "Folklore, Anthropology, and Social History." *The Indian Historical Review* 3, no. 2 (1977): 248–66.

Todorov, Tzvetan. *The Conquest of America: The Question of the Other.* Translated by Richard Howard. New York: Harper Colophon, 1985. Reprint, New York: HarperPerennial, 1992.

Totoricagüena, Gloria P. *Identity, Culture, and Politics in the Basque Diaspora.* Reno: University of Nevada Press, 2004.

Townshend, Charles. *Terrorism: A Very Short Introduction.* Oxford: Oxford University Press, 2002.

Trask, R. L. *The History of Basque.* London: Routledge, 1997.

Tuñón de Lara, Manuel, Julio Valdeón Baruque, and Antonio Domínguez Ortiz. *Historia de España.* Barcelona: Editorial Labor, 1991.

Tusell, Javier. *La España de Franco: El poder, la oposición y la política exterior durante el franquismo.* Madrid: Historia 16, 1989.

Ucelay Da Cal, Enric. "The Nationalisms of the Periphery: Culture and Politics in the Construction of National Identity." In *Spanish Cultural Studies: An Introduction*, edited by Helen Graham and Jo Labanyi, 32–39. Oxford: Oxford University Press, 1995.

Ugalde, Martín de. *Nueva síntesis de la historia del País Vasco.* Vol. 2. Donostia: Elkar, 1983.

———, Eugenio Goienetxe, Federico Zabala, María Mina, and Ramón Sota. *Mesa Redonda en torno a: Sabino de Arana y Goiri.* Bilbao: La Editorial Vizcaína, 1977.

Ugarte, Javier. "Represión como instrumento de acción política del 'nuevo estado' (Álava, 1936–1939)." In *II Euskal mundu-biltzarra/II Congreso mundial vasco.* Sec. 2, *Euskal Herriaren historiari buruzko biltzarra/Congreso de historia de Euskal Herria.* Vol. 7, *Aro moderno eta gaur egungoa/Edad moderna y contemporánea*, 247–72. Vitoria-Gasteiz: Eusko Jaurlaritzaren Argitalpen-Zerbitzu Nagusia/Servicio Central de Publicaciones del Gobierno Vasco, 1988.

Ugarte, Javier, and Antonio Rivera. "La guerra civil en el País Vasco: La sublevación en Alava." *Historia Contemporánea*, no. 1 (1988): 181–201.

Unzueta, Patxo. *Los nietos de la ira: Nacionalismo y violencia en el País Vasco.* Madrid: El País/Aguilar, 1988.

———. "El alma de Sabino Arana." In Juan Aranzadi, Jon Juaristi, and Patxo Unzueta. *Auto de terminación (Raza, nación y violencia en el País Vasco)*, 157–70. Madrid: El País/Aguilar, 1994. First published in *Claves*, no. 28 (December 1992).

Urla, Jacqueline. "Being Basque, Speaking Basque: The Politics of Language and Identity in the Basque Country." Ph.D. diss., University of California, Berkeley, 1987.

Urquijo y Goitia, Joseba Mikel. "La crisis de 1917: Las reivindicaciones autonómicas en el País Vasco." In *II Euskal mundu-biltzarra/II Congreso mundial vasco*. Sec. 2, *Euskal Herriaren historiari buruzko biltzarra/Congreso de historia de Euskal Herria*. Vol. 7, *Aro moderno eta gaur egungoa/Edad moderna y contemporánea*, 273–78. Vitoria-Gasteiz: Eusko Jaurlaritzaren Argitalpen-Zerbitzu Nagusia/Servicio Central de Publicaciones del Gobierno Vasco, 1988.

Urquijo Goitia, Mikel. "Carlismo y guerra en el orígen del nacionalismo vasco." *Muga*, no. 93 (September 1995), 38–47.

Vicens Vives, Jaime. *Approaches to the History of Spain*. Translated and edited by Joan Connelly Ullman. Berkeley: University of California Press, 1967.

Waldmann, Peter. *Militanter Nationalismus im Baskenland*. Frankfurt am Main: Vervuert Verlag, 1990.

Waldron, Arthur N. "Theories of Nationalism and Historical Explanation." *World Politics* 37, no. 3 (1985): 416–33.

Walton, John K. "Planning and Seaside Tourism: San Sebastián, 1863–1936." *Planning Perspectives* 17 (2002): 1–20.

Walton, John K., Martin Blinkhorn, Colin Pooley, David Tidswell, and Michael J. Winstanley. "Crime, Migration and Social Change in North-West England and the Basque Country, c.1870–1930." *British Journal of Crimniology* 39, no. 1, special issue (1999): 90–112.

Walton, John K., and Jenny Smith. "The Rhetoric of Community and the Business of Pleasure: The San Sebastián Waiters' Strike of 1920." *International Review of Social History* 39 (1994): 1–31.

———. "The First Spanish Seaside Resorts." *History Today* 44, no. 8 (August 1994): 23–29.

Watson, Cameron J. "Basque Nationalism during the Dictatorship of Primo de Rivera, 1923–1930." Master's thesis, University of Nevada, Reno, 1992.

———. "Folklore and Basque Nationalism: Language, Myth, Reality." *Nations and Nationalism* 2, no. 1 (1996): 17–34.

———. *Modern Basque History: Eighteenth Century to the Present*. Reno: Center for Basque Studies, University of Nevada, Reno, 2003.

Weber, Eugen. *Peasants into Frenchmen: The Modernisation of Rural France*. London: Chatto & Windus, 1977.

White, Hayden. "The Question of Narrative in Contemporary Historical Theory." *History and Theory* 23, no. 1 (1984): 1–33.

White, Julian. "The Musical Avant-garde: Modernity and Tradition." In *Spanish Cultural Studies: An Introduction*, edited by Helen Graham and Jo Labanyi, 79 81. Oxford: Oxford University Press, 1995.

———. "Music and the Limits of Cultural Nationalism." In *Spanish Cultural Studies: An Introduction*, edited by Helen Graham and Jo Labanyi, 225–28. Oxford: Oxford University Press, 1995.

Williams, Martin. "Ancient Mythology and Revolutionary Ideology in Ireland, 1878–1916." *The Historical Journal* 26, no. 2 (June 1983): 307–28.

Williams, Raymond. *Culture and Society*. London: Chatto & Windus, 1958. Reprint, with a postscript, Harmondsworth, England: Penguin Books, 1963.

———. *Marxism and Literature*. Oxford: Oxford University Press, 1977.

———. "Culture is Ordinary." In *Resources of Hope: Culture, Democracy, Socialism*, edited by Robin Gable, with an introduction by Robin Blackburn, 3–18. London: Verso, 1989.

Woodworth, Paddy. *Dirty War, Clean hands: ETA, the GAL and Spanish Democracy*. Cork: Cork University Press, 2001.

Zeldin, Theodore. *An Intimate History of Humanity*. London: Sinclair-Stevenson, 1994. Reprint, London: Minerva, 1995.

Zirakzadeh, Cyrus Ernesto. *A Rebellious People: Basques, Protests, and Politics*. Reno: University of Nevada Press, 1991.

Zulaika, Joseba. *Basque Violence: Metaphor and Sacrament*. Reno: University of Nevada Press, 1988.

———. "Terror, Totem, and Taboo: Reporting on a Report." *Terrorism and Political Violence* 3, no. 1 (Spring 1991): 34–49.

———. *Caza, símbolo y eros*. Translated by Lurdes Azurmendi. Madrid: Nerea, 1992.

———. *Del Cromañon al Carnaval. Los vascos como museo antropológico*. Donostia: Erein, 1996.

———. "Tropics of Terror: From Guernica's 'Natives' to Global 'Terrorists.'" *Social Identities* 4, no. 1 (1998): 93–108.

———. "Anthropologists, Artists, Terrorists: The Basque Holiday from History." *Journal of Spanish Cultural Studies* 4, no. 2 (2003): 139–50.

———. "Nourishment by the Negative: National Subalternity, Antagonism, and Radical Democracy." In *Empire and Terror: Nationalism/Postnationalism in the New Millennium*, edited by Begoña Aretxaga, Dennis Dworkin, Joseba Gabilondo, and Joseba Zulaika, 115–36. Reno: Center for Basque Studies, University of Nevada, Reno, 2005.

———. *ETAren hautsa*. Irun: Alberdania, 2006.

———, and William A. Douglass. *Terror and Taboo: The Follies, Fables, and Faces of Terrorism*. London: Routledge, 1996.

Index